Notting Hill Gate 6B

Für Klasse 10 an Gesamtschulen
und anderen integrierenden Schulformen

Diesterweg

Notting Hill Gate 6B

Für Klasse 10 an Gesamtschulen
Differenzierende Ausgabe
Basic course

Herausgegeben von: Dr. phil. h.c. Christoph Edelhoff, StD a.D., Vorsitzender THE ENGLISH ACADEMY
Erarbeitet von: Michael Biermann (Hamburg), Otfried Börner (Hamburg), Hannelore Debus (Mörfelden-Walldorf), Phil Mothershaw-Rogalla (Siegen), Ingrid Preedy (Dortmund), Kathleen Unterspann (Halstenbek), Jürgen Wrobel (Oberursel) **sowie** Ingrid Gebhard (Wetzlar) und Pat Jüngst (Kassel)
Fachliche Beratung: Natalie Beer (Duisburg), Lieselotte Bohnsack (Essen), Melanie Dahm (Wiesbaden), Arno Esser (Ebsdorfergrund), Rolf-Olaf Geisler (Gelsenkirchen), Susanne Hooß-Biehl (Buseck), Axel Jonuschat † (Oer-Erkenschwick), Stephanie Mayer (Bochum), Angelika Pohlmann (Hanau), Bettina Röper (Ritzerau), Cornelia Scherer (Bielefeld), Dr. Annegret Staufer (Dortmund), Noah Tauche (Kassel), Michael Tetzlaff (Mörfelden-Walldorf)

Zusatzmaterialien zum vorliegenden Schülerbuch

Schülermaterialien

• Workbook	978-3-425-11616-7
• Audio-CDs für Schüler	978-3-425-10666-2
• Workbook mit Audio-CDs	978-3-425-11626-6

Lehrermaterialien

• Teacher's Manual mit Unterrichtskommentaren und Lösungen	978-3-425-11676-1
• Vorschläge für Lernerfolgskontrollen mit CD-ROM	978-3-425-11686-0
• Copymasters mit Unterrichtskommentaren	978-3-425-11696-9
• Audio-CDs + DVD für Lehrer	978-3-425-11716-4
• Lehrersoftware	978-3-425-11706-5

Dieses Werk folgt der reformierten Rechtschreibung und Zeichensetzung 2006. Ausnahmen bilden Texte, bei denen künstlerische, philologische oder lizenzrechtliche Gründe einer Änderung entgegenstehen.

© 2012 Bildungshaus Schulbuchverlage
Westermann Schroedel Diesterweg
Schöningh Winklers GmbH, Braunschweig
www.diesterweg.de

Das Werk und seine Teile sind urheberrechtlich geschützt. Jede Nutzung in anderen als den gesetzlich zugelassenen Fällen bedarf der vorherigen schriftlichen Einwilligung des Verlages. Hinweis zu § 52a UrhG: Weder das Werk noch seine Teile dürfen ohne eine solche Einwilligung gescannt und in ein Netzwerk eingestellt werden. Dies gilt auch für Intranets von Schulen und sonstigen Bildungseinrichtungen.
Für Verweise (Links) auf Internet-Adressen gilt folgender Haftungshinweis: Trotz sorgfältiger inhaltlicher Kontrolle wird die Haftung für die Inhalte der externen Seiten ausgeschlossen. Für den Inhalt dieser externen Seiten sind ausschließlich deren Betreiber verantwortlich. Sollten Sie bei dem angegebenen Inhalt des Anbieters dieser Seite auf kostenpflichtige, illegale oder anstößige Inhalte treffen, so bedauern wir dies ausdrücklich und bitten Sie, uns umgehend per E-Mail davon in Kenntnis zu setzen, damit beim Nachdruck der Verweis gelöscht wird.

Druck A[4] / Jahr 2018
Alle Drucke der Serie A sind im Unterricht parallel verwendbar.

Redaktion: Doris Bos, Barbara Drauschke, Jutta Eckardt-Scheurig, Amy Koerner, Laura Lanik, Dr. Katja Nandorf und Verena Nungesser sowie Matthew Emery
Karten: Joachim Zwick, Gießen
Illustrationen: Ulf Marckwort, Kassel
Umschlaggestaltung: blum design und kommunikation GmbH, Hamburg
Layout: Claudia Ehrlich, Jesse Konzept & Text GmbH, Hannover
Druck und Bindung: westermann druck GmbH, Braunschweig

ISBN 978-3-425-**11606**-8

Inhalt

Seite	Kapitel / Theme	Sprechabsichten	Methoden-kompetenzen
9	**1** ● **Figure, food and famine**		
10	A Looks and image	sich über Werbeanzeigen austauschen über retuschierte Fotos sprechen über Schönheitsideale diskutieren über Essstörungen sprechen	How to talk, listen, mediate, discuss, read, work with a dictionary and statistics, write, present
17	B Hunger in a land of plenty	die Essgewohnheiten in verschiedenen Ländern vergleichen über die Lebensmittelindustrie sprechen über eine Kampagne gegen Hunger in der Welt berichten	How to write, read, write a summary, talk about lyrics, mediate
24 26	P Practice matters O How they eat in heaven		How to work with a dictionary
27	**2** ● **Project: Pages from America's past***		How to work on a project
28 30 32 36 38 40	Introduction P1 A long journey, the first Thanksgiving P2 Moving the Native Americans from their lands P3 Slaves, a president killed, another war P4 Hollywood, Charles Lindbergh, Al Capone P5 The nuclear bomb, the Cold War, Apollo 11 and more weapons	über die USA sprechen eine Präsentation über die ersten Siedler und die Unabhängigkeit von England halten eine Präsentation über *Native Americans* und ihre Vertreibung halten eine Präsentation über den Sklavenhandel und Gleichberechtigung der Afroamerikaner halten eine Präsentation über die Industrialisierung der USA halten eine Präsentation über die Weltmacht Amerika halten	How to write, talk, present, talk about lyrics, poems and films, write a comment, listen, mediate
42	GR Grammar revision		
45	**3** ● **Human rights and wrongs**		
46	A Human rights for everyone	über die eigenen Rechte sprechen über Menschenrechte und Menschenrechtsverletzungen sprechen über eigene Menschenrechte im Alltag diskutieren	How to listen, write a summary and comment, read, discuss, present, do an interview
52	B The death penalty	über Statistiken sprechen über die Todesstrafe diskutieren sich mit einem Film auseinandersetzen	How to work with statistics, read, mediate, discuss, talk about films, present
60 62	P Practice matters O Let the posters speak		

Die Projekt-*Themes* in diesem Band Notting Hill Gate 6B sind modular und können in beliebiger Reihenfolge bearbeitet werden. Sie sind nicht obligatorisch. Die Auswahl der Texte und Aufgaben richtet sich nach den Schwerpunkten des schulinternen Curriculums.

Textsorten	Info-Texte	Sprachliche Mittel / LiF
Fragebogen, Werbeanzeigen, Videoclip, Interview, Hörtext, Infotext, Zeitungsartikel		1R Steigerung der Adjektive 2R Verlaufsform der Vergangenheit 3R Einfache Vergangenheit oder Verlaufsform? 4 Adjektive nach Verben der Sinneswahrnehmung 5R Fragenbildung 6R Modalverben
Zeitschriftenartikel, Videoclip, Sachtext, Liedtext, Webseite		
Erzählung		
Zitate, Sachtexte, Gedichte, Liedtexte, Hörtexte, Videoclips, Plakate, Zeitstrahl		7R Das Passiv 8R Die Vorvergangenheit 9R Formen des Futurs
Interview, Hörtext, Artikel aus den Menschenrechtserklärungen, Informationstexte, Videoclip, Auszug aus einer Rede	The Universal Declaration of Human Rights S. 48	10R Bedingungssätze 2 11 Indirekte Fragen mit Zeitverschiebung
Statistik, Landkarte, Auszug aus einem Brief, Nachruf, Webseite, Zitate, Inhaltsangabe eines Films	Sister Helen Prejean S. 58	12R Unregelmäßig gesteigerte Adjektive 13 Partizipien zur Verkürzung von Nebensätzen 14R Die ing-Form nach Präpositionen 15R Besonderheiten bei manchen Nomen
Poster		

* = fakultatives Zusatzangebot

Inhalt

Seite	Kapitel / Theme		Sprechabsichten	Methoden-kompetenzen
63	4	Project: Living together*		How to work on a project
64		Introduction	über Lebens- und Familienkonzepte sprechen	How to talk, write a comment and a summary, present, discuss, read comics, mediate, write, listen, talk about lyrics and films
66	P1	Roles in relationships	eine Präsentation über Geschlechterrollen halten	
68	P2	Arranged marriages	Ansichten über die Ehe diskutieren	
70	P3	Love and laughter	*Chat-up lines* erklären	
72	P4	A love song and a love letter	ein Liebeslied/einen Liebesbrief interpretieren	
73	P5	My stories		
74	P6	Films about families	eine Präsentation über Familienfilme halten	
76	GR	Grammar Revision		
79	5	Global player		
80	A	India	über Fakten zum Thema Indien sprechen über die Geschichte Indiens sprechen über den indischen Arbeitsalltag sprechen	How to read, listen, mediate, present, work on a project
88	B	Global economy and sweatshops	über Herstellerinformationen in der eigenen Kleidung sprechen die Lebensumstände von zwei Teenagern vergleichen seine Meinung zu Sweatshops ausdrücken	How to listen, read comics, mediate, talk, discuss, read, write a comment, present
94	P	Practice matters		
96	O	An Indian invention		
97	6	Project: Hopes and dreams*		How to work on a project
98		Introduction	sich über Zukunftsvorstellungen austauschen	How to talk, read, write, talk about poems and lyrics, listen, present
99	P1	People about the future	Äußerungen vergleichen	
100	P2	Poems about the future	eine Präsentation über ein Gedicht oder Lied halten	
101	P3	Make a change		
102	P4	How green is your future?	über Umweltinitiativen sprechen über die Zukunft spekulieren	
104	P5	Songs about the future		
106	GR	Grammar Revision		

Textsorten	Info-Texte	Sprachliche Mittel/LiF
Zitate, Sachtext, Satire, Auszug aus Jugendroman, Liedtext, Jugendzeitschrift, Romanauszug, Zeitungsartikel, Comic, Dialog, Gedicht, *Chat-up lines*, Liedtext, Liebesbrief, Bericht, Poesie, Rezept Inhaltsangaben	Living together S. 65 Arranged marriages S. 68	16R Partizip Präsens und Partizip Perfekt 17R Das Perfekt
Sachtext, Informationstext, Aussagen, Videoclip		18 *used to* 19 Konjunktionen 20 Bedingungssätze 3 21 Relativsätze, bei denen man das Relativpronomen weglassen kann
Labels, Aussagen, Hörtext, *graphic novel*, Bericht, Cartoon, Landkarte		22 Das Partizip Perfekt nach *have* und *get* in der Bedeutung von „(veran)lassen"
Sachtext		
Aussagen, Gedichte, Liedtext, Webseite, Bröschüre		23 Ortsbezeichnungen mit und ohne Artikel

* = fakultatives Zusatzangebot

Inhalt

110	Book stop
110	BS 1 Uglies
112	BS 2 Hunger in a world of plenty
114	BS 3 The Absolutely True Diary of a Part-Time Indian
118	BS 4 Squanto
120	BS 5 Dead Man Walking
122	BS 6 Star Rubbish
124	BS 7 The end of a friendship?
126	BS 8 BollyWhat? – The Bollywood FAQs
127	BS 9 Suniti Namjoshi, Bird woman

128	How to …
128	How to talk/listen
129	How to read
130	How to write/do an interview
131	How to present
132	How to work on a project
133	How to mediate
134	How to work with a dictionary
135	How to write a summary/comment
136	How to discuss
137	How to work with statistics
138	How to prepare for an exam
140	How to talk about films
142	How to read and analyse comics
143	How to talk about poems and lyrics

144	Wordbank
144	Looks and image
145	Food
146	American politics
147	Human rights
148	Justice
149	Relationships
150	Economy
152	Hopes and dreams

153	Classroom phrases
155	Glossary
157	Language in Focus

170	Words mit Einführung
198	English-German dictionary
242	German-English dictionary
255	Names
258	Numbers
259	Irregular verbs
261	Bild- und Textquellen

CD	Der Hörtext ist auf der Schüler-CD.
CD	Der Hörtext ist auf der Lehrer-CD.
DVD	Das Video ist auf der Lehrer-DVD.
workbook A1	Hierzu gibt es Übungen im Workbook.
LiF 1	Hierzu gibt es eine Erklärung im LiF-Teil.
wordbank food	In den *wordbanks* findest du die wichtigsten Wörter und Ausdrücke zu einem Thema.
how to … talk	Auf den *How to*-Seiten findest du Lernhilfen.
project	Projekte sind umfangreiche Aufgaben für Gruppen.
portfolio dossier	Du kannst deine Arbeit im Portfolio-Dossier (Mappe) aufbewahren.
portfolio I can listen	Zu dieser Aufgabe gibt es in den Portfolio-Bögen im Workbook einen Eintrag.
model	Ein *model text* ist eine Vorlage für deinen eigenen Text.
film	Aufgaben zum Hör-Seh-Verstehen
★	leichte Aufgabe
☀	schwere Aufgabe
Choose	Suche dir eine Aufgabe aus oder denke dir eine eigene Aufgabe aus.
○○○○	Diese Aufgaben gehören nicht zum Basisweg und bieten Vertiefungsmöglichkeiten.

Figure, food and famine

1

In diesem *Theme* ...

- beschäftigst du dich mit Schönheitsidealen.
- erfährst du etwas über Fotobearbeitung.
- sprichst du über Essstörungen.
- beschäftigst du dich mit Essgewohnheiten in verschiedenen Ländern.
- erfährst du etwas über eine Organisation, die Essen an Bedürftige verteilt.

Figure, food and famine

A1 ○ The "Do I feel good about myself?" test

a) Read the test and write down your answers in your exercise book.

Do I feel good about myself?

1 You have to talk to your class about something important. What do you do?
  a) You write down what you want to say and learn it by heart.
  b) You write down what you want to say, read from the paper and don't look at the group.
  c) You just say what you feel and hope it sounds good.
  d) You ask your friend to talk for you.

2 Who or what has the biggest influence on the way you feel about yourself?
  a) media or celebrities
  b) peers
  c) friends or family
  d) nobody else but me

3 What do you do if you look in the mirror in the morning and you see that you have a spot on your face?
  a) You tell your mother you don't feel well and you stay in bed.
  b) You cover the spot.
  c) You go to school but hide in dark corners.
  d) You don't care.

4 Your friend says that someone that you like wants to go out with you. What's your first reaction?
  a) You don't believe your friend.
  b) You compare yourself to other people this person has been out with before.
  c) You are happy and don't know what to do.
  d) You phone and invite the person you like to the cinema.

5 You have problems with other pupils at school. What do you do?
  a) You ask your mother if you can go to another school.
  b) You talk to those pupils and ask them what the problem is.
  c) You eat lots of chocolate and crisps in your room while you watch TV.
  d) You avoid those pupils and hope the problems will go away.

6 When you try something new and it doesn't work …
  a) You think: "I'm such an idiot" for days afterwards.
  b) You think about what went wrong and try again.
  c) You feel bad but then you do something that you know you can do.
  d) You decide never to try anything new again.

7 The person you sit next to in class has got a higher mark than you for their homework.
  a) You are disappointed but you will work harder next time.
  b) You don't care, you got what you expected and that's fine.
  c) It reminds you that your classmate is just better than you at everything.
  d) You try to sit next to somebody else.

8 Teams are being chosen during P.E.
  a) You don't want to play because you know you will be picked last.
  b) You want to pick the teams.
  c) You tell the person picking teams why you should be picked.
  d) You know you won't be picked first but you don't worry.

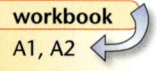

b) Look at page 25. Add up your points and check your results.

Figure, food and famine

A2 ● The advert effect

a) Look at these adverts and read the statements. What do the products promise? Talk to a partner.

how to …
talk

portfolio
I can talk

b) Do you buy any products like these? Why or why not?

c) Look at the adverts. How do you think the people in these adverts feel? Why?

> feel good about themselves ·
> feel confident · are full of life ·
> happy · …

d) ★ Choose oneof the adverts and describe it to a partner.

 Do you think these adverts work? Why or why not? Discuss with a partner.

wordbank
looks and image

portfolio
I can work with words, work with grammar, talk

11

Figure, food and famine

A3 ● She's got the looks

a) Look at the photos. What is the difference between the two of them? Make a list.

Before

After

> looks thinner · prettier · more confident · younger · older · longer neck · slimmer nose · brighter eyes · darker hair · fewer shadows under eyes · …

b) Watch the video clip on the DVD or on the Internet:
http://www.youtube.com/watch?v=iYhCn0jf46U

☆ Say in German what you have seen and what you think about "beautiful" people now.

☼ Print out a few "freeze" shots and write subtitles for them to say what is happening.

c) Why do you think some people, and especially celebrities, have their photos retouched?

> look more beautiful · don't want to look old / fat / tired / stressed · must look perfect · pressure from fans · must keep up image · want to look the same as when they were younger · whiter / brighter teeth · …

A4 ○ In my opinion

According to magazines, TV and advertising the ideal beauty is skinny, young and flawless. Why do they show unrealistic ideals of beauty? And why do people respond to these ideals by trying to change? Discuss in class.

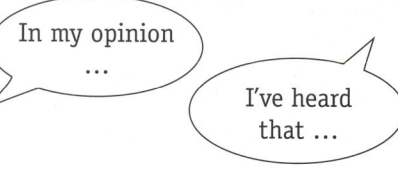

- In my opinion …
- I've heard that …
- No, I don't think so. I think …
- What I mean is …
- I see your point, but …

Figure, food and famine

A5 ● Eating disorders

a) Listen to Amy Kowalik and read along. What happened to her?

ANNOUNCER: This week our program is about eating disorders. Here to talk about her experience is Amy Kowalik. Good morning, Amy. Nice of you to come and talk to our listeners. Can you tell us something about your experience?

AMY: Yes, good morning. And thanks for inviting me. Well, it all started in high school: there, I was the girl who always got good grades. I had lots of friends and a cool boyfriend.

ANNOUNCER: I see.

AMY: My friends thought I was happy and were always talking to me about their problems. But I never talked to them about mine. I guess I thought I didn't have any.

ANNOUNCER: Mhmm.

AMY: But, you see, I always wanted to be the best at everything I did. If I got an average grade, I would work harder and harder. By the time fall came, I was totally burned-out. Plus, things weren't so great at home. My mom and dad were fighting a lot. I started eating less. I didn't eat at home because my mom and dad were always fighting at the dinner table. I didn't eat out much because I was always running around trying to be the best. I started losing weight, more and more all the time. At first I didn't realise I had lost much weight, but then my family and friends started telling me how great I looked. It felt really good to hear that.

ANNOUNCER: What happened then?

AMY: Well, first I really felt great. I had finally found something in my life I could take control of – my weight. I weighed myself all the time. For a month or so, everyone said how good I looked. But soon my mother and my friends started telling me I looked too skinny. But I didn't believe them. In the mirror I couldn't see what they saw. I told them that I had lost so much weight because of a cold and that they needn't worry.

ANNOUNCER: And, did they believe you?

AMY: Yes, actually, at first they did. You see, I would eat snacks when my family or friends were around. Then I'd eat nothing else for the rest of the day, which they didn't notice. I just couldn't stop dieting at that stage.

ANNOUNCER: I see. And then?

AMY: I soon became exhausted from not eating enough. I didn't even have enough energy to dance – and I used to love dancing. I couldn't concentrate at school and I was sick quite often. I was always freezing cold because my body didn't have the energy to keep me warm. Then, one day at school, I got really sick and had to see a doctor. The doctor told me I was too thin and that I was actually suffering from anorexia. That was when things started to change.

ANNOUNCER: Well, thank you Amy. We'll take a short break now and afterwards we'll hear from Amy's doctor about how she helped her. Now let's listen to …

CD
1/2 1/1

portfolio
I can listen

LiF
2R, 3R

b) Answer the questions in your exercise book.

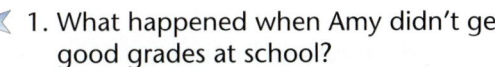

1. What happened when Amy didn't get good grades at school?
2. Why didn't Amy eat at home?
3. And why didn't she eat out?
4. Was it Amy's plan to lose weight?
5. What did Amy do so that her friends and family did not notice that she was not eating?
6. Why did she always feel cold?

1. Why do you think Amy didn't talk to her friends about her problems?
2. Why do you think Amy wanted to be the best at everything?
3. Why do you think Amy kept eating less and less even when her friends and family told her she looked too skinny?
4. What advice do you think the doctor gave Amy?

c) Why do you think it was important for Amy to control her weight? Discuss in small groups.

how to …
read

portfolio
I can read

wordbank
looks and image

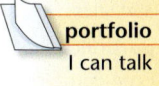
portfolio
I can talk

workbook
A4

13

how to ... work with a dictionary

portfolio I can learn English

A6 What are eating disorders?

a) Look up the words or phrases from the box that you do not understand.

- anorexia
- bulimia
- go on a diet
- being obsessed with one's weight
- body weight a lot less than the average
- malnutrition
- infection
- being afraid of gaining weight
- obsessive exercise
- usually look pale
- eating binge
- induce vomiting

CD 1/3

portfolio I can listen

b) Listen to the second part of the radio programme from A5. What is the main difference between anorexia and bulimia? Take notes.

c) Listen again and make notes on what comes to mind while listening. Is there anything that the doctor says that surprises you? Talk about it with a partner.

A7 Eating disorders – some statistics

portfolio I can read

a) Read the facts. What do you find surprising?

Did you know that ...

- approximately 8 million people in the United States have an eating disorder such as anorexia and bulimia?
- an estimated 10–15% of people with anorexia or bulimia are males?
- 95% of those who have eating disorders are between the ages of 12 and 25?
- 5–10% of anorexics die within 10 years after contracting the disease?
- in the UK, approximately 1 in 150 fifteen-year-old females and 1 in 1000 fifteen-year-old males suffer from anorexia?
- approximately 1% of all sixteen- to eighteen-year-olds have anorexia?
- about 40% of people with anorexia recover completely?

b) Match the sentence halves.

1. 85–90% of people with eating disorders
2. Approximately 8 million people in the United States
3. Only 5% of the people with eating disorders
4. In the UK, approximately 1 in 150
5. In the UK, approximately 1 in 1000
6. About 60% of people with anorexia

a. never recover completely.
b. fifteen-year-old males suffer from anorexia.
c. are females.
d. have an eating disorder.
e. fifteen-year-old females suffer from anorexia.
f. are not between the ages of 12 and 25.

how to ... work with statistics

portfolio I can combine skills, mediate

Choose one or more of the facts in a) and make a graphical representation of the figures (for example a pie chart). Then write down what it shows.

workbook A5–A7

c) Find statistics about eating disorders in Germany. Report the facts back to the class.

Figure, food and famine

A8 ● The perfect figure

a) Listen to this report about George and read along. Find out what went wrong and why.

CD
1/5 1/3

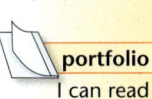
portfolio
I can read

George Ramsay, from Taunton, Somerset, developed an eating disorder at the age of 15, and his weight dropped to 41 kilos.

He told the BBC: "I was always, not fat, but fairly chunky. I wanted to get fit for the rugby season and I thought that by losing weight I would get fit. I stopped eating fats in meals and avoided carbohydrates as much as possible. My mother said what I was doing was not good. I thought it was good. I lost a lot of weight and felt great at first but soon I noticed this was not ideal. My energy levels were zilch. I felt tired all the time and it was difficult for me to eat at all. Everything tasted terrible. I felt awful. Soon I became very ill.

My mother took me to the doctor's to get help. He did a lot of tests – but he never thought I might have an eating disorder. When the test results came back and there was nothing physically wrong with me he didn't really know what to do."

George's trainer, Gordon Brown, came to visit him one day because George had stopped going to training. "No energy. I couldn't run to catch my grandma," said George.

George and Mr Brown talked for a while. They talked about the team's performance in the last game and the new sponsors who were going to buy new balls and shoes for the team. However, Mr Brown did not say anything about the fact that George looked so thin.

But after a long time George started to open up. He told his trainer how he had wanted to get fit for the rugby season by losing weight.

Mr Brown was shocked. He told George that he had had the perfect figure for rugby. He told him that now he would have to put on a lot of weight and gain muscle if he wanted to play again. And that's what George wanted. He had always lived for rugby and wanted to return to playing. So they sat together and worked out a plan.

b) What do you think the plan was? How might George's story go on? Discuss with a partner and make notes.

c) Now listen to the end of the report on the CD and find out if you were right. Compare the facts to your notes from b).

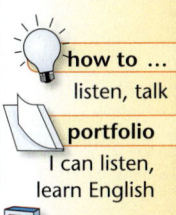
how to …
listen, talk

portfolio
I can listen,
learn English

wordbank
looks and
image

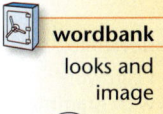
CD
1/6

A9 ● I feel tired

a) Go through the report in A8 again. Write down the sentences which tell you how George "felt" or "looked" or how something "tasted". What do you notice about the words that follow the verbs?

b) Complete the sentences.

1. People suffering from eating disorders usually ??? .
2. They often ??? .
3. They don't have a lot of energy and ??? all the time.
4. They often get colds easily and with a cold the food they eat ??? .
5. Although they have lost so much weight they usually think they ??? . To others they ??? .

> look fat · feel tired · look pale ·
> look too thin · feel exhausted ·
> tastes terrible

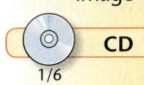
LiF
4

portfolio
I can work
with grammar

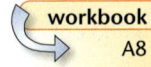
workbook
A8

15

Figure, food and famine

A10 • Questions and answers

a) While George and his trainer Mr Brown were talking, they asked each other a lot of questions. Read the answers and write the questions. The first word has been given.

LiF
5R

1   Q: Did …?
    A: No, we didn't win last Saturday.
2   Q: Why …?
    A: We lost because two good players were missing. The score was 24–18!
3   Q: Did …?
    A: Yes, Bobby played.
4   Q: Was …?
    A: Yes, one person was hurt. Jack broke the little finger on his right hand.
5   Q: Did …?
    A: Yes, I watched the rugby game between Scotland and New Zealand on TV with my father.
6   Q: Are …?
    A: No, I'm not doing any sports at school at the moment.
7   Q: When …
    A: My last pizza? I think I ate my last pizza about four months ago.
8   Q: Do …?
    A: Yes, I feel tired all the time.
9   Q: Why …?
    A: Because I thought I was too chunky to play rugby.
10 Q: Who …?
    A: Nobody told me to lose weight but all the other boys were much fitter and less chunky.

portfolio
I can work with grammar

workbook
A9

b) Read through the questions that you just wrote down. Who asked them, George or Mr Brown? Put the names in front of the questions.

Write down at least six questions you could ask George and his trainer.

A11 ○ Choose

portfolio
I can combine skills, write

1. Take a digital photograph of yourself. Retouch the photo with graphics software. How do you feel about it? Present your photo in class and tell the others what you have changed and how you did it.

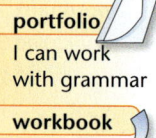

wordbank
looks and image

2. Design an ad for a beauty product. Present it.

3. You are one of Amy's or George's friends. Write a letter to a magazine help page. Describe his or her problems and situation. Ask for help.

how to …
write, present

4. Draw up a fitness plan for an unfit football player or another sports person. Think about food and exercise. Make a poster and present it.

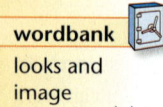

workbook
A10

5. Write a different ending to the report about George's eating disorder.

Figure, food and famine

B1 ● What the world eats

Imagine you had dinner with 30 different families in 24 different countries. That's what photographer Peter Menzel and writer Faith D'Aluisio did for their book, *Hungry Planet: What the World Eats*. Each chapter of their book shows a photo of a family, with their food for one week. Here are some of the families.

a) What food items do you recognize?
   What do you find unfamiliar?
   What surprises you?
   If you want to see more details,
   have a look at the next two pages.

> fresh · packaged ·
> comes in sacks · frozen ·
> cooked · ready to eat

workbook B1

portfolio I can talk

wordbank food

A

B

C

D

b) Match the photographs to these countries.

> China · Ecuador ·
> Mali · USA

c) Compare what the families eat.

d) Choose one of the photos. What are the differences and similarities between what you see in that photograph and what you are used to in your own life?

   ★ Make a list with two columns: "similar" and "different".

   ☼ Make notes and write about what is similar and what is different.

how to … write

portfolio I can write

workbook B2

17

Gwaltney
BROWN SUGAR
Maruchan Ramen
TEXAS
RAGU
BURGER KING
MOTT'S
HOT POCKETS
Flatout
Diet Coke
Bud

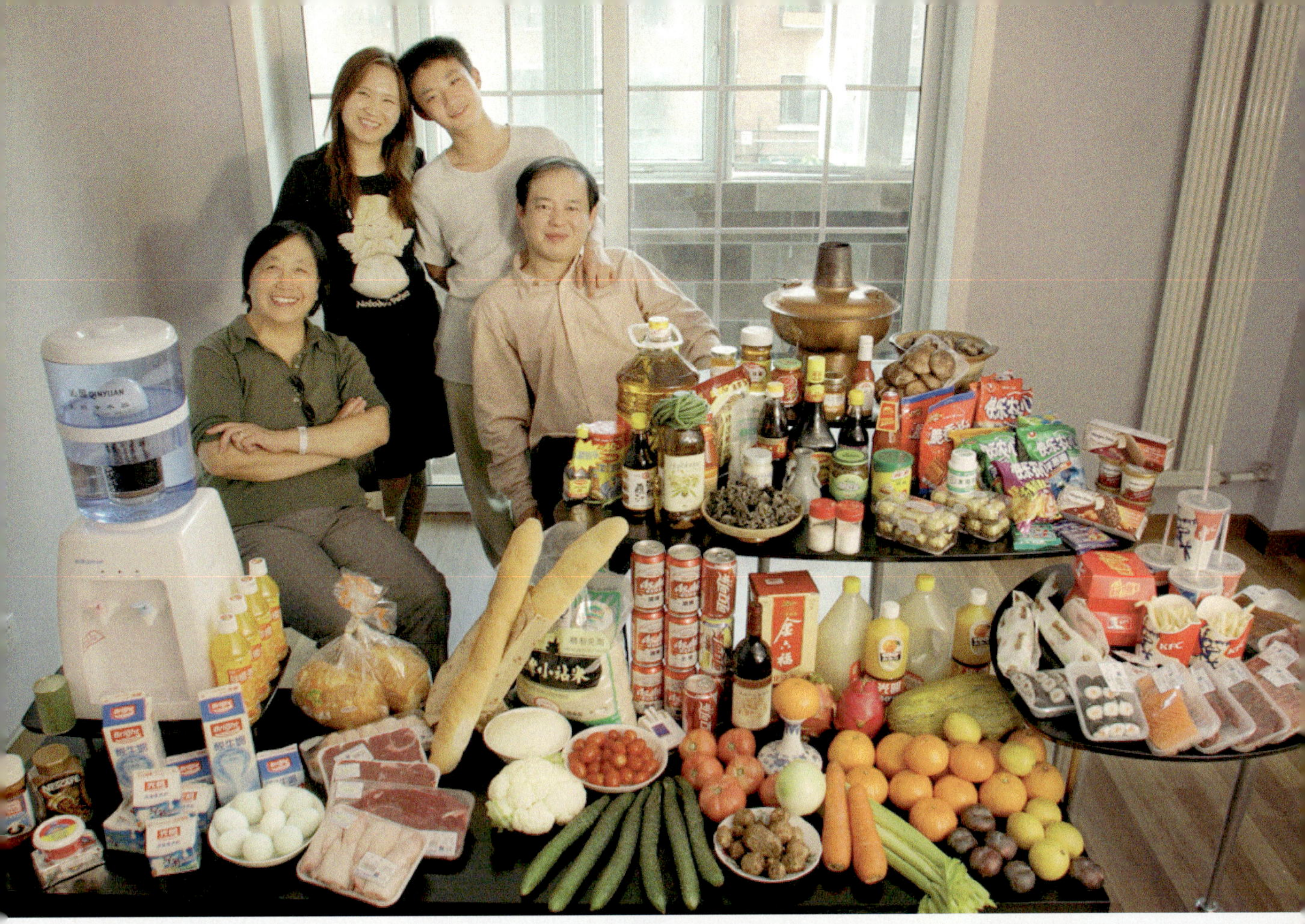

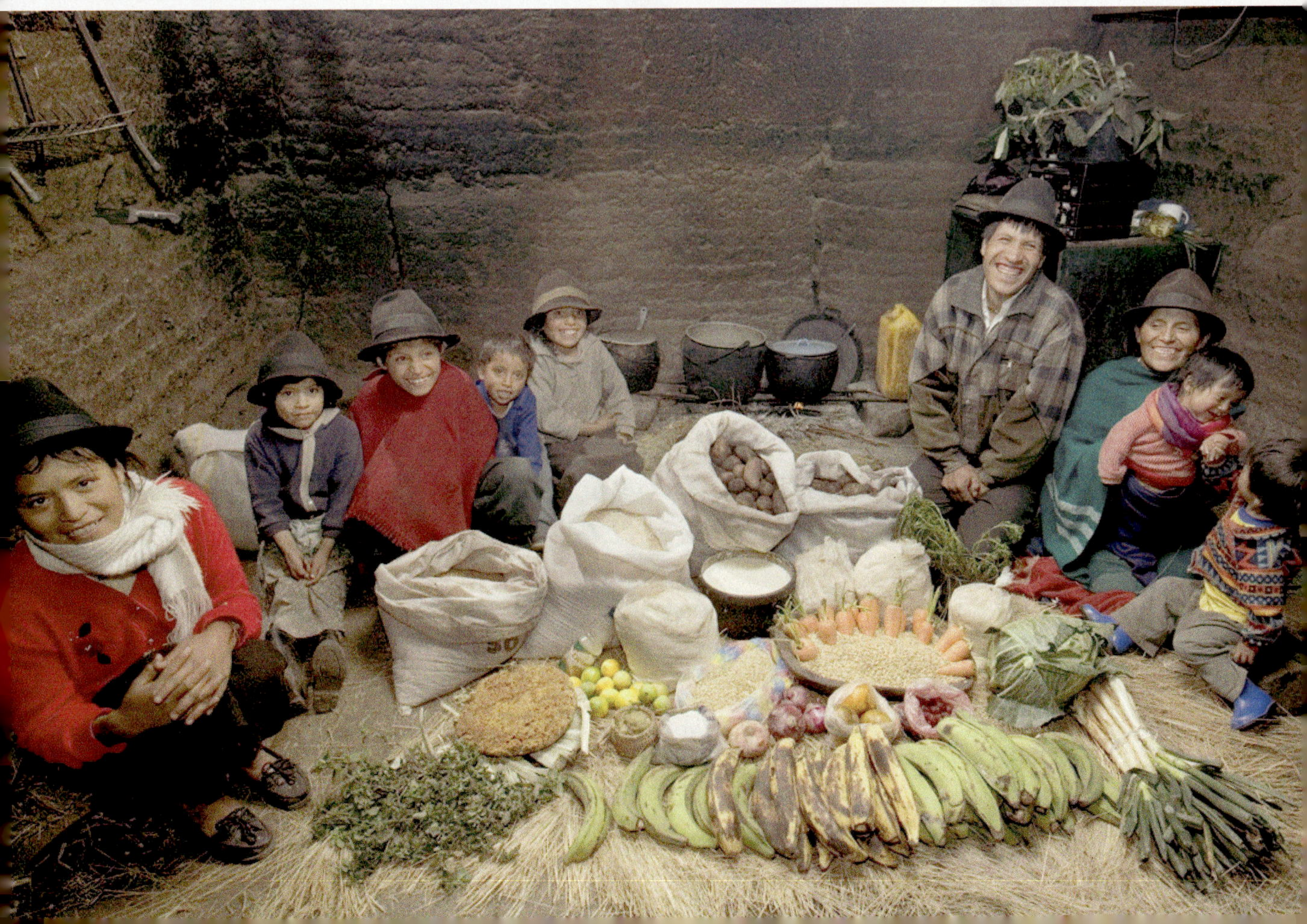

Figure, food and famine

B2 ● Hunger in a land of plenty

a) Skim the article. Then write down in two or three sentences what it is about.

> SYDNEY, Australia, July 6, 2010 (IPS) – Devina Celeste, 50, waits in a queue of about 40 people for the only hot meal she will get on this cold winter night.

The queue is getting longer. Nearly half of the people in the queue who are teenagers and students have become good friends while waiting for this only-meal-a-day they have on weekdays.

"This is my only real meal. I need almost half of the money that I earn to pay for my little flat. The rest goes on bills and buying the basic things like bread and milk and soap and toilet paper", says Celeste, a massage therapist. Celeste is one of the "working poor" in Australia who are not able to earn enough to feed themselves. And this group is getting bigger all the time.

They are finding it hard to fight off hunger in this land of plenty, where three million tonnes of food are thrown away every year. This food is worth 5.2 billion Australian dollars.

Yet there are 60,000 low-income families who cannot afford at least one meal every day, and there are two million people who have to ask for food at least once a year, says a November 2009 report.

Some volunteer groups have started to act. They collect surplus food to feed the poor and hungry. OzHarvest is one such food bank that collects unwanted food from restaurants, food outlets and corporate kitchens. Its founder, Ronni Kahn, remembers being shocked while she was working as an events organizer, to see good food being thrown away.

When Kahn set up OzHarvest in November 2004, the organization collected and delivered food for about 13,000 meals to eight charities. Today it delivers over 340,000 meals each month to people in need across Australia.

By Neena Bhandari

b) Read the article again and find the following information.

1. Who are the "working poor"?
2. How much food do Australians throw away every year?
3. What is OzHarvest and when was it set up?
4. Who started OzHarvest and why?

c) Find out about a similar organization in your area. Who are the volunteers? How is the charity run? Where does it get support? Why is this charity necessary? Write a report.

Why do you think Australia is called a "land of plenty" in this article? Would you call Germany a land of plenty, too? Why? Write a statement.

d) Watch the video clip about Ronni Kahn, the founder of OzHarvest food bank and winner of the "Australian Local Hero" award in 2010. What do you find out about her? How did she get the idea to start OzHarvest? Take notes and share your findings in class.

Figure, food and famine

B3 ◯ Not fair

a) Read this Canadian brochure about the agri-food chain and find the one sentence in the text that sums it up best.

Imagine food production as a long chain. The first link is oil and natural gas companies. Moving up to the next link, the oil is made into diesel fuel and natural gas into fertilizer. The next links are the chemical companies which make the pesticides, the companies which make the farm machinery, the companies which prepare the seeds and finally the banks.

Now we have the farmer, in the middle of the chain, who combines fuel, seed and technology with the earth, rain and sun to produce food.

The rest of the chain links are the companies that buy the farm produce, the railways which move the produce from A to B, the factories which process the food, the people who pack it, the shops that sell it and the restaurants which cook it.

Almost every link in this chain is in the hands of between two and ten big multi-billion-dollar multinational corporations. The only link that is not is the farmer. In Canada, that link is made up of over 170,000 family farms.

Every day people spend millions of dollars on food. Food prices go up each year. So where does this money go? The farmers do not get it. In 2010 Canadian farmers had a turnover of about CAN $317,916 each. Their profit however was only about CAN $51,117.

The companies that buy from the farmers, transport it, process it, package it and sell that food make billions of dollars in profit. So do the companies that make tractors, fertilizer, and pesticides. There is no shortage of money in the process, it is just shared unfairly.

b) Collect all the "economy words" in the text.

c) In groups, make a chart or diagram to help you to visualize the agri-food chain. Use your economy words to explain it.

According to the brochure, what is the main problem with the agri-food chain? Write a brief summary. Use your economy words.

how to …
write a summary

wordbank
food, economy

portfolio
I can work with words

workbook
B5–B7

Figure, food and famine

B4 Who's gonna feed the hungry?

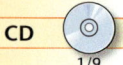

a) Listen to the song and say who the song is about and what this person is praying for.

Hunger Song

When I wake up in the morning
To face another day
Hunger's hanging over my head
There's a weakness in my stomach, Lord
It's always been that way
Hunger's hanging over my head

Chorus:
Who's gonna feed the hungry?
Who's gonna feed the poor?
Who's gonna stand and help me fight?
That lean wolf that's howling at my door?

When the kids come in from playing
And there's nothing there to eat
Hunger's hanging over my head
It makes me feel so helpless
From my head down to my feet
Hunger's hanging over my head

Chorus

And when the day is over
And it's time to go to bed
Hunger's hanging over my head
My prayers look for tomorrow, Lord
To see my family fed
Hunger's hanging over my head

Chorus

Music and lyrics: Joyce Brookshire

b) Do you think the lyrics and the music go together well? Why?

c) Do you know any other songs about hunger? Find some and present them to the class.

Figure, food and famine

B5 ○ Walk the world

a) Look at the photos and read the article. What does this campaign do to help fight world hunger?

---

www.wfp.org

On 6 June 2010 about 150,000 people in 70 countries around the world walked. Why? They wanted to collect money for the United Nations World Food Programme (WFP) in the fight against world hunger. In 2010 the annual "End Hunger: Walk the World" sponsored walk made enough money to give more than 10,000 children school meals for a whole year.

Walking the World for School Meals

The idea of a "World Walk" against hunger started in 2003. The idea came from seeing the millions of poor children around the world who walk several kilometres to school every day – often hungry and barefoot – because they want to learn and have a better future.

WFP gives tens of millions free school meals to these children. Good, healthy food helps students learn better and helps children develop their full physical and mental potential.

---

b) Go to the World Food Programme website (www.wfp.org) and find out more about "Walk the World". Take notes and report back to your partner in German.

c) What is your opinion on "Walk the World"? Would you join in? Why or why not? Discuss your points of view in class. Then write a statement.

B6 ○ Choose

1. Look at the photos in B1 again. What would a photo of your family and your food for one week look like? Make a sketch and describe it.
2. Look at the photos in B1 again. Choose one of the families. Do some research on their home country and its economic situation. Present your findings to the class.
3. Find out about fair trade. Give a presentation of your findings to the class.
4. Go to http://freerice.com and find out how it works. What can you do on this website? Who pays for the donated rice? What do you think about the website? Report to the class.
5. If you were a politician, how would you change things so that the money within the agri-food chain was distributed more fairly?

how to ...
mediate

portfolio
I can talk,
mediate

workbook
B10

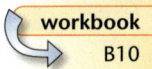

wordbank
food

portfolio
I can
combine skills

workbook
B11

Figure, food and famine

Practice matters

P1 ○ Say it in English

Match the sentences.

1. Zeitschriften, Fernsehen und Werbung zufolge ist die ideale Schönheit dünn, jung und makellos. Wie sagst du das?
2. Wie fragst du, warum Menschen auf diese Idealvorstellungen reagieren?
3. Du wolltest in allem immer der/die Beste sein. Wie drückst du das aus?
4. Wie drückst du aus, dass jemand es schwierig findet, den Hunger zu bekämpfen?
5. Wie fragst du, was jemand nicht kennt?

a. I always wanted to be the best at everything I did.
b. Why do people respond to these ideals?
c. What do you find unfamiliar?
d. According to magazines, TV and advertising the ideal beauty is skinny, young and flawless.
e. They are finding it hard to fight off hunger.

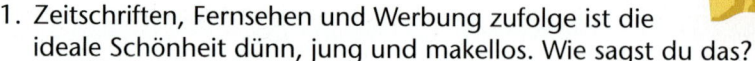

P2 ○ George

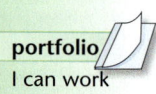
LiF 1R

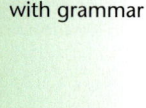
portfolio
I can work with grammar

a) Use the right form of the adjective to complete the sentences.

1. George thought the other boys were (fit) than he was.
2. His mother was (worried) about George than his father.
3. Mr Brown thought that George's problem was the (bad) that he had seen all year.
4. Mr Brown was (helpful) than the doctor.
5. He told George that the team was (good) when George played with them.
6. The plan George and his trainer worked out was the (successful) one that George had ever heard.

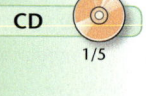
CD 1/5

b) Listen to the CD and check your sentences.

P3 ○ Amy

LiF 2R, 3R

a) Put the verb in brackets in the past progressive.

Amy told the listeners that when she (not listen) to her friends' problems, she (learn) for school. She lost so much weight because she (run) around all the time. She didn't want to eat at home because her parents always (fight). Her friends said that she (look) really good but soon she just felt tired. She found that she (not feel) good any more.

Amy told the listeners that when she was not listening to her friends' problems, ...

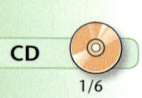
CD 1/6

b) Listen to the CD and check your sentences.

c) Now read what Amy's mother says. Decide if the verb is in the simple past or past progressive.

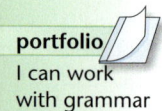
portfolio
I can work with grammar

My daughter (start) to lose weight when she was fifteen. In the first month she (lose) 4 kilos. Every day, while we (eat) lunch, she just (drink) a bottle of water. Even when we (watch) TV in the evening she (eat) nothing. I (start) to worry. I (take) her to the doctor. While he (talk) to her I (find) an article about anorexia in a magazine in the waiting room. When my daughter came out I (still read) the article. I (think) I (know) what the problem (be).

CD 1/7

d) Listen to the CD and check your sentences.

Practice matters

Figure, food and famine

P4 Opposites

a) Copy the table. Find words or phrases that have the opposite meaning to the words in the box and fill in the table.

word or phrase	opposite
gain weight	

chunky · spend money · I began eating more. · gain weight · thin · familiar · similar · go together badly · unrealistic · Everything tasted delicious.

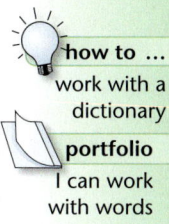

how to …
work with a dictionary

portfolio
I can work with words

b) Work with a partner and compare your words and phrases.

P5 How are things?

a) Complete the sentences.

1. When Sally went to school in her new dress her friends thought she ??? ???.
2. "Thank you for inviting me for dinner, Mrs Black. Everything ??? ???."
3. Peggy went to the doctor after many people had told her how ??? she ???.
4. "How do you feel about moving to Australia?" – "I ??? very ???."
5. I think honey and olives together must ??? ???.
6. He likes how he looks and feels. He ??? ???.
7. A bad fish ??? ???.
8. I like this new band. I think their music ??? ???.

feel · sound · taste · look · smell

excited · pretty · horrible · exhausted · delicious · good · terrible · confident

LiF 4

1. When Sally went to school in her new dress her friends thought she looked pretty.

b) Listen to the CD and check if you were right.

CD 1/8

P6 Silent letters

Listen to the words on the CD and repeat them. Which letter is silent?

mirror · talking · weight · campaign · whole · exhausted · half · thought · sign · Wednesday

CD 1/9

Do I feel good about myself? – Test results

	1	2	3	4	5	6	7	8
a)	3 points	1 point	1 point	1 point	1 point	1 point	3 points	1 point
b)	2 points	2 points	3 points	2 points	4 points	4 points	4 points	4 points
c)	4 points	3 points	2 points	3 points	3 points	2 points	1 point	3 points
d)	1 point	4 points	4 points	4 points	3 points	2 points	2 points	2 points

32 – 27 points: You have high self-esteem. You're confident and it sounds as if you really know and like who you are.

26 – 16 points: It sounds like most days you feel happy about yourself but sometimes you are shy and doubt what you can do.

15 – 8 points: You seem to be very hard on yourself and always look at what you did wrong or can't do. It's time to make a list of all the things that are good about yourself and you might be surprised.

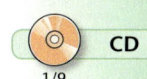

25

Figure, food and famine

Optional

○ How they eat in heaven

The following excerpt is taken from *The Bean Trees*, a novel by Barbara Kingsolver. It describes a young woman's journey through the United States. Taylor Greer, the young woman, is sitting down to dinner with some refugees from Guatemala. One of them tells the following story.

THE BEAN TREES

"Tortolita, let me tell you a story," Estevan said. "This is a South American, wild Indian story about heaven and hell."

Mrs Parsons made a prudish face, and Estevan went on. "If you go to visit hell, you will see a room like this kitchen. There is a pot of delicious stew on the table, with the most delicate aroma you can imagine. All around, people sit, like us. Only they are dying of starvation. They are jibbering and jabbering," he looked extra hard at Mrs Parsons, "but they cannot get a bite of this wonderful stew God has made for them. Now why is that?"

"Because they're choking? For all eternity?" Lou Ann asked. […]

"No," he said. "Good guess, but no. They are starving because they only have spoons with very long handles. As long as that." He pointed to the mop, which I had forgotten to put away. "With these ridiculous, terrible spoons the people in hell can reach into the pot but they cannot put food in their mouths. Oh, how hungry they are! Oh, how they swear and curse each other!" he said, looking again at Virgie. He was enjoying this.

"Now," he went on, "you can go and visit heaven. What? You see a room just like the first one, the same table, the same pot of stew, the same spoons as long as a sponge mop. But these people are all happy and fat."

"Real fat, or do you mean just well-fed?" Lou Ann asked.

"Just well-fed," he said. "Perfectly, magnificently well-fed, and very happy. Why do you think?"

36

CD

What could be the answer to Estevan's question? You can find it when you listen to the CD.

Project: Pages from America's past 2

Project 1

A long journey, the first Thanksgiving, a war and tea in the sea

Project 2

Moving the Native Americans from their land and killing the buffalo

Project 3

Slaves, a president killed, another war, the KKK and four famous black Americans

Project 4

Hollywood, Charles Lindbergh, Al Capone and Black Thursday

Project 5
The nuclear bomb, the Cold War, Apollo 11 and more weapons

Pages from America's past

> In this Theme you will be dealing with topics from America's past.
>
> Have a look at these pictures. You might recognize them from Notting Hill Gate textbooks and workbooks from the last few years. Do you remember any of the topics?
>
> What other topics come to mind when you think of America's past?

Once the religious, the hunted and weary
Chasing the promise of freedom and hope
Came to this country to build a new vision
Far from the reaches of kingdom and pope

Steppenwolf, Monster

The first mobile phone call was made from the streets of New York in 1973. Martin Cooper, back then a manager at Motorola, called one of the company's biggest rivals.

Lacrosse is a ball sport originating from Native Americans.

Timeline

About 17,000 BC
People walk from Siberia to Alaska and in the course of time further south.

Pages from America's past

You can have a car painted any colour you want so long as it is black.

Henry Ford

I don't drink coffee, I take tea my dear
I like my toast done on one side
You can hear it in my accent when I talk
I'm an Englishman in New York

I'm an alien, I'm a legal alien
I'm an Englishman in New York
I'm an alien, I'm a legal alien
I'm an Englishman in New York

Sting, Englishman in New York

Tip
Nimm zur Kenntnis, dass manche Informationen aus den Ursprungsquellen variieren.

- In this Theme you will find glimpses of America's past. You can choose any of the five projects, and any topic you find interesting.
- Discuss in your group who wants to deal with which topic and text. You can also choose one of the additional facts from the timeline and research it.
- Find ways to present your results. You may wish to present text or picture collages, a short scene (live, as a short film or a listening sequence), posters for a gallery walk or a reading session.
- Draw your own timeline onto large sheets of paper and hang it on the wall in your classroom. Display the results of your individual projects on the appropriate part of the timeline so it will give orientation to everyone in the class and to all visitors.

project

workbook p. 17

1492
Columbus reaches the New World.

Pages from America's past

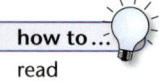
how to...
read

Project 1 ○ A long journey, the first Thanksgiving, a war and tea in the sea

Why did people from England cross the Atlantic in small boats to start a new life in another country? Some farmers left because their land was taken over for sheep farming, others because they were poor. Sons of rich people left because only their oldest brothers got their father's land. Some Protestants were becoming more and more unhappy with the Church of England and wanted to start their own church.

The first ships arrive
In December 1606, three ships left England with 144 boys and men who wanted to settle in America. When they reached the East Coast of America the following year in April, only 104 of them were still alive. They started the first permanent European settlement in America in May 1607 in the southern part of what is now called Virginia, and called it Jamestown.
Many of them were not familiar with physical work which caused a lot of problems, and then some of the Native Americans they met were unfriendly and attacked them. Within half a year, about half of the settlers had died of starvation and disease.

Pocahontas
One of the settlers, John Smith, played an important role in the survival of the colony. With his diplomatic skills and the help of Pocahontas, the daughter of the chief of the Powhatan Indians, peace was arranged between the Native Americans and the settlers. Pocahontas later married one of the settlers, John Rolfe, who introduced the tobacco plant to that area. Tobacco became the most important export of that time and essential to the survival of the colonists.

POCAHONTAS, ca. 1616

The Pilgrim Fathers
The second English settlement was founded by the so-called Pilgrim Fathers, settlers who had left Europe on a ship called the *Mayflower* to look for religious freedom. They established a colony in Plymouth, Massachusetts, in 1620. They got help from a Native American called Squanto, who was able to speak English. He showed them how to cultivate maize, how to fish and hunt, and mediated between the settlers and the local tribes, the Wampanoag. Together with some Wampanoag the Pilgrims celebrated the colony's first harvest with a Thanksgiving feast in autumn 1621.

Timeline Project 1

- **1607** The first English colony, Jamestown, is founded in Virginia.
- **1612** John Rolfe plants tobacco in Virginia.
- **1614** John Rolfe marries Pocahontas.
- **1619** The first black slaves are sold at Jamestown.
- **1620** The Pilgrims land at Plymouth Rock.

The Boston Tea Party

By the late 18th century, the American colonials were increasingly angry with the British parliament. More and more taxes were put on things they imported, and finally the East India Company was given a monopoly on the tea trade with America and taxes were put up. The settlers started to protest and sent back ships with tea. In Boston, the ships were not sent back, but dozens of angry protesters disguised as Native Americans went onto the ships on 16 December 1773, and threw all the 342 boxes of tea into the sea. This event is known as the Boston Tea Party.

The War of Independence

As a response, the British government sent soldiers to make the colonials pay the tax. The colonials answered by fighting the British soldiers. This was one of the conflicts between the colonials and the British government that eventually led to the War of Independence (1775–1783).

The first president

The War of Independence was won by the Americans, led by George Washington in 1775. America was no longer under British rule. George Washington became the first President of the USA (1789–1797).

Tasks to choose from

For this project, you can focus on one or more of these tasks. You could even find your own task.

1. Find out more about the Powhatan Indians, or Virginia Algonquins, as they were also called. How was their life influenced by the early settlers?
2. Find out more about Pocahontas, especially her role in peace making. Present her life to the class.
3. Find out more about Squanto's life. Then make up a scene in which he meets some Pilgrims for the first time. Act out the scene. You could also film it.
4. Imagine you have survived the journey on the Mayflower. Write a letter to your relatives back home about the journey and your new home.
5. Research how the English emigrants had lived before they came to the New World.
6. Find out how the first Thanksgiving came about and how the Americans celebrate it today.
7. Find out about the Declaration of Independence (1776). What was special about it?

how to ...
work on a project, write, talk, present

wordbank
American politics

workbook
p.18–20, 25, 26

portfolio
I can read, write, combine skills, present

portfolio
dossier

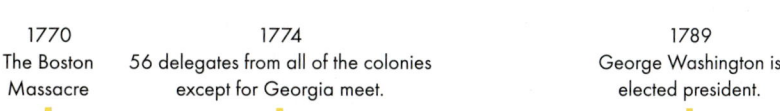

Timeline:
- 1625 The Dutch West Indies Company establishes a colony called New Amsterdam.
- 1770 The Boston Massacre
- 1774 56 delegates from all of the colonies except for Georgia meet.
- 1774 The "Intolerable" Acts
- 1776 On 4 July Congress formally adopts the Declaration of Independence.
- 1789 George Washington is elected president.

Pages from America's past

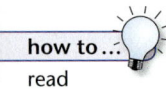
how to... read

Project 2 Moving the Native Americans from their land and killing the buffalo

The Native Americans were forced to move west because the "white men" wanted their land.

The Trail of Tears

Under President Andrew Jackson the Indian Removal Act was passed in Congress in 1830. It forced Native American tribes west of the Mississippi and Missouri to move to what is now Oklahoma. Within seven years, more than 46,000 Native Americans were forced to move thousands of kilometres under inhumane conditions – thousands of them died on the way.

Sitting Bull

"What treaty that the whites have kept has the red man broken? Not one. What treaty that the white man ever made with us have they kept? Not one."

Sitting Bull, Lakota Sioux chief who defeated the US government's forces in the Battle of Little Bighorn

Timeline Project 2

1737
"Walking Purchase": Delaware Indians are forced to give up most of their land.

1766
Chief Pontiac and his Ottawa tribe surrender after years of war with the settlers.

1836
Battle of the Alamo

Pages from America's past

Buffalo Bill (1846–1917)

William Frederick Cody got his nickname after he had killed 4,280 buffalo in eighteen months to feed the Kansas Pacific Railroad workers. This was not the only job he had. He was a gold prospector, a scout for the Union during the Civil War, a stagecoach driver and an actor. He became world-famous for his Wild West Shows.

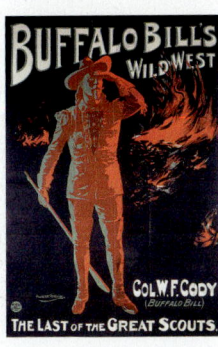

"This song was on my first album and I'd have thought it would be obsolete by now. But governments are still breaking promises and stealing indigenous lands, and I still believe that informed people can help make things better."

Buffy Sainte-Marie

Tasks to choose from

For this project, you can focus on one or more of these tasks. You could even find your own task.

1. Research the life of the Cherokee or another Native American tribe before they were forced to move. How did they live afterwards?
2. Find out more about the Indian Removal Act. Were there also people in Congress who were against it and why?
3. Give a talk about the Battle of Little Bighorn.
4. Give a presentation about the life of Sitting Bull.
5. Give a presentation about the life of Buffalo Bill.
6. Give a talk about the role of the buffalo in the lives of the Native Americans.
7. Who is Buffy Sainte-Marie? Present her biography and her music to the class.
8. Find out about Native Americans in the United States today.

 **how to …**
work on a project, write, talk about lyrics, present

workbook
p. 21, 22, 25, 26

portfolio
I can read, write, combine skills, present

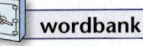 **wordbank**
American politics

Now that the buffalo's gone

…
Oh it's written in books and in songs
that we've been mistreated and wronged
Well over and over I hear the same words
from you good lady and you good man
Well listen to me if you care where we stand
and you feel you're a part of these ones
…
Has a change come about Uncle Sam
or are you still taking our lands?
A treaty forever George Washington signed

He did dear lady, he did dear man
and the treaties being broken by Kinzua Dam
and what will you do for these ones

Oh it's all in the past you can say
but it's still going on here today
The government now wants the Iroquois land
that of the Seneca and the Cheyenne
It's here and it's now you must help us dear man
Now that the buffalo's gone.

Music and lyrics: Buffy Sainte-Marie

(Adjusted text. You can find the full lyrics on the Internet.)

 CD 1/12

- **1848** Beginning of Californian Gold Rush
- **1864** Sand Creek Massacre
- **1869** Transcontinental railroad is completed.
- **1874** Red River War against joint forces of Kiowa, Comanche, Arapaho and Cheyenne
- **1876** Custer and his troops are defeated at Little Bighorn.
- **1886** Apache chief Geronimo surrenders.
- **1890** Sitting Bull is shot dead in a reservation.
- **1890** Wounded Knee Massacre

Newspaper Rock, Canyonlands National Park, Utah – pictures drawn by Native American tribes over a period of 2,000 years up until the early 20th century

Pages from America's past

Project 3 ○ Slaves, a president killed, another war, the KKK and four famous black Americans

how to… read

A lot of Africans were brought to America to work as slaves. Four hundred years later, on 20 January 2009, an African American became President of the United States of America. What happened in the 400 years between?

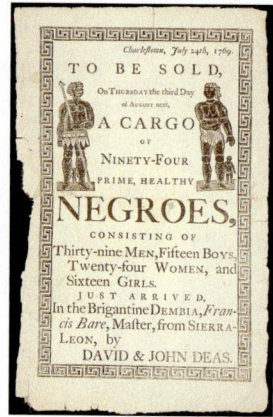

Slavery
In 1619 the first 20 slaves from Africa were brought to America to work in the tobacco fields.
In 1815, there were already about 1 million slaves. By 1860, according to statistics, their number was over 1.7 million. Most of them lived in the agricultural South where cheap workers were needed. But there had also always been people who thought slavery to be unchristian and fought for the freedom of the slaves, especially in the North where slavery was eventually abolished by 1840.

The American Civil War 1861–1865
There were many other differences of opinion between the states in the North and in the South. In February 1861 the Southern States declared their independence from the North, the "Union". This was the beginning of the American Civil War.

Abraham Lincoln (1809–1865)
Abraham Lincoln was President of America during the Civil War. He didn't want the South to become independent. When the Union won the war in 1865, America stayed a united country and slavery was also abolished in the South. Lincoln was assassinated in 1865.

The Ku Klux Klan
The Ku Klux Klan (KKK) was founded in 1865. They terrorized blacks in the South. Hundreds of African Americans were beaten, driven from their homes or brutally murdered by this group.

Rosa Parks
On 1 December 1955 Rosa Parks was arrested by the police. The reason was that she did not obey the bus driver's order to give her seat on the bus to a white man. Parks became a symbol for peaceful protest.

Timeline Project 3

- **1827** New York State abolishes slavery.
- **1850–1860** "Underground Railroad", a network to help slaves escape, is at its height.
- **1861** Abraham Lincoln is elected president.
- **1861** Civil War starts.
- **1863** Battle of Gettysburg.
- **1865** Lincoln is assassinated.

Pages from America's past

Martin Luther King (1929–1968)

Martin Luther King was a clergyman and non-violent civil rights activist. He was a brilliant orator, and in his speeches he talked about an American nation free from racial prejudice. King was assassinated in 1968.

Malcolm X (1925–1965)

Not all African Americans were aiming at a peaceful integration into American society. One of the best-known militant black activists was Malcolm X. He was assassinated in 1965.

Barack Obama

"There is not a black America and white America and Latino America and Asian America – there is the United States of America."

Barack Obama, 44th President of the United States, 2009

I, too, sing America.

I am the darker brother.
They send me to eat in the kitchen
When company comes,
But I laugh,
And eat well,
And grow strong.

Tomorrow,
I'll be at the table
When company comes.
Nobody'll dare
Say to me,
"Eat in the kitchen,"
Then.
Besides,
They'll see how beautiful I am
And be ashamed –

I, too, am America.

Langston Hughes

Tasks to choose from

For this project, you can focus on one or more of these tasks. You could even find your own task.

1. Find out which states belonged to the Confederacy during the Civil War and illustrate this on a map of the United States. What was the economic situation of the Northern and the Southern states then? How did this influence their attitude towards slavery?
2. Find out about the Ku Klux Klan today.
3. Who was Rosa Parks? Write a short biography.
4. There was a song written about Rosa Park's protest called *Back of the Bus*. Present the song as well as the story behind it.
5. One of Martin Luther King's most famous speeches is the "I have a dream" speech. Watch it on the Internet and do some research. Make a poster to illustrate the speech.
6. In 1964, Martin Luther King received the Nobel Peace Prize. Find out about this prize and why he got it.
7. Watch the film *Malcolm X* and write a review. Why was it OK for Malcolm X to use the word "negro" and why is it not OK today? What does the "X" in "Malcolm X" mean?
8. Find out about Langston Hughes. Use your material to understand the poem "I, too, sing America.".
9. Find more poems by Langston Hughes on the life of African Americans. Illustrate the poems and make an exhibition.
10. Watch Barack Obama's inaugural speech on the Internet. What strikes you most about it?

how to …
work on a project, write, talk about poems, present, talk about films

wordbank
American politics, human rights

portfolio
I can read, write, combine skills, present

workbook
p.22, 23
25, 26

film

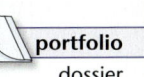

CD
1/13 1/11

portfolio
dossier

1875	1920s and 1930s	1961	1963	2009
Civil Rights Act is passed.	Harlem Renaissance cultural movement is at its height.	John F. Kennedy is elected president.	March on Washington with Martin Luther King	Barack Obama becomes the first African American president.

Pages from America's past

Project 4 ○ Hollywood, Charles Lindbergh, Al Capone and Black Thursday

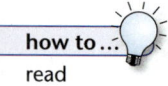
how to...
read

America was a country full of hope and success, but then the crash came. How did it happen and what did America do about it?

Modern Times
By 1920 Hollywood had become world-famous for its film industry. All the films were silent. In 1927 *The Jazz Singer*, the first film with sound, was produced. This was the beginning of the "talkies" era.
In 1936, Charlie Chaplin's voice was heard for the first time as he performed "The Nonsense Song" in his famous comedy *Modern Times*. This film shows how industrialization and the Great Depression (see next page) changed the lives of ordinary people.

Atlantic Crossing
In 1927 Charles Lindbergh flew non-stop from New York City to Paris in his aircraft *Spirit of St Louis*. The flight took more than 30 hours.
Lindbergh became a national hero and public interest in the air travel exploded.

Prohibition
During the Prohibition Era alcohol was forbidden. The police arrested anyone who made, sold or transported alcohol. Organized crime took over, alcohol was smuggled and bootlegged on a grand scale. Bloody gang wars were fought. Gangsters such as Al Capone made a fortune selling alcohol in illegal pubs, the so-called "speakeasies". In 1933 Prohibition ended.

Timeline Project 4

- 1908 — The first Model T Ford is built.
- 1920 — Prohibition in the USA is established.
- 1924 — National Origins Act
- 1927 — Sacco and Vanzetti are executed.

Pages from America's past

2

Black Thursday and the Great Depression
Stock prices in the USA rose during the 1920s. In 1925 the market value of all stocks was $27 billion; by October 1929 it was $87 billion. On 24 October 1929, called "Black Thursday", the stock market collapsed. This was the beginning of the Great Depression, a time of high unemployment and low economic production.

The New Deal
When Franklin D. Roosevelt became President in March 1933, he found an answer to the Great Depression. This was called the New Deal. The New Deal was a series of economic programmes that the state established between 1933 and 1936. These programmes aimed at social reform and economic recovery.

○ Tasks to choose from

For this project, you can focus on one or more of these tasks. You could even find your own task.

1. Find out more about Hollywood, its beginnings and the development of the American film industry.
2. Find out more about other industries at the beginning of the 20th century, for example the car industry.
3. Research how American aviation developed after Charles Lindbergh.
4. Why was alcohol forbidden in the Prohibition Era and why was it allowed again later? In which countries or cultures is alcohol forbidden today?
5. Find out more about the Chicago gang wars, Al Capone and the Mafia.
6. Watch the film *The Untouchables*, which shows how Al Capone was finally imprisoned. Report to the class what he was tried for and why.
7. What did the Great Depression mean for the lives of families at the time? You might find an individual case and present it to the class.
8. How do stock markets work? What does it mean if a stock market collapses?
9. What exactly happened on Black Thursday? What happened before?
10. Find out more about the New Deal. Compare the economic programme with programmes today. What is similar, what is different? Write a comment.

how to …
work on a project, write, present, talk about film, write a comment

workbook
p.23–26

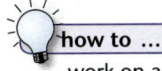
film

wordbank
American politics, economy

portfolio
I can read, write, combine skills, present

portfolio
dossier

1929
Hallelujah, the first all-black movie by a major film studio, is released.

1936/37
Autoworkers' sit-down strike

1936
Franklin D. Roosevelt is re-elected.

1939
Albert Einstein writes to Franklin D. Roosevelt about developing the nuclear bomb.

Pages from America's past

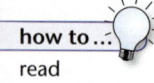

Project 5 ○ The nuclear bomb, the Cold War, Apollo 11 and more weapons

After the Allied victory in World War II, the United States grew to be the world's leading power – a role they first shared with the Soviet Union.

From Pearl Harbour to Hiroshima
On 7 December 1941, the Japanese bombed Pearl Harbour, Hawaii. This brought the United States into World War II. Four days later Hitler declared war on America.
On 8 May 1945 Germany surrendered. But Japan would not surrender. On Monday, 6 August 1945, a nuclear bomb was dropped on Hiroshima by an American bomber. About 80,000 of the 340,000 inhabitants of the city died that day and between 10,000 and 60,000 more people died later that year from injury and radiation.
On 9 August 1945, another nuclear bomb was dropped on Nagasaki. Japan surrendered and World War II was over.

The Cold War
The world became divided: there was the Communist world, the "East", on the one side, and the alliance of democratic societies, the "West", on the other. The United States was the biggest power in the West and the Soviet Union was the biggest power in the East. Both superpowers had nuclear weapons and, knowing of the effect their use would have on both sides, they didn't declare war – the war between them stayed "cold".
The Cold War came to its end in the late 1980s when the superpowers agreed on ending the arms race.

A split world
Although the superpowers did not attack each other, there were wars all over the world. The United States got involved in a lot of them – for example, it sent forces to fight in the Vietnam War. But when pictures of massacres of civilians were shown on TV around the world, a huge international protest movement forced the United States to leave Vietnam in 1975. Another most controversial aspect of the US military effort in South-East Asia was the use of chemical weapons.

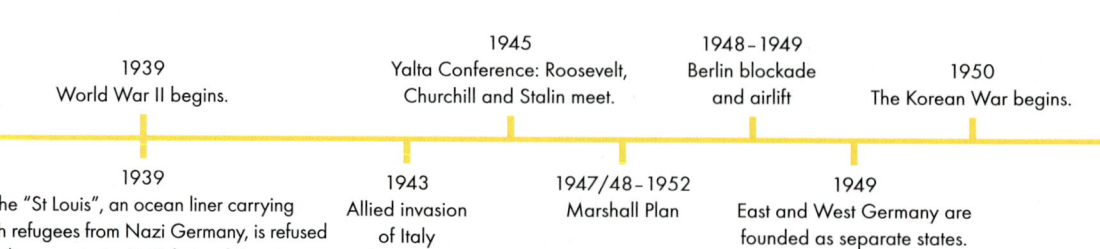

Timeline Project 5

- 1939 — World War II begins.
- 1939 — The "St Louis", an ocean liner carrying Jewish refugees from Nazi Germany, is refused landing permission in Cuba and America.
- 1943 — Allied invasion of Italy.
- 1945 — Yalta Conference: Roosevelt, Churchill and Stalin meet.
- 1947/48–1952 — Marshall Plan
- 1948–1949 — Berlin blockade and airlift
- 1949 — East and West Germany are founded as separate states.
- 1950 — The Korean War begins.

Pages from America's past

Sputnik and "Flopnik"

On 4 October 1957, the Soviet Union launched the first satellite, "Sputnik". Two months later, the United States launched its first satellite. But the rocket exploded. The newspapers wrote of America's "Flopnik". In July 1958, NASA was founded which had, among others, one specific goal: to land a man on the moon. This was achieved by the Apollo 11 mission on 20 July 1969 according to US time which was the early morning of 21 July in Europe, when astronauts Neil Armstrong and Buzz Aldrin walked on the moon.

"That's one small step for man, one giant leap for mankind."   *Neil Armstrong, first man on the moon*

A new order and new challenges

On 11 September 2001, terrorists hijacked four jet planes and attacked the United States. The United States answered by invading Afghanistan because it was suggested that the terrorists were hiding there. In 2003, the United States and their allies invaded Iraq to prevent President Saddam Hussein from using his "weapons of mass destruction". (It turned out that he did not have any!)

Silicon Valley

Silicon Valley in Northern California is home to many of the world's largest technology corporations. After World War II, Stanford University founded Stanford Research Park for high technology companies. Among the first to move there in 1954 were Stanford graduates William Hewlett and David Packard, who had started their business in a garage.

Tasks to choose from

For this project, you can focus on one or more of these tasks. You could even find your own task.

1. Find out more about Pearl Harbour.
2. Watch the video about the Pearl Harbour memorial. What role do it and other war memorials play for Americans today?
3. Listen to one of the veterans' oral histories at http://www.britannica.com/dday and present what he said.
4. Research the bombing of Hiroshima and Nagasaki. Make a collage, a text, a presentation, a poem, a song, … to comment on the operation.
5. Research a Cold War incident, such as the Berlin airlift from 1947–1948, or the Cuban missile crisis in 1962.
6. Find out more about the protest against the Vietnam War.
7. Present a brief history of the Apollo programme.
8. Find out more about NASA. Present their activities in an interesting way.
9. Interview your teachers, parents and neighbours and find out what they were doing on 11 September 2001. Make a speech bubble display.
10. Make a list of companies based in Silicon Valley. Pick five of them and write a fact file on each one. To get an idea of Silicon Valley, watch the clip on the DVD.

how to … work on a project, write, present, listen, mediate

DVD 4

workbook p.24–26

wordbank American politics, economy

portfolio I can read, write, combine skills, present

DVD 5

1958	1965	1975	2001
Lebanon crisis and US military intervention	American bombing of North Vietnam	End of Vietnam War	US invasion of Afghanistan

1962	1970
Cuban missile crisis	Four students are shot dead in an anti-war demonstration in Ohio.

Grammar revision

G1 ○ Comparisons

a) Use the right form of the adjectives to complete the sentences.

1. There are many famous American speeches. It is hard to say which one is the (famous).
2. The mission to put a man on the moon was (successful) than the launch of the satellite "Flopnik".
3. When Charles Lindbergh flew from New York to Paris in 1927 it took (long) than it does today.
4. Rosa Parks' protest was (peaceful) than many other protests in American history.
5. There were many bad days in the history of the stock market but 24 October 1929 was one of the (bad) days.
6. Some of the (large) technology corporations in the world are in Silicon Valley.

1. *There are many famous American speeches. It is hard to say which one is the most famous.*

b) Listen to the CD and check your sentences.

G2 ○ News from the past

a) Put the verbs in brackets into the past progressive.

1. "Were you listening on the afternoon of 20 January 2009, as Barack Obama (give) his inaugural speech?"
2. People in Hiroshima and Nagasaki (live) normal lives before August 1945.
3. Stock prices in the USA (rise) right up until "Black Thursday".
4. Al Capone (open) illegal saloons during prohibition.
5. Buffalo Bill (perform) his Wild West Shows in the late 19th century.

1. *"Were you listening on the afternoon of 20 January 2009, as Barack Obama was giving his inaugural speech?"*

b) Listen to the CD and check your sentences.

G3 ○ What were you doing when …?

a) Complete the sentences with the simple past and the past progressive forms of the verbs.

1. While she (sit) on a bus, Rosa Parks (start) a peaceful protest.
2. William Hewlett and David Packard (start) their business while they (use) a garage as their office.
3. Many Cherokee people (die) while they (move) west.
4. "I wonder what Neil Armstrong (think) as he (walk) on the moon."
5. While they (sail) from England to America, about 40 men and boys (die).
6. Custer (die) while he (fight) at Little Bighorn.

1. *While she was sitting on a bus, Rosa Parks started a peaceful protest.*

b) Listen to the CD and check your sentences.

Grammar revision

G4 ○ You look beautiful

a) Complete the sentences with an appropriate adjective.

1. Celebrities have their photos retouched because they want to look ??? .
2. If you do not eat enough, you will have no energy and feel ??? all the time.
3. When Amy started to lose weight her family told her that she looked ??? .
4. Then she lost more and more weight and began to look ??? .
5. Do you think the food they eat in Mali tastes ??? .
6. People with eating disorders often feel ??? with their bodies.

1. Celebrities have their photos retouched because they want to look perfect.

G5 ○ Questions

a) Form questions from the following sentences. The underlined parts will form the answers to the questions.

1. Columbus reached the New World in 1492.
2. John Rolfe brought tobacco to Virginia.
3. Pocahontas married John Rolfe.
4. The English won the first war against the Native Americans in Virginia.
5. Japanese bombers attacked Pearl Harbour in 1941.
6. In 1620 the Pilgrims landed at Plymouth Rock.

1. When did Columbus reach the New World?

b) Listen to the CD and check your sentences.

G6 ○ Should, must, can …?

a) Complete the sentences with the correct form of modal verb.

> couldn't · be able to · must ·
> should · shouldn't · have to

1. As he spoke some English, Squanto ??? help Captain Smith.
2. "In my opinion, celebrities ??? have their photos retouched."
3. Someone with an eating disorder ??? see a doctor.
4. You do not ??? be skinny to be beautiful.
5. George Ramsay was so ill that he ??? play rugby.
6. "I think everyone ??? study history, it's so important."

1. As he spoke some English, Squanto was able to help Captain Smith.

b) Listen to the CD and check your sentences.

Grammar revision

G7 ○ It was done …

a) Rewrite these sentences using the past passive.

1. The American government moved many Native Americans west of the Mississippi river.
2. A man killed Martin Luther King in Memphis.
3. The Americans won the War of Independence.
4. The British government sent soldiers to make the settlers pay tax.
5. Sitting Bull and the Lakota Sioux defeated Custer at Little Bighorn.
6. The American people elected Barack Obama as President.
7. The American government gave blacks the vote in 1870.

1. Many Native Americans were moved west of the Mississippi river by the American government.

b) Listen to the CD and check your sentences.

G8 ○ What had happened?

a) Complete the sentences using the past perfect.

> about 80,000 people (die) · Native Americans (be moved) ·
> Neil Armstrong and Buzz Aldrin (walk) · the Southern States (declare) ·
> about 40 people (die) · the superpowers (agree)

1. By the time the ships arrived in America in 1607, …
2. By 1840, more than 100,000 …. west to Oklahoma.
3. The American Civil War began after … their independence from the North.
4. By the end of Monday, 6 August 1945, the day when Hiroshima was attacked, …
5. Once … on ending the arms race, the Cold War came to an end.
6. Once … on the moon, NASA achieved its main goal.

1. By the time the ships arrived in America in 1607, about 40 people had died.

b) Listen to the CD and check your sentences.

G9 ○ Talking about the future

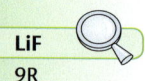

a) Complete the sentences with either the going to-future or will-future.

1. "Look! The Mayflower is setting sail. They (leave) the country."
2. "Now, Barack, if you work hard at school, maybe you (be) President one day."
3. "William, if you go on killing buffaloes like this, maybe you (be called) Buffalo Bill one day!"
4. "And now Neil Armstrong is descending the ladder on the lunar module. He (be) the first man on the moon!"
5. "Look at that! They have climbed onto the British ships. They (throw) all the tea into the sea!"
6. "The police are coming. Rosa Parks (be arrested)."

1. "Look! The Mayflower is setting sail. They are going to leave the country."

b) Listen to the CD and check your sentences.

Human rights and wrongs

3

In diesem *Theme* ...

- erfährst du etwas über Menschenrechte und Menschenrechtsorganisationen.
- sprichst du über Menschenrechtsverletzungen.
- erfährst du etwas über die Todesstrafe in den USA und der Welt.
- liest du etwas über einen Todesstrafe-Fall und erfährst etwas über verschiedene Meinungen zum Thema Todesstrafe.
- bearbeitest du ein Filmprojekt zu *Dead Man Walking*.

Human rights and wrongs

A1 I have the right to …

a) Read the following statements and think of more.

I have the right to …

1. get enough to eat.
2. have a room of my own.
3. go to school.
4. get medicine when I am ill.
5. decide what to do in my free time.
6. get pocket money.
7. have my own opinion.
8. protest against injustice.
9. sleep as long as I like.
…

b) Now discuss in class: which statements should be rights for everyone?

> Everybody should be able to / allowed to … · It is important that … ·
> I need / I can't do without … · It would be OK if I couldn't … · If I was not allowed
> to …, I would … · I've got the right to … · I've got the right not to …

portfolio
I can talk

workbook
A1

Which of the statements are also human rights? Compare your list with the human rights on pages 48/49.

A2 We all have the right to …

Talk about these photos. What do you think they show?
How are the photos connected to human rights?

I think the first one shows …

I've seen this kind of picture before in / on …

The children in photo number …

Maybe …

Could it be that …?

Human rights and wrongs

A3 ● Human rights issues

a) Listen to the interview between a newspaper reporter and a representative from a human rights organization and look at the photos in A2. Do you find any issues that match the photos?

CD
1/14 1/25

portfolio
I can listen, read, learn English

b) Now read the interview. Which human rights issues are they talking about? Take notes.

> **Reporter:** Which human rights violations are taking place around the world?
> **Representative:** Well, in some countries you find what are called "honour killings". In those families there are strict social rules about marriage. Some family members have kidnapped and murdered the husband or wife because they have married someone from the wrong caste or religion.
> **Reporter:** What is the motive behind this?
> **Representative:** They believe that by killing them they will protect the family honour.
> **Reporter:** Are there any human rights issues that involve children?
> **Representative:** Oh, yes of course. Some families are often so poor that the children as well as the parents have to work to earn enough money for the family.
> **Reporter:** What are the consequences for the child?
> **Representative:** Well, in most cases we are looking at 12 hour working days, six or even seven days a week. It means that children can't go to school. But if they got a proper school education they would get a better job and have a better life in the future.
> **Reporter:** Are human rights violations against children a big part of your campaigns?
> **Representative:** Definitely. Even here in Europe the situation for some children is not as positive as we would think. Recently, the Spanish government has been criticized for keeping African migrant children in terrible conditions.
> **Reporter:** Why has that happened?
> **Representative:** Four emergency centres have been set up on the Canary Islands for Africans who are trying to reach Europe to start a new life. We discovered that more than 900 children had to live in rooms without windows. As long as the government continues to violate human rights, we will campaign against this.

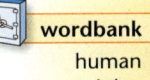
LiF 10R

wordbank
human rights

LiF 11

c) Discuss in small groups: which human rights violations do you find the most outrageous? Why?

d) Write reported questions from the interview questions.

   1. The reporter asked which human rights violations were taking place around the world.

e) Listen to the CD and check your sentences.

portfolio
I can talk, work with grammar

CD
1/26

how to ...
listen, write a summary, comment

A4 ● The stories behind the issues

a) Listen to three stories about victims of human rights violations. What happened to them?

b) Which issues in A3 match these people's stories?

c) Find out more details about one of the human rights issues on the Internet: where, when, who, why? Make notes and report the most important facts in class.

CD
1/15

d) ★ Summarize your notes from c) in a short text.
   ☼ The name of one of the centres on the Canary Islands is "La Esperanza". What does that mean? How do you feel about the name? Write a comment.

portfolio
I can listen, write, combine skills

workbook
A2, A3

EVERYONE'S RIGHT TO **LIFE** SHALL BE PROTECTED BY LAW

Everyone has the right to marry and to start a family

The Universal Declaration of Human Rights

The Universal Declaration of Human Rights was drawn up by the United Nations on 10 December 1948. In the declaration, basic human rights that each of us should have in order to lead a life in peace and freedom were set out.
These rights apply to each person on our planet, whatever his or her race, religion, sex or cultural background.
Here are some examples.

INFO BUBBLE

Everyone is entitled to attend school

EVERYONE HAS THE RIGHT TO PARTICIPATE IN ELECTING HIS COUNTRY'S GOVERNMENT BY MEANS OF FREE ELECTIONS BY SECRET BALLOT

Everyone shall enjoy the rights secured in the Convention whatever the colour of their skin, their sex, language political or religious convictions or their origins

Human rights and wrongs

A5 ○ Defending human rights

how to...
read

a) Read about these organizations for human rights.

Human Rights Watch   www.hrw.org

Human Rights Watch is a non-governmental organization. It is based in New York with offices in Berlin, Tokyo, Moscow, Johannesburg and other cities around the world. It …

- helps victims and activists to prevent discrimination
- supports political freedom
- protects people from cruelty in wartime
- fights human rights violations
- supports human rights for everybody.

The Council of Europe   www.coe.int

The Council of Europe works to defend human rights, democracy and the rule of law in Europe. It …

- protects and promotes human rights in the 47 member states
- tries to find solutions for issues such as human trafficking, racism, violence against women and child abuse
- wants to ensure social human rights, like the right to health protection, for everyone

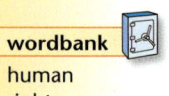
wordbank
human rights, justice

Amnesty International   www.amnesty.org

Amnesty International is a worldwide movement of people. They have more than 2.2 million members in over 150 countries. Amnesty …

- campaigns against human rights abuses
- works to abolish the death penalty
- fights for the rights of refugees
- takes care of political prisoners.

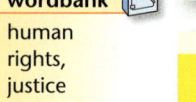
portfolio
I can mediate, talk

workbook
A8, A9

b) Which aims do these organizations have? Present them in German.

c) Would you like to be active in one of the organizations? Why? Why not?

A6 ○ One face of Amnesty

Kalaya'an Mendoza has been working for Amnesty International and campaigning for human rights for 15 years. He organizes workshops for community groups, high school and university students, using platforms like Facebook and Twitter. Kalaya'an was part of a team of Tibet activists who were arrested, interrogated and forced to leave China because they were protesting against human rights abuses during the Opening Ceremonies of the 2008 Olympic Games in Beijing.

portfolio
I can listen

DVD
6

workbook
A10

Watch the video clip of Kalaya'an Mendoza's account about what happened to him during a protest in Beijing. What did the Chinese police do to him and his friends?

Human rights and wrongs

A7 ◯ Human rights are everywhere

a) Read this statement about human rights. It comes from Eleanor Roosevelt, who was a member of the UN Human Rights Commission. What is her message?

"Where, after all, do universal human rights begin? In small places, close to home – so close and so small that they cannot be seen on any maps of the world. Yet they are the world of the individual person; the neighbourhood he lives in; the school or college he attends; the factory, farm, or office where he works. Such are the places where every man, woman, and child seeks equal justice, equal opportunity, equal dignity without discrimination. Unless these rights have meaning there, they have little meaning anywhere."

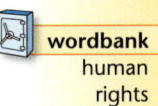

wordbank
human rights

b) Which rights does Eleanor Roosevelt mention?

Write down rights from pages 48/49 that match the rights Eleanor Roosevelt mentions.

c) What do these rights mean to you? Find examples from your own life. Are there any situations in which you feel that these rights are not taken seriously enough? Discuss with a partner.

how to …
discuss

portfolio
I can talk

workbook
A11

A8 ◯ Choose

1. Find out about the history of a human rights organization. Make a timeline and present it.
2. With a partner or in a small group make a poster of human rights which are important for you and your school.
3. Find out about your nearest Amnesty International group and contact them. What action(s) are they working on at the moment? What can a person of your age do to help?
4. What activities are the human rights organizations from page 50 involved in at the moment? Find out from the Internet, television, newspapers and magazines. Take notes and write short statements: organization, where, what, why, expected result, …
5. Think of a slogan and design a T-shirt, a badge, or a flyer for one of the organizations.
6. Find out about Eleanor Roosevelt's life. Who was she? What did she do?
7. Watch a speech on the DVD which Eleanor Roosevelt gave in Carnegie Hall, New York. When is Human Rights Day and why does she think it is a good idea?

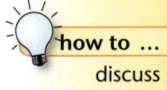

how to …
present, do an interview, write

portfolio
I can combine skills

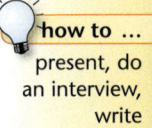

DVD
7

3 Human rights and wrongs

B1 ● The death penalty worldwide

CD 1/16

a) What do you know about the death penalty? Collect information in class.

b) Listen to the CD and take notes. Talk about your notes in class.

how to ... work with statistics

c) Read the facts below and study the bar chart. Name positive and negative aspects.

wordbank
human rights, justice

portfolio
I can combine skills

- More than two-thirds of the countries of the world have abolished the death penalty.
- While 67 countries still had the death penalty in 2011, most did not use it.
- 20 countries were known to have carried out executions, killing a total of at least 676 people.
- However, this figure does not include the thousands of executions that are likely to have taken place in China. China again refused to publish figures on its use of the death penalty.

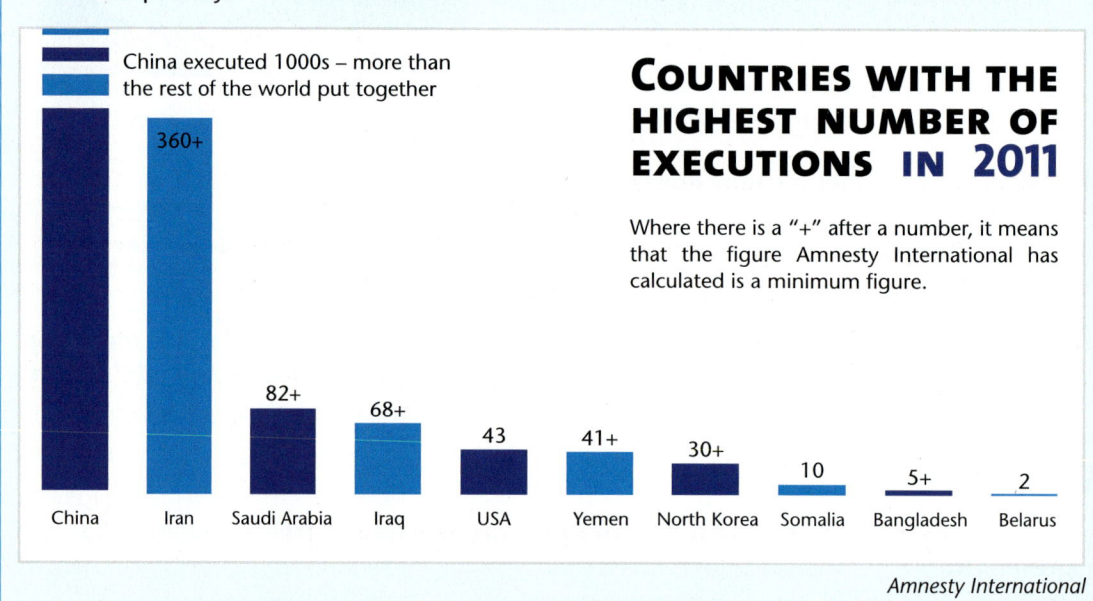

LiF
12R

d) Complete these sentences using the following expressions:

1. Amnesty International has ??? knowledge about executions in China.
2. There were ??? executions in Iran than in Bangladesh.
3. ??? people were executed in Somalia than in Yemen.
4. Amnesty International has ??? knowledge about executions in the USA than in Saudi Arabia.
5. ??? of the countries that have the death penalty did not use it.
6. ??? countries in the world which have the death penalty actually use it.

few · very little ·
many more · most ·
fewer · better

CD 1/28

portfolio
I can listen

e) Listen to the CD and check your sentences.

f) Write a short report about the article in b). It should contain the most important facts. You can also use the information from c).

☀ What is special about the figures for the USA, Somalia and Belarus?

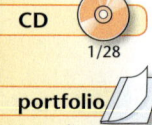
workbook
B1–B3

Human rights and wrongs

B2 ● Death penalty in the USA

a) Look at the map of the USA. What does it tell you about the death penalty in the USA?

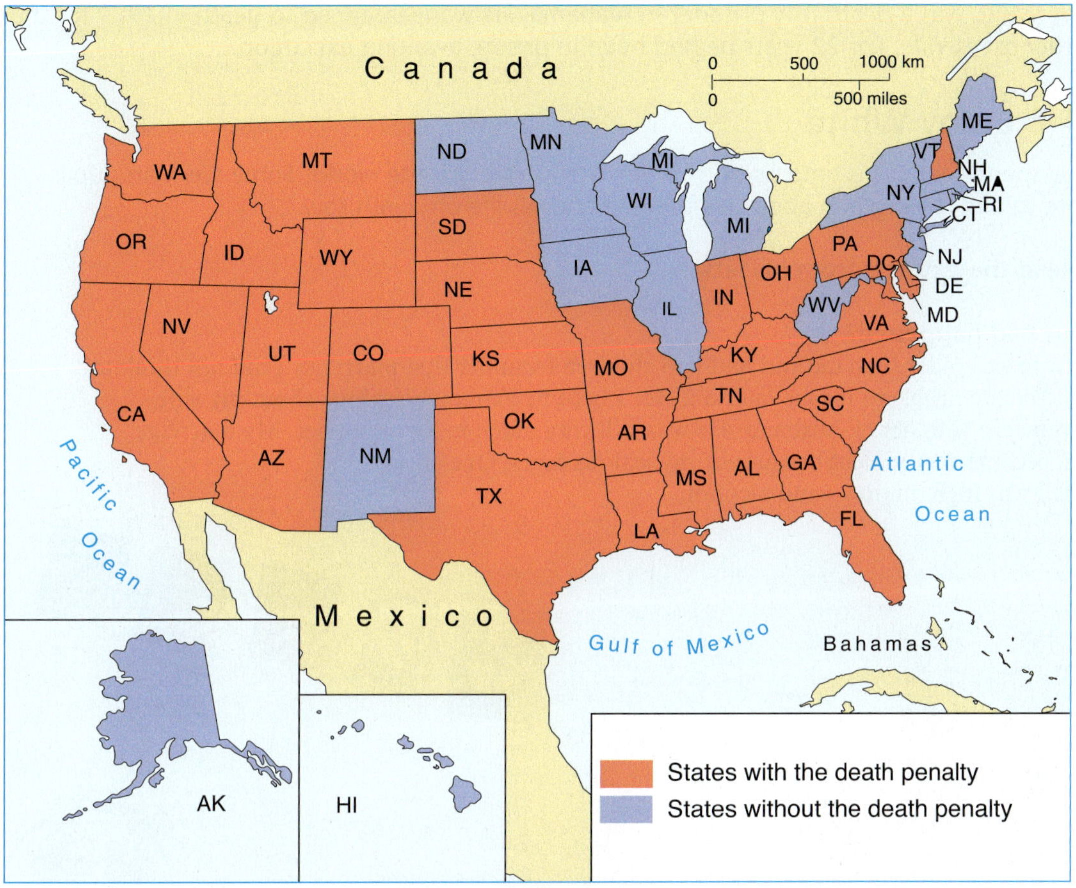

Tipp
Du findest die Namen der US-Staaten auf der Karte vorne im Buch.

Find out which state was the last to abolish the death penalty.

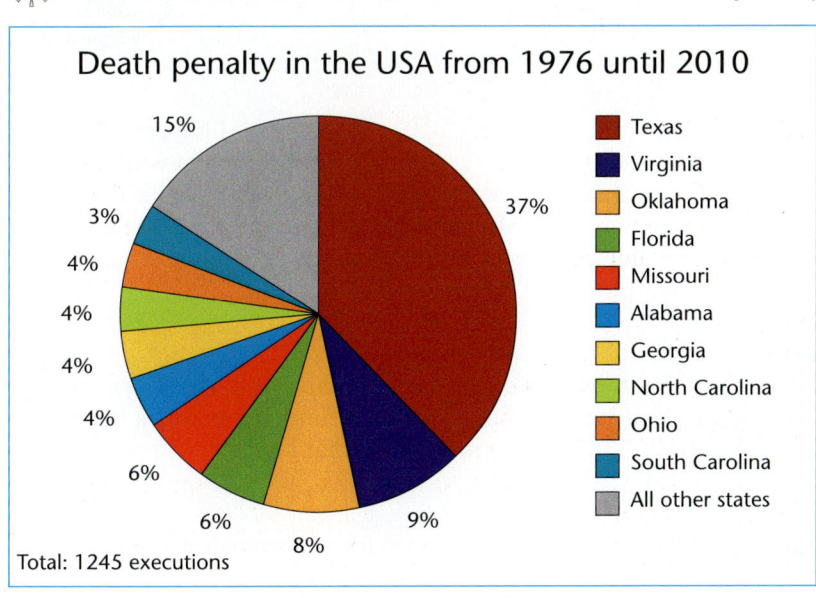

b) What additional information do you get from this pie chart?

c) Find the states named in the pie chart in the US map above. Describe where they are on the map.

portfolio
I can combine skills

how to ...
work with statistics

workbook
B4

Human rights and wrongs

B3 ● On death row in Alabama

Read the following information. What is your first reaction? Talk about it.

Leroy White was a death row prisoner in Alabama. He was sentenced to death in 1989 for the murder of his wife. For 22 years he had been in prison, awaiting execution.

B4 ● Leroy White

Leroy spent a lot of his time writing to pen friends around the world. Some German pupils wrote to him, asking him about his past life and his life on death row.

how to... read

a) Read the extracts from his letters.

What had happened?
My wife was older than me and had two children from her first marriage. I did not think this would create problems for me later on. But I became extremely jealous about my wife's relationship with her ex-husband. He was still very much in love with her. My marriage soon became very violent because of my jealous rages. One day, while I was high on drugs and alcohol,

I happened to get into a heated argument with my wife's sister. My rage of violence was so fierce that I shot my sister-in-law and my wife. Miraculously, my sister-in-law lived through it. Sadly, my wife and mother of my only child, was murdered by my raging jealousy and inability to control my anger.

How he feels about the crime
I wish so much I could take back those few moments of my life but I can't. But what I can do is try to be a better person from now on. We do stupid stuff in life sometimes but taking a life is something that can never be changed back. I'm angry at myself for what I did.

His mother
Of course she loved me, but raising 12 children was just too much for one woman without a strong helper.

His dreams
The life I had always wanted for myself was to get a college education and a good paying job, a lovely home and wife and 3 children.

His life on death row
I am very unhappy with the life I have created for myself. But I have managed not to lose hope and happiness.
Every day I go on a group walk with 40 or 50 other prisoners, depending on how many decide to go outside that particular day. On group walk I get to lift weights, play basketball, volleyball, walk around the big fenced-in walk yard or just stand around and talk to others. Yes, there are lots of friendships between inmates and you can meet other prisoners at church services, on the walk yard or in the library. My cell has my own personal TV, radio (headset) and access to a telephone. I rarely make phone calls because they are too expensive nowadays from inside prisons.

I can always find things positive to do to avoid boredom. Writing letters is one thing I do. Writing and getting to know people and their lives through letter-writing has been one of my biggest prison hobbies. I like cooking, music and dancing, especially hip hop but I can't really dance. I try to make the most of life in prison. I don't think I would be afraid of daily life if I was able to leave prison. I would be totally happy! […]

His advice to young people
I don't want you thinking that partying and drinking and having a good time can always solve every problem you might face in life. I love fun and parties too but there's a lot more to life as well. I bet if you guys decided one weekend instead of partying to go to bed early and get up to cut some old folk's lawn, you would feel different and see another purpose in life.

> †
> After 22 years on death row, **Leroy White** was executed on 13 January 2011 by lethal injection despite pleas from the victim's family for his life to be spared.

b) Answer the following questions.
1. Why did Leroy kill his wife?
2. What did he write about his crime in his letters?
3. Do you think he had changed? Give reasons.

Which of the following statements are true? Write them down and find passages in Leroy's letter to back them up.

1. Leroy White was sorry for murdering his wife.
2. Leroy was jealous of his wife's ex-husband.
3. His mother had no time to look after him as a child.
4. He had learned how to stay optimistic on death row.
5. He did not often make phone calls because they cost a great deal of money.
6. He could only watch television in the library.
7. He thought that fun is not the only purpose of life.

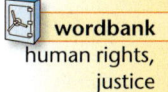
wordbank
human rights, justice

c) Which questions do you think the German pupils asked him in their letters? Which additional questions would **you** have asked? Work in small groups and discuss.

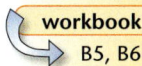
workbook
B5, B6

Human rights and wrongs

B5 ● The life of Leroy White

LiF 13

portfolio
I can work with grammar

Make one sentence from two. Use the present participle (ing-form).

1. Leroy White married. He did not think this would create problems.
2. He became extremely jealous. He got into heated arguments with his wife.
3. He shot his wife. He couldn't control himself.
4. Later he tried to become a better person. He was angry at himself for what he had done.
5. He was very unhappy with his life. He wished he could be free again.

workbook
B7, B8

1. Leroy White married, not thinking this would create problems.

B6 ● Teenage action

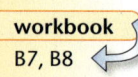
how to … read

a) Read this online report. Why did the three boys start their campaign?

We are the future

The nephews of Jeffrey Wood, a man waiting for his execution on Texas death row, started an anti-death penalty organization, Kids Against the Death Penalty (KADP).

LiF 14R

Gavin, Nick and Nathan Been (12, 13 and 15) are just like any American teenagers. But something is different. Their uncle Jeffrey Wood is on Texas death row. That's why they go to protest meetings and public debates on the death penalty rather than baseball matches or birthday parties. They're interested in finding out about government decisions and reading everything on death penalty laws and regulations.

Their campaigning started within the family, who were not all on their side. "Grandpa is for the death penalty, but we keep on trying to get him to our side," they said. Not everyone agreed with their campaign in a state where most of the public support the death penalty. "Some people screamed at us when we were protesting and tried to run us over with their truck," Nathan said.

But the kids were determined and in 2010, they were in Geneva to tell World Congress participants about their experience. Gavin, the youngest of the nephews, talked about the effect of the death sentence on the whole family.

Their main arguments against the death penalty:

- The death penalty makes a murderer of someone.
- The death penalty allows for the murder of innocent people.
- The death penalty creates more victims and violates human rights.
- The death penalty is a cruel and unusual form of torture.
- The death penalty is not a deterrent to murder, or other violent crimes.

wordbank
human rights, justice

portfolio
I can work with grammar

b) Find headlines for each paragraph.

c) Find the two nouns in the text that use a plural form of the verb although the noun is in the singular. Can you think of a reason why?

LiF 15R

☼ Write an introduction for Gavin's talk in Geneva. Use two of the KADP arguments against the death penalty in your introduction.

workbook
B9–B13

56

B7 Can we end the death penalty?

a) Read the quotes.

"The death penalty is a symptom of a culture of violence, not a solution to it. It is an affront to human dignity."
Amnesty International

"To take a life when a life has been lost is revenge, not justice".
Desmond Tutu

"I don't think you should support the death penalty to seek revenge. I don't think that's right. I think the reason to support the death penalty is because it saves other people's lives."
George W. Bush

"Government … can't be trusted to control its own bureaucrats or collect taxes equitably or fill a pothole, much less decide which of its citizens to kill."
Sister Helen Prejean, author of the book Dead Man Walking

"I have never heard a murderer say they thought about the death penalty as consequence of their actions prior to committing their crimes."
Gregory Ruff, police lieutenant in Kansas

"… I was a firm believer in the American system of justice and the death penalty. Today, three days before I end my term as Governor, I stand before you to explain my frustrations and deep concerns about both the administration and the penalty of death … Our capital system is haunted by the demon of error, error in determining who among the guilty deserves to die. Because of all these reasons today I am commuting the sentences of all death row inmates."
George Ryan, former Governor of Illinois in a speech on January 11, 2003

"This decision is supposed to be about human rights. Well, when I think of human rights, I think of my wife, Kathy. My wife's rights were violated by Paul Taylor [her murderer], so I don't see why his rights should be placed ahead of hers."
John Woodhouse in a letter about Governor Ryan's decision, 2003

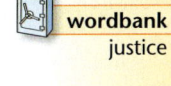
wordbank
justice

b) Write down the gist of four of the quotes in German.

c) Find out more about Desmond Tutu, George W. Bush or Sister Helen Prejean. Present your findings to the class.

Find out more about one or more of the people who are quoted. Does the quote fit in well with the information you can find? Take notes and tell the class.

d) Collect all the arguments you can find for and against the death penalty. Don't forget the arguments in B6.

e) What do **you** think about the death penalty? Discuss in class.

how to …
mediate

portfolio
I can mediate, combine skills, talk

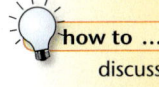
how to …
discuss

3

Human rights and wrongs

film

how to...
talk about films

B8 ○ Dead Man Walking – the film

a) Look at the pictures from the film. What kind of film do you expect?

b) What do you think "dead man walking" means?

c) Order the following text blocks to get a short summary of the film.

INFO BUBBLE

Sister Helen Prejean

was born on 21 April 1939. She is a Roman Catholic sister and spent a lot of time working as a spiritual advisor for prisoners on death row. She also helped the victims of crimes. In 1993 she wrote a book called *Dead man walking*. It is about her experience with inmates on death row. The film from 1996 is based on this book.

A Sister Helen decides to visit Poncelet, and he seems arrogant, sexist, and racist. He is not even pretending to feel sorry for what he did.

B As the day of his execution comes closer and closer, Poncelet asks Sister Helen to help him with a final appeal.

C During his execution, he asks the boy's parents to forgive him and tells the girl's parents he hopes his death brings them peace.

D Sister Helen tells Poncelet that his redemption is possible only if he takes responsibility for what he did.

E Matthew Poncelet has been on death row for six years. He is awaiting his execution for killing a teenage couple.

F Sister Helen's application for a pardon is declined.

G Poncelet asks Sister Helen to be his spiritual advisor on the day of his execution, and she agrees.

H Just before he is taken from his cell, Poncelet admits to Sister Helen that he killed the boy and raped the girl.

portfolio
I can listen, learn English

d) Before you watch the film look up the following words:

- pardon board hearing
- life sentence / life imprisonment
- lethal injection
- jury
- lawyer
- victim
- burial

e) Now watch the film. Did you put the text blocks in the correct order? Were your ideas in a) and b) right?

Human rights and wrongs

B9 Quotes from the characters

a) What do you know about the main characters in the film? Collect information in class. Then match the following quotations with the people. Who says what?

Matthew Poncelet   Poncelet's mother   Sister Helen Prejean

"My boys are having a real hard time at school. Kids picking on 'em, beating 'em up …"

"I just keep … tryin' to figure out what I done wrong."

"You're not gonna find many rich people on death row."

"We just sit there quietly, nod our heads and say 'Justice has been done.'"

"My name, my family name dies with me. There will be no more Delacroixs, Sister."

"How can you come here? How can you do that? How can you sit with that scum?"

"This is not a person. This is an animal. … Matthew Poncelet is God's mistake."

"It's easy to kill a monster, but it's hard to kill a human being."

"Nobody called me no son of God before."

"I want the last face you see in this world to be the face of love, so you look at me when they do this thing. I'll be the face of love for you."

Mr and Mrs Percy (the dead girl's parents)

Mr Delacroix (the dead boy's father)

Mr Barber (Poncelet's lawyer)

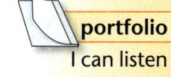
portfolio
I can listen

B10 Choose

1. What can you find out about Kansas and New Hampshire in connection with the death penalty? Present the information to the class.

2. Listen to the song "Ellis Unit One" written for the film *Dead Man Walking*. Find the lyrics on the Internet. Present the song and the story behind it to the class.

3. Watch minutes 42:27–43:05 from the film *Dead Man Walking*. Pay attention to the demonstration banners. Which of the quotations have you heard before? What do you think of them?

4. Have a look at the home page of KADP: www.kadp.webs.com. Write a short introduction to one of their videos or some of their pictures and present it to the class.

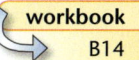
workbook
B14

how to …
talk, present

portfolio
I can combine skills

3

Human rights and wrongs

Practice matters

P1 ○ Say it in English

Match the sentences.

1. Wie fragst du, welche Ziele diese Organisationen haben?
2. Wie sagst du, dass diese Rechte für jeden Menschen auf unserem Planeten gelten?
3. Wie drückst du aus, dass man die Hauptaussage der Zitate auf Deutsch aufschreiben soll?
4. Wie drückst du aus, dass eine Organisation seinen Sitz in einer bestimmten Stadt hat?
5. Wie sagst du, dass ein Bericht die wichtigsten Tatsachen enthalten soll?
6. Wie sagst du, dass ein Land sich weigerte, Zahlen zu veröffentlichen?

a. The organization is based in New York.
b. Which aims do these organizations have?
c. China refused to publish figures.
d. The report should contain the most important facts.
e. Write down the gist of the quotes in German.
f. These rights apply to each person on our planet.

P2 ○ What would you do?

Complete the sentences and think of some more.

If
- someone stole my mobile phone
- we had the death penalty in Germany
- I were a friend of the Been brothers
- I could be a member of Human Rights Watch
- I lived in the USA
- someone beat up my best friend
- I were 18 years old
- I could choose
- …

I would …
I could …
I'd …

P3 ○ What did you ask?

A newspaper reporter took some notes before interviewing someone about his job. Later, he told his boss which questions he had asked.

a) Write reported questions.

1. What's your name?
2. Which organization do you work for?
3. What are you doing at the moment?
4. How many hours a week do you work?
5. Is your work dangerous?
6. What have you been doing so far?
7. Who did you help last year?
8. In which countries did you work in the last few years?

1. I wanted to know what his name was.
2. I asked …

b) Listen to the CD and check your sentences. Note: if you have started your sentences with "I wanted to know …" or "I asked …" – both are correct.

Practice matters

Human rights and wrongs

P4 ○ More or less

a) Complete the text using adjectives from the box.

> a lot of · little · bad ·
> much · less · worse ·
> more · worst

We have ??? information about what is going on in Korea, but we have even ??? information about what is going on in China. We don't have ??? knowledge about North Korea. We have ??? knowledge about Spain and even ??? knowledge about Germany. We are getting some ??? news from the Italian economy at the moment, but even ??? news from Spain, and the ??? from Greece.

b) Listen to the CD and check your sentences.

P5 ○ Shortening sentences

a) Rewrite the following sentences using a present participle.

1. When people have to go to prison, they sometimes start thinking.
2. As prisoners have a lot of time, they have to look for something to do.
3. When the inmates find a hobby they like, they spend a lot of time on it.
4. While the prisoners spend time in prison, they get to know a lot of other prisoners.
5. While the prisoners discuss things in prison, they often plan what they want to do later on.
6. As many people find it difficult to change their lives, they have to work hard at it.

1. Having to go to prison, people sometimes start thinking.

b) Listen to the CD and check your sentences.

P6 ○ Leroy White

Read B3 again and write at least eight sentences about what Leroy White writes that he is good at / looks forward to / is happy about / is afraid of / dreams of …

Leroy White writes that he is happy about writing letters. He …

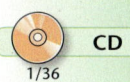

P7 ○ Unusual nouns

a) Decide whether to use the plural or the singular form of the verb in brackets.

1. Their family ??? not all on their side. (was / were)
2. Only one family member always ??? . (helps / help)
3. The police ??? to help the girl. (comes / come)
4. The staff ??? very friendly in this restaurant. (is / are)
5. The boss ??? always polite. (is / are)
6. The media ??? a lot of power. (has / have)

b) Listen to the CD and check your sentences.

c) Decide whether or not to use "a" or "an".

1. Have you got ??? homework?
2. Have you got ??? pet?
3. Is there ??? room available in this hotel?
4. When you've got ??? accommodation at a hotel, you have to check in first.
5. Do you need ??? advice?
6. If you need ??? holiday tip, search the Internet.

d) Listen to the CD and check your sentences.

3 Human rights and wrongs *Optional*

○ Let the posters speak

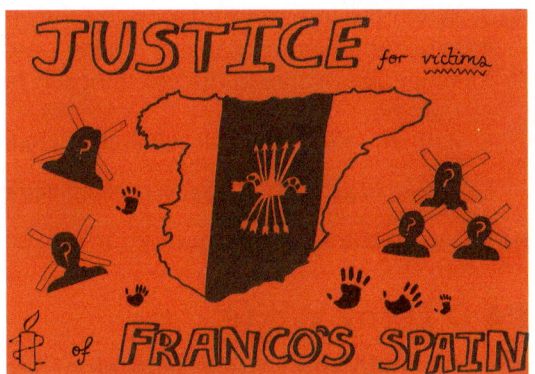

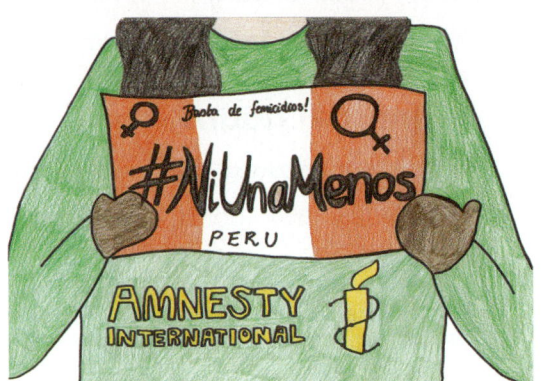

Which is the most impressive poster for you?

Project: Living together 4

Project 1

Roles in relationships

Project 2

Arranged marriages

Project 3

Love and laughter

Project 4

A love song and a love letter

Project 5

My stories

Project 6

Films about families

Living together

This Theme deals with different kinds of relationships and family models.

a) What family models do you know? Collect ideas in class.

b) Talk about the pictures. Do they show family models that you have thought of?

c) Read the statements and match them with the pictures. Are all of your ideas represented? Think of pictures that could go with the remaining statements and describe them.

A

B

C

D

E

1 Two kids and a dog – that's my idea of a perfect family.

2 I've got two mums.

3 I live alone with my father.

4 I love my big family.

5 I want to have a career and no family.

6 I live with my granddaughter.

Living together

F

7. The life of a single mum can be hard.
8. I can't imagine having kids.
9. I'm happy my grandfather lives with us.
10. I want to marry a rich man and live in a villa.
11. We're a blended family.
12. Old and young living together? – A nightmare!

H

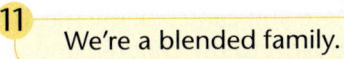

G

13. I'm an adopted child.
14. I'm dreaming of marrying a woman with a big family.

I

K

Living together

Mum, Dad and two kids, the traditional family model – also the perfect family system? Today there are a lot of other types of families, such as blended (or: patchwork) families, the extended family with children, parents and grandparents living together, single parent families (father and children or mother and children), or forms of co-housing where all kinds of different families live together.

INFO BUBBLE

In this Theme you can read about different relationships and family models and how they work for some people.

- Look through the six projects and decide which one you want to work on for the next couple of weeks.
- Find people who want to work on the same project. Read the tasks that go with your project and decide who wants to work on which task.
- Find ways of presenting your results. Remember that people who listen to your presentation may not know the story, poem, song or film. Your presentation could be part of an English afternoon, a literary café or an open day at your school.

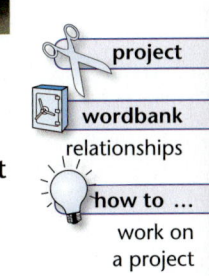

project

wordbank
relationships

how to …
work on a project

workbook
p. 58

Living together

Project 1 ○ Roles in relationships

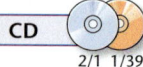

The frog and the princess

Once upon a time, a beautiful princess was sitting beside a pond near her castle dreaming of her future. Suddenly, a little green frog hopped up into her lap. Looking up at her, he said: "An evil old witch cast a spell on me. But one kiss from you and I will turn back into the handsome, charming, intelligent prince that I used to be. Then we can get married and live in my castle with my mother. There you can cook my meals for me, wash my clothes, give birth to my children and forever feel grateful and happy doing so."
That night, eating frogs' legs in a white wine and cream sauce, the princess chuckled to herself and thought: "I don't think so!"

Adrian and Pandora

Adrian Mole is the "hero" of Sue Townsend's novel *The Secret Diary of Adrian Mole Aged 13 ¾*. In his diary Adrian records his problems, for example those with his friend Pandora:

Friday Nov 13th

Pandora and I had a frank talk about our relationship tonight. She doesn't want to marry me in two years' time! She wants to have a career instead!
Naturally I am devastated by this blow. I told her I wouldn't mind her having a little job in a cake shop or something after our wedding, but she said she intended to go to university and that the only time she would enter a cake shop would be to buy a large crusty. Harsh words were exchanged between us. (Hers were harsher than mine.)

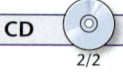

Put another log on the fire

Put another log on the fire
Cook me up some bacon and some beans
And go out to the car and change the tire
Wash my socks and sew my old blue jeans.

Come on baby you can fill my pipe and then go
    fetch my slippers
And boil me up another pot of tea
Then put another log on the fire babe
And come and tell me why you're leaving me.

Now don't I let you wash the car on Sunday?
Don't I warn you when you're gettin' fat?
Ain't I gonna take you fishin' with me someday?
Well, a man can't love a woman more than that.

Ain't I always nice to your kid sister?
Don't I take her driving every night?
So sit here at my feet cause I like you
    when you're sweet
And you know it ain't
    feminine to fight.

So put another log
    on the fire …

*Music and lyrics:
Shel Silverstein*

4 Living together

Are we from the same planet?

Confused girls ask:
"Are we from the same planet?"

Boys and girls might live on the same planet, but sometimes it seems like girls come from one planet, and boys from another. Girls and boys are sometimes so different from one another, that they just don't understand each other.

There are lots of things girls just don't understand about boys, things like:

- Why do boys find it so hard to talk about their feelings?
- Why are boys obsessed with computer games?
- Why do boys act stupidly to try and impress us?
- What's a good way to ask a boy out?
- Would boys go out with a girl taller than them?
- How do boys feel when you make the first move?
- Why don't boys want their friends to go out with their sisters?
- Do boys talk to each other about girls they fancy?
- Why do boys … ?

Boys have questions too!
They want to know things like:

- Why do girls always giggle?
- What do girls really want?
- Why can't girls make the first move?
- Do girls like boys who are not interested in dancing?
- Are girls put off by spots?
- Do girls prefer muscular boys?
- What kind of chat-up-lines do girls like?
- Do girls … ?

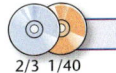
CD
2/3 1/40

○ Tasks to choose from

For this project you can focus on one or more of these tasks. In your group, decide who wants to work on which task. You could even create your own task.

1. Choose one of the texts ("The frog and the princess", "Adrian and Pandora" or "Put another log on the fire") and write a scene to act out.
2. Pandora meets the princess in a chat room. Write a dialogue.
3. Read "The frog and the princess", "Adrian and Pandora" and "Put another log on the fire". What do the three texts have in common? What do the frog, Adrian and the man in the song think about a woman's role in life? Do you agree? Write a comment.
4. "Are we from the same planet?" Choose the questions you find most interesting and find answers. The answers can be serious or funny. You could present them in a web page with FAQs.
5. What is typical of men? What is typical of women? Collect ideas and present them in a funny, perhaps even provocative way.

workbook
p. 59, 60

how to …
work on a project, talk, write a comment, present

wordbank
relationships

portfolio
I can read, write, combine skills, present

Living together

Project 2 ○ Arranged marriages

In his novel *(Un)arranged Marriage* Bali Rai tells the story of Manjit, a British Asian boy whose family came from India. Manjit was born in Britain and has an English girlfriend, Lisa. Because Manjit feels more British than Indian, he often has problems with his parents.

INFO BUBBLE

Arranged marriages

An arranged marriage is a marriage organized by the families of the couple, not the couple themselves. Often the couple don't date at all. This is because these marriages are not about falling in love, but instead are organized for financial or social reasons. In the past, arranged marriages were often found in royal or upper-class families around the world, including Europe. Today there are fewer arranged marriages in Europe, but they are still commonly practised in South Asia, Africa and the Middle East. They are not the same as forced marriages.

While we waited for Lisa's mum after school, I talked a little more to Lisa about the whole deal to do with arranged marriages the way my parents saw it. Lisa told me again to say "no" and keep on saying it until my parents gave up.

"They can't make you do something you don't want to do."

"You don't understand, Lisa. It isn't that simple. My old man is threatening to take me to India if I don't agree. My mum just cries every time we talk about it."

"So, what are you going to do then? Say yes to keep them happy? What about what YOU want?"

That was the problem. I knew that I didn't want to get married young to some girl who I didn't even know. I didn't want to spend my life looking after my parents in their old age and having to go to the weddings of some distant cousins because it was the right thing to do. And deep down inside I was scared that if I did say no, my dad would kill me and my mum would kill herself because of the shame. How could I do that to them? How? And how was I going to explain that to Lisa who was never going to have to choose between what she wanted out of life and her family? She didn't have to fight to be seen as an individual.

"I told you what they've been like. All my mum does is cry."

"But she did that with your brothers too. And you know she doesn't mean it, don't you?"

"Yeah, but what if she does?"

"She won't, Manny, I promise." She held my hand and squeezed it really hard, trying to reassure me. "It'll be fine after a while. When they've accepted you for you."

"I really don't think that will ever happen, Lisa. They're just too set in their old ways to accept what I want to do with my life."

Lisa kissed me on the cheek and squeezed my hand again. I looked at her and tried to smile.

"On a more selfish level, what about me?"

"You know how I feel about you, Lisa."

"And you know that I love you too. But if you end up having an arranged marriage, provided we're still together at that point, are you going to just cast me aside?"

This time I kissed her on the lips and gave her a big hug. "Never. And we will still be together – I know we will."

"Oh, Manny, what are we going to do?"

read

I can read

The perfect couple?

Part 5 of our series *Multicultural Cardiff* — by John Stetson

Different cultures have different ways of finding the perfect partner for life. We spoke to Saju Chahal from India, who has lived in Britain for 23 years. His wife was chosen for him by his parents. It was an arranged marriage in the Hindu tradition. When we interviewed Mr Chahal, we wanted to know what he thought about arranged marriages.

"In India, most people still think that arranged marriages are better than love marriages. A lot of people still arrange the marriages of their children, even when they live here in Britain. I have seen both sides of it. Both of my sons got married in Britain. Their wives are English, so both of them had love marriages. Luckily, they are very happy. But quite often, these love marriages don't last. So many people are getting divorced here in Britain. I think they expect too much of their partners and are really disappointed to find out that they have weaknesses, too. But nobody is perfect!

In my opinion, arranged marriages are good because they often seem to last longer. People don't have unrealistic expectations. My wife and I didn't expect love right from the start, you know. In most arranged marriages, love grows with time. Over the years, we learned to live with each other and accept each other's weaknesses. And if there are problems, everyone tries to help: in a traditional Indian family, everyone feels responsible for the marriage.

It's a difficult topic for me. Here in Britain, people are often shocked to hear about arranged marriages. Last week, a neighbour said to me that arranged marriages were old-fashioned and cruel … Someone had told him that people had to get married to a man or woman they didn't like. Unfortunately, that really does happen. For example, a cousin of mine wasn't allowed to get married to the woman he loved because she was too poor. He was very unhappy and had to get married to a woman his parents had chosen for him. The marriage wasn't happy. But my wife and I have had a happy marriage for over 30 years. That is why I think that arranged marriages are a good idea."

○ Tasks to choose from

For this project you can focus on one or more of these tasks. In your group, decide who wants to work on which task. You could even create your own task. But first of all, write a short summary of the story and add some information about the author.

1. After the conversation with Lisa, Manjit talks to his father again. Write and act out the dialogue.
2. What happened next? Think of several different endings to the story. Read them out to the audience and have them decide which ending they like best.
3. Imagine you were one of Mr Chahal's sons. Write an e-mail to him. Tell him that you respect his views but that you have different ideas about marriage. Give reasons.
4. Write a scene where a family discusses how they could help a couple whose arranged marriage is in trouble.
5. Read up on the term "arranged marriage" and its traditions in different cultures. Think of an interesting way of presenting your results.
6. Write a screenplay for the first meeting of two partners of an arranged marriage.

workbook p. 61

wordbank relationships

how to … work on a project, write a summary, discuss

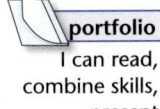

portfolio I can read, combine skills, present

Living together

Project 3 o Love and laughter

The talk

Boy: I need someone to talk to.
Girl: I'm always here for you.
Boy: I know.
Girl: What's wrong?
Boy: I like her so much.
Girl: Talk to her.
Boy: I don't know. She won't ever like me.
Girl: Don't say that … you're amazing.
Boy: I just want her to know how I feel.
Girl: Then tell her.
Boy: She won't like me.
Girl: How do you know that?
Boy: I can just tell her …
Girl: Well just tell her.
Boy: What should I say?
Girl: Tell her how much you like her.
Boy: I tell her daily.
Girl: What do you mean?
Boy: I'm always with her … I love her.
Girl: I know how you feel. I have the same problem … but he'll never like me.
Boy: Wait. Who do you like?
Girl: Oh, some boy.
Boy: Oh, she won't like me either.
Girl: She does.
Boy: How do you know?
Girl: Because who wouldn't like you?
Boy: You.
Girl: You're wrong. I love you.
Boy: I love you too.
Girl: So are you going to talk to her?
Boy: I just did.

Love letter

I hold my breath,
drop the letter on his desk,
watch him pick it up,
mouth the words he reads
following as his finger traces them.

  'Dear Rodger
  I love you
  love from Alison.'

He looks up
And I can read nothing in his eyes;
Picks up his pencil,
Shields paper with his arm.
I pray Miss Forshaw isn't looking.

The folded note begins its journey
– Godfrey – Colin – John – Carol –
I wrench it open, desperate to know.

  'Dear Alison
  There is no d in Roger.'

Alison Chisholm

Living together

Chat-up lines

I must be lost. I thought paradise was further south?

Do you have a plaster? I hurt my knee when I fell for you.

Do you believe in love at first sight, or do you think I should walk past again?

Did the sun come out or did you just smile at me?

Was that an earthquake, or did you just rock my world?

There is something wrong with my mobile phone. It doesn't have your number in it.

How much does a polar bear weigh? Enough to break the ice – can I get your number?

Tasks to choose from

For this project you can focus on one or more of these tasks. In your group, decide who wants to work on which task. You could even create your own task.

1. Copy the comic strip and add thought and speech bubbles for the frog and Nemi.
2. Imagine Nemi had turned into a frog after the kiss. What could have happened? Write the "froggy" conversation.
3. Practise reading "The talk" with a partner and present it to the class. You can also present it as a short film.
4. Draw the outline of Alison's head and fill it with words that express her feelings (embarrassed, unhappy, furious, angry, …) after she has read Roger's message. Make a collage of all the pictures from your class.
5. Chat-up lines
   - Do any of these work for boys and girls? Would any of these work in German? Explain why or why not.
   - Could you use typical German chat-up lines and translate them into English? Do you think they would work? Explain why or why not.
6. Create your own chat-up line and write the resulting dialogue.

workbook p. 62

how to … work on a project, read comics, mediate, write

wordbank relationships

portfolio I can combine skills, present

portfolio dossier

Living together

Project 4 ○ A love song and a love letter

This ain't a love song

Every night I remember that evening
The way you looked when you said you were leaving
The way you cried as you turned to walk away
The cruel words and the false accusations
The mean looks and the same old frustrations
I never thought that we'd throw it all away
But we threw it all away.

Chorus:
And I'm a little bit lost without you
And I'm a bloody big mess inside
And I'm a little bit lost without you
This ain't a love song this is goodbye

I've been lost, I've been out, I've been losing
I've been tired, I'm all hurt and confusion
I've been mad, I'm the kind of man that I'm not
I'm going down, I'll be coming back fighting
I may be scared and a little bit frightened
But I'll be back, I'll be coming back to life
I'll be coming back to life

Chorus
And you can try (you can try)
And you can try but you'll never keep me down
(I won't be lost, I won't be down)

Chorus
It's alright (It's alright) cause you can try but
   you'll never keep me down
It's alright (It's alright) I may be lost but you'll
   never keep me down
You can try (you can try) you can try
   but you'll never keep me down
You can try (you can try) I know
   I'm lost but I'm waiting
   to be found
you'll never keep me down
you'll never keep me down
never keep me down

Music and lyrics: Lane / Chagnon / Lee

Dylan Thomas to his wife

Cat: my cat: If only you would write to me: My love, oh Cat. [...]   March 16, 1950
*Have you forgotten me? I am the man you used to say you loved. I used to sleep
in your arms – do you remember? But you never write. You are perhaps mindless of me. I am not of
you. I love you. There isn't a moment of any hideous day when I do not say to myself, 'It will be alright.
I shall go home. Caitlin loves me. I love Caitlin.' But perhaps you have forgotten. If you have forgotten, or
lost your affection for me, please, my Cat, let me know. I Love You.*

Dylan

This love letter was written by the Welsh poet Dylan Thomas. He sent it to his wife Caitlin while he was on a reading tour in North America.

○ Tasks to choose from

For this project you can focus on one or more of these tasks. In your group, decide who wants to work on which task. You could even create your own task.

1. Present your favourite love songs in an interesting way. You could, for example, combine the songs into a musical.

2. Answer Dylan Thomas' letter as if you were Caitlin. Prepare a reading session where you read out both letters.

3. Do some research and find out more about the relationship of Dylan and Caitlin. Think of reasons why Caitlin did not write.

4. Search for another famous love letter and present it with some background information.

Living together

Project 5 ○ My stories

I'd be a proper house husband!

My name is Geoffrey. I'm 17 and I live in Croydon. I'm at college now, but after that I want to work in a hotel as a manager. I haven't got a girlfriend at the moment. It's not a big problem because I'm working hard for my exams but I know that when I've started my career I'd like to live with someone. But I don't want to feel trapped in a relationship. You should always be able to spend some time on your own or with your mates without it causing a problem in the relationship. I know it can be hard to keep a relationship going but I think you just have to work at it. The most important thing is that you can trust each other.

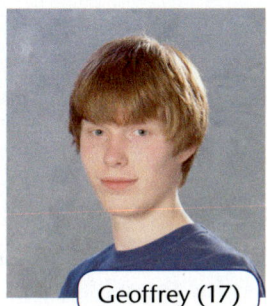
Geoffrey (17)

I'm from a big family so I'd really love to have children. I want to do loads with my kids! My partner should have a good job, a proper career and not only have the kitchen and the kids to talk about. I could work part-time for a while, too, and stay at home with the kids whilst my partner was at work. We could share the housework as well as taking it in turns to look after the children – I'd be a proper house husband! So, all in all: yes, I want to get married once I've got a good job and I want a partner who is satisfied both with her career and with her family.

A house of my own

Not a flat. Not an apartment in back. Not a man's house. Not a daddy's. A house all my own. With my porch and my pillow, my purple pretty petunias. My books and my stories. My two shoes waiting beside my bed. Nobody to shake a stick at. Nobody's garbage to pick up after. Only a house quiet as snow, a space for myself to go, clean as paper before the poem.

Sandra Cisneros

CD
2/9 1/47

○ Tasks to choose from

For this project you can focus on one or more of these tasks. In your group, decide who wants to work on which task. You could even create your own task.

1. Write about your ideal home. You can use Sandra Cisneros' "A house of my own" as a model.
2. "A house of my own" was written by a female writer. Write a similar text from a male point of view.
3. Write a "perfect relationship recipe".
4. Write about your ideas of your future life. You can use Geoffrey's text as a model.

First take two people that trust each other. Then add a cup of love. Mix in one tablespoon of time, a teaspoon of forgiveness and 80 grams of faith. Top it with 100 grams of loyalty and a pinch of joy.

workbook
p. 64

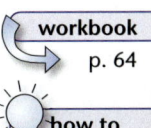
how to …
work on a project, write

model

wordbank
relationships

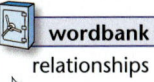
portfolio
I can write, combine skills

Living together

Project 6 ◯ Films about families

how to ...
talk about films, listen

film

workbook
p. 65

There are a lot of films about families and relationships. Choose one of the five films or find another one. All the people who have chosen Project 6 can make a film guide on relationship films together. Find help with the structure in your workbook.

East is East

It's 1971 and George Khan, a Pakistani immigrant, and his British wife Ella, run a fish and chip shop in Salford. Although George has lived in England for over 30 years, he expects his family to lead strict Muslim lives. When he starts arranging marriages for his eldest sons, the problems begin ...

- Describe the structure of the Khan family.
- What kinds of relationships are presented in the film?
- Watch the scene (1:10:30-1:13:42): How do Abdul and Tariq deal with the fact that their father arranged marriages for them?

Four weddings and a funeral

Always the best man, never the groom. Charles fears that he's going to spend the rest of his life attending weddings without ever getting married himself. But then he meets Carrie ...

- How many love stories are told in the film? Which ones are happy and which aren't?
- All of the weddings take place either in England or in Scotland.
  What can you find out about wedding ceremonies in Great Britain?
  Is there anything different from the wedding ceremonies you are familiar with?
- Watch the scene (0:42:26) where Charles asks himself: "Why am I always at weddings and never actually getting married?"
  What is his answer? Do you think he is right?
- Listen to the conversation between Charles and Tom after the funeral (1:26:05). What are Tom's expectations and what happens to him later?
- The last scene shows Charles' relationship problems being solved (1:48:28). What do you think of this solution?

Living together

Dan in real life

For Thanksgiving, widower Dan Burns takes his three daughters to his parents' house for a family get-together. In a bookshop Dan meets Marie and they immediately connect. Although she has a boyfriend, Marie agrees to meet Dan again. But when Dan returns to his parents' house he finds out that Marie is his brother's new girlfriend.

film

- Thanksgiving is a traditional family holiday. Describe how Dan's family celebrates it.
- Dan is a newspaper advice columnist who sometimes needs some advice himself. What kind of advice would you give him?
- "You're a good father, but sometimes a bad dad." Select scenes that support or disprove what Dan's youngest daughter says at the beginning of the film. What do you think of Dan as a father?

About a boy

Will is a rich Londoner in his thirties. He is looking for a new way to meet women. He invents a son so that he can go to single parent meetings. Through one of the women he meets Marcus, a 12-year-old boy with no friends and problems at home. Slowly, Will and Marcus become friends …

- Watch the opening credits (0:00:50-0:02:00). What does the phrase "No man is an island" mean to Will?
- Now watch the final scene (1:30:05-1:32:17). How has Will's view changed throughout the film? Give a presentation about these changes using screenshots.
- Select scenes which show how Will and Marcus' relationship develops and present them to the class.

Juno

16-year-old Juno is bored and decides to have sex for the first time with her friend Paulie. She soon finds herself pregnant, but doesn't want to have an abortion. Instead, she chooses adoptive parents and gets drawn further and further into their lives …

- How do Juno's family, friends and the father of the baby react when they find out that she is pregnant? What changes during the pregnancy?
- Imagine that Juno kept her baby and raised it with Paulie, the father. Write an alternative plot.
- What is important when choosing an adoptive family for a baby? What was important for Juno? Do you think her decision was right? Set up your own categories and explain them.

4 Grammar revision

G1 Sound check

a) Listen to these words and repeat them. Is the stress on the first or second syllable? Draw a table and write the words into two columns.

> model · adopted · marry · alone · career · patchwork
> traditional · extended · together · single

b) Listen to the CD and check your table.

G2 Questions for a future partner

What questions would you ask a future partner in order to find out how well-suited you are?

> Do you like … ?   What kind of … ?   How many … ?
> Would you ever … ?   Where would you … ?   How often … ?
> Would you like to … ?   How long … ?   …

G3 Asking about the past

Imagine interviewing someone who has had an arranged marriage. Write down at least 10 questions you would like to ask them.

Where did you … ?   Why did / didn't you … ?   What did … ?
Why did your parents … ?   How long have you … ?   When did … ?
Do you think … ?   Did you wish you … ?   …

Now exchange your questions with a partner. Correct mistakes if necessary and write down the questions using the indirect form. Don't forget the tense shift!

My partner wanted to know whether the person he/she interviewed …

G4 Diary entry: My future life

a) Complete the diary entry using modals.

I really ??? find a partner! He/She ??? be clever, friendly and really nice. He/She ??? hate children, because I want at least four children. He/She ??? be poor because I would love to spend lots of money and not think about it. But he/she ??? be a millionaire, that's not necessary. He/She ??? be famous, as I don't want to be photographed all the time, I want my peace. But he/she ??? have a good job. As I ??? dance well, he/she must ??? dance too, so we can go dancing together.

Tipp
Achtung: *should* verändert sich nicht.

I really must find a partner! I wrote that he/she should …

b) You found your diary and talk about what you wrote with a friend. Write down the sentences from a) in the past tense.

I wrote that I had to find a partner. I wrote that he/she should …

Grammar revision

G5 ○ Dreaming of the weekend

a) You dream about your next weekend. Use the correct form of the future.

On Saturday I ??? go to a concert. I bought the tickets two months ago. After the concert my friend and I ??? meet other friends at the new burger bar in town. Hopefully they ??? already be there waiting for us when we come from the concert. Perhaps the weather ??? be good, so we ??? go to the lake for a swim on Sunday. If the weather is bad, we ??? perhaps go to the cinema or I might go and visit my grandmother. I have been planning to visit her for a long time. Last time I spoke to her I told her: "I ??? visit you soon" – so I should really do that. Before I go, I ??? go into town to get her some flowers as she ??? hopefully be happy then.

b) Listen to the CD and check your text.

LiF 9R

CD 1/51

G6 ○ What would happen if … ?

a) Complete the sentences using the verbs in brackets in the correct form.

1. If I ??? better marks my parents ??? much happier. (have, be)
2. I ??? a new laptop if I ??? the money. (buy, have)
3. If I ??? to university I ??? a doctor. (go, become)
4. If I ??? a doctor I ??? other people. (become, help)
5. They ??? me a lot of money. (pay)
6. With that money I ??? a lot of nice things. (buy)

b) Listen to the CD and check your sentences.

LiF 10R

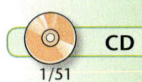

CD 1/52

G7 ○ I keep thinking …

a) Rewrite the following sentences using the correct form of the verb.

1. I am so afraid of (do) badly in my exams.
2. Everyone else seems to be good at (learn).
3. My teachers say I have a good chance of (get) good enough marks to go to university.
4. Why am I so awful at (do) exams?
5. I can't even look forward to (go) on holiday because I know that I must do the exams first.
6. I'm not interested in (find out) the results!

1. I am so afraid of doing badly in my exams.

b) Listen to the CD and check your sentences

LiF 14R

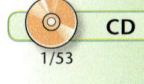

CD 1/53

G8 ○ Life can be hard

a) Shorten the sentences using a participle.

1. A beautiful princess, who was sitting beside a pond, was dreaming of her future.
2. A frog that came up from the bottom of the pond looked up at her.
3. While he looked at her, he told her about a spell that was cast on him.
4. But the princess, who had her own opinion, did not do what the frog wanted.
5. That night the princess, who was eating frogs' legs, smiled to herself.
6. The frog, who was dead now, would never marry her.

Sitting beside a pond, a beautiful princess was dreaming of her future.

b) Listen to the CD and check your sentences.

LiF 16R

CD 1/54

4

Grammar revision

G9 How long?

a) Write "How long …?" questions using the "present perfect progressive":

1. live / Frankfurt
2. learn / English
3. attend / your present school
4. play / in your school's handball team
5. play / piano
6. learn / to drive
7. have / school lunches
8. see / your boyfriend

1. How long have you been living in Frankfurt?

b) Listen to the CD and check your sentences.

G10 What have you been doing?

a) Answer the question "What have you been doing?" for each situation.

1. prepare for a maths test
2. tidy my bedroom
3. clean my bike
4. do my homework
5. play computer games
6. prepare a presentation on Shakespeare
7. work on a project about chat-up lines
8. practise English grammar

1. I've been preparing for a maths test.

b) Listen to the CD and check your sentences.

G11 Guess what has been happening!

a) Explain what has been happening in each situation.

1. Jack's really out of breath. (jog)
2. It's all white outside. (snow)
3. Jennifer looks so tired. (work / all night)
4. Sonya's eyes are all red. (cry)
5. Kirsty's hands are dirty. (fix / bike)
6. Sam has lost his voice. (shout / football match)

1. Jack's really out of breath. He has been jogging.

b) Listen to the CD and check your sentences.

G12 Happy endings

a) Find correct endings for the words in the yellow box. In some cases, there is more than one possibility.

danger	man	nation
differ	inform	beautiful
govern	import	perfect
know	success	bad
real	resist	national

ledge	ly	age
ist	ant	ment
ation	ent	al
ful	ance	s
ous	ful	ness

b) Make sure that you know the German meaning of the words you found.

Global player 5

In diesem *Theme* …

- erfährst du etwas über Indien und die Menschen in Indien.
- liest du etwas über die Geschichte Indiens.
- hörst du, was Menschen in Indien von ihrem Leben berichten.
- erfährst du etwas über *sweatshops* und die globale Wirtschaft.
- beschäftigst du dich mit der Mode- und Textilindustrie.

Global player

A1 Journey to India

a) What comes to mind when you look at the pictures and listen to the sounds?

b) Which captions and pictures match?

> auto rickshaw · Taj Mahal · cricket · sacred animal · street market in Calcutta ·
> sari · film industry in Mumbai · flag · Mahatma Gandhi

c) What do *you* know about India? What would you like to know? Talk about your ideas in class.

Global player

A2 ● Did you know that …

… India is the country with the second largest population, 1.2 billion people, after China with 1.35 billion?

… New Delhi is the capital of India?

… the largest city in India is Mumbai with about 13 million inhabitants?

… the flag of India has three colours: orange-yellow stands for courage, white stands for peace and green stands for faith?

… the yearly rainfall in some parts of India is about 3 metres, compared to about 60 cm in Germany?

… India used to be a British colony and did not become independent until 1947?

… Hinduism plays an important role in India? More than 80 % of the population are Hindus.

… for Hindus the Ganges is the most sacred river on earth?

… cows are sacred in Hinduism?

… the Taj Mahal is thought to be one of the most beautiful buildings in the world? It is a symbol of eternal love.

… Mahatma Gandhi was the leader of the Indian nationalist movement against British rule?

… Bollywood is not only the largest film producer in India but also one of the largest centres of film production in the world?

… Diwali, the festival of lights, is one of the most important festivals in India?

… there are several hundred different languages spoken in India? 22 of them are official languages with Hindi and English being the most important ones?

… pyjamas were originally invented in India to be worn outdoors and were later imported by the British to be sleepwear?

… the sari is a typical garment for women in India?

… the sitar is a famous Indian string instrument which is also used in some modern European pop music?

… cricket is the national game?

… India is home to several well-known large animals, like the Asian elephant, Bengal tiger, leopard and Indian rhinoceros?

… IT is an important industry in India?

how to …
read

a) Read the facts. Discuss the most interesting ones with a partner.

b) Close your books. Which facts do you remember?

c) Complete the sentences with phrases from the box.

1. There **???** fewer than 10 million people in Mumbai, but now there are about 13 million.
2. There **???** a lot of tigers and leopards in India, but now there are not many left.
3. All women **???** saris but today many wear other clothes.
4. Bollywood **???** known in Europe but today it is well-known.

didn't use to be ·
used to be ·
used to wear ·
used to be

d) Listen to the CD and check your sentences.

portfolio
I can listen, read, talk, work with grammar

LiF
18

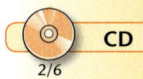
CD
2/6

workbook
A1, A2

81

Global player

A3 ● A short history of India

a) Look at the pictures. Does anything look familiar?

b) Now read about India's history. Which part do you find the most interesting?

1. **3300 BC:** Civilization started in the Indus River Valley. People used to live in brick buildings.

2. **From the 4th century BC,** India was divided into a very large number of small kingdoms. It was a period of great economic wealth.

3. **326 BC:** Alexander the Great of Macedonia went to India with his soldiers. They fought battles against Indian kings and conquered parts of northern India. They stayed in India until 316 BC.

4. **1st and 2nd century AD:** trade between India and the Roman Empire was very successful. The Romans used to come across the Indian Ocean with gold and silver and sail back with pearls, spices, silk and ivory.

5. **4th / 5th century:** Hinduism became a major religion in India. It is the world's oldest religion. Hindus believe in reincarnation. Their god, Brahman, appears in different forms and is present in all things. The 4th to 6th centuries are called the "golden age" of Indian history when literature, art and science were of the highest quality.

6. **Between the 10th and the 16th century:** Islam grew as another important religion in India. Muslims believe in one god, Allah. Today Islam is the second largest religion practised in India. However, there were, and still are, severe conflicts between Hindus and Muslims.

7. **1498:** Portuguese sailors under Vasco da Gama were the first "modern" Europeans who came to India. They were followed by colonists from Britain, Denmark, France, the Netherlands and Portugal. Trade was their main interest.

8. **1858:** After a large number of conflicts and wars the British took control of India, which then included today's Pakistan, Bangladesh, Sri Lanka and Myanmar (Burma). The country was named the Indian Empire. In 1876 Queen Victoria became Empress of India.

9. **1915:** Mahatma Gandhi started a campaign of non-violent resistance against British rule in India. Gandhi's 24-day-long salt march as a protest against the British salt taxes in 1930 was an important campaign against British rule. Gandhi was murdered in New Delhi in 1948.

Global player

10. **1947:** India won independence from Britain. The country was divided into India and the Muslim-controlled Pakistan. On 15 August the national flag of India was raised on the Red Fort in Delhi, which had been used as a military camp by the British.

11. **1947–1964:** Nehru was the first prime minister of the Republic of India. Together with Gandhi he had been a leading figure in India's fight for independence. Nehru became a successful leader of the new republic. To make India a single, unified country he used to warn, "Integrate or perish".

12. **Since 1947:** There have been permanent conflicts and wars with Pakistan over Kashmir in the north-west of India.

13. **1998:** India carried out five underground nuclear tests and became the sixth member of the so-called "nuclear club".

14. **2000:** India's population grew to more than 1 billion.

15. **Today** India is the seventh-largest and the second-most populous nation. It's the world's ninth largest and one of the fastest-growing economies in the world. India is a big power in South Asia. However, there are still severe problems with poverty, illiteracy, corruption and public health.

c) Which three events do you think were most important in the history of India? Say why.

d) Make a timeline of the history of India.

A4 ● The many aspects of India

 a) Unscramble the sentences.

1. was very successful – Trade with India – because – pearls, spices, silk and ivory – the Indians had
2. are called – when – The 4th to 6th centuries – the "golden age" – literature, art and science – of the highest quality – were
3. the major religion – in India – the major religion – in Pakistan – Hinduism – Islam – while – is – is
4. India – 1947 – was – a British colony – before
5. India – with poverty – the world's ninth largest economy – is – there are – although – severe problems

b) Listen to the CD and check your sentences.

 a) Make two sentences from one using a conjunction.

> while · and · because ·
> before · when · although

1. The Romans came with gold and silver. They sailed back with pearls, spices, silk and ivory.
2. The 4th to 6th centuries are called the "golden age". Literature, art and science were of the highest quality.
3. Many Europeans came to India in the 15th century. Trade was their main interest.
4. India became independent in 1947. It used to be a British crown colony.
5. Hinduism is the major religion in India. Islam is the major religion in Pakistan.
6. India is the world's ninth largest economy. There are severe problems with poverty.

b) Listen to the CD and check your sentences.

portfolio
I can read, talk, learn English

workbook
A3, A4

LiF
19

portfolio
I can listen

CD
2/9

portfolio
I can work with grammar, listen

workbook
A5

CD
2/10

83

Global player

A5 • People in India

a) Close your books and listen to three people talking about their lives in India. One of them is not from India. Who is it?

1. Sunil Chettira was born and brought up in Mumbai and is one of the many English-speaking tour guides who work for Reality Tours & Travel.

"I was given extensive training by Reality Tours. If I hadn't had this training I wouldn't have been able to do the job and I wouldn't have met such a lot of people from all over the world. Contact within the tourist groups is good – there are only six people in a group – so a kind of cultural exchange takes place.
People who come on the tours usually want to see India as it really is. The village tours are great and very popular; the tourists don't just observe and learn about life in the village but are encouraged to take part in village activities such as milking the cows, ploughing the fields, fishing or just playing cricket. They stay as guests of an Indian family and spend at least a night with them. Some of our guests told me that our tour was the part of their holiday they enjoyed most."

2. André from Germany wanted to gain some experience working in the film industry abroad after graduating from university.

"At the moment, I work as an intern on a Bollywood film set. When I first got to India, I was shocked at how different it was from Germany. People, traffic, noise, dirt and damaged streets are everywhere! Public transport is always full of people. The train is sometimes so packed that the Indians will even sit on the roofs – no joke!
Even on the film set there are a lot more people than I am used to. I think it's great that the film industry employs so many people who would otherwise perhaps just be sitting on the street. In terms of communication, I never really have any problems. Many people speak English, although it takes a while to get used to their accents."

3. Bhumika Chaturvedia, 24, works in a call centre in Gurgaon, Delhi.

"I call people to remind them of their credit card payments. We have been dealing with American clients a lot lately. I don't think this would have been the case if the Americans hadn't suffered so much in the recent financial crisis. Most of my colleagues are young and educated, and we earn quite well – $5,000 a year. The downside is that we usually have to work late into the night, because we're 10 hours ahead of the United States. We used to think that America was a paradise full of high-paying jobs and big houses. It is strange to be sitting here in India, listening to Americans who cannot pay their credit card bills. People cry on the phone because they are scared of losing their jobs, their houses or their cars. Of course, we cannot do much for them but try and show empathy and patience. My boss always says that in this business, we're part therapists."

Global player

b) Scan the texts and find the person who …

… deals with Americans a lot.
… is from Mumbai.
… works in Delhi.
… talks about everyday problems in India.
… meets people from other countries.
… talks about language.
… goes on tours with people.
… has to deal with other people's problems.

c) Discuss in groups: whose job is the most interesting? Whose job is the least interesting?

d) Complete the sentences using the sentence parts in the green box.

1. If Sunil hadn't been given training …
2. If Sunil's guests hadn't been on tour with him, they …
3. If the Americans hadn't lost so much money in the financial crisis …
4. If Bhumika hadn't started working in a call centre …

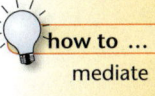

have problems with their credit card payments · be able to do the job · know that Americans were scared of losing their houses · see India as it really is

1. *If Sunil hadn't been given training he wouldn't have been able to do the job.*

e) One of your relatives wants to travel to India. Tell him or her in German about what Sunil says about the village tours.

A6 About their jobs

Write about the lives of the three people using "that", "who" and "which".

1. Some guests told me that the tour was the part of their holiday
2. The film industry employs many people
3. André knows good English
4. Bhumika's American customers worry a lot about the bills
5. Her boss is the person

who
that
which

helps him a lot in India.
she asks for advice about difficult customers.
they cannot pay.
they enjoyed most.
would otherwise just be sitting on the street.

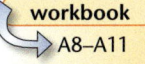

In which sentences can you leave out "that", "who" or "which"? Why can you leave them out? Find the rule.

A7 A class project on India

Do a project on India. Choose a topic.

- famous cities and sights
- famous Indians
- jobs and globalization
- religions
- Bollywood

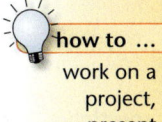

Start by collecting information. Make notes and plan your presentation. Decide as a group on how you are going to present your topic to the class. You can also find information on some of the topics on the DVD. Give each other feedback after the presentation.

87

Global player

B1 What's behind the labels?

a) Look at the labels. What information do you get? What information is missing?

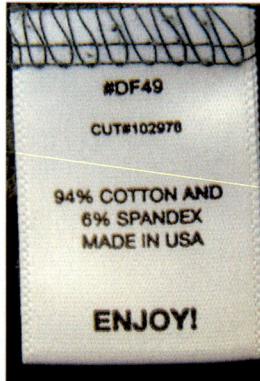
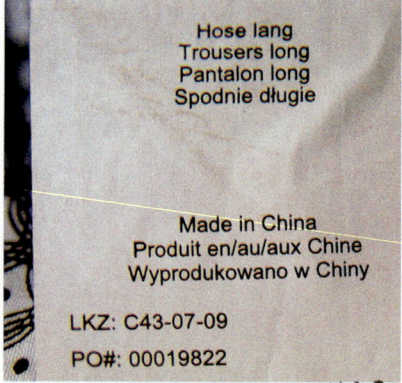
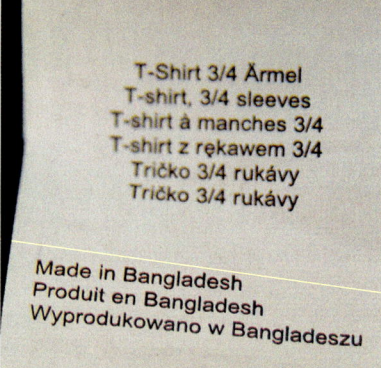

> The label does not tell us anything about …
> I would like to know …
> I have heard of …
> The label does not give any information on …
> How can I be sure that …?
> Why do they not give any information about …?

wordbank
economy

portfolio
I can learn English

b) Look at the labels in your own clothes. What information do you get? Compare with your findings from a).

c) In which countries were the clothes produced? Make a list from the labels in the pictures and your own clothes. Which country do you find most often? Why do you think this is the case?

Global player

B2 ● Where do my clothes come from?

a) Look at the photos of the two teenagers and compare them.

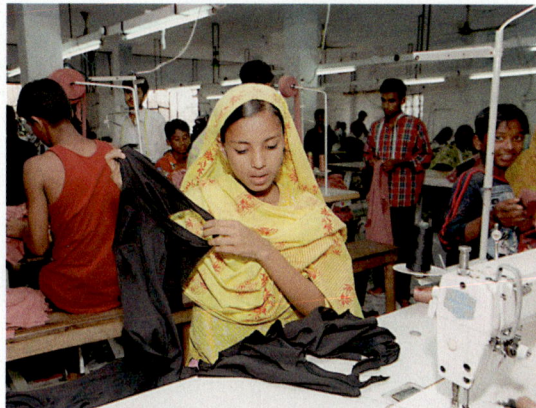

b) What questions come to mind when you see these pictures? Think about it, then work with a partner. Agree on at least three questions to share with the class.

☼ Find questions that cover the same aspects and group them together. Find headings for each aspect.

c) Now listen to the two girls and read along. Which of your questions are answered?

CD
2/13 2/17

portfolio
I can listen

Chantelle

My name's Chantelle, I'm 15 and I'm from Bristol. I get 40 pounds a month pocket money, which I spend on clothes. I just love clothes shopping. I try to keep up to date with the latest fashions, although that's sometimes hard with the tiny amount of money I get from my parents. There are so many awesome things to buy, it's so hard! I even try to save money elsewhere. I don't get my hair done very often, for example.

Mantheesh

My name is Mantheesh. I'm 14 and I come from Sri Lanka. I had to leave my home country and I'm now in a refugee camp in India. I've found work in a textile factory which is good because we wouldn't have enough money otherwise. I start at 7 in the morning and work all day, often into the night. If we work late we often have to work by candlelight because the electricity here is poor. It makes my eyes hurt.

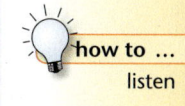

how to ...
listen

d) Now listen to the rest of the girls' stories. What else do you get to know about them? Take notes in your workbook (B1a).

e) Unscramble the following sentences.
1. doesn't get – Chantelle – very often – her hair done
2. at all – can't get – her hair done – Mantheesh
3. her clothes washed – she – can't get
4. onto the clothes – has the beads sewn – her boss
5. has the work done – her boss – if Mantheesh works late – by candlelight

CD
2/14 2/18

portfolio
I can listen,
work with
grammar

LiF
22

workbook
B1–B3

89

B3 Journey of a cheap T-shirt

The story of the cheap T-shirt begins in a big textile company in Europe. Here, the T-shirt is designed and the managers of the company discuss how to make the T-shirt cheap enough so that everyone can afford it. They decide that the price must be just under 5 Euros.

price now: €0.90

The managers decide to buy cotton from a farmer in the US. The cotton here is cheap, because the United States government pays the farmers money for it to support the cotton farming industry in the US.

The cotton is made into fabrics which are sewn together in a factory in Bangladesh. Mainly girls and young women work here. The wages in Asia are very low. This helps to keep the price of the T-shirt down.

price now: €0.908

This is Nazneen. It's her job to cut out T-shirts. She has to do 250 T-shirts every hour, and works 10 hours a day.

Nazneen and the other women get paid very little. Nazneen earns about €36 a month, that means €1.18 a day and as little as 15 cents an hour. Nazneen gets far less than one cent for every T-shirt she cuts, so the T-shirt stays cheap.

Global player

price now: €1.35

The manager of the factory in Bangladesh sells the T-shirts to a buyer from the company in Europe. Now that they have been sewn together, the T-shirts cost €1.35 each.

The T-shirts are now shipped from Bangladesh to Europe. They are loaded into containers and onto a ship. The cost for transport is about 6 cents per T-shirt.

price now: €1.41

T-shirt €4.99

Our cheap T-shirt has arrived in a store in Europe. It is sold at the price of €4.99. After taxes and other costs, the textile company makes a profit of about 60 cents per T-shirt. Considering that they sell millions of cheap T-shirts around the world, it means that the company is making lots of money.

Who is really paying to keep the price of the T-shirt so cheap? Give reasons for your answer.

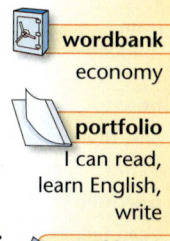

wordbank
economy

portfolio
I can read, learn English, write

workbook
B4

Global player

B4 ● Sweatshops and child labour

wordbank
economy

portfolio
I can read

a) Before you read the statements, make sure you know the meaning of the following words:

- sweatshop
- retailer
- child labour
- turnaround
- wages
- ethical

b) Now read the statements.

A Mum-of-three Katrina Reddie, 34, from East London: "I can't stop shopping at cheap stores. Of course, I think it's wrong that our clothes are made in sweatshops, but I can't afford to shop anywhere else."

B Human rights groups representative: "Consumers need to make it clear to retailers that the use of child labour cannot be accepted. Children have a right to an education!"

C Manager of an ethical clothing store: "Many people will benefit from our business. Customers can shop at our store safe in the knowledge it is an ethical organization that helps give people in the developing world a higher standard of living and a better quality of life."

D Government officials in developing countries: "We don't want children working on our clothes. The people in our factories work in proper working conditions. We want people paid properly."

E Student: "The root of the problem is our 'fast fashion' culture because it means a lot of retailers ask for a fast and flexible turnaround, and low prices."

F Economist: "36 Euros may not be a lot of money for a month's work, but what will it buy in India? You cannot make a direct comparison between UK wages and Indian wages."

c) Report what the people and organizations say.

1. The mother says that …
2. The Human rights group representative says that …
3. The manager of an ethical clothing store says that …
4. Government officials in developing countries claim that …
5. A student …
6. The economist is of the opinion that …

1. The mother says that she thinks it's wrong that our clothes are made in sweatshops, but she can't afford to shop anywhere else.

how to…
mediate

portfolio
I can mediate

d) Ask some family members or friends about their opinion of child labour and the fashion industry. Report back to the class in English. Also say which statement in B4 you agree with most and why.

how to…
talk, discuss

B5 ○ Your opinion

a) Which statement in B4 do you agree with most? Say why.

portfolio
I can talk

b) Work with a partner. One of you argues for a company selling cheap clothes and the other argues that the company should make certain changes. Make notes. Have a group discussion.

Global player

B6 ● Child labour in India

a) Read this report. It names one reason for child labour. What is it?

India has the largest number of children in work in the world. Some experts put the figure at 100 million children. Often young children are forced to work for long hours for low pay and sometimes in unhealthy or even dangerous conditions.

Many of them work because their families are poor and rely on the extra money they earn for the family. This form of child labour is very common in India.

There is also another form of child labour, the so-called bonded labour. This means that children are sold by their families to work for others. They are often forced to live in the place where they work, and in very poor conditions. This modern form of slavery is illegal in India, but still in practice.

But banning all child labour would not help the poor children. The best way to solve the problem would be to help families to get a better income. Then they would be able to afford to send their children to school. A good education would mean a better paid job later on. There are projects and initiatives that help families to get a better income, which means that their children can get an education and escape poor health, malnutrition and child labour.

how to …
read, write a comment

b) ★ What is bonded labour? Write down a definition in your own words.

☼ What are the effects of child labour and bonded labour? Write a comment.

portfolio
I can read, write

B7 ○ Choose

1. Read the diary of a trip to India. Choose one entry and talk to your partner about it.
   www.oxfam.org.uk/coolplanet/kidsweb/diary/index.htm

2. B3 shows the journey of a cheap T-shirt. Find out how other products, e. g. sports shoes, are made and present your findings to the class as a comic, a diagram or a report.

3. Read about Mantheesh in B2 again. Describe a week in the girl's life. Use the information in this Theme and make up what you don't know.

4. Find out about child labour in other countries. Compare your findings to the situation in Germany.

5. Could you imagine being a sweatshop worker?
   Try out what it would be like by playing the "Unfair factory game" on www.playfair2012.org.uk. Report back to the class.

6. Look at the cartoon and write a comment.

how to …
write, present, write a comment

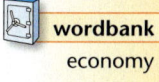
wordbank
economy

portfolio
I can write, combine skills

93

Global player

Practice matters

P1 ○ Say it in English

Match the sentences.

1. Du sagst, dass Kinder ein Recht auf Bildung haben.
2. Wie drückst du aus, dass du versuchst, auf dem neuesten Stand zu bleiben?
3. Wie sagst du, dass du es dir nicht leisten kannst, woanders einzukaufen?
4. Wie drückst du den Wunsch aus, dass Menschen angemessen bezahlt werden?
5. Wie sagst du, dass du als Praktikant bzw. Praktikantin arbeitest?
6. Wie sagst du, dass es Projekte und Initiativen gibt, die Familien helfen, ein besseres Einkommen zu erzielen?

a. I try to keep up to date.
b. There are projects and initiatives that help families to get a better income.
c. Children have the right to an education.
d. We want people paid properly.
e. I cannot afford to shop anywhere else.
f. I work as an intern.

P2 ○ Facts about India

a) All the statements are wrong. Correct them.

1. Mumbai used to be called Bumbai.
2. Indira Gandhi used to be the leader of the Indian nationalist movement.
3. Pyjamas didn't use to be worn outdoors.
4. India used to be a German colony.
5. The Romans used to buy gold and silver in India.
6. Today's Pakistan didn't use to be part of the British colony.

1. Mumbai used to be called Bombay.

b) Listen to the CD and check your sentences.

P3 ○ Child labour

Complete the sentences, using the conjunctions from the box.

1. ??? I had heard about child labour I didn't think twice about where to go shopping.
2. ??? many people know about child labour they go shopping at places that get their clothes from Asia.
3. ??? they knew under which conditions their clothes were made maybe they would not buy them.
4. ??? people are very poor they have to do jobs they don't like.
5. ??? I go to school, children in other countries have to work.
6. ??? , lots of people don't want to think about it.

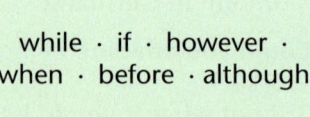

while · if · however · when · before · although

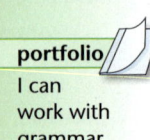

I can work with grammar

Practice matters

Global player

P4 O Another look at the history of India

a) Write what you would have done.

1. If I (wish) to own spices and silk in the 1st century I (sail) to India.
2. If I (be) Vasco da Gama I (try) to be a friendly visitor.
3. If I (live) in India at the end of the 19th century I (lead) a totally different life.
4. If I (meet) Gandhi I (ask) him about his life in London.
5. If I (know) about Gandhi's protest march I (follow) him.
6. If I (hear) about India's nuclear tests in 1998 I (be) shocked.

1. *If I had wished to own spices and silk in the 1st century I would have sailed to India.*

b) Listen to the CD and check your sentences.

LiF 20

portfolio
I can work with grammar

CD 2/25

P5 O Touring India

a) Complete the sentences with a relative pronoun only when it is necessary.

Sunil works for Reality Tours, a company ??? offers village tours in India. People ??? come on the tours usually want to see India as it really is. Sunil has met a lot of people on these tours ??? he really liked. The tourists ??? go on the tours observe, learn and take part in activities ??? the people ??? live in the villages have to do, like fishing or milking the cows. They stay as guests of an Indian family ??? they spend a night with. Some of his guests had told him that this tour was the part of their holiday ??? they enjoyed most.

b) Listen to the CD and check your sentences.

LiF 21

CD 2/26

P6 O Trouble with prepositions

a) Find the correct prepositions.

for · in · of · to · on · by

1. New Delhi is the capital ??? India.
2. White in the Indian flag stands ??? peace.
3. The Ganges is the most sacred river ??? earth.
4. The Taj Mahal is a symbol ??? love.
5. Pyjamas were imported ??? the British.
6. The sari is a garment ??? women.
7. India is home ??? several large animals.
8. India became independent ??? 1947.

b) Listen to the CD and check your sentences.

portfolio
I can work with words

CD 2/27

P7 O Journey of a cheap T-shirt

a) Complete the sentences using the past participle of the verb in brackets.

The managers of the clothes company in the story have new T-shirts ??? (design). They have the cotton ??? (buy) in the USA because it is cheap there. The company has the cotton ??? (make) into fabrics. They have the fabrics ??? (sew) together in Asia by women and young girls. The manager of the factory in Asia has the women and young girls ??? (pay) very little. He has the T-shirts ??? (sell) to a buyer from the European company. They then have them ??? (ship) to Europe. Finally they have them ??? (sell) in shops in Europe.

b) Listen to the CD and check your text.

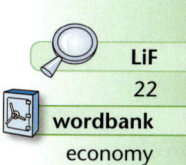

LiF 22

wordbank
economy

CD 2/28

Global player

Optional

○ Meet the Nano

Tata Nano is the name of a car made in India. It is small, cheap and it was meant to be "the people's" car that almost everyone can afford. The Nano has been designed and is manufactured by Tata Motor Limited, the largest automobile company in India. They saw a great opportunity for expanding their business. The price the company aimed at was around 1 lakh or 100,000 Indian rupees which is approximately 2000 US dollars.

How did they make the Nano so cheap? Basically, by making things smaller and lighter, and by doing away with all parts that are not essential. There is no air conditioning, radio or CD player, no air bags and just one windscreen wiper. As labour costs in India are low, this also keeps the price low.

When the company first said they were making this car, they received over 5,500 orders. Sales of other cheap cars dropped because people were so excited about this even cheaper car.

But then a few problems appeared. The company wanted to build a factory in the countryside to lower costs but some people did not want the factory to be built on their land. This delayed the release of the car. Now the Nano is also not as cheap as it was. The price has gone up by over half to more than $3000. This is because manufacturing costs have increased. People also have to wait more than a year after ordering their car before it is built. It is nevertheless a success story and still the cheapest car in the world. They even plan to sell the car in Europe. If you want to drive fast though, this is probably not the car for you as its maximum speed is only 105 kph!

"We are happy to present the people's car in India and we hope it brings the joy, pride and utility of owning a car to families who need personal mobility."
Ratan Tata 2008

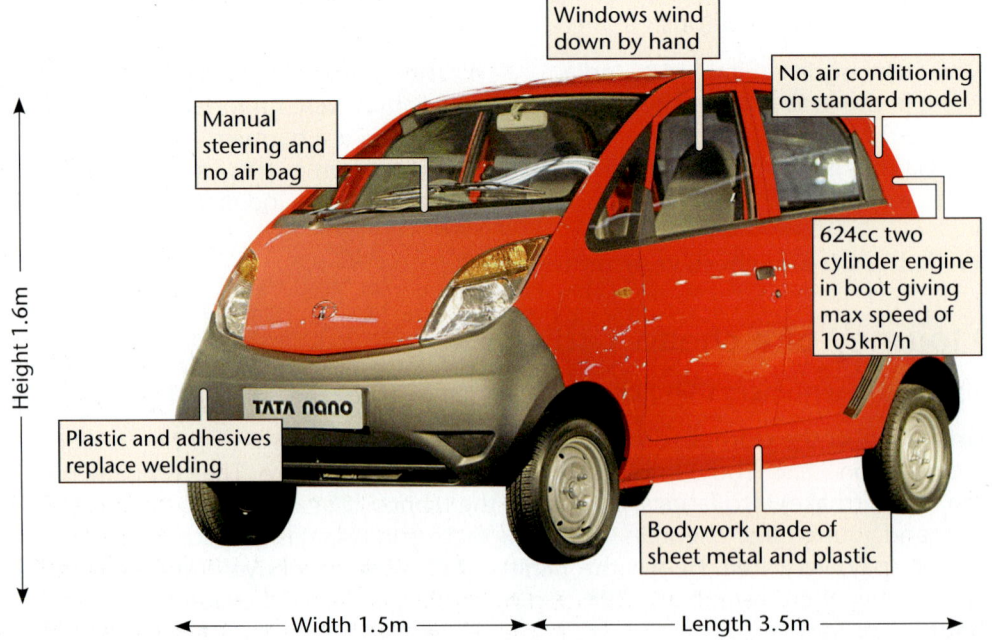

Do you think the Nano is a desirable car?

Project: Hopes and dreams 6

Project 1

People about the future

Project 2

Poems about the future

Project 3

Make a change

Project 4

How green is your future?

Project 5

Songs about the future

Hopes and dreams

- This Theme is all about the future. It includes bits and pieces about people's hopes and dreams for the future and there is room for your contribution.
- In this Theme there are various projects which aim to combine English with art. In each project we give you different ideas for producing an artistic display of some kind. These might be, for example, sculptures with English texts, banners with photos or installations combining light, sound and text.
- You might even be able to create public displays of land art in parts of your school or even outside your school, in the community.

As a starting point, have a look at the picture. What does it make you think of?

project

how to …
talk

Now think about the following questions:

1. What will you be doing after you leave school?
2. On which of your plans and wishes for the future do you and your family agree?
3. Are there any differences between your dreams and your plans?

wordbank
hopes and dreams

- Look through this Theme and its five projects. Decide which project you are most interested in working on for the next few weeks.
- Get together with people who would like to work on the same project. Discuss in your group who wants to deal with which task. Decide on one or more tasks or find your own.
- This is your chance to be especially creative, bringing together your work and ideas for your English and art lessons – a chance to do something special at the end of the school year!

workbook
p. 97

Hopes and dreams

Project 1 ○ People about the future

In an ideal world ...

This week we asked young people from Britain about their priorities, hopes and ambitions for the future. Here are four answers to this week's questions:

Graham (22)

The pressure to have a well-paid job and stuff like that used to make me feel unhappy. I only began feeling I had a purpose in life when I started to work with the charity *Young Minds*. We help young people who've had mental health problems. And since I've started helping other people, I've felt like I'm really part of something, it is so rewarding.

Alice (21)

I want to live in a world where it's possible for each human being to live a good life. A world with no environmental disasters, food shortages or scandals, no military invasions.

Felix (24)

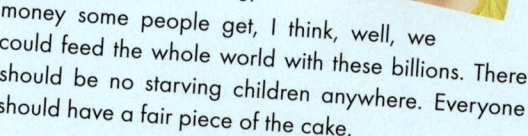

I'd like to see people from different social classes get a bit closer. If you make your money, you make your money, fair enough. But when I hear these astronomical sums of money some people get, I think, well, we could feed the whole world with these billions. There should be no starving children anywhere. Everyone should have a fair piece of the cake.

Farah (22)

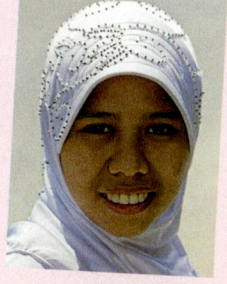

For me, most important would be having a stable family, a house, a good career. Home is important to me, and I need the security of a nice house to live in and pleasant green surroundings. It shouldn't be in the middle of nowhere, but I need peace and quiet – no busy roads or noisy aircraft.

○ Tasks to choose from

For this project you can focus on one or more of these tasks. In your group, decide who wants to work on which task. You could even create your own task. Remember that your aim is to contribute to some sort of art exhibition.

1. Read what Graham thinks. For him having a purpose in life is the most important thing. Imagine you wanted to start an organization that aims to help others. What sort of organization would it be and how would you get people to join you? Think of designing a home page, a poster, an advertising campaign, …
2. Read what Alice has to say. Make a text and picture collage that shows your idea of living in harmony or make a film.
3. Read what Felix thinks, then design buttons or T-shirt prints to make people stop, think and act! Think of a slogan as well.
4. Read what Farah thinks. Imagine a day in Farah's future life, write a screenplay and make a video.

workbook p. 98

how to … work on a project

portfolio I can read, write, combine skills

Hopes and dreams

Project 2 ○ Poems about the future

Features of the future

I'm closer to the future
Than I was yesterday.
The highway of the future
Is in each break of day.
I frame my future
By the decisions I make.
I encounter the future
If diligent steps I take.
Plans for the future
I made in the past.
Today I face the future
Yet it won't last.
Depending on the future
Is so inefficient.
Because the so-called future
Is vague and transient!
"you'll live well in the future
If the present is well lived!"

Robert Reuben

Dreams

Hold fast to dreams
For if dreams die
Life is a broken-winged bird
That cannot fly.
Hold fast to dreams
For when dreams go
Life is a barren field
Frozen with snow

Langston Hughes

Look to the future

Look to the future
Detach from the past
Let the people go
Start anew this time
Look to the future
Love like it'll last
Dream like it's forever
No more envy
Look to the future
Have the star life
Learn from others
Take it in
Look to the future
Be proud with yourself
No more lies
No more disguises
Look to the future
Solve the unresolved
Be someone's firefly
Stop living for yourself
Look to the future
Be the person
You dream to be
Stop fantasizing
Look to the future
It only gets brighter
From here on out
Detach from the past
Look to the future

Leah Harlow

The future

Is it true?
that the future is always bright
in the past
there was not much light

The future is ours to behold
but what I was told
in the future
you get old

The future will come
this is sure
yours and mine
one second at a time

Until the final curtain
our lives uncertain
what the future will bring
will be exciting

David Darbyshire

○ Tasks to choose from

For this project you can focus on one or more of these tasks. In your group, decide who wants to work on which task. You could even create your own task. But first of all try to capture the ideas of one of the poems in a piece of art using sound and images.

1. Choose one of the poems and rewrite it in a different graphical form, e.g. different line breaks, fonts, colours or layout. Be prepared to explain what you did and why.
2. Search the Internet for more poems about the future and present them in an interesting way.
3. Write your own poem about your future and think about an eye-catching illustration.
4. Choose one or more of the poems to recite and make a group audio recording. Find suitable background music.

CD
2/17 2/30
2/18 2/31
2/19 2/32
2/20 2/33

workbook p. 99

how to ... work on a project, read, write, talk about poems, present

wordbank hopes and dreams

portfolio I can read, write, combine skills, present

Hopes and dreams

Project 3 ○ Make a change

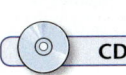
CD 2/24

Breakaway

Grew up in a small town,
And when the rain would fall down,
I'd just stare out my window,
Dreamin' of what could be,
And if I'd end up happy
I would pray.

Trying hard to reach out,
But when I tried to speak out,
Felt like no one could hear me.
Wanted to belong here,
But something felt so wrong here,
So I prayed I could break away.

Chorus:
I'll spread my wings, and I'll learn how to fly.
I'll do what it takes till I touch the sky, now
Make a wish, take a chance,
Make a change and breakaway
Out of the darkness and into the sun,
But I won't forget all the ones that I love.
I'll take a risk, take a chance,
Make a change and break away.

Wanna feel the warm breeze,
Sleep under a palm tree,
Feel the rush of the ocean.
Get on board a fast train,
Travel on a jet plane,
Far away and breakaway

Chorus

Buildings with a hundred floors,
Swinging 'round revolving doors,
Maybe I don't know where they'll take me,
but gotta keep movin' on movin' on,
Fly away, breakaway

I'll spread my wings and I'll learn how to fly
Though it's not easy to tell you goodbye
Take a risk, take a chance, make a change
And breakaway
Out of the darkness and into the sun
But I won't forget the place I come from
I gotta take a risk, take a chance, make a change
And breakaway.
Breakaway
Breakaway

Music and lyrics: Benenate / Gerrard / Lavigne

○ Tasks to choose from

For this project you can focus on one or more of these tasks. In your group, decide who wants to work on which task. You could even create your own task. Remember that your aim is to contribute to some sort of art exhibition.

1. "Take a risk. Make a wish. Take a chance. Make a change and breakaway." What does that mean to you? Express your ideas in writing or even a dance performance.
2. Draw or paint and describe the place where the singer feels wrong. Why does she not want to forget the place?
3. Make a collage that illustrates the images in the song and add your associations.

workbook
p. 100

how to …
listen, talk about lyrics

wordbank
hopes and dreams

portfolio
I can write, combine skills

Hopes and dreams

Project 4 o How green is your future?

Some people believe that for environmental reasons, there will have to be big changes to the way we live, work and travel in the future. Here is something that you can do already. One experiment in low-impact housing is taking place in south-west Wales: Lammas is a so-called "eco-village", where everything is planned specifically to reduce the impact on the environment. Here is a page from the Lammas website.

http://www.lammas.org.uk

Low Impact Living

Home | Eco Village 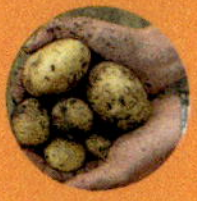 | Get Involved 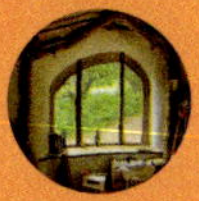 | Low Impact Living

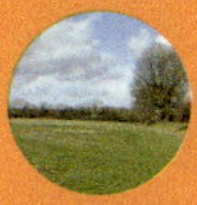

Pioneering low-impact developments

- carbon-neutral houses which blend into the landscape
- independent and self-sufficient

We are building an eco-village in Pembrokeshire, Wales. It combines the traditional small farmhouse model with the latest innovations in environmental design, green technology.

- a new settlement of nine eco-houses
- a campsite
- a community building
- meadows and woodland

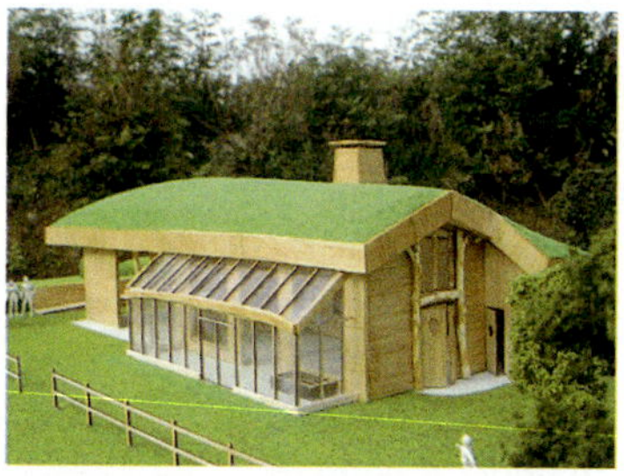

The houses: low-impact architecture

A combination of recycled and natural materials and styles is used:
- straw bale
- earth sheltered
- timber frame
- cob (clay, sand and straw)
- grass roofs

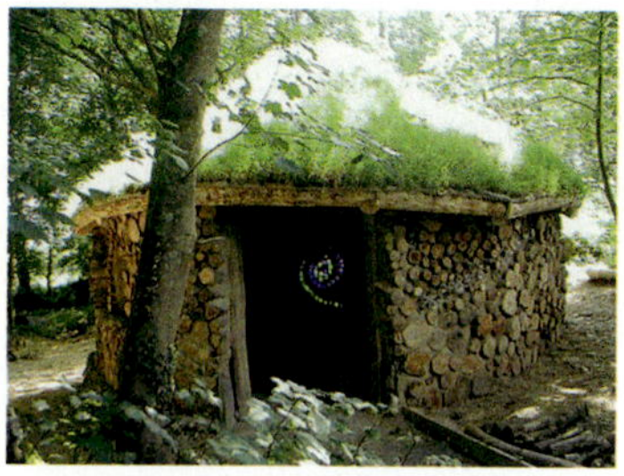

The houses include the latest environmental technologies and design techniques.

Services

- The eco-village will be completely independent of all mains services.
- The water supply is taken from a local spring and uses rainwater from rooftops.
- All electricity is produced on site using renewables.
- All organic waste is composted on site (compost toilets and compost heaps).
- We grow our own heating fuel (willow trees and elephant grass).

Hopes and dreams

Size matters! Measure your carbon footprint

So, what is a carbon footprint?

A carbon footprint is an estimate of how much carbon dioxide (CO_2) is released into the atmosphere as a result of a person's actions. The size of the footprint is affected by the CO_2 emissions we cause when we burn fossil fuels – for example, when we travel by car or by plane, or when we heat our homes with fossil fuels. Also, the products we use have an influence on our carbon footprint, as a result of the carbon dioxide emissions which resulted from their manufacture.

Size matters!

As lifestyles and the use of energy vary widely around the world, people in different countries have different sizes of carbon footprint. The average US footprint is over twice as big as the average in the UK, and the UK average is more than ten times bigger than the average in Africa.

Calculate your carbon footprint

Calculating your carbon footprint can be tricky, but there are many online carbon footprint calculators you can try.

○ Tasks to choose from

For this project you can focus on one or more of these tasks. In your group, decide who wants to work on which task. You could even create your own task. Remember that it is your aim to contribute to a class exhibition. Be prepared to explain to your visitors what you did and why.

New designs for living

1. Design your own eco-village and present your ideas with drawings or models. For ideas, watch the video "The Sustainable Village" on the DVD.
2. Design an eco-house and make a model or diagram of it.
3. Find other projects for future living on the Internet and exhibit them.

Carbon footprint

4. Design a campaign or make a short film to motivate people to reduce their carbon footprint.
5. Design a display to show the advantages and disadvantages of:
   - biofuels
   - energy-saving light bulbs. The film *Bulb Fiction* has interesting details about energy-saving light bulbs.
6. Watch the video "The Electricity of Tomorrow" and present the facts to the class.

workbook p. 101

how to …
work on a project, read, listen, present

DVD 14, 15

portfolio
I can read, listen, write, combine skills, present

film

103

Hopes and dreams

Project 5 ◯ Songs about the future

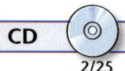

CD
2/25

One Tribe

One tribe, one time, one planet, one race
It's all one blood, don't care about your face
The color of your eye or the tone of your skin
Don't care where ya are
Don't care where ya been
Cause where we gonna go
Is where we wanna be
The place where the native language is unity
And the continent is called Pangaea
And the main ideas are connected like a sphere
No propaganda, they tried to upper hand us
Cause man I'm loving this peace
Man, man, I'm loving this peace
I don't need no leader
That's gonna force feed a
Concept to make me think I need to
Fear my brother and fear my sister
And shoot my neighbor with my big missile
If I had an enemy, then my enemy is gonna
   try to come and kill me
Cause I'm his enemy
There's one tribe ya'll

One tribe ya'll
We are one people
Let's cast amnesia, forget about all that evil
Forget about all that evil, that evil that they
   feed ya
Remember that we're one people
We are one people
One people, one people

One tribe, one time, one planet, one race,
One love, one people, one
Too many things that's causing one
To forget about the main cause
Connecting, uniting
But the evil is seeded and alive in us
So our weapons are colliding
And our peace is sinking like Poseidon

 But, we know that the one
The evil one is threatened by the sum
So he'll come and try and separate the sum
But he dumb, he didn't know we had a way
   to overcome
Rejuvenated by the beating of the drum

Come together by the cycle of the hum
Freedom when all become one
Forever

One tribe ya'll
We are one people
Let's cast amnesia
Forget about all that evil
That evil that they feed ya
Let's cast amnesia
Forget about all that evil
That evil that they feed ya
Remember that we're one people
We are one people, one people

One love, one blood, one people
One heart, one beat, we equal
Connected like the Internet
United that's how we do
Let's break walls, so we see through
Let love and peace lead you
We could overcome the complication cause
   we need to
Help each other, make these changes
Brother, sister, rearrange this
Way of thinking that we can change this
   bad condition
Wait, use your mind and not your greed
Let's connect and then proceed
This is something I believe
We are one, we're all just people

One tribe ya'll
We are one people
Let's cast amnesia
Forget about all that evil, that evil that
   they feed ya
Let's cast amnesia, forget about all that
   evil
That evil, that they feed ya
One tribe ya'll
One people, one people
Let's, let's cast amnesia
Lord help me out
Trying to figure out what it's all about
Cause we're one in the same
Same joy, same pain

Hopes and dreams

And I hope that you're there when I need ya
Cause maybe we need amnesia
And I don't wanna sound like a preacher
But we need to be one

One world, one love, one passion
One tribe, one understanding
Cause you and me can become one.

Music and lyrics: Ferguson / Adams / Gomez / Pineda / Board

(Adjusted text. You can find the full lyrics on the Internet.)

If I ruled the world

If I ruled the world,
every day would be the first day of spring.
Every heart would have a new song to sing,
and we'd sing of the joy every morning would
   bring.

If I ruled the world,
every man would be as free as a bird.
Every voice would be a voice to be heard,
take my word, we would treasure each day that
   occurred.

My world would be a beautiful place
where we would weave such wonderful dreams.
My world would wear a smile on its face,
like the man in the moon has, when the moon
   beams.

If I ruled the world,
every man would see the world was his
   friend. Yeah
There'd be happiness that no man could end,
no my friend, not if I ruled the world.

Every head would be held up high.
There'd be sunshine in everyone's sky.
If the day ever dawned,
when I rule the world.

Every head would be held up high.
Sunshine in everyone's sky.
If the day ever dawned …

Music and lyrics: Ornadel / Bricusse

CD 2/26

○ Tasks to choose from

For this project you can focus on one or more of these tasks. In your group, decide who wants to work on which task. You could even create your own task. Remember that it is your aim to contribute to a class exhibition. Be prepared to explain to your visitors what you did and why.

1. Choose one of the songs and make a video clip, a presentation with photos or make a stop-motion film.
2. Create your own version of one of the songs or write your own song about the future.
3. Find out about the continent Pangaea. Find a way to describe and depict it.
4. What does it take to rule the world? What if you ruled the world? Display your ideas.

workbook
p. 102

how to …
work on a project, talk about lyrics

portfolio
I can listen, write, work with words, combine skills

105

Grammar revision

G1 ○ You used to love me

a) A girl is complaining to her boyfriend, reminding him about all the things he used to do, but does not do any more. Make sentences with "used to".

1. You don't buy me flowers any more.
2. You hardly ever text me now.
3. You never look happy to see me.
4. You hardly ever take me to the cinema these days.
5. You don't pay me nice compliments any more.
6. You don't listen to me any more.

1. *You used to buy me flowers.*

b) Listen to the CD and check your sentences.

G2 ○ What you used to do

Make sentences about things you used to do, but don't do any more.

I used to take the bus to school, but now I usually walk or take my bike.

G3 ○ Using conjunctions

Complete the sentences with conjunctions.

1. ??? many people are now trying to reduce their carbon footprints, global warming is still a problem.
2. A community in Wales is building an eco-village ??? they want to reduce their impact on the environment.
3. ??? lifestyles are not the same around the world, people in different countries have different sizes of carbon footprint.
4. Calculating your carbon footprint is not easy, ??? there are lots of carbon footprint calculators online.
5. ??? you started walking or riding your bike to school instead of going by car, you would reduce your carbon footprint.
6. ??? we heat our homes with fossil fuels or travel by plane we are adding to our carbon footprint.

1. *Although many people are now trying to reduce their carbon footprints, global warming is still a problem.*

G4 ○ When I was at school

a) Rewrite the text below using the third type of conditional clauses.

When I was at school I didn't work very much. If I (work) harder, I (get) better exam results. If I (get) better exam results, I (go) to university. If I (go) to university, I (find) a better job. If I (find) a better job, I (make) more money. If I (make) more money, I (have) lots of holidays abroad in the sun. However, if (have) lots of holidays abroad, I (not go) to Scotland on holiday in the summer of 1956. If I (not go) to Scotland that year, I (not meet) my wife. So really it's a good thing I didn't work hard at school!

When I was at school I didn't work very much. If I had worked harder I would have got better exam results. ...

b) Listen to the CD and check your text.

Grammar revision

G5 ○ Which, who, that or nothing?

a) In some of these sentences you can leave out the relative pronoun. Rewrite the sentences where this is the case.

1. The thing which I am most worried about is finding a good job.
2. I want to live in a world which has no wars or food shortages.
3. The person who I think is right for me might not be the same person my parents would choose.
4. It would be amazing if I got the job that I applied for last week!
5. It's not fair that there are some people in the world who make lots of money, while others have nothing.
6. The house that I dream of has a big garden and is in a peaceful area.

1. *The thing I am most worried about is finding a good job.*

LiF 21

b) Listen to the CD and check your sentences.

CD 2/41

G6 ○ What shall I have done?

a) Complete each sentence with the correct form of the verb in brackets.

1. If I make enough money when I'm older, I will get my hair (do) every week.
2. I don't really understand what "carbon footprint" means. I need to have it (explain) to me again.
3. If I can't find my perfect house in the future, I will have a house (build) for me!
4. I love wearing interesting clothes. When I'm older and I can afford it, I will get my clothes (make) especially for me, so that I won't look like everyone else!

1. *If I make enough money when I'm older, I will get my hair done every week.*

LiF 22

b) Listen to the CD and check your sentences.

CD 2/42

G7 ○ I'd love to go to …

a) Rewrite the following sentences with the place names and an article if needed.

1. I walked along part of (Great Wall of China) last year.
2. I'd love to visit (Czech Republic) and (Poland), both members of (European Union).
3. To fly from (England) to (United States of America) you have to fly over (Atlantic).
4. I have always wanted to visit (Paris) and climb (Eiffel Tower).
5. I'd love to climb (Mount Everest) and (Mount Snowdon).
6. (Nile) is the longest river in the world.
7. I've always wanted to live near the coast of (North Sea).
8. When I was in (London) last year, I arrived at (Heathrow Airport), took the train to (Paddington Station) and went to see (Buckingham Palace) and (Thames).

LiF 23

1. *I walked along part of the Great Wall of China last year.*

b) Listen to the CD and check your sentences.

CD 2/43

Grammar revision

G8 Next year

Complete the following sentences with a form of the "will" future, the "going to" future or the future with the simple present.

1. I don't know if I (get married) when I am older or not.
2. I (apply) for that job in the supermarket tomorrow.
3. My interview (be) at 11 o'clock tomorrow.
4. Do you think you (go) to university?
5. My brother (find) a good job eventually, I'm sure.
6. Today I (study) for my English exam all day.
7. Our exam (start) at 9 o'clock on Tuesday morning.
8. Next week we (begin) our class project.

1. I don't know if I will get married when I am older or not.

G9 The future of the planet

Say what changes will have to be made in the future for ecological reasons. Make sentences using the will-future.

wordbank
hopes and dreams

live in low-energy homes · use public transport · walk to school or work more often · cars more fuel-efficient · solar water heating · use more renewable energy · use fewer fossil fuels · use more solar and wind power · live in energy-efficient houses · recycle more materials

1. More people will live in low-energy homes.

G10 I'm pretty sure …

Write sentences about what is going to happen. Use the "going to future".

portfolio
I can work with words

   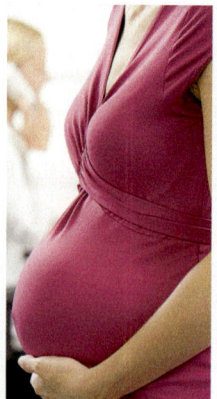 

It's going to rain.
He's …

Was ist wo im Anhang?

 Book stop — S. 110–127
Nimm dir Zeit zu lesen. Wenn du alle Texte, die dir gefallen, schon gelesen hast, dann schau doch mal in eurer Schülerbücherei oder Stadtbücherei nach englischsprachigen Büchern.

 How to … — S. 128–143
Hier kannst du nachschauen, wenn du wissen möchtest, wie du strukturierter lernen oder mit bestimmten Anforderungen aus dem Unterricht umgehen kannst.

 Wordbank — S. 144–152
Hier sind alle wichtigen Wörter und Ausdrücke aus den Kapiteln, nach Themen gesammelt.

 Classroom phrases — S. 153–154
Hier stehen die wichtigsten Redewendungen aus dem Englischunterricht.

 Glossary — S. 155–156
Im *Glossary* findest du wichtige grammatikalische Begriffe mit ihrer englischen Übersetzung und einem Beispiel.

 Language in Focus — S. 157–169
In *Language in Focus* (LiF) wird die englische Sprache genauer unter die Lupe genommen. Es gibt zwei Unterkapitel:
Say it in English
Hier findest du Sätze und Redewendungen, die im Theme vorgekommen sind. Du kannst sie benutzen, um dich besser auszudrücken.
Sprachliche Mittel
Hier kannst du nachschlagen, welche Grammatikregeln es in der englischen Sprache gibt. Du kannst nachschauen, wenn du eine neue Regel besser verstehen willst, und auch wenn du dir bei einer schon gelernten Regel nicht mehr ganz sicher bist.

 **Words – Die Wortlisten nach Kapiteln** — S. 173–197
In diesem Teil findest du alle Wörter und ihre Bedeutung in der Reihenfolge, in der sie im Text erscheinen. Auf den Seiten 171 und 172 findest du auch Hinweise zur richtigen Aussprache.

 ***Dictionary* – Die alphabetischen Wortlisten** — S. 198–241
English–German
Hier schaust du nach, wenn du nicht mehr weißt, was ein englisches Wort bedeutet.
German–English — S. 242–254
Hier kannst du nachschauen, wenn du einen englischen Text schreiben willst und dir nur ein deutsches Wort dafür einfällt. Wenn du das gesuchte Wort nicht findest, überlege, ob es ein ähnliches deutsches Wort gibt.

 Names — S. 255–257
Das ist die Liste der Namen und Ortsnamen mit ihrer Aussprache.

 Irregular verbs — S. 259–260
In dieser Liste findest du alle unregelmäßigen Verben, die in TB1 bis TB6 vorgekommen sind.

Book stop

BS1 Uglies

Fifteen-year-old Tally lives in a world where everyone has an operation when they turn sixteen. This operation makes them as beautiful as a supermodel. They are changed from an "Ugly" into a "Pretty". Tally cannot wait for her life to change. Not only will she be good-looking, but this will be the beginning of her new life – a life all about having fun. But then she meets Shay, who is also fifteen, but with very different opinions to Tally …

The following excerpt from Scott Westerfeld's science fiction novel begins with Tally and Shay returning from a trip to the dormitory of some of the younger "Uglies".

"Oh, that was perfect!"

"Did you see their faces?"

"Not actually," Shay said. "I was kind of busy watching the floor coming at me."

"Yeah, I remember that from jumping off the roof. It does catch your attention."

"Speaking of faces, love the nose."

Tally giggled, pulling it off. "Yeah, no point in being uglier than usual."

Shay's face clouded. She wiped off an eyebrow, then looked up sharply. "You're not ugly."

"Oh, come on, Shay."

"No, I mean it." She reached out and touched Tally's real nose.

"Your profile is great."

"Don't be weird, Shay. I'm an ugly, you're an ugly. We will be for two more weeks. It's no big deal or anything." She laughed.

"You, for example, have one giant eyebrow and one tiny one."

Shay looked away, stripping off the rest of her disguise in silence.

They were hidden in the changing rooms beside the sandy beach, where they'd left their interface rings and a spare set of clothes. If anyone asked, they'd say they were swimming the whole time. Swimming was a great trick. It hid your body-heat signature, involved changing clothes, and was a perfect excuse for not wearing your interface ring. The river washed away all crimes.

A minute later they splashed out into the water, sinking the disguises. The bungee jacket would go back to the art school basement that night.

"I'm serious, Tally," Shay said once they were out in the water.

"Your nose isn't ugly. I like your eyes, too."

"My eyes? Now you're totally crazy. They're way too close together."

"Who says?"

"Biology says."

Shay splashed a handful of water at her. "You don't believe all that crap, do you - that there's only one way to look, and everyone's programmed to agree on it?"

"It's not about believing, Shay. You just *know* it. You've seen pretties. They look … wonderful."

"They all look the same."

"I used to think that too. But when Peris and I would go into town, we'd see a lot of them, and we realized that pretties do look different. They look like themselves. It's just a lot more subtle, because they're not all freaks."

"We're not freaks, Tally. *We're* normal. We may not be gorgeous, but at least we're not hyped-up Barbie dolls."

"What kind of dolls?"

She looked away. "It's something David told me about."

"Oh, great David again." Tally pushed away and floated on her back, looking up at the sky and wishing this conversation would end. They'd been out to the ruins a few more times, and Shay always insisted on setting off a sparkler, but David had never showed. The whole thing gave Tally the creeps, waiting around in the dead city for some guy who didn't seem to exist. It was great exploring out there, but Shay's obsession with David had started to sour it for Tally.

"He's real. I've met him more than once."

"Okay, Shay, David's real. But so is being ugly. You can't change it just by wishing, or by telling yourself that you're pretty. That's why they invented the operation."

"But it's a trick, Tally. You've only seen pretty faces your whole life. Your parents, your teachers, everyone over sixteen. But you weren't *born* expecting that kind of beauty in everyone, all the time. You just got programmed into thinking anything else is ugly."

"It's not programming, it's just a natural reaction. And more important than that, it's fair. In the old days it was all random – some people *kind of* pretty, most people ugly all their lives. Now everyone's ugly ... until they're pretty. No losers."

Shay was silent for a while, then said, "There are losers, Tally."

Tally shivered. Everyone knew about uglies-for-life, the few people for whom the operation wouldn't work. You didn't see them around much. They were allowed in public, but most of them preferred to hide. Who wouldn't? Uglies might look goofy, but at least they were young. *Old* uglies were really unbelievable.

"Is that it? Are you worried about the operation not working? That's silly, Shay. You're no freak. In two weeks you'll be as pretty as anyone else."

"I don't want to be pretty."

Tally sighed. This again.

"I'm sick of this city," Shay continued. "I'm sick of the rules and boundaries. The last thing I want is to become some empty-headed new pretty, having one big party all day."

"Come on, Shay. They do all the same stuff we do: bungee jump, fly, play with fireworks. Only they don't have to sneak around."

"They don't have the imagination to sneak around."

"Look, Skinny, I'm with you," Tally said sharply. "Doing tricks is great! Okay? Breaking the rules is fun! But eventually you've got to do something besides being a clever little ugly."

"Like being a vapid, boring pretty?"

"No, like being an adult. Did you ever think that when you're pretty you might not *need* to play tricks and mess things up? Maybe just being ugly is why uglies always fight and pick on one another, because they aren't happy with who they are. Well, I want to be happy, and looking like a real person is the first step."

"I'm not afraid of looking the way I do, Tally."

"Maybe not, but you are afraid of growing up!"

Shay didn't say anything. Tally floated in silence, looking up at the sky, barely able to see the clouds through her anger. She wanted to be pretty, wanted to see Peris again. It seemed like forever since she'd talked to him, or to anyone else except Shay. She was sick of this whole ugly business, and just wanted it to end.

A minute later, she heard Shay swimming for shore.

Book stop

BS2 ○ Hunger in a world of plenty

A light came wobbling up the Banbury Road, Oxford, in the dead of night. It stopped near a garbage bin and an elderly figure dismounted from an equally elderly bicycle. It was a man, slim and upright, if a little tremulous, dressed in faded but impeccably pressed clothes, a clip on his right ankle to guard the indeterminate grey of the trouser leg against any chance encounter with bike grease.

First he looked up and down the road. Then, very carefully, he extricated a neatly folded plastic carrier bag from a pocket and set about methodically searching through the contents of the bin. From amongst the day's detritus he picked up some half-eaten items, inspected them for decay, then placed them in his carrier bag. In a few minutes he was through and set off in the direction of Summertown, wobbling to a stop from time to time.

All of North Oxford seemed to be asleep, every locked house silent, and I knew I had witnessed a routine which was meant to be invisible. I couldn't help but feel that had it happened in broad daylight in front of curious passers-by it would have been just as dignified.

In my mind this memory dovetails with a much older one from when I was a child living in my family home in Indore – a city in India's Deccan heartland which has grown pell-mell around industry's magnet.

One day a very old and skeletal man wearing only a loincloth came and sat down by the potted cactus at the end of our drive. Unlike other alms seekers he sat silently until my mother noticed him – there was no telling how long he had been there. He was immediately given some money which he took with the kind of abundant gratitude that puts the giver to shame.

He returned once a week, every week, more emaciated each time. He weighed heavy on our conscience – watching the bones straining through his skin with every movement he made was a lesson in anatomy and ethics rolled into one.

We became more watchful, looking out several times a day to see if he was there. He was persuaded to come round to the back of the house and sit in the shade. My mother took to giving him larger sums of money and food which he would take away to eat elsewhere. He was nearly blind and had to be told the value of the coins. We all feared that in reality it made little difference because he would probably be cheated anyway. We asked him to come around more often, but he had his own code of honour and would only visit once a week. Eventually he stopped and then we knew he was dead. To be honest it was a relief not to have to watch the skin hang from him or his slow, angular, careful walk.

In Indian folklore the gods often come down to earth to test human beings. We felt as though we had been through such a test but couldn't say whether we had passed it or not.

Increasingly sophisticated lifestyles often distort our relationship with food: we are even able to forget that its basic purpose – apart from the obvious pleasure it gives – is to keep us going. Another person's hunger is a reminder that there is something as simple as eating to live. Yet nowhere are

people guaranteed a right to food. If the presence of hunger is an affront to our notions of justice, then it is doubly unjust that those who have the least power – the elderly, women and their dependent children, refugees, the disabled – are the most likely to go hungry.

The shame of hunger is a double shame – it burns the hungry with the brand of humiliation, despair and dependency and it burns us with guilt and a feeling of powerlessness at being unable to help. For the hungry it can mean being reduced to surrender the dignity that attends being able to provide for oneself. Sometimes this can be perceived oddly – as though the hungry had no dignity to lose, as though they had no emotions to expend, as though they were ciphers filled only by need, as though they were Martians.

The wealthy often go into denial – putting up walls around their homes, sending their kids to special schools, policing their malls, making sure that the poor are 'elsewhere'. This distance is essential to making Martians of the poor – they are completely alien, they have no connection to us, they are illegal immigrants to our neighbourhood or our nation, they are a problem. An aunt of mine once suggested that poor people should be taken out at the dead of night and shot – such 'cleaning-up' happens for real in some parts of the world.

Today it is estimated there are nearly 800 million people who don't have enough to eat – 12 million die of hunger every year. Two billion have vitamin and mineral deficiencies in their diets which can cause serious health problems.

Book stop

BS3 ○ The Absolutely True Diary of a Part-Time Indian

The Absolutely True Diary of a Part-Time Indian by Sherman Alexie is a novel about the young Indian Junior who lives on the Spokane Indian Reservation. Junior wants to escape the hopelessness of the reservation, which he calls „the rez", and decides to change from his local school to Reardan High School where all the students are white.

How to fight monsters

The next morning, Dad drove me the twenty-two miles to Reardan.
"I'm scared," I said.
"I'm scared, too," Dad said. He hugged me close. His breath smelled like mouthwash and lime vodka.
"You don't have to do this," he said. "You can always go back to the rez school." "No," I said. "I have to do this." Can you imagine what would have happened to me if I'd turned around and gone back to the rez school? I would have been pummeled. Mutilated. Crucified. You can't just betray your tribe and then change your mind ten minutes later. I was on a one-way bridge. There was no way to turn around, even if I wanted to.
"Just remember this," my father said. "Those white people aren't better than you."
But he was so wrong. And he knew he was wrong. He was the loser Indian father of a loser Indian son living in a world built for winners.
But he loved me so much. He hugged me even closer. "This is a great thing," he said. "You're so brave. You're a warrior."
It was the best thing he could have said. "Hey, here's some lunch money," he said and handed me a dollar.
We were poor enough to get free lunch, but I didn't want to be the only Indian *and* a sad sack who needed charity. "Thanks, Dad," I said.
"I love you," he said.
"I love you, too." I felt stronger so I stepped out of the car and walked to the front door. It was locked. So I stood alone on the sidewalk and watched my father drive away. I hoped he'd drive right home and not stop in a bar and spend whatever money he had left. I hoped he'd remember to come back and pick me up after school.
I stood alone at the front door for a few very long minutes. It was still early and I had a black eye from Rowdy's good-bye punch. No, I had a purple, blue, yellow, and black eye. It looked like modern art.
Then the white kids began arriving for school. They surrounded me. Those kids weren't just white. They were *translucent*. I could see the blue veins running through their skin like rivers.
Most of the kids were my size or smaller, but there were ten or twelve monster dudes. Giant white guys. They looked like men, not boys. They had to be seniors. Some of them looked like they had to shave two or three times a day. They stared at me, the Indian boy with the black eye and swollen nose, my going-away gifts from Rowdy. Those white kids couldn't believe their eyes. They stared at me like I was Bigfoot or UFO. What was I doing at Reardan, whose mascot was an Indian, thereby making me the only *other* Indian in town?
So, what was I doing in racist Reardan, where more than half of every graduating class went to college? Nobody in my family had ever gone near a college.
Reardan was the opposite of the rez. It was the opposite of my family. It was the opposite of me. I didn't deserve to be there. I knew it; all of those kids knew it. Indians don't deserve shit.
So, feeling worthless and stupid, I just waited. And pretty soon, a janitor opened the front door and all of the other lads strolled inside.

I stayed outside. Maybe I could just drop out of school completely. I could go live in the woods like a hermit. Like a real Indian. Of course, since I was allergic to pretty much every plant that grew on earth, I would have been a real Indian with a head full of snot.

"Okay," I said to myself. "Here I go."

I walked into the school, made my way to the front office, and told them who I was. "Oh, you're the one from the reservation," the secretary said.

"Yeah," I said. I couldn't tell if she thought the reservation was a good or bad thing. "My name is Melinda," she said. "Welcome to Reardan High School. Here's your schedule, a copy of the school constitution and moral code, and a temporary student ID. We've got you assigned to Mr. Grant for homeroom. You better hustle on down there. You're late."

"Ah, where is that?" I asked.

"We've only got one hallway here," she said and smiled. She had red hair and green eyes and was kind of sexy for an old woman. "It's all the way down on the left."

I shoved the paperwork into my backpack and hustled down to my homeroom. I paused a second at the door and then walked inside. Everybody, all of the students and the teacher, stopped to stare at me. They stared hard. Like I was bad weather.

"Take your seat," the teacher said. He was a muscular guy. He had to be a football coach. I walked down the aisle and sat in the back row and tried to ignore all the stares and whispers, until a blond girl leaned over toward me. Penelope! Yes, there are places left in the world where people are named Penelope! I was emotionally erect.

"What's your name?" Penelope asked.

"Junior," I said. She laughed and told her girlfriend at the next desk that my name was Junior. They both laughed. Word spread around the room and pretty soon everybody was laughing.

They were laughing at *my name*. I had no idea that Junior was a weird name. It's a common name on my rez, on any rez. You walk into any trading post on any rez in the United States and shout, "Hey, Junior!" and seventeen guys will turn around. And three women.

But there were no other people named Junior in Reardan, so I was being laughed at because I was the only one who had that silly name.

And then I felt smaller because the teacher was talking roll and he called out my *name* name.

"Arnold Spirit," the teacher said. No, he yelled it. He was so big and muscular that his whisper was probably a scream.

"Here," I said as quietly as possible. My whisper was only a whisper.

"Speak up," the teacher said. "Here," I said.

"My name is Mr. Grant," he said.

"I'm here, Mr. Grant." He moved on to other students, but Penelope leaned over toward me again, but she wasn't laughing at all. She was mad now.

"I thought you said your name was Junior," Penelope said. She *accused* me of telling her my *real* name. Well, okay, it wasn't completely my real name. My full name is Arnold Spirit Jr. But

B Book stop

nobody calls me that. Everybody calls me Junior. Well, every other *Indian* calls me Junior.

"My name is Junior," I said. "And my name is Arnold. It's Junior and Arnold. I'm both." I felt like two different people inside of one body.

No, I felt like a magician slicing myself in half, with Junior living on the north side of the Spokane River and Arnold living on the south.

"Where are you from?" she asked. She was so pretty and her eyes were so blue. I was suddenly aware that she was the prettiest girl I had ever seen up close. She was movie star pretty.

"Hey," she said. "I asked you where you're from."

Wow, she was tough.

"Wellpinit," I said. "Up on the rez, I mean, the reservation."

"Oh," she said. "That's why you talk so funny."

And yes, I had that stutter and lisp, but I also had that singsong reservation accent that made everything I said sound like a bad poem.

Man, I was freaked.

I didn't say another word for six days. And on the seventh day, I got into the weirdest fistfight of my life. But before I tell you about the weirdest fistfight of my life, I have to tell you:

THE UNOFFICIAL AND UNWRITTEN (but you better follow them or you're going to get beaten twice as hard) SPOKANE INDIAN RULES OF FISTICUFFS :

1. If somebody insults you, then you have to fight him.
2. If you think somebody is going to insult you, then you have to fight him.
3. If you think somebody is thinking about insulting you, then you have to fight him.
4. If somebody insults any of your family or friends, or if you think they're going to insult your family or friends, or if you think they're thinking about insulting your family or friends, then you have to fight him.
5. You should never fight a girl, unless she insults you, your family, or your friends, then you have to fight her.
6. If somebody beats up your father or your mother, then you have to fight the son and/or daughter of the person who beat up your mother or father.
7. If your mother or father beats up somebody, then that person's son and/or daughter will fight you.
8. You must always pick fights with the sons and/or daughters of any indians who work for the bureau of indian affairs.
9. You must always pick fights with the sons and/or daughters of any white people who live anywhere on the reservation.
10. If you get in a fight with somebody who is sure to beat you up, then you must throw the first punch, because it's the only punch you'll ever get to throw.
11. In any fight, the loser is the first one who cries.

I knew those rules. I'd memorized those rules. I'd lived my life by those rules. I got into my first fistfight when I was three years old, and I'd been in dozens since. My all-time record was five wins and one hundred and twelve losses. Yes, I was a terrible fighter. I was a human punching bag. I lost fights to boys, girls, and lads half my age. One bully, Micah, made me beat up myself. Yes, he made me punch myself in the face three times. I am the only Indian in the history of the world who ever lost a fight with *himself*.

Okay, so now that you know about the rules, then I can tell you that I went from being a small target in Wellpinit to being a larger target in Reardan.

Well, let's get something straight. All of those pretty, pretty, pretty, pretty white girls ignored me. But that was okay. Indian girls ignored me, too, so I was used to it.

And let's face it, most of the white boys ignored me, too. But there were a few of those Reardan boys, the big jocks, who paid special attention to me. None of those guys punched me or got violent. After all, I was a reservation Indian, and no matter how geeky and weak I appeared to be, I was still a potential killer. So mostly they called me names. Lots of names. And yeah, those were bad enough names. But I could handle them, especially when some huge monster boy was insulting me. But I knew I'd have to put a stop to it eventually or I'd always be known as "Chief" or "Tonto" or "Squaw Boy."

But I was scared. I wasn't scared of fistfighting with those boys. I'd been in plenty of fights. And I wasn't scared of losing fights with them, either. I'd lost most every fight I'd been in. I was afraid those monsters were going to kill me.

And I don't mean "kill" as in "metaphor." I mean "kill" as in "beat me to death."

So, weak and poor and scared, I let them call me names while I tried to figure out what to do. And it might have continued that way if Roger the Giant hadn't taken it too far.

It was lunchtime and I was standing outside by the weird sculpture that was supposed to be an Indian. I was studying the sky like I was an astronomer, except it was daytime and I didn't have a telescope, so I was just an idiot. Roger the Giant and his gang of giants strutted over to me.

"Hey, Chief," Roger said. It seemed like he was seven feet tall and three hundred pounds. He was a farm boy who carried squealing pigs around like they were already thin slices of bacon.

I stared at Roger and tried to look tough. I read once that you can scare away a charging bear if you wave your arms and look big. But I figured I'd just look like a terrified idiot having an arm seizure.

"Hey, Chief," Roger said. "You want to hear a joke?"

"Sure," I said.

"Did you know that Indians are living proof that niggers fuck buffalo?"

I felt like Roger had kicked me in the face. That was the most racist thing I'd ever heard in my life. Roger and his friends were laughing like crazy. I hated them. And I knew I had to do something big. I couldn't let them get away with that shit. I wasn't just defending myself. I was defending Indians, black people, and buffalo.

So I punched Roger in the face. He wasn't laughing when he landed on his ass. And he wasn't laughing when his nose bled like red fireworks. I struck some fake karate pose because I figured Roger's gang was going to attack me for bloodying their leader. But they just stared at me. They were *shocked*.

"You punched me," Roger said. His voice was thick with blood. "I can't believe you punched me."

He sounded insulted. He sounded like his *poor little feelings* had been hurt. I couldn't believe it. He acted like he was the one who'd been wronged.

"You're an animal," he said.

I felt brave all of a sudden. Yeah, maybe it was just a stupid and immature school yard fight. Or maybe it was the most important moment of my life. Maybe I was telling the world that I was no longer a human target.

"You meet me after school right here," I said.

"Why?" he asked. I couldn't believe he was so stupid.

"Because we're going to finish this fight."

"You're crazy," Roger said. He got to his feet and walked away. His gang stared at me like I was a serial killer, and then they followed their leader. I was absolutely confused. I had followed the rules of fighting. I had behaved exactly the way I was supposed to behave. But these white boys had ignored the rules. In fact, they followed a whole other set of mysterious rules where people apparently DID NOT GET INTO FISTFIGHTS.

"Wait," I called after Roger.

"What do you want?" Roger asked.

"What are the rules ?"

"What rules?"

I didn't know what to say, so I just stood there red and mute like a stop sign. Roger and his friends disappeared. I felt like somebody had shoved me into a rocket ship and blasted me to a new planet. I was a freaky alien and there was absolutely no way to get home.

Book stop

BS4 ○ Squanto

Book stop

BS5 ○ Dead Man Walking

The following text was taken from *Dead Man Walking*, written by Sister Helen Prejean, a nun who counselled prisoners on death row. It is the story of her work with Pat Sonnier, who brutally killed two teenagers, David Le Blanc and Loretta Bourque in 1977, and was executed on the electric chair in 1984. In these passages, Sister Helen describes Sonnier's last hours before his execution.

I look at my watch and Pat looks at his. It is 10:30. Everything is ready now. All Pat needs to do now is die. He asks the guard for a pen and writes in his Bible, up in the front, where there is a special place for family history – births, marriages, deaths.

"There," he says, "I wrote it in my own hand."

The guard unlocks the door and hands me the Bible. I look at the front page. He has written loving words to me, words of thanks. Then I see under "Deaths" his name and the date, April 4, 1984.

I remember Jesus' words that we do not know the day nor the hour. But Pat knows. And in knowing he dies and dies again.

Two guards inside the tier stand on stepladders and hang black curtains over the windows along the top.

"They don't want other inmates to see the lights dim when the switch is pulled," Pat tells me. He is smoking and talking now, his talk a torrent, a flood, all coming together now, snatches from childhood and teasing Eddie and school with the sugar-cane fields gleaming in the sun and Star, what will happen to her, and his Mama, to please see about his Mama, and Eddie, will he be able to keep his cool in this place, and if only he knew when the current first hit that he would die right away ...

He begins to shiver. "It's cold in here," he says, and the guard gets a blue denim shirt from the cell and puts it around his shoulders, then goes back into his position at the end of the tier.

People are chatting nervously in the front and lobby now. The witnesses must all be inside by now, the press, all prison officials. You can hear the hum of talk and some snatches of conversation. You can hear when someone inserts coins into one of the drink machines and the clunk of the can when it comes out. [...]

People are still milling around in the large room. The witnesses have not been seated yet. Mr. LeBlanc and Mr. Bourque must be here. What are they going through? Will this help heal their loss? I wonder. I hear the toilet flush in Pat's cell.

Rabelais summons us back to the door. Pat comes from his cell, his legs and hands cuffed. Anger flickers in his eyes. "A grown man, and I have to leave this world with a diaper on," he says.

"I'll be free of all this," he says, shaking his handcuffs. "No more cells, no more bars, no more life in a cage," he says.

He reaches in his pocket for a cigarette. He turns and shows the guard, "Look, the last one. It'll see me out."

Warden Maggio approaches us. He is flanked by six or seven large guards. It must be midnight. "Time to go, Sonnier," Maggio

Book stop

says. […] I stand to the side of the door. I will walk with Pat. I am holding his Bible. I have selected an Isaiah passage to read as we walk, the words that were in the song, words that Pat has heard and the words will be there for him to hear again, if he can hear words at all, when he will be trying to put one foot in front of another, walking from here to there across these polished tiles. "Warden," he asks, "can I ask one favour? Can Sister Helen touch my arm?"
The Warden nods his head.
I am standing behind him. Guards, a mountain of blue, surround us. I put my hand on his shoulder. He is tall. I can barely reach. It is the first time I have ever touched him. We walk. Pat walks and the chains scrape across the floor. God has heard his prayer. His legs are holding up, he is walking.

Book stop

BS6 ◯ Star Rubbish

This is an excerpt from Joanna Trollope's short story "Star rubbish". It tells the story of a girl who is struggling with the new family situation that she finds herself in.

The therapist they sent me to when my mother left us wanted me to acknowledge that I was grieving, so that I could reconcile myself to the end of one stage of my relationship with my mother, and start more fruitfully (for us both) on the next. I didn't want to be fruitful. I sat in the therapist's cream-painted room with the flower prints on the walls and the kind of half-comfortable chairs that try and suggest a bit of home and a bit of hospital and glared at him. He wanted me to try and empathise with my mother, to try and imagine – 'You are fourteen, after all,' he said. 'You have feelings, emotional feelings' – how strongly she must have felt to leave her family for a man the other side of the world, in Australia.

My brother Nat had said bitterly, flicking Coco Pops at the wall with his knife, 'She said she'd die if she couldn't be with him.'

'And if she had to?'

'She'd feel,' said my father from behind the newspaper, 'like we do now.'

'Like bloody rubbish.'

'Don't say bloody –'

'Like bloody, bloody rubbish,' Nat said, and threw his knife after the Coco Pops.

'I don't want to imagine that,' I said to the therapist.

'You don't want to feel better?' said the therapist in his calm, knowing voice. 'You don't want to try to understand in case it makes you feel better?'

'Right,' I said.

He looked out of the window. He'd asked to see a picture of my mother, and since he'd seen it, he'd started wanting me to be generous, to do the giving. It was the effect my mother had on most people. It was the effect, presumably, that she'd had on the man in Australia.

After four sessions, I told my father I wasn't going to see the therapist any more. He sighed. He sighed a lot back then, as if he'd always expected life to be disappointing, and oh boy, it hadn't let him down. He said, 'Isn't it helpful to talk to someone?'

'No,' I said. 'It's unhelpful.'

'Would you like to talk to me?'

'No, thanks,' I said.

'Could – could you explain why?'

I looked at him. I looked at someone who had been around all my life but to whom I couldn't honestly feel much sense of belonging.

I said, 'I don't know you very well,' and then I looked at him again, and I said, 'Sorry,' and then I said, 'I don't know myself very well, either,' because of the expression on his face.

He did his best, I know he did. He took the fourth chair away from the kitchen table, and tried to make a life designed exclusively for three people, three people who had chosen this life deliberately, and not by default. He didn't try and take my mother's place, he just tried to squeeze shut the gap she'd left. I don't blame him. In his place, I'd probably have tried to do the same, and it would have taken so much effort and energy that I wouldn't have noticed, either, that my son and my daughter, in all respects but the physical, were living on the moon.

[…]

Then something happened. When it first happened, neither Nat nor I took much notice because it all looked so unlikely, weird even. I suppose, even if we had never allowed the thought anywhere near our lips, we had vaguely sort of considered the notion that our father would find someone else. No. Let me pull myself together. Even people of sixteen and seventeen, sunk in self-absorption, are not going to expect a man of forty-two to live without a woman for ever. Not even us.

But this woman? This noisy, not young, redhaired woman in jeans, and big awful jumpers with pictures on the front, banging round our kitchen and making prawn jambalaya? This – well, this fat woman? Who didn't seem afraid of us or made awkward by us and whom our father watched with the expression of a little kid opening something on Christmas morning and finding he'd got exactly what he'd been hoping for?

We were stunned. We were too stunned, I think, even to know what our reaction was to her, to him, to them. She was called Shirley. Sometimes, she skewered her hair up on top of her head with what looked suspiciously like swizzle sticks nicked from the pub, and sometimes she tied it back with a bit of purple tinsel. As with everything, she didn't seem to notice what she did, she didn't seem to care, and nor, did it seem to me, did she care whether we liked her or not. 'I'm not here to mother you,' she said to me. 'You've got a perfectly good mother of your own to do that.'

I was bent over looking into the fridge hoping, as you do, to see something that would catch my stomach's eye. I muttered into the fridge, 'Except she isn't perfectly good.'

'You wait till you're a mother,' Shirley said from across the kitchen. 'You wait to see what a picnic it is.'

I straightened up, holding a cold sausage. There were never any cold sausages, before Shirley…

'You're not a mother,' I said rudely.

'I'm a teacher,' she said. 'Next best thing. It gives you a view of mothering.'

I took my sausage upstairs. I was beginning to revisit some of the feelings I'd had when the therapist had encouraged me to be generous, had wanted me to see that joining the rest of the human race in terms of emotional intelligence might benefit me in the long run. I bent to look at myself in my bedroom mirror, chewing my sausage. 'Hello, stranger,' I said to myself with my mouth full. 'Don't let them near you.'

[…]

Shirley moved in. She painted her and my father's bedroom yellow and shunted the kitchen around so that the table was somehow in the middle and not crammed in a corner with its wall end stacked with sliding piles of newspapers. Then she said those were all the changes she proposed making. But of course they weren't. There were changes everywhere, in every aspect. I don't mean stuff like her passion-fruit shampoo in the shower, but timetables and food and atmosphere and requirements to live with a communal conscience instead of in three sealed units. Naturally, I looked to my father and my brother to resist all these unspoken but irresistible changes, but I looked in vain. It was plain from the very beginning that my father and brother, thankfully surrendering any domestic initiative, actually liked it.

Book stop

BS7 The end of a friendship?

Book stop

Book stop

BS8 ○ BollyWhat? – The Bollywood FAQs

Bollywood is an often used nickname for the most popular cinema on the planet: the Hindi-language film industry based in Bombay (also known as Mumbai), India. Hundreds of millions of people worldwide recognize Bollywood as their first choice in entertainment. If you, too, are in the mood for high drama then there's no other cinema for you.

However, Bollywood films can pose a considerable challenge if you are not familiar with Indian culture, because gestures and manners might be considerably different from what you're used to. But don't worry, we'll explain.

Why don't the characters ever kiss? Sometimes the characters do. But it's rare. The censor board is notoriously unpredictable; no one wants to risk getting a rating that would scare away families. Also, Bollywood films are made for a diverse range of people, from the illiterate and provincial to the worldly and urban. Ideas of morality differ widely from group to group. Why include a kiss when you can easily leave it out and avoid the risk of offending customers?

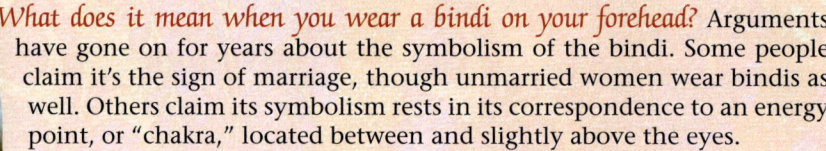

What does it mean when you wear a bindi on your forehead? Arguments have gone on for years about the symbolism of the bindi. Some people claim it's the sign of marriage, though unmarried women wear bindis as well. Others claim its symbolism rests in its correspondence to an energy point, or "chakra," located between and slightly above the eyes.

What does it mean when you touch someone's feet? Touching someone's feet is a sign of respect usually accorded to elders. Why is this considered respectful, you ask? Well, Hindu theology, and Indian culture in general, holds the feet to be the most polluted part of the body. This is why you take off your shoes upon entering a temple, and also why you should never point the soles of your feet at someone. Therefore making a point to touch someone's feet is a sign of your immense respect for them: you honour them so greatly that touching even their feet is a privilege.

What does it mean when you press your palms together? You'll see in the films that, upon first meeting someone, a character will press his or her palms together and say "Namaste." You can equate this to a handshake if you'd like, but pressing your palms together suggests a respect the handshake no longer does.

What does it mean when a woman wears red colour in the parting of her hair? Wearing a red colour in your hair has one clear meaning – a woman is married, and her husband is alive. Legend has it that this ceremony began due to a bride being kidnapped at the wedding ceremony. The groom would fight for his bride, and if he killed the kidnapper, he would smear his bride's parting with the fallen man's blood. Hindi film-makers love this: watch a few action movies and you're sure to see the hero smearing the villain's blood into his beloved's hair.

What does it mean when you put kohl on someone's cheek? When someone looks especially beautiful, it's assumed that she'll attract a great deal of jealousy. Putting a dot of black on her face as a makeshift "blemish" serves to ward off the evil eye that might otherwise be attracted by her perfection. This is most often done to babies, but women occasionally place a black smudge on their faces when they're especially well dressed.

Book stop

BS9 Suniti Namjoshi, *Bird woman*

Once there was a child who sprouted wings. They sprang from her shoulder blades, and at first they were vestigial. But they grew rapidly, and in no time at all she had a sizeable wing span. The neighbours were horrified. "You must have them cut," they said to her parents. "Why?" said her parents. "Well, it's obvious," said the neighbours. "No," said the parents, and this seemed so final that the neighbours left. But a few weeks later the neighbours were back. "If you won't have them cut, at least have them clipped." "Why?" said the parents. "Well, at least it shows that you're doing something." "No," said the parents, and the neighbours left. Then for the third time the neighbours appeared. "On at least two occasions you have sent us away," they informed the parents, "but think of that child. What are you doing to the poor little thing?" "We are teaching her to fly," said the parents quietly.

How to talk / How to listen

Remember? ● How to talk

- Wenn du einen Vortrag, ein Interview oder ein Gespräch zu einem bestimmten Thema vorbereiten willst, kann es dir helfen, wenn du dir vorher auf Kärtchen Notizen dazu machst.
- Versuche aber immer, frei zu sprechen und nicht einfach deine Notizen abzulesen.
- Achte dabei auch auf deine Aussprache, Betonung und die Satzmelodie, damit das, was du sagst, lebendig und nicht eintönig klingt.
- Das Sprechen wird dir leichter fallen, wenn du ein Gespräch oder einen Vortrag gut vorbereitest und übst.
- Achte beim Sprechen auch auf deine Körpersprache, deinen Gesichtsausdruck und deine Gesten.
- Schau deine Zuhörer beim Sprechen an.
- Hab keine Angst vor Fehlern!
- Nutze jede Gelegenheit, Englisch zu sprechen, dann wirst du mit der Zeit immer sicherer.

Remember? ● How to listen

- Wenn du einem Gesprächspartner zuhörst, schau ihn dabei an. Es hilft nämlich, beim Zuhören auch die Lippenbewegungen zu sehen, wenn der andere spricht. Achte im Gespräch auf Körpersprache, Gesichtsausdruck und Gesten. Dies hilft dir zu verstehen, was der andere sagen will.
- Wenn du dir einen Hörtext, z. B. von CD, anhörst, musst du dich beim ersten Hören noch nicht auf alle Details konzentrieren. Hör erst einmal, worum es im Großen und Ganzen geht. Wichtig ist dabei auch, um welche Sorte Hörtext es sich handelt: Ist es z. B. ein Radiobericht, eine Geschichte, ein Telefongespräch oder ein Interview? Dies hat einen Einfluss darauf, wie die Sprecher sprechen und was für Hintergrundgeräusche zu hören sein können. Besonders bei einem Interview oder einem Gespräch verraten die Stimmen der Sprechenden oft viel darüber, wie sie sich fühlen (z. B. aufgeregt, fröhlich, traurig, …).
- Willst du bei einem zweiten Hören genauer verstehen, worum es in dem Hörtext geht, dann können dir folgende Fragewörter helfen, die wichtigsten Informationen herauszuhören:
  – **Who?** Wer ist beteiligt? Um wen geht es?
  – **What?** Worum geht es? Was passiert?
  – **Where?** Wo spielt sich das Gehörte oder die Geschichte ab?
  – **When?** Wann passiert etwas?
  – **Why?** Warum passiert etwas?
- Wenn es zu dem Hörtext eine Aufgabe gibt, dann lies diese vorher genau durch und konzentriere dich beim Hören auf die Aufgabe. Mache dir Notizen, allerdings nur in Stichworten, z. B. in einer Tabelle.
- Übe das Hörverstehen so oft du kannst, achte z. B. einmal auf englische Songtexte oder höre dir englischsprachige Podcasts an.

How to read

Remember? ● How to read

Verschaffe dir vor dem Lesen zunächst einen Eindruck, worum es überhaupt geht: Was verrät die Überschrift? Was sagen Zwischenüberschriften aus? Gibt es Hinweise durch Abbildungen? Jetzt kommt es darauf an, mit welcher Absicht du den Text lesen willst.

Reading for fun
Du möchtest zu deinem eigenen Vergnügen lesen, zum Beispiel eine längere Geschichte oder einen Roman. Du liest wie bei einem deutschen Buch drauflos und versuchst, dir unbekannte Wörter zu erschließen. Wenn du den Zusammenhang nicht mehr richtig verstehst, brauchst du Hilfe durch ein Wörterbuch. Aber schlage nicht *jedes* unbekannte Wort nach, damit dir nicht der Spaß am Lesen vergeht.

Scanning
Du suchst in einem Text gezielt nach bestimmten Informationen, zum Beispiel möchtest du etwas über eine bestimmte Person (etwa ihr Alter) oder eine Begebenheit (wann etwas stattgefunden hat) herausfinden. Du überlegst dir Schlüsselwörter *(keywords)*, mit deren Hilfe du nach den Informationen suchst. Beim Scanning kommt es darauf an, dass du schnell liest. Du musst nicht jedes einzelne Wort verstehen.

Skimming
Auch beim Skimming kommt es darauf an, den Text schnell zu lesen. Hier sammelst du erste Eindrücke, zum Beispiel worum es überhaupt geht oder was für Personen vorkommen. Auch beim Skimming musst du nicht jedes einzelne Wort verstehen.

Reading for detail
Wenn du detailliert lesen musst, um zum Beispiel eine Zusammenfassung *(summary)* eines Textes zu schreiben, musst du den gesamten Text schon recht gut verstehen. Das kannst du mit den Fragestellungen *who, where, when, what, why* erreichen. Dabei hilft dir auch das Wörterbuch (siehe „How to work with a dictionary", S. 134). Wie du eine Zusammenfassung schreibst, kannst du in „How to write a summary" (S. 135) nachlesen.

In *Notting Hill Gate* gibt es sehr vielseitige und unterschiedliche Texte, zum Beispiel E-Mails, Berichte, Erzähltexte, Gedichte, Dialoge oder Informationstexte.
- Den Bericht „Fitness Drive" in Theme 1, A8 musst du genau lesen, um herauszufinden, was mit George passiert ist und warum *(reading for detail)*.
- In Theme 2 sollst du dir anhand von kurzen Informationstexten ein Projektthema aussuchen, das dich interessiert. Dafür überfliegst du die Texte *(skimming)* und suchst dir heraus, was dich am meisten anspricht.
- Den Briefauszug in Theme 3, B4 musst du genau lesen *(reading for detail)* um die Fragen dazu beantworten zu können.
- Die *Book-stop*-Seiten kannst du zum reinen Vergnügen lesen und dich dabei daran gewöhnen, Originaltexte zu verstehen, ohne dass du anschließend geprüft wirst.
- Im Workbook (zum Beispiel in Theme 1 bei A6) kannst du mit Hilfe der QAR-Methode verschiedene Lesestrategien üben.

How to write/How to do an interview

Remember? ● How to write

- Wenn du eine Geschichte schreiben willst, kannst du mit Hilfe von *who*, *what*, *where*, *when* und *why* Ideen sammeln und die Geschichte planen.
- Außerdem kann es helfen, in einem *word web* wichtige Wörter zu sammeln. Du kannst auch in den *wordbanks* im Buch oder in einem Wörterbuch nachschauen, um noch mehr passende Wörter zu finden.
- Überlege dir eine Reihenfolge für deine Geschichte: Was sollte am Anfang stehen, wie weckst du Interesse? Was folgt darauf? Wie könnte das Ende der Geschichte aussehen?
- Bei jeder Art von Texten gilt, dass du zunächst einen Entwurf schreiben solltest *(draft)*.
- Dann solltest du deinen Text überarbeiten und verbessern *(edit)*. Du kannst ihn auch jemand anderem zu lesen geben und ihn nach seiner Meinung und nach Verbesserungsvorschlägen fragen.
- Ist dein Text fertig, sollte er „veröffentlicht" werden *(publish)*. Stelle ihn aus und bewahre ihn dann z. B. in deinem Portfolio auf.

Remember? ● Ein Interview führen

Interviews können verschiedenen Zwecken dienen. Du willst vielleicht etwas über deinen Interviewpartner erfahren, unterschiedliche Meinungen zu einem bestimmten Thema sammeln oder dich über ein Thema genauer informieren.

1. **Bereite dein Interview gut vor, um gezielt Fragen stellen zu können.**
   - Wenn du z. B. zu Theme 3 ein Interview mit einem Mitarbeiter von Amnesty International führen möchtest, solltest du vorher so viel wie möglich über die Hintergründe in Erfahrung bringen.
   - Überlege dir dann, was genau du in deinem Interview erfahren möchtest, und notiere dir deine Fragen auf Karteikarten, um sie später leicht sortieren zu können.
   - Vermeide Ja-Nein-Fragen, denn schließlich möchtest du ja möglichst viel von deinem Gesprächspartner erfahren.

2. **Beim Interview:**
   - Stelle dich höflich vor und sage, warum du das Interview machen möchtest.
   - Reagiere auf Antworten, indem du z. B. nachfragst, ob die Person noch mehr zu diesem Punkt sagen könnte, oder indem du eine Antwort in eigenen Worten nochmals zusammenfasst, um sicherzugehen, dass du sie richtig verstanden hast.
   - Bedanke dich für das Interview.

> Hello, my name is … and I would like to ask you a few questions about …

> Is it okay if I record the interview?

> My first question is …

> Well, does that mean …?

> That last point sounded interesting. Could you tell me more about that?

How to present

Remember? ● Präsentieren leicht gemacht

Bei einer Präsentation vor der Klasse kommt es darauf an, das Interesse deiner Mitschüler zu wecken und dafür zu sorgen, dass sie sich das Wichtigste leicht merken können. Dafür beschränkst du dich am besten auf drei bis vier zentrale Punkte des Themas. Diese Informationen präsentierst du dann auf verschiedene Art und belegst sie mit möglichst gut verständlichen Beispielen.

Deine Zuhörer können dir besser folgen, wenn du ihnen auch Anschauungsmaterial präsentierst. Das können die wichtigsten Stichworte an der Tafel sein, ein Poster, eine Overheadfolie oder eine Computerpräsentation.

So kannst du im Einzelnen vorgehen:

1. Wähle einige Hauptpunkte zu deinem Thema aus.
2. Sage in deiner Einleitung, worüber du sprechen wirst und in welcher Reihenfolge.
3. Überlege dir, welche Hilfsmittel du einsetzen möchtest (z. B. Poster, Overheadprojektor, Computer mit Beamer). Wenn du technische Hilfsmittel benötigst, kläre das mit dem Lehrer / der Lehrerin ab und mache dich mit ihrer Bedienung vertraut.
4. Überlege, was deine Zuhörer schon wissen, damit du sie weder über- noch unterforderst.
5. Fertige Notizen zum Hauptteil deiner Präsentation an. Versuche jeden Hauptpunkt durch Beispiele, Statistiken usw. zu belegen.
6. Notiere für die Zusammenfassung noch einmal klar deine Hauptpunkte.

Deine Klasse wird dir gespannter zuhören, wenn du frei sprichst, dabei gestikulierst, deine Mitschüler ansiehst und auch ab und zu lächelst, anstatt nur einen Text abzulesen. Ein paar Stichworte auf Karteikärtchen oder ein Spickzettel genügen, damit du nicht den Faden verlierst, insbesondere wenn du deinen Vortrag schon ein paar Mal geübt hast. Das hilft dir auch dabei, vor deiner Präsentation nicht zu nervös zu werden.

Hier ein paar sprachliche Tipps:

Für die Einleitung:
- First of all, I'm going to …
- Then I'll talk about …
- Finally I'll …
- Please feel free to interrupt me if you have any questions.

Etwas Neues einleiten:
- So let's start with …
- OK, my first / next / last point is …

Auf Hilfsmittel hinweisen:
- If you look at the poster / overhead transparency / handout / screen, you'll see …

Etwas anders ausdrücken:
- In other words, …
- What I'm saying is …

Aufmerksamkeit aufrechterhalten:
- You see?
- Do you see what I mean?
- Don't you agree?

Zum Schluss kommen:
- So, to summarize …
- Thank you for listening.
- If you have any questions or comments, I'll be happy to answer them.

How to work on a project

Remember? • An einem Projekt arbeiten

Mittlerweile habt ihr vermutlich schon viele kleinere und einige größere Projekte im Englischunterricht durchgeführt und seid mit den Schritten *plan it – do it – check it – present it* vertraut.

In diesem Buch gibt es drei Kapitel, die sich größeren Projekten widmen. In Theme 2 geht es um *America,* in Theme 4 um *relationships* und in Theme 6 um *hopes and dreams.* An der grundsätzlichen Vorgehensweise bei der Projektarbeit ändert sich dabei nichts. Ihr könnt euch aber länger und intensiver mit einem Teilthema beschäftigen. Das bedeutet auch, dass ihr die Arbeit in der Gruppe besonders gut planen und dabei immer das Ziel vor Augen behalten solltet. Im Workbook findet ihr Hilfen und Anregungen für eure Projektarbeit.

Das folgende Beispiel aus Theme 4 Project 6 zu „Films about families" zeigt, welche Schritte bei der Planung eines Projektes wichtig sind.

Eure Gruppe hat sich den Film *Dan in real life* ausgesucht. Nachdem ihr den Film angesehen habt, möchtet ihr euch intensiver mit der Rolle des Thanksgiving-Fests beschäftigen.

- Sammelt erste Ideen in einem *brainstorming.*
  Zunächst einmal überlegt ihr euch, in welcher Form ihr euch mit dem Film und seiner Thematik auseinandersetzen möchtet. Welche Bedeutung hat das Thanksgiving-Fest in den USA und wie wird es von der Familie im Film begangen?

- Beim *brainstorming* sind folgende Regeln zu beachten:
  1. Erst einmal werden spontane Ideen gesammelt – Kritik, Bewertungen und abfällige Bemerkungen sind verboten.
  2. Jede Idee ist willkommen.
  3. Je mehr Ideen gesammelt werden, desto besser.
  4. Die Ideen anderer können weiterentwickelt werden, z. B. durch Kombination oder Verbesserung einiger Punkte.

  Erst nach dem *brainstorming* werden die Vorschläge diskutiert. Wenn ihr z. B. alle eure Ideen in einer Zettelsammlung zusammengetragen und sortiert habt, erfolgt die Abstimmung über die Auswahl. Damit nichts verloren geht, was später vielleicht doch noch einmal wichtig sein könnte, solltet ihr einen Platz einrichten, an dem auch zunächst verworfene Ideen aufbewahrt werden.

- Überlegt in der Gruppe, welche Informationen, Materialien und technischen Geräte ihr braucht.
  Eine Filmbesprechung wird viel lebendiger, wenn ihr eure Ausführungen um interessante Hintergrundinformationen, passende Filmausschnitte, Zitate und Standbilder aus zentralen Szenen ergänzt.

How to work on a project / How to mediate

- Verteilt die Aufgaben innerhalb der Projektgruppe gerecht.
  Ihr teilt euch zum Beispiel die Recherche zu Thanksgiving im Allgemeinen und dessen Darstellung im Film auf: Einer liest nach, warum Thanksgiving begangen wird und welche Bedeutung es in den USA hat. Jemand anderes informiert sich darüber, wie Thanksgiving heutzutage gefeiert wird und vergleicht dies mit den Feierlichkeiten in der Filmhandlung. Gibt es jemanden in eurer Gruppe, der Spaß an der Gestaltung des Layouts hätte? Er oder sie könnte beispielsweise die wichtigsten Informationen zu Thanksgiving auf einem Factsheet zusammentragen und dort die Gemeinsamkeiten und Unterschiede mit Dans Familienfeier vermerken.
- Überlegt, wie euer Endprodukt bzw. eure Präsentation aussehen soll.
  Möchtet ihr den Film im Rahmen einer elektronischen Präsentation vorstellen oder möchtet ihr einen Clip drehen, der einem Kinomagazin entnommen sein könnte?
- Erstellt einen Zeitplan.
- Ein (in englischer Sprache geführtes) Lerntagebuch hilft euch außerdem, den Verlauf eurer Arbeit zu dokumentieren. Diese Dokumentation könnt ihr in eure Präsentation einbeziehen, um die Ergebnisse eurer Arbeit transparenter zu machen.

Remember? • How to mediate

- Bei der Sprachmittlung (auf Englisch *mediation*) geht es darum, jemandem sprachlich weiterzuhelfen, der zum Beispiel nicht genug Englisch oder Deutsch versteht. So kannst du etwa im Englandurlaub für deine Eltern dolmetschen oder einem ausländischen Besucher in Deutschland beim Bestellen in einem Restaurant helfen. Auch wenn du jemandem in einer anderen Sprache wiedergibst, was in einem Radiobericht gesagt wird, handelt es sich um Sprachmittlung.
- Dabei kommt es darauf an, die wichtigsten Informationen von einer Sprache in die andere zu übertragen.
- Du musst nicht alles wörtlich übersetzen, konzentriere dich nur auf die wesentlichen Inhalte.
- Benutze kurze, einfache Sätze.
- Sprachliche Richtigkeit ist dabei nicht so wichtig. Es geht darum, sich verständlich zu machen. Das geht auch mit Wortumschreibungen oder Gesten, wenn dir ein Wort nicht einfällt.
- Wenn es dir gelingt, bei der Verständigung behilflich zu sein und wenn du siehst, wie nützlich deine Englischkenntnisse sein können, wird dir die Sprache künftig noch mehr Spaß machen.

How to work with a dictionary

Remember? ● How to work with a dictionary

- Wörterbücher sind alphabetisch sortiert.
- Auf jeder Seite stehen am oberen Rand die Leitwörter. Das sind jeweils das erste und letzte Wort, deren Übersetzungen auf dieser Seite zu finden sind.
- Auf die fett gedruckte Vokabel folgen Informationen über das Wort sowie die möglichen Übersetzungen und Beispielsätze.

dictionary /ˈdɪkʃənəri/ *SUBST* **1** Wörterbuch: *I have to look it up in a dictionary. nt* **2** Lexikon

Vokabel   Aussprache in Lautschrift   Wortart   Übersetzungsvorschläge   Beispielsatz

- Nimm nicht einfach den erstbesten Übersetzungsvorschlag, sondern behalte immer den Textzusammenhang im Auge, für den du die Übersetzung benötigst.

● Ein einsprachiges Wörterbuch verwenden

Ein einsprachiges Wörterbuch kann dir helfen, dein gesprochenes und geschriebenes Englisch zu verbessern, da es mehr Details und Informationen enthält.

Wichtige Hinweise:

> **Tipp**
> Lesen macht mehr Spaß, wenn du nicht jede Vokabel nachschlägst. Meist kannst du die Bedeutung aus dem Zusammenhang erschließen. Erst wenn ein Wort mehrfach vorkommt und sich als wichtig erweist, schlägst du es nach.

- Sieh dir zunächst an, welche **abbreviations** (Abkürzungen) für *uncountable noun, adjective, verb, conjunction, British English* und *American English* in deinem Wörterbuch verwendet werden.

- Ein wichtiger Punkt in deinem einsprachigen Wörterbuch sind die **collocations** – Wörter, die in der Regel mit anderen Wörtern kombiniert werden. Das Wort *advice* verwendet man zum Beispiel oft mit den Verben *follow* und *give*.

- Neben den Kategorien *formal* und *informal* verwenden viele Wörterbücher auch Begriffe wie *spoken, literary, impolite, offensive* oder *humorous* als **style labels**, um die üblichen Verwendungsmöglichkeiten eines Wortes deutlich zu machen.

- **Idioms** sind Redewendungen und Ausdrücke, die nicht das gleiche bedeuten wie die Wörter, aus denen sie bestehen. Nur wenige *idioms* sind im Deutschen und Englischen gleich, deshalb ist es wichtig, sie in einem Wörterbuch zu überprüfen. In Wörterbüchern sind *idioms* im Eintrag des ersten wichtigen Wortes der Redewendung aufgeführt.

Hier ein Beispiel aus einem Wörterbuch:

abbreviation → **cook** /kʊk/ verb ★★★ **1** [I/T] to prepare food and heat it so that it is ready to eat: *Cook the apple slowly until it is soft.* • **cook sth for sb** *Joe's cooking dinner for me tonight.* • **cook sb sth** *He offered to cook me lunch.* **1a.** [I] when food cooks, it is heated so that it is ready to eat: *The potatoes need to cook for about 20 minutes.* **2** [T] *informal* to change information

dishonestly: *They cooked the scripts to make Adams look stupid.* **2a. cook the books** to change accounts and figures dishonestly, usually in order to get money **be cooking** *spoken* to be happening or being planned, often secretly: *I'll try and find out what's cooking.* **cook sb's goose** *informal* to cause a lot of problems for someone or spoil their plans.

— idiom
— style label
— idiom

Beispielsatz

134

How to write a summary / How to write a comment

Remember? ● Eine Zusammenfassung schreiben

Wenn du eine Zusammenfassung eines Texts oder eines Buchs schreibst, möchtest du keine Details oder eigenen Interpretationen schildern, sondern nur einen generellen Eindruck vermitteln, worum es in dem Text oder dem Buch geht.

- Bevor du eine Zusammenfassung schreibst, musst du die wichtigsten Aussagen des Buchs oder des Texts ausfindig machen. In deinem Workbook kannst du sie farbig unterstreichen, ansonsten solltest du sie dir stichwortartig notieren.
- Um den Aufbau eines Buchs oder Texts zu erkennen, hilft es dir, Stichworte oder Überschriften für die einzelnen Absätze oder Kapitel zu formulieren.
- Beginne deine Zusammenfassung mit einem Einleitungssatz, in dem du kurz beschreibst, wovon der Text handelt.

   The book "The Absolutely True Diary of a Part-Time Indian" by Sherman Alexie is about …
   The song "Ellis Unit One" deals with …

Tipp
Lies dir auch *How to write* auf Seite 130 noch einmal durch.

- Führe nur die wesentlichen Informationen aus dem Text an. Lass alle Beispiele, detaillierten Beschreibungen, direkte Rede oder deine eigene Meinung weg.
- Zitiere nicht aus dem Text, sondern benutze eigene Formulierungen.
- Achte auf die Zeitform: Die Zusammenfassung steht in der Regel im Präsens.

Remember? ● Einen Kommentar schreiben

In einem Kommentar nimmst du Stellung zu einem bestimmten Thema oder Problem. Dabei vergleichst du Argumente dafür und dagegen und begründest deine Meinung.

- Bilde dir deine Meinung, indem du zunächst Argumente, Informationen und Beispiele zum Thema sammelst. Eine Tabelle mit *pros* und *cons* oder *examples* und *reasons* kann helfen, dir einen Überblick zu verschaffen.
- Beginne mit einer kurzen Einleitung, die das Thema deines Kommentars vorstellt und Interesse weckt.
- Bringe die Argumente, die du gesammelt hast, in eine sinnvolle Reihenfolge und finde Beispiele oder Belege für die Argumente.

   Firstly, …   *Finally, …*   *The reason is …*
   Secondly, …   *Let me give an example …*   *It is a fact that …*

- Führe nicht nur Argumente für deine Meinung auf, sondern auch Gegenargumente, die du dann entkräftest.

   Many people say … but I think …,   *I believe …*
   On the one hand … but on the other hand …,   *In my opinion …*
   Although I can understand …,   *I am sure …*

- Im letzten Absatz deines Kommentars ziehst du die Schlussfolgerung aus den genannten Argumenten und fasst deine eigene Meinung zusammen.

   All in all, I would say …   *That is why I think …*

How to discuss

Remember? ● An einer Diskussion teilnehmen

Die Grundregeln einer normalen Diskussion kennt ihr bereits: einander aufmerksam zuhören, höflich bleiben, auf die Argumente der anderen eingehen. Wenn ihr ernsthaftere Fragen in der Klasse diskutieren wollt, wie z. B. in Theme 3 zum Thema Todesstrafe, ist es sinnvoll, eure Argumente vorzubereiten und euch auf einige Regeln zu einigen, die ihr beim Diskutieren einhalten möchtet.

Vor der Diskussion

- Teilt euch in Pro- und Contra-Gruppen auf und sammelt in der Gruppe Argumente, um eure Meinung zu begründen. Stichpunkte und *word webs* helfen, nichts Wichtiges zu vergessen. Ihr könnt die Argumente auch auf Karteikarten schreiben.
- Denkt auch an Argumente, die gegen eure Meinung sprechen und überlegt euch mögliche Antworten darauf.
- Legt gemeinsam einige Diskussionsregeln fest, z. B. dass jeder eine Redezeit von drei Minuten nicht überschreiten darf und dass man sich per Handzeichen zu Wort meldet.

Tipp:
- Bestimmt einen Diskussionsleiter/eine Diskussionsleiterin. Er/Sie sollte darauf achten, dass alle zu Wort kommen können, beim Thema bleiben und die vereinbarte Redezeit einhalten.
- Bildet eine neutrale Gruppe, die während der Diskussion Notizen macht und nachher Feedback gibt.

Beim Diskutieren

- Lasst am besten eure/n Diskussionsleiter/in beginnen, indem er oder sie das Thema kurz vorstellt und dann das Wort an jemanden weitergibt, der das erste Argument nennt oder seine Karte vorliest.
- Jemand anderes reagiert auf das Argument und sagt, ob er/sie es richtig findet oder nicht. Macht in dieser Weise weiter.
- Hört genau zu, was die anderen sagen. Fragt nach, wenn ihr etwas nicht versteht.
- Am Ende könnt ihr in der Klasse noch einmal gemeinsam abstimmen.

Hier ein paar sprachliche Tipps:

Meinung äußern:
- I am convinced that …
- I strongly believe …
- In my opinion …

Meinung begründen:
- I think so because …
- Let me give an example …
- I have heard / read that …
- Statistics show that …

Widersprechen:
- Sorry, I don't agree with you.
- I'm afraid I don't agree at all …
- I see your point, but …

Zustimmen:
- I agree with / that …
- … is completely right in saying …

In anderen Worten zusammenfassen:
- So what you are saying is …
- What I mean is …
- Let me put it another way: …

Wenn man ein Argument nicht verstanden hat und nachfragen möchte:
- I don't understand what you mean (by …).
- What exactly do you mean by …?
- So you mean …?

How to work with statistics

Remember? • Wie man mit Statistiken arbeiten kann

Informationen verschiedener Art lassen sich in Statistiken optisch darstellen. Die Art der Darstellung ist abhängig von der Information und natürlich davon, was man veranschaulichen will.

1. Tortendiagramm / *pie chart*:

Mit einem Tortendiagramm könnt ihr Prozentanteile veranschaulichen. In Theme 3, B2 auf S. 53 zum Beispiel wird so gezeigt, wie viel Prozent aller Gefangenen in welchen Staaten der USA hingerichtet wurden.

Tipp: Du verfügst über ein Tabellenkalkulationsprogramm wie Excel und kannst damit umgehen? Dann kannst du dir z. B. von deinem Informatiklehrer zeigen lassen, wie du *pie charts* und *bar charts* mit diesem Programm erstellen kannst.

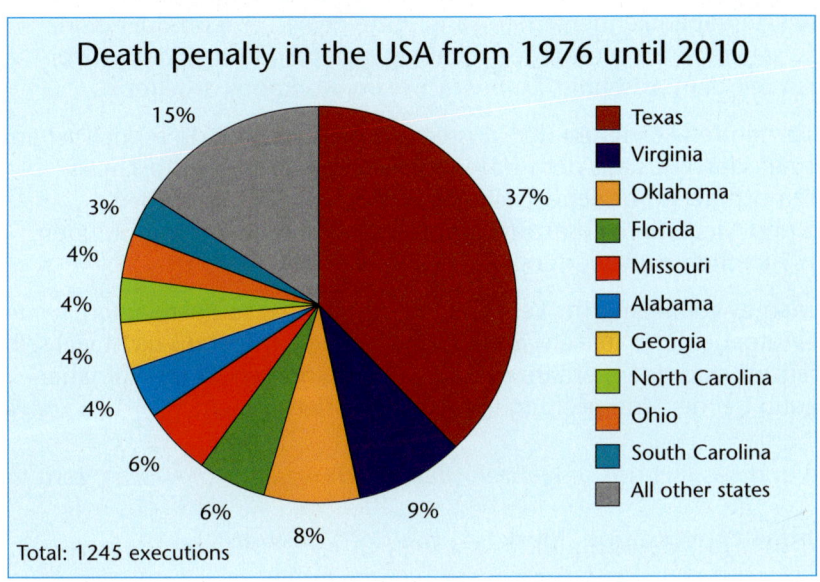

... per cent of all executed prisoners were executed in ...

Most of the executions ...

2. Säulendiagramm / *bar chart*:

Mit einem Säulendiagramm lassen sich übersichtlich Zahlen vergleichen. Nehmt beispielsweise B1 in Theme 3 auf S. 52, wo die Anzahl der Hinrichtungen pro Land dargestellt wird.

More than ... were executed ...

Most people ...

137

How to prepare for an exam

● Gut vorbereitet in die Prüfung

Das Wichtigste zuerst: Eine Abschlussprüfung kommt nicht unvorhergesehen und sie bringt eigentlich nichts Neues. Alles, was dir in der Abschlussprüfung begegnet, hast du in der einen oder anderen Form bereits im Unterricht gemacht und geübt. Bewahre also Ruhe und bereite dich gezielt in den Bereichen vor, wo du dich noch unsicher fühlst. Für diese Vorbereitungen solltest du dir allerdings einen Plan machen und feste, am besten regelmäßige Zeiten vorsehen.

Bei der Vorbereitung ist es wichtig, die Art der Aufgabenstellungen zu kennen, wie sie für Abschlussprüfungen deiner Schulform (und deines Bundeslandes) üblich sind. Die Landesinstitute und Kultusministerien, die die Prüfungen erarbeiten, bieten auf ihren Webseiten in der Regel „Musterprüfungen" aus früheren Jahren zum Herunterladen an, mit denen man die so genannten Formate der Aufgaben kennenlernen kann. Bitte deine Lehrerin oder deinen Lehrer um Hilfe, wenn du solche Musterprüfungen nicht eigenständig finden kannst; vor allem aber kannst du auch mit dem Abschnitt *Exam practice* im Workbook arbeiten.

Wenn du dich dann näher mit den Formaten der Mustertests befasst, wirst du schnell sehen, dass dir die Aufgabenformen durchaus aus dem Unterricht vertraut sind. Alle Abschlussprüfungen im Bereich Fremdsprachen beziehen sich auf die Bereiche Leseverstehen, Hörverstehen, Schreiben und Mediation; zusätzlich gibt es oft auch mündliche Prüfungen, um deine Fähigkeiten im Sprechen zu bewerten.

Bei den Bereichen, in denen es vor allem ums Verstehen geht *(listening comprehension, reading comprehension)*, sind die Aufgabenformate sehr ähnlich. In der Regel musst du nicht viel selber schreiben, sondern ankreuzen, zuordnen, ergänzen und vervollständigen. Diese Aufgabenformen begegnen dir häufig bei der Überprüfung von Verstehensleistungen:

- eine Auswahl treffen und das Richtige ankreuzen *(multiple choice* oder *true-false)*, zum Beispiel:
  Listen to the telephone conversation. Mark (✓) the right answer.
- Sätze/Aussagen in die richtige Reihenfolge bringen, zum Beispiel:
  This is what Leonora said to a newspaper afterwards. Put her statements in the right order.
- Zuordnen, zum Beispiel:
  Match the correct sentence parts.
  oder
  Match the four texts with these headlines.
  oder
  Read the following adverts for different sports. Then match the pictures with the right text.
- Sätze/Aussagen vervollständigen, zum Beispiel:
  Listen again and complete the sentences with the right information.
  oder
  Complete the notes with the missing information.
- Notizen machen, zum Beispiel:
  Read the questions below. Listen to the interview again and take notes. Then answer each question in one sentence.
- umschriebene (anders ausgedrückte) Textstellen im Originaltext finden (nur bei Leseverstehensaufgaben), zum Beispiel:
  Read these statements. Then find phrases in the text with the same meaning. Write them next to the statements.

How to prepare for an exam

Bezüglich der Schreibfertigkeit *(writing)* findest du vor allem folgende Aufgabenstellungen:

- einen Brief / eine E-Mail schreiben, zum Beispiel:
  Read the following two letters. Then choose one of them and answer it.

- zu einer oder mehreren Aussagen Stellung nehmen, zum Beispiel:
  Choose one of the following statements and write down your opinion. Give reasons for your opinion.

- einen Text für einen bestimmten Zweck verfassen, zum Beispiel:
  You are on an exchange visit at an English school and want to organize a 'German evening' with films and / or music. Write a text for a poster or a flyer for this evening.

- eine Geschichte (zu Ende) schreiben, zum Beispiel:
  Write a story that starts with this sentence:
  The first day of my work experience started with a huge problem.

Bei den Mediationsaufgaben kommt es darauf an, aus einem gelesenen oder gehörten Text gezielt die Informationen für jemanden zu entnehmen, der selbst diesen Text nicht verstehen kann. Zum Beispiel musst du aus einem englischen Text die gewünschten Informationen auf Deutsch wiedergeben, oder umgekehrt. Es geht dabei aber keineswegs um wörtliche Übersetzung; du musst also nicht jedes einzelne Wort übertragen, sondern nur die Informationen, die derjenige wissen möchte, dem du hilfst. Wenn dir dabei ein wichtiges Wort nicht einfällt, kannst du versuchen, es zu umschreiben.

Eine typische Mediationsaufgabe sieht so aus:

You are in London with your parents. In a mobile phone shop you see this advert. Your parents are quite interested. Tell them what this advert is about and give them the most important information in German.

Die Aufgaben einer mündlichen Prüfung können den Bereich „Zusammenhängend Sprechen" betreffen oder den Bereich „Miteinander Sprechen". Im ersten Fall musst du etwas vortragen, zum Beispiel zu einem vorgegebenen oder von dir gewählten Thema oder zu einem Bild, zum Beispiel:

Choose one of the pictures and describe it. Then talk about it.

Im zweiten Fall wirst du dich entweder mit den Prüfenden oder mit anderen Prüflingen über etwas unterhalten; das kann wiederum ein gestelltes Thema oder ein Bild sein, oder du erhältst zu einer bestimmten Situation eine Rollenvorgabe und musst dich entsprechend verhalten, zum Beispiel:

Two friends are talking about a film. Act out their conversation.

Wie gesagt: Wenn du dich noch einmal im Zusammenhang mit den Aufgabenstellungen in Musterprüfungen befasst, wirst du schnell sehen, dass nichts Unerwartetes von dir verlangt wird. Bewahre Ruhe und lies vor allem die Aufgaben in der „echten" Prüfung sehr genau durch. Achte genau auf die Verben, die meistens in der Befehlsform stehen, und beachte ihre Bedeutung genau. Wenn Beispiele vorgegeben sind, schau sie dir sehr genau an und halte dich an die Muster. Stelle sicher, dass du die Situation, die in manchen Aufgaben vorgegeben wird, genau verstanden hast, bevor du mit der Lösung der Aufgabe beginnst. Und schließlich, ebenso simpel wie wichtig: Achte bei mehrgliedrigen Aufgaben (zum Beispiel a), b), c) usw.) ganz genau darauf, dass du keinen Schritt übersehen hast. Und wenn du am Ende noch Zeit hast, lies alles noch einmal aufmerksam durch – auch wenn du es eigentlich schon gar nicht mehr sehen magst. Good luck!

How to talk about films

● Filme analysieren

Wie du eine kurze Filmkritik schreibst und wie du Filme beschreiben kannst, hast du in den letzten Jahren bereits gelernt. Wie kannst du nun Filme genauer analysieren? Stell dir dazu einfach vor, du würdest einen Film drehen: Mit welchen Einstellungen wird die Kamera geführt? Wie sollen die Bilder auf den Zuschauer wirken? Welcher Mittel kann sich ein Filmemacher beim Drehen bedienen? Hier geben wir dir einige zentrale Begrifflichkeiten an die Hand, die dir beim Analysieren ebenso helfen können wie beim Erstellen eines eigenen Films.

A **long shot** puts the camera at a great distance from the person being filmed and gives a view of the setting, thus of the context of the action taking place.

A **medium long shot** shows a person or people in interaction with their surroundings.

A **full shot** gives a view of a figure's entire body, e.g. to show (inter)action and/or a constellation of characters.

A **medium shot** shows a subject down to his/her waist, e.g. to show two people in conversation.

A **close-up** draws the viewer's attention to someone or something specific, e.g. to show the emotions on someone's face or to stress the importance of an object.

How to talk about films

Camera Angle

= the perspective from which an object is viewed

In an **aerial shot** or **overhead shot**, the camera is placed at an angle above the scene of action, making objects and people appear smaller and less important. This shot is also called a **bird's eye view**.

A **high angle shot** shows people or objects from above, i.e. higher than eye level, making the viewer more powerful than the character.

An **eye-level shot** or **straight-on angle** views a subject from the level of a person's eyes. It is often used to express objectivity.

A **low angle shot** shows people or objects from below, i.e. lower than eye level, exaggerating and stressing the importance of a character.
A very low angle shot is called a **below angle shot** or **worm's eye perspective**.

Camera Movement

= the movement of the camera during a shot

- **panning shot:** the camera moves (= pans) horizontally from left to right or vice versa across the picture.
- **tilt shot:** the camera moves up and down (= tilts up and down) on a vertical line.
- **tracking shot / trucking shot:** the camera follows along next to or behind a moving object or person.
- **zoom:** the stationary camera appears to approach a subject by "zooming in" or to move further away by "zooming out".

How to read and analyse comics

Remember? • Comics lesen und analysieren

Comics erzählen eine Geschichte in Bildern. Meist werden die Bilder mit Sprechblasen, Geräuscheffekten und Bildunterschriften kombiniert, das Hauptgewicht liegt aber auf den Abbildungen.

Wollt ihr z. B. den Comic aus Theme 5 näher analysieren und in der Klasse präsentieren, helfen euch die jeweiligen Fachbegriffe für die Bild- und Sprachelemente von Comics:

Bildelemente:

- Als *panel* wird das einzelne Bild eines Comics bezeichnet. Der Rahmen *(frame)* des *panels* kann quadratisch, rechteckig, rund oder unregelmäßig sein.
- Das *gutter* ist der Raum außerhalb des *panels* und enthält normalerweise keine zeichnerischen Elemente.
- Die Sprechblasen *(speech bubbles)* und Gedankenblasen *(thought bubbles)* teilen dem Leser mit, was die Figur sagt oder denkt.
- Die *splash bubbles* (meistens mit gezackten Ecken) enthalten sehr wichtigen oder besonders dramatischen Text, wie z. B. einen Warnruf oder einen Wutschrei.
- Die Zeiger *(pointers)* einer Sprechblase zeigen an, welche Figur den Text in der Sprechblase spricht.

Sprachelemente:

- *Sound effects* sind alle Arten von Text, die ein Geräusch beschreiben (z. B. *wham, boom, biff*).
- *Captions* (spezielle Textrahmen) enthalten meist Text, der direkt an den Leser gerichtet ist oder dienen als Ersatz für Sprech- und Gedankenblasen.
- *Lettering* (die Gestaltung der Buchstaben) wird häufig benutzt, um Informationen hervorzuheben. Dafür verwendet man heutzutage den Computer mit seinem Angebot an verschiedenen Schriftarten und Schriftschnitten wie **fett (bold)**, *kursiv (italic)* usw.

Wie man einen Comic liest

- Versucht zunächst einen allgemeinen Überblick zu bekommen über das, was in den Bildern gezeigt wird. Achtet neben der Handlung selbst auch auf die Kleidung der Figuren, auf den Ort der Handlung usw.
- Sprech- und Gedankenblasen bieten nicht sehr viel Platz, jedes Wort im Comic muss wohlüberlegt sein. Aus diesem Grund ist es wichtig, genau auf den Wortlaut zu achten.
- Jetzt geht es mehr ins Detail: Wie werden die Farben eingesetzt? Wie drücken Gesichter eine bestimmte Atmosphäre und Gefühle aus?
- Versucht herauszufinden, welche Einzelheiten die einzelnen *panels* miteinander verbinden.
- Gefällt euch die Geschichte? Gefällt euch der Zeichenstil und passt er zur Geschichte? Was genau findet ihr gut oder schlecht daran?

How to talk about poems and lyrics

● Ein Gedicht oder einen Liedtext interpretieren

Lieder und Gedichte haben einiges gemeinsam. Sie drücken Gefühle oder Erfahrungen anders aus als eine Kurzgeschichte oder ein Roman. Die Sprache wird anders – auch freier – eingesetzt. Lieder und Gedichte nutzen Rhythmus, Laute oder Reime, um Stimmungen zu vermitteln. Die üblichen Sprachregeln, sogar die der Grammatik, werden in Gedichten und Liedern häufig verändert. Die folgenden Fragen können dir helfen, ein Gedicht oder einen Liedtext besser zu verstehen:

- **Thema** *(topic)*: Was ist das Thema? Wird es im Titel genannt?

- Erzählt das Gedicht / Lied eine **Geschichte** *(story)*? Oder wird eine bestimmte **Erfahrung** *(experience)* oder ein **Ereignis** *(occurrence)* geschildert? Fasse den Inhalt in wenigen Worten zusammen.

    The poem ... is about ...,
    The song lyrics give a description of ...,
    The song is an attack on those people who ...

- **Gefühle** *(feelings)*: Welche Gefühle drückt das Gedicht / der Liedtext aus? Mit welchen Ausdrücken werden die Gefühle dargestellt? Werden konkrete Bilder *(images)* benutzt, um die Gefühle auszudrücken?

    The song writer uses the image of ... to express ...,

- **Erzähler** *(narrator)*: Gibt es in dem Gedicht / Lied direkte oder indirekte Hinweise auf den Erzähler? Gibt es Hinweise auf die Person, zu der der Erzähler spricht?

    The speaker seems to be ...,
    The speaker talks to ...

- **Klang** *(sound)*: Lies das Gedicht laut oder spiele das Lied und konzentriere dich auf die Klänge. Markiere die betonten Silben und schreibe die Wörter auf, die sich reimen. Gibt es Alliterationen (d. h. Wörter, die mit dem gleichen Laut beginnen)? Gibt es einen bestimmten Klang, der auffallend oft vorkommt?

- **Ungewöhnlicher Sprachgebrauch** *(unusual language)*: Kommen ungewöhnliche Wortkombinationen vor? Oder eine ungewöhnliche Wortstellung? Oder grammatikalische Konstruktionen, die wiederholt werden *(repetition)*? Gibt es personifizierte Dinge oder Ideen? Werden Symbole verwendet (wie Taube für Frieden oder Herz für Liebe)?

    In her "Hunger Song", Joyce Brookshire uses the phrase "the lean wolf that's howling at my door" to describe ...
    Repetition is used to ...
    In the poem ... is used as a symbol for ...

- **Wirkung** *(critique)*: Wie fühlst du dich, wenn du das Gedicht / Lied liest bzw. hörst? Was drückt es für dich aus? Welche Wörter drücken für dich das meiste aus?

    The image of ... reminds me of ...
    When I read ... I feel ...

Wordbank

Looks and image

Happy people usually …

> feel good about themselves
> feel confident
> are full of life

People sometimes want to be …

> thinner
> prettier
> more confident
> younger
> slimmer
> more beautiful
> perfect
> skinny
> flawless

People usually don't want to look …

> old
> fat
> tired
> stressed

weight loss and gain:

> only eat low-fat food
> control one's weight
> go on a diet
> being obsessed with one's weight
> weigh oneself
> lose weight
> gain weight
> avoid carbohydrates
> stop eating fats

eating disorders:

> anorexia
> bulimia

possible side effects of eating disorders:

> inducing vomiting   extreme weight loss
> obsessive exercise   eating binges
> self-starvation   feeling burnt out
> loss of periods   feeling exhausted
> looking pale   feeling out of
> malnutrition   control
> infection   feeling faint
> low energy levels   feeling chunky

> retouch a photo · have a photo retouched

Wordbank

Food

eating habits:

food production:

agri-food chain
oil companies
natural gas companies
diesel fuel
fertilizer
chemical companies
pesticides
farm machinery
farm seed companies
banks
farmers
buyers of farm produce
transport
food processing factories
shops
restaurants
consumers

food can …
- be processed
- be packaged
- be fresh
- be frozen
- be cooked
- be ready to eat
- come in sacks

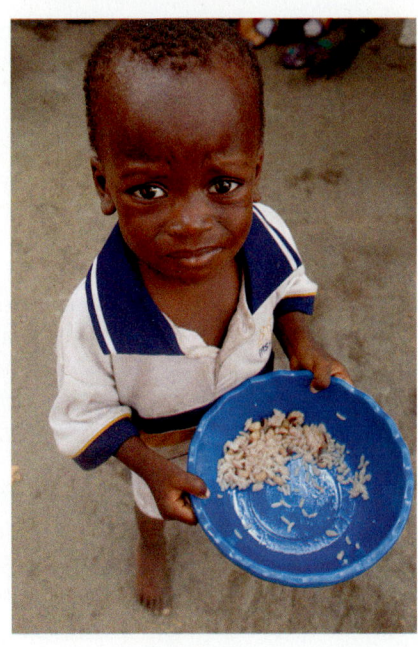

not enough food:

collect money to feed the hungry
fight against world hunger
school meals
donated rice
good, healthy food to develop full
    physical and mental potential
food banks

Wordbank

American politics

Native Americans:

tribe
chief / leader
tomahawk / bow / knife
reservation
wagon
Indian Removal Act
Trail of Tears
move somebody

Cherokee · Algonquian · Navaho ·
Apache · Kiowa · Cheyenne · Comanche ·
Seneca · Lakota Sioux · Iroquois · Arapaho ·
Powhatan · Wampanoag

government and politics:

British rule
pay tax
sign/keep/break a treaty
break a promise
pass an act/a law

freedom
equality
justice

leading power
the superpowers

conflicts and wars:

battle · rebellion · War of Independence ·
civil war · the Cold War · a split world ·
peaceful protest · protest movement ·
anti-war demonstration ·
nuclear or chemical weapons · missiles ·
the arms race · forces · massacres ·

Black America:

slaves from Africa
fight for freedom of slaves
abolish slavery
African Americans
peaceful protest
civil rights activists
non-violent activists
militant activists
racial prejudice

declare war on
declare independence
defeat
invade a country
surrender
mistreat someone
wrong someone
drop a bomb
die from injuries

take/steal someone's land
be ready to fight for
force someone to move from the land
end arms race

Wordbank

Human rights

injustice:

honour killings
imprisonment
torture
terrorism
organized crime
corruption
racism
human trafficking
abuses
discrimination
executions
violate human rights
child labour
slavery
servitude
human rights violations
death penalty

human rights:

the Universal Declaration of Human Rights
set out basic human rights
human dignity
have the right to life/ to be free from
    torture/ to a fair trial / to go to school
universal rights
democracy
political freedom
equal justice
lead a life in freedom
fair trial

free elections
freedom of thought
freedom of conscience
freedom of religion

human rights supporters:

- protest against injustice
- campaign against …
- fight for the rights of …
- organize workshops
- support political freedom
- fight human rights violations
- help victims
- protect people
- support human rights
- work to abolish the death penalty
- take care of political prisoners

- activists
- victims
- political prisoners
- supporters

Treat others in the same way you want to be treated.

Wordbank

Justice

governments can:

- carry out executions
- use the death penalty
- abolish the death penalty
- pass a law
- put people on trial
- sentence people to death
- commute a sentence

the death penalty:

death row
death row inmate
death row prisoner
sentence someone to death
execution
revenge
capital system
capital punishment
life sentence
lethal injection
laws
regulations

campaigns against the death penalty:

- protest meetings
- public debates
- talks
- finding out about government decisions
- working to defend human rights
- working to defend democracy
- protecting and promoting human rights
- a non-governmental organization
- a worldwide movement of people
- fighting human rights violations

Capital punishment is a violation of human rights.

The KADP think that the death penalty should be abolished.

Leroy White was sentenced to death in 1989.

the legal system:

jury
lawyer
final appeal
application for a pardon
pardon board hearing
imprisonment
life sentence

Wordbank

Relationships

family members:

- wife
- husband
- granddaughter
- grandson
- grandparents
- grandmother
- grandfather

family models:

traditional family model · blended family · patchwork family · extended family · living together · partner · alone · divorce · (get) divorced · single (parent) · couple · love marriage · (pre-)arranged marriage · community · co-housing · adopted/adoptive

relationships:

in the beginning …
- fancy someone
- be fond of someone
- be interested in someone
- seeing someone
- making the first move
- chat-up line

getting to know each other …
- share feelings
- fall in love
- trust each other
- date someone
- go out with someone
- connect
- kiss (on the cheek)
- squeeze one's hand

a life together …
- (deep) love
- keep a relationship (going)/ work at a relationship
- be/live with someone
- be/get engaged
- marry/get married
- wedding
- good job/ proper career
- pregnant/pregnancy
- having/raising children
- housewife
- house husband
- work part-time

making it work …
- share housework
- take turns
- accept each other's weaknesses

problems in a relationship …
- blame someone
- cry
- turn away
- cruel words
- (false) accusations
- feel trapped
- have unrealistic expectations
- fight about
- hurt
- leave

149

Wordbank

Economy

industries:

IT industry	food production industry
film production	high technology companies
film industry	technology corporations
tourism	
textile industry	
textile factory	cotton farming industry
automobile company	

positions and jobs:

intern · tourist guide · call centre agent · manager · textile worker · retailer · consumer · buyer

economy verbs:

earn well
work late into the night
manufacture
be educated
deal with other people's problems
give training to someone
gain (some) experience
get paid
make some money
be in work
earn extra money
find work
earn/get paid very little
start a business
found a company
take over a business
invest into something
build roads or public buildings
expand a business
support
be able to afford something

global player
high paying jobs
labour costs
turnaround
production
transport
major order
wages
profit
income
fast-growing economy

economic production
employment
(high) unemployment
industrialization
turnover
shortage of money
distribution of money
stock market
depression
economic recovery
pocket money

The IT industry is one of the fastest growing businesses in India.

Educated workers generally get higher wages and make more money. Their income is much higher than that of people who do simple jobs.

Child labour is often used in industries where little training is needed.

Profit is what is left over after the company has paid out wages and covered their costs.

Wordbank

textile industry:

label
clothing
garment
cotton
fabrics
sweatshop
child labour
low pay
low wages
stay cheap
bonded labour
costs
find work
work on a garment

design a T-shirt
sew together fabrics
cut out T-shirts
pay the price
earn / get very little money
made in
sew beads onto clothes
be loaded into containers
be loaded onto ships
be shipped

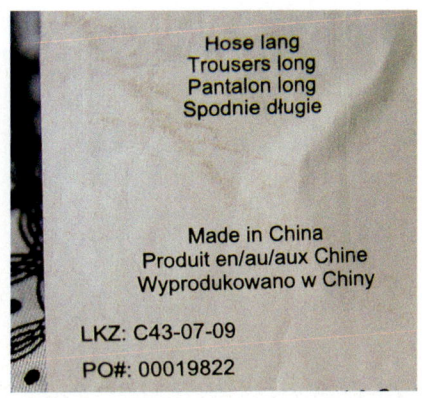

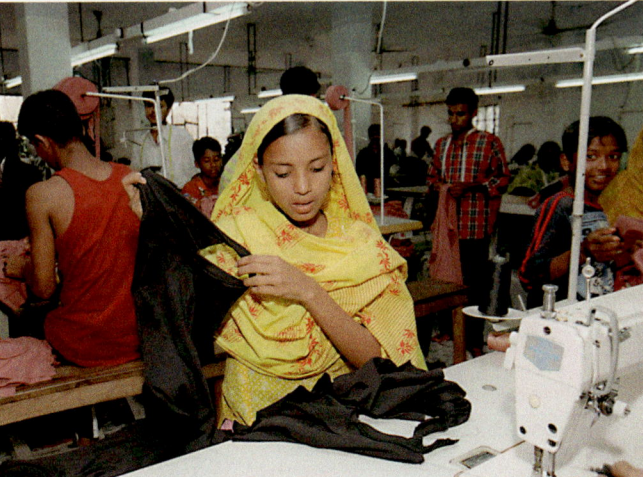

Consumers need to make it clear to retailers that the use of child labour cannot be accepted.

Ethical organizations help give people in the developing world a higher standard of living and a better quality of life.

The root of the problem is our 'fast fashion' culture.

Wordbank

Hopes and dreams

> hopes · dreams · important things in life · priorities for the future · ambitions for the future · plans for the future

thinking of others:

> charity
> helping other people
> having a purpose in life by helping others

what you may hope to be:

> rich
> famous

what you may hope for:

> well-paid job
> good career
> security
> purpose in life
> someone to share one's dreams with
> stable family
>
> good life
> good career
> home
> nice house
> pleasant green surroundings

a world without:

> military invasions
> environmental disasters
> food shortages
> scandals
> busy roads
> noisy aircraft
> starving children

the future of the planet:

> carbon-neutral houses
> eco-village
> recycled materials
> natural materials
> green technology

ways to be green/ environmentally friendly:

> be self-sufficient
> be independent
> composting organic waste
> growing heating fuel
> using rainwater

Classroom phrases

Allgemeines

Sorry, I'm late.	Tut mir leid, dass ich zu spät bin.
Sorry, I haven't got my exercise book / homework with me.	Tut mir leid, ich habe mein Heft / meine Hausaufgaben nicht dabei.
What's the matter?	Was ist los?
I'm fine. / I feel sick.	Mir geht's gut. / Mir ist schlecht.
I've got a headache.	Ich habe Kopfschmerzen.
Can I open the window, please?	Kann ich bitte das Fenster öffnen?
Can I go to the toilet, please?	Kann ich bitte zur Toilette gehen?

Was der Schüler oder die Schülerin sagt

Could you help me, please?	Können Sie mir bitte helfen?
I don't understand this.	Ich verstehe das hier nicht.
Could you explain that (again), please?	Können Sie das bitte (noch einmal) erklären?
Sorry, I didn't quite get that. Could you repeat it, please?	Tut mir leid, das habe ich nicht verstanden. Können Sie das bitte wiederholen?
What's … in English / German?	Was heißt … auf Englisch / Deutsch?
Sorry, I don't know.	Tut mir leid, das weiß ich nicht.
This question is quite difficult.	Diese Frage ist ziemlich schwer.
What page, please?	Auf welcher Seite bitte?
Could you write it on the board, please?	Können Sie das bitte an die Tafel schreiben?
Could we listen to the CD again?	Können wir die CD bitte noch einmal hören?
Could you turn the volume up / down, please?	Können Sie den Ton bitte lauter / leiser stellen?
I can't see the board / transparency properly.	Ich kann die Tafel / die Folie nicht richtig sehen.
We are almost finished.	Wir sind fast fertig.
Could we have an extra five minutes, please?	Können wir bitte noch fünf Minuten haben?
What's for homework?	Was haben wir als Hausaufgabe auf?

Was die Lehrerin oder der Lehrer sagt

Can we have some quiet now, please?	Seid bitte still.
Turn to page …	Blättert zu Seite …
Look at the next paragraph / line …	Seht euch den nächsten Absatz / die nächste Zeile … an.
Who wants to go first?	Wer möchte anfangen?
Work in pairs / in groups.	Arbeitet zu zweit / in Gruppen.
Listen to track number …	Hört euch Nummer … an.

Classroom phrases

Make up your own dialogue.	Entwerft selbst einen Dialog.
Change roles.	Tauscht die Rollen.
Please speak up.	Sprich bitte lauter.
You can do better.	Das kannst du besser.
Try again.	Versuch es noch einmal.
Good question / point.	Das ist eine gute Frage / ein gutes Argument.
That's it.	Das ist alles. / Richtig!

Wenn du mit dem Computer arbeitest

What's your e-mail address?	Wie ist deine E-Mail-Adresse?
You can click on this link.	Du kannst auf diesen Link klicken.
Enter the word in a search engine.	Gib das Wort in eine Suchmaschine ein.
Can I print it out / download it?	Kann ich das ausdrucken / herunterladen?
I saved it.	Ich habe es gespeichert.
My computer has crashed.	Mein Computer ist abgestürzt.

Wenn man zusammen arbeitet

Why don't we do this together?	Wollen wir das nicht zusammen machen?
What are we going to do first?	Was machen wir zuerst?
Let's compare our …	Lass uns unsere … vergleichen.
Can I help you with …?	Soll ich dir bei … helfen?
Could you please check my spelling?	Kannst du bitte meine Rechtschreibung überprüfen?
What's another word for …?	Wie kann man … noch ausdrücken?
Can you look that word up, please?	Kannst du das Wort bitte nachschauen?
Whose turn is it?	Wer ist dran?
Do you follow me?	Verstehst du, was ich meine?
I forgot my … Can I borrow yours for a moment?	Ich habe mein … vergessen, kann ich mir deines kurz ausleihen?
You're welcome.	Gern geschehen.
We're running out of time.	Unsere Zeit ist fast um.
It's time to finish.	Es ist Zeit aufzuhören.
Don't forget to bring … tomorrow.	Denk dran, morgen … mitzubringen.
Thanks for your help.	Danke für deine Hilfe.

Glossary

Deutscher Begriff	Englischer Begriff mit Aussprache	Beispiele
Adjektiv (Eigenschaftswort)	adjective [ˈædʒɪktɪv]	typical, easy, delicious
Adverb (Umstandswort) pl. Adverbien	adverb [ˈædvɜːb]	happily, easily, well
Begleitsatz (in Berichteter Rede)	report clause [rɪˈpɔːt ˌklɔːz]	*The trainer told* George that he had had the perfect figure for rugby.
Berichtete / Indirekte Rede	reported speech [rɪˌpɔːtɪd ˈspiːtʃ]	George told his trainer how he had wanted to get fit.
Ersatzform (eines Hilfsverbs)	substitute [ˈsʌbstɪtjuːt]	have to, be able to, be allowed to
Fragewort	question word [ˈkwestʃən wɜːd]	who, what, where, which, why
Futur mit *will*	will-future [ˈwɪl ˌfjuːtʃə]	In this Theme you will find glimpses of America's past.
Imperativ (Befehlsform)	imperative [ɪmˈperətɪv]	*Be* punctual. *Don't talk* on the phone.
Indirekter Fragesatz	reported question [rɪˌpɔːtɪd ˈkwestʃən]	The reporter asked *whether there were any human rights issues that involved children.*
Infinitiv (Grundform des Verbs)	infinitive [ɪnˈfɪnətɪv]	go, live, do, be, have
Konditionalsatz (Bedingungssatz)	conditional clause [kənˈdɪʃnəl ˌklɔːz]	If they got a proper school education, they would get a better job.
Modalverben	modals [ˈməʊdlz]	can, can't, must, mustn't, needn't
Nebensatz (mit *if*)	(if-)clause [ˈɪf klɔːz]	*If I hadn't had this training I wouldn't have been able to do this job.*
Negation (Verneinung)	negation [nɪˈgeɪʃn]	You *don't* have to finish your meal if you are full.
Objekt (Satzergänzung)	object [ˈɒbdʒɪkt]	George asked *his trainer questions.*
direktes Objekt	direct object [dɪˌrekt ˈɒbdʒɪkt]	questions
indirektes Objekt	indirect object [ˌɪndɪrekt ˈɒbdʒɪkt]	his trainer
Passiv	passive [ˈpæsɪv]	The animals *are kept* in cages.
Perfekt	present perfect [ˌpreznt ˈpɜːfɪkt]	She *has written* a long text.
Prädikat (Satzaussage)	predicate [ˈpredɪkət]	India *is* different from Europe.
Präsens (Gegenwartsform)	simple present [ˌsɪmpl ˈpreznt]	Who *knows* where the time goes?
Präteritum (Vergangenheitsform)	simple past [ˌsɪmpl ˈpɑːst]	went, knew, asked, was, did
Relativpronomen	relative pronoun [ˌrelətɪv ˈprəʊnaʊn]	who, which, that
Relativsatz	relative clause [ˌrelətɪv ˈklɔːz]	Some of our guests told me that our tour was the part of their holiday *that they enjoyed most.*

Glossary

Deutscher Begriff	Englischer Begriff mit Aussprache	Beispiele
Satzgliedstellung	word order [ˈwɜːd ˌɔːdə]	S P O Kids love burgers. *Kids* love burgers.
Subjekt (Satzgegenstand)	subject [ˈsʌbdʒekt]	
Verb	verb [vɜːb]	
regelmäßiges Verb	regular verb [ˈregjʊlə ˌvɜːb]	ask, asked, asked
unregelmäßiges Verb	irregular verb [ɪˈregjʊlə ˌvɜːb]	go, went, gone
Vergleichsformen (des Adjektivs oder Adverbs)	comparison (of adjectives or adverbs) [ˈkɒmˈpærɪsn]	happy, happier, happiest happily, more happily, most happily
Verlaufsform	progressive (form) [prəʊˈgresɪv ˌfɔːm]	
im Perfekt	present perfect progressive [ˌpreznt ˈpɜːfɪkt prəʊˈgresɪv]	The Been brothers *have been campaigning* against the death penalty since their uncle was sentenced to death.
in der Vergangenheit	past progressive [ˌpɑːst prəʊˈgresɪv]	My mom and dad *were always fighting* at the dinner table.
Verstärkung	emphasis [ˈemfəsɪs]	*Do* come to an end with this!
Vorvergangenheit	past perfect [ˌpɑːst ˈpɜːfɪkt]	He got his nickname after he *had killed* 4,280 buffalo.
Wiedergegebene Aussage (in Berichteter Rede)	reported clause [rɪˈpɔːtɪd ˌklɔːz]	Mr Brown told George that now he would have to put on a lot of weight and gain muscle.
Zeitform (des Verbs)	tense (form) [ˈtens fɔːm]	went, done, will look, is running
Zeitverschiebung (in Berichteter Rede)	tense shift [ˈtens ʃɪft]	Mr Brown told George *that now he would have to put on a lot of weight and gain muscle.*

Language in Focus

Theme 1 ● Figure, food and famine

Say it in English

So kann man…

fragen, ob man glaubt, dass etwas funktioniert.
sagen, dass jemand an einer Erkrankung leidet.

auffordern, seinen Standpunkt zu diskutieren.
sagen, wie eine Idee entstanden ist.

ausdrücken, dass etwas dazu beiträgt, ein Potenzial zu entwickeln.

Do you think these adverts **work**?
The doctor told me that I was **suffering from** anorexia.
Discuss your points of view in class.
The idea came from seeing children walk to school.
Good, healthy food **helps** children **develop their** full physical and mental **potential**.

 ### Remember? Steigerung der Adjektive ● comparison of adjectives

- Um Personen, Gegenstände oder Aktivitäten zu vergleichen, steigert man die Adjektive, die sie beschreiben.

- Alle einsilbigen Adjektive und die zweisilbigen Adjektive, die auf **-le**, **-y**, **-er** und **-ow** enden, werden mit **-er** und **-est** gesteigert.
  fit – fitter – the fittest
  little – littler – the littlest
  hungry – hungrier – the hungriest
  clever – cleverer – the cleverest
  slow – slower – the slowest

- Alle anderen Adjektive werden mit **more** und **most** gesteigert.
  helpful – more helpful – most helpful

 ### Remember? Verlaufsform der Vergangenheit ● past progressive

- Das **past progressive** drückt aus, dass eine Handlung in der Vergangenheit über einen längeren Zeitraum ablief:
  I was always **running** around trying to be the best.

- Du bildest das **past progressive** mit **was/were** + Verb + **-ing**.
  My friends **were** always **talking** to me about their problems.
  My friends **were** not **talking** to me.
  Were my friends **talking** to me?

Language in Focus

 ## Remember? Einfache Vergangenheit oder Verlaufsform? ● simple past or past progressive?

- Für Ereignisse und Handlungen, die in der Vergangenheit liegen und abgeschlossen sind, verwendest du das **simple past**.
  Signalwörter: **yesterday, last week, two days ago, in 1965,** …
- Das **simple past** von regelmäßigen Verben bildest du, indem du **-ed** an den Infinitiv anhängst.
  My daughter started to lose weight when she was 15.
  Die Verbformen der unregelmäßigen Verben musst du auswendig lernen.
  I took her to the doctor.

- Das **past progressive** drückt aus, dass eine Handlung in der Vergangenheit über einen längeren Zeitraum ablief.
  My mom and dad were always fighting at the dinner table.
  Es wird ebenfalls benutzt, wenn man mehrere gleichzeitig ablaufende Handlungen in der Vergangenheit beschreibt.
  While we were eating lunch she was just drinking a bottle of water.

- Die Verlaufsform der Vergangenheit benutzt man auch zur Beschreibung einer Hintergrundhandlung. Die Handlung, die sich hier im Vordergrund abspielt, wird allerdings in der einfachen Vergangenheit ausgedrückt.
  While he was talking to her I found an article about anorexia in a magazine.

While the old man was crossing the road two cars crashed.

 ## Adjektive nach Verben der Sinneswahrnehmung ● adjectives used after link verbs

- Normalerweise benutzt man ein Adverb, um ein Verb genauer zu umschreiben.
  She runs quickly.
  He works well.

- Es gibt aber bestimmte Verben, die mit einem Adjektiv und nicht mit einem Adverb verwendet werden. Dies sind:
  Verben der Sinneswahrnehmung: feel, taste, smell, sound
  Verben des Werdens: get, become
  Verben des Scheinens oder Seins: be, seem, look

  Everything tasted terrible.
  I felt awful.
  George looked so thin.

This flower smells so good!

Language in Focus

 ## Remember? Fragenbildung ● formation of questions

- Fragen in der Gegenwart und in der Vergangenheit werden mit einer Form von „do" gebildet, außer, wenn „be" das Verb im Satz ist.

PRESENT TENSE	PAST TENSE
Do you feel tired?	**Did** you watch the rugby game?
Does he often feel tired?	**Were** you watching the rugby game when the telephone rang?
Are you tired?	
Is he tired?	**Was** he a good rugby player?

Bei Fragen mit Fragewort rückt das Fragewort noch vor **do** oder **does**:
How much did he weigh? **When did** you eat your last pizza?
What did you do? **Why does** she like pizza so much?

Bei Fragen mit **who** als Subjekt braucht man kein **do** oder **does**:
Who told you so?

- In den anderen Zeitformen bildet man mit dem jeweiligen Hilfsverb (**will, have/has**) die Fragen.

PRESENT PERFECT	WILL-FUTURE
Has he played rugby for many years?	**Will** you play again?

 ## Remember? Modalverben ● modals

Modalverben geben zum Beispiel an, ob etwas erlaubt oder notwendig ist. Die meisten Modalverben kannst du nur in der Gegenwartsform benutzen.
Im **past, present perfect** und im **will future** musst du deshalb Ersatzformen benutzen.

a) Fähigkeit: **can / be able to**

	PRESENT	PAST	PRESENT PERFECT	FUTURE
MODALVERB	can	could	–	–
	can't	couldn't	–	–
ERSATZFORM	be able to	was/were able to	has/have been able to	will be able to
	not be able to	wasn't/weren't able to	hasn't/haven't been able to	won't/will not be able to

- Mit **can** und **be able to** drückst du aus, was jemand kann.
  When we visited Germany ten years ago, we **weren't able to** speak German.

- **Could** benutzt du auch für höfliche Bitten und Aufforderungen:
  Could someone open the window, please?

Language in Focus

b) Erlaubnis: **can / be allowed to – mustn't / not be allowed to**

	PRESENT	PAST	PRESENT PERFECT	FUTURE
MODALVERB	can	could	–	–
	can't	couldn't	–	–
	mustn't	–	–	–
ERSATZFORM	be allowed to	was / were allowed to	has / have been allowed to	will be allowed to
	not be allowed to	wasn't / weren't allowed to	hasn't / haven't been allowed to	won't / will not be allowed to

- **Can, mustn't** und **(not) be allowed to** benutzt du, wenn du um etwas bittest, um Erlaubnis fragst oder jemandem etwas erlaubst oder verbietest.
  You **can** swim in the pool but you **aren't allowed to** swim in the lake.

c) Empfehlung: **should / shouldn't**
Hier gibt es nur die Formen **should / shouldn't** bzw. **should have / shouldn't have**.

- Mit **should (not)** drückst du aus, dass etwas deiner Meinung nach (nicht) so sein sollte oder erfragst die Meinung einer anderen Person.
  You **should** be in a good physical condition to play a sport.
  Producers **should** pay good wages.

d) Notwendigkeit: **must / have to – needn't / don't have to**

	PRESENT	PAST	PRESENT PERFECT	FUTURE
MODALVERB	must	–	–	–
	needn't / doesn't / don't need to	–	–	–
ERSATZFORM	has / have to	had to	has / have had to	will have to
	doesn't / don't have to	didn't have to	hasn't / haven't had to	won't have to

- Du benutzt **must** oder **has to / have to**, wenn du sagen willst, was jemand tun muss.
  I **had to** go to the post office yesterday.

- Wenn du sagen willst, dass jemand etwas nicht tun muss, d. h. nicht zu tun braucht, benutzt du **doesn't have to / don't have to** oder **needn't / doesn't need to / don't need to.**
  You **don't have to** finish your meal if you are full.

You must tidy your room!

You don't need to stand up. Please remain seated.

Language in Focus

Theme 2 ● Pages from America's past

Say it in English

So kann man…

sagen, womit man sich beschäftigen wird.

fragen, welche Themen einem noch einfallen, wenn man an etwas denkt.
sagen, in welchem Jahr etwas geschah.
ausdrücken, bis zu welchem Zeitpunkt etwas war.
sagen, an welchem Tag etwas passierte.

In this Theme **you will be dealing with** topics from America's past.
What other topics come to mind when you think of America's past?
Lincoln was assassinated **in** 1865.
By 1860 their number was over 1.7 million.

On 24 October 1929 the stock market collapsed.

 Remember? Das Passiv ● the passive

- Wenn mit einer Person, einem Tier oder einer Sache etwas getan wird, kannst du das durch das Passiv ausdrücken. Man benutzt es dann, wenn nicht wichtig oder nicht klar ist, wer handelt oder gehandelt hat.

  Das Passiv in der Gegenwart bildest du so:
  am / is / are + past participle
  In this Theme topics from America's past **are dealt with**.

  Das Passiv in der Vergangenheit bildest du so:
  was / were + past participle
  In 1927 the first film with sound **was produced**.

  Das Passiv in der Zukunft bildest du so:
  will be + past participle
  We hope that one day worldwide pollution **will be reduced**.

- Wenn du in einem Passiv-Satz die handelnde Person oder die Ursache für etwas nennen willst, musst du sie mit **by** an den Satz anhängen.
  In 1607 the first permanent European settlement in America **was started by** settlers from England.

Language in Focus

  Remember? Die Vorvergangenheit ● past perfect

- Wenn eine Handlung vor einer anderen in der Vergangenheit stattfand und beide Handlungen abgeschlossen sind, drückst du das mit dem **past perfect** und dem **simple past** aus. Die Handlung, die vor der anderen stattgefunden hat, steht im **past perfect**.

- Das **past perfect** bildest du so:
  had + past participle
  William Frederick Cody got his nickname after he had killed 4,280 buffalo.

  Remember? Formen des Futurs ● forms of the future

Es gibt verschiedene Möglichkeiten, Futurformen zu bilden.

I am going to fly to Paris.

Futur mit „going to"
- Wenn man sagen will, was jemand für die Zukunft plant oder beabsichtigt, oder ausdrücken will, dass etwas mit großer Wahrscheinlichkeit passieren wird, verwendet man **going to**.
  Das **going to**-Futur bildest du so:
  Form von **be + going to + infinitive**
  In the picture you can see Charles Lindbergh who is going to fly to Paris.

Futur mit „will"
- Wenn man darüber sprechen möchte, was in der Zukunft wahrscheinlich oder vermutlich passieren wird, benutzt man **will**.
  Das **will**-Futur bildest du so: **will + infinitive**
  In this Theme you will find glimpses of America's past.

Futur mit dem simple present
- Wenn du über einen festgelegten Zeitplan redest, der in der Zukunft liegt, zum Beispiel über einen Fahrplan von Bussen oder Zügen, benutzt du das simple present.
  The bus leaves at 10 pm.   The concert starts at 7 pm tomorrow.

Futur mit dem present progressive
- Wenn du einen Plan für die Zukunft hast, der schon abgesprochen oder arrangiert ist, kannst du auch das **present progressive** benutzen.
  I am taking a gap year before I go to university.

Futur mit „would"
- Wenn du einfach ausdrücken möchtest, was du in der Zukunft gerne machen würdest, kannst du auch einfach **would like to** benutzen.
  After school I would like to work with children.

Language in Focus

Theme 3 ● Human rights and wrongs

Say it in English

So kann man…

jemanden auffordern, über bestimmte Themen mehr Einzelheiten herauszufinden.
fragen, welche Ziele diese Organisationen haben.
fragen, bei was sich jemand engagieren könnte.
ausdrücken, dass etwas der Grund für etwas ist.

Find out more details about one of the human rights **issues**.
Which aims do these organizations have?
What can a person of your age **do to help**?
That's why they go to protest meetings.

 Remember? Bedingungssätze 2 ● conditional clauses 2

- Ein Bedingungssatz der zweiten Form drückt aus, was unter bestimmten Bedingungen geschehen könnte. Es ist möglich, aber eher unwahrscheinlich, dass diese Bedingung eintritt.
  if + simple past   **would/could/might** + infinitive
  If they got a proper school education, they **would get** a better job.

 Indirekte Fragen mit Zeitverschiebung ● reported questions with tense shift

- Wenn du eine Frage wiedergeben willst, die jemand anderes in der Vergangenheit gestellt hat, benutzt du **if** oder **whether** und beachtest die Regeln für die Zeitverschiebung: PRESENT wird zu PAST, und PAST und PRESENT PERFECT werden zu PAST PERFECT. WILL wird zu WOULD.
  "Are there any human rights issues that involve children?"
  The reporter asked **whether** there were any human rights issues that involved children.

When Robinson Crusoe was on the island he wondered if he **would** ever **get** home again.

- Werden Fragen mit Fragewort wiedergegeben, so bleibt das Fragewort stehen.
  "**What** is the motive behind this?"
  The reporter asked **what** the motive behind this **was**.

Language in Focus

Remember? Unregelmäßig gesteigerte Adjektive ● comparison of adjectives (irregular forms)

- Um Personen, Gegenstände oder Aktivitäten zu vergleichen, steigert man die Adjektive, die sie beschreiben.

    The figure in Iran is larg**er than** the figure in Yemen. The figure in China is **the** larg**est**.

- Einige Adjektive, die häufig verwendet werden, haben unregelmäßige Formen.

good – better – best	gut – besser – am besten
bad – worse – worst	schlecht – schlechter – am schlechtesten
little – less – least	wenig – weniger – am wenigsten
little – smaller – smallest	klein – kleiner – am kleinsten
much – more – most	viel – mehr – am meisten (unzählbar)
many – more – most	viele – mehr – die meisten (zählbar)

    Amnesty International has very **little** knowledge about executions in China.

Partizipien zur Verkürzung von Nebensätzen ● participles used for shortening subordinate clauses

- Das **present participle**, das auf **-ing** endet, kannst du benutzen, um Nebensätze, die mit **when, as** oder **while** anfangen, zu verkürzen.

When he thought about what he had done, Leroy White was very unhappy.
Thinking about what he had done, Leroy White was very unhappy.

As he had a lot of time, Leroy wrote to pen friends around the world.
Having a lot of time, Leroy wrote to pen friends around the world.

While he was in prison, Leroy White met a lot of other prisoners.
Being in prison, Leroy White met a lot of other prisoners.

- Mit dem **present participle** kannst du auch zwei Sätze verbinden, die das gleiche Subjekt haben.

For 22 years he had been in prison. He had been awaiting execution.
For 22 years he had been in prison, **awaiting** execution.

Some German pupils wrote to him. They asked him about his life.
Some German pupils wrote to him, **asking** him about his life.

Language in Focus

 Remember? Die ing-Form nach Präpositionen ● -ing-nouns after prepositions

- Wenn du im Englischen ein Verb zu einem Nomen umformen willst, benutzt du die **-ing**-Form.

  Read*ing* **is fun.**

  Sehr oft stehen solche **ing**-Nomen nach Ausdrücken wie **be good at, be bad at, look forward to, be happy about, be afraid of, keep on, dream of, be interested in** …

  They're interested in finding out about government decisions.

 Remember? Besonderheiten bei manchen Nomen ● unusual forms of some nouns

- Bestimmte Nomen werden nur mit Verben im Plural verwendet, weil sie eine Gruppe von Menschen bezeichnen, z. B. **people** oder **the police**.

- Andere Nomen, die eine Gruppe von Menschen bezeichnen, kann man sowohl mit Verben im Plural als auch mit Verben im Singular verwenden, z. B. **family, government, team, staff, firm**. Mit der Verwendung der Pluralform des Verbs drückt man aus, dass die Gruppe nicht als Ganzes betrachtet wird, sondern als Ansammlung einzelner Mitglieder.

  The police are arresting a man.

  Their campaigning started within the family, who were not all on their side.
  The public support the death penalty.

  Man benutzt die Singularform des Verbs, wenn man die Einheit der Gruppe betonen möchte.

  My family is big.

- Bestimmte Nomen (z. B. **information, advice, accommodation, homework**) sind im Englischen nicht zählbar, d. h. man kann sie nicht mit **a/an** verwenden.

  What information do you get? (Welche Information**en** …?)

- Will man eine Menge oder Zahl des Nomens angeben, so sagt man **a piece of** oder **a form of**:

  That's an interesting piece of information.

Language in Focus

Theme 4 ● Living together

Say it in English

So kann man…

sagen, welche Vorstellung man von etwas hat.	**T**hat's my idea of a perfect family.
ausdrücken, dass einem etwas nichts ausmachen würde.	I **wouldn't mind** her having a little job.
sagen, dass etwas ein schwieriges Thema für einen ist.	It **is a difficult topic** for me.
fragen, woher jemand etwas weiß.	**How do you know?**

 Remember? Partizip Präsens und Partizip Perfekt zur Verkürzung von Relativsätzen ● present participle and past participle for shortening relative clauses

- Im Englischen gibt es zwei Partizipien, das **present participle**, das auf **-ing** endet, und das **past participle**, d. h. die dritte Verbform, die bei regelmäßigen Verben auf **-ed** endet.
- Diese Verbformen kannst du auch benutzen, um einen Relativsatz zu verkürzen.

  Some of the sentences (that are) **written** are not true.
  Have you ever experienced an adult **behaving** like a teenager? (Have you ever experienced an adult who behaved like a teenager?)
  He told me of an old man **crossing** the road. (He told me of an old man who was crossing the road.)

 Remember? Das Perfekt ● present perfect

- Du benutzt das **present perfect**, um über Handlungen oder Ereignisse zu sprechen, die in der Vergangenheit begonnen haben und bis in die Gegenwart andauern oder gerade beendet wurden. Oft drückst du damit auch aus, dass ein Ergebnis sichtbar ist.

I**'ve read** this book.	(Es wird betont, dass die Handlung gerade beendet wurde.)
She **has written** a long text.	(Das Ergebnis kann gezeigt werden.)

- Wenn es wichtiger ist, die Handlung selbst oder die Dauer zu betonen, benutzt du das **present perfect progressive**.
  Das **present perfect progressive** bildest du so:
  has/have + been + -ing-Form des Verbs

What **have** you **been doing** all morning?	
I**'ve been preparing** for a maths test.	(Die Dauer der Handlung wird betont.)
I**'ve been living** in London for a year now.	(Die Handlung dauert immer noch an.)

Language in Focus

Theme 5 ● Global Player

Say it in English

So kann man …

sagen, dass etwas eine wichtige Rolle spielt.
ausdrücken, dass etwas früher der Fall war.
sagen, dass man an etwas gewöhnt ist.

sagen, dass man eine Weile braucht, um sich an etwas zu gewöhnen.
ausdrücken, dass man sich in letzter Zeit mit etwas beschäftigt.
fragen, was die Auswirkungen von etwas sind.

Hinduism **plays an important role** in India.
India **used to be** a British colony.
On the film set there are a lot more people than **I am used to**.
It takes a while to get used to their accents.

We have been dealing with American clients a lot **lately**.
What are the effects of child labour and bonded labour?

 ## Used to

- Den Ausdruck „used to" benutzt du, um auszudrücken, was früher, was über einen längeren Zeitraum, oder regelmäßig oder gewohnheitsmäßig der Fall war.

  India used to be a British colony.

- Die Verneinung bildest du mit „didn't use to".

  India didn't use to be a German colony.

 ## Konjunktionen ● conjunctions

- Du benutzt eine Konjunktion, um Sätze oder Satzglieder zu verbinden. Mit Konjunktionen wie **and, but, so** oder **or** verbindest du Hauptsätze.

  They fought battles and conquered parts of northern India.

- Mit Konjunktionen kannst du auch Haupt- und Nebensätze verbinden, z. B. mit **before, because, although, if, when** oder **while**.

  The 4th to 6th centuries are called the "golden age" of Indian history when literature, art and science were of the highest quality.

- Du kannst einen Satz auch mit einem Nebensatz beginnen. In diesem Fall steht die Konjunktion am Satzanfang.

  However, there were, and still are, severe conflicts between Hindus and Muslims.

Language in Focus

 Bedingungssätze 3 ● conditional clauses 3

- Du kennst bereits zwei Arten von Bedingungssätzen. Es gibt noch eine dritte Art, die man benutzt, wenn man über Möglichkeiten in der Vergangenheit reden möchte, die weder Wirklichkeit wurden noch jemals Wirklichkeit werden können.

if-Satz	Hauptsatz
if + past perfect	would + have + past participle

  If I hadn't had this training   I wouldn't have been able to do this job.

  If the boys had been more careful, the vase wouldn't have fallen.

 Relativsätze, bei denen man das Relativpronomen weglassen kann ● contact clauses

- Wenn ein Relativpronomen das Objekt eines Relativsatzes ist, kann man es auch weglassen. Diese Sätze werden **contact clauses** genannt, weil Haupt- und Nebensatz in direktem Kontakt zueinander stehen.
  Some of our guests told me that our tour was the part of their holiday (which) they enjoyed most.

 Das Partizip Perfekt nach *have* und *get* in der Bedeutung von „(veran)lassen" ● the past participle after "have" and "get"

- „have sth done" oder „get sth done" drückt aus, dass man etwas machen lässt, d. h. veranlasst, dass etwas getan wird und man es nicht selber tut. Die Übersetzung lautet meist „lassen".
  have/get + object + past participle
  I don't get my hair done very often.
  Many factory owners have their carpets woven or their fireworks made by children.

- Wenn man ausdrücken will, dass man von jemandem etwas getan haben will, benutzt man „want sb to do sth".
  The boss wants us to finish everything in no time.

  He has his shoes cleaned by a shoeshine boy.

Language in Focus

Theme 6 ● Hopes and dreams

Say it in English

So kann man …

sagen, was für einen wichtig im Leben ist.

ausdrücken, dass es große Veränderungen geben muss.

sagen, wovon etwas beeinflusst wird.

ausdrücken, dass etwas mehr als zweimal so groß ist wie etwas anderes.

Home is **important** to me.

There will have to be big changes to the way we live.

The size of the footprint **is affected by** the CO_2 emissions we cause.

The average US footprint **is over twice as big as** the average in the UK.

 ## Ortsbezeichnungen mit und ohne Artikel ● Place names with and without articles

- Mit ganz wenigen Ausnahmen werden Ortsbezeichnungen <u>ohne</u> Artikel verwendet, z. B. **America, Europe, London**.

    We are building an eco-village in Pembrokeshire, Wales.

- Bei den Namen von Inseln, (z. B. **Tenerife**), einzelnen Bergen (z. B. **Ben Nevis**) oder Seen (z. B. **Loch Ness**) und bei vielen Namen, die aus zwei oder mehreren Wörtern bestehen, (z. B. **Windsor Castle, John F. Kennedy Airport, Victoria Station**) wird auch <u>kein</u> Artikel verwendet.

- Ist aber das erste Wort kein eigentlicher Name, wie z. B. **great** oder **empire**, dann wird **the** verwendet (z. B. **the Great Barrier Reef, the Empire State Building**).

- Man verwendet **the** auch bei Ortsbezeichnungen, die die Wörter **states, republic, kingdom** oder **union** enthalten, z. B. **the United States, the Dominican Republic, the United Kingdom, the EU**.

- Ebenso verwendet man **the** vor den Namen von Meeren, Flüssen, Wüsten und Bergketten oder Inselgruppen (z. B. **the Pacific, the Thames, the Sahara, the Himalayas, the Philippines**.)

- Man verwendet **the** auch vor den Namen von Hotels, Kneipen, Theaterhäusern, Kinos oder Museen (z. B. **the Sheraton, the King's Arms, the Globe, the Odeon, the Tate Gallery**).

- Man verwendet ebenfalls **the**, wenn ein Bestandteil des Namens **of** ist (z. B. **the Great Wall of China, the Houses of Parliament, the Bank of England**).

Words

So funktionieren die Wortlisten

Es gibt alphabetische Wortlisten und Wortlisten nach Kapiteln.

Alphabetische Wortlisten

Wenn du nicht mehr weißt, wo ein Wort zum ersten Mal vorgekommen ist, kannst du es in der alphabetischen Wortliste *(Dictionary English – German)* ab Seite 198 nachschlagen. Dort findest du auch die Wörter aus den einzelnen Projektkapiteln, die Wörter, die in den Optionals vorkommen, die Wörter, die im *Book Stop* ab Seite 110 vorkommen, und die neuen Wörter aus den Randleisten im Buch.
Wörter mit einem ° gehören zu den Texten aus den *Optionals*.
Wörter, hinter denen „BS" steht, sind aus den *Book Stop*-Texten.

Wortlisten nach Kapiteln

Hier siehst du, wie du diese Wortlisten (ab Seite 173) benutzen kannst.

Die Lautschrift zeigt an, wie man ein Wort ausspricht.

Hier findest du die Übersetzungen.

Links stehen die englischen Wörter mit ihrer Lautschrift.

Fett gedruckte Wörter solltest du dir merken.

Theme 1

chase [tʃeɪs] — verfolgen; nachjagen
promise [ˈprɒmɪs] — Versprechen
vision [ˈvɪʒn] — Vorstellung, Vision
reach [riːtʃ] — Reichweite
kingdom [ˈkɪŋdəm] — Königreich
pope [pəʊp] — Papst/Päpstin
break [breɪk] — *hier:* Ausbruch
simple [ˈsɪmpl] — einfach
paint [peɪnt] — malen, streichen
Cherokee [ˈtʃerəkiː] — Cherokee/der Cherokee
nation [ˈneɪʃn] — Nation, Land
reservation [ˌrezəˈveɪʃn] — Reservat
take away [ˌteɪk əˈweɪ] — wegnehmen
tomahawk [ˈtɒməhɔːk] — Tomahawk, Kriegsbeil
caste [kɑːst] — Kaste
religion *(no pl)* [rɪˈlɪdʒən] — Religion; Glaube
increase [ˈɪŋkriːs] — Anstieg, Zunahme
dramatically [drəˈmætɪkli] — dramatisch
kidnap [ˈkɪdnæp] — entführen
couple [kʌpl] — Paar
in order to [ɪn ˈɔːdə tʊ] — um zu
honour [ˈɒnə] — Ehre
migrant [ˈmaɪɡrnt] — Zuwanderer/Zuwanderin
keep [kiːp] — halten; *hier:* unterbringen
cell [sel] — Zelle
criticize [ˈkrɪtɪsaɪz] — kritisieren
African [ˈæfrɪkən] — Afrikaner/in; afrikanisch
living conditions *(only plural)* [ˈlɪvɪŋ kənˌdɪʃnz] — Lebensbedingungen
move [muːv] — umziehen
Native American [ˌneɪtɪv əˈmerɪkən] — amerikanische/r Ureinwohner/in
native [ˈneɪtɪv] — einheimisch, eingeboren
buffalo *(pl* buffalo *or* buffaloes*)* [ˈbʌfələʊ] — Büffel
slave [sleɪv] — Sklave/Sklavin
president [ˈprezɪdənt] — Präsident/in
opening [ˈəʊpnɪŋ] — Eröffnung
loads [ləʊdz] — jede Menge
way *(informal)* [weɪ] — weit(aus)
textile company [ˈtekstaɪl ˌkʌmpni] — Textilunternehmen
Sweden [ˈswiːdn] — Schweden
fall *(AE)* [fɔːl] — Herbst
burnt out [ˌbɜːntˈaʊt] — ausgebrannt, völlig erschöpft
mom *(AE = mum BE)* [mɒm] — Mama
fight [faɪt] — (sich) streiten; (be)kämpfen
dining room [ˈdaɪnɪŋ ˌruːm] — Esszimmer
rush [rʌʃ] — eilen, hetzen

A5

The girl *is painting* her cupboard.
A *nation* is a country, or a large group of people who live in one area, with their own government, culture etc.

They are such a happy *couple*!

A *cell* is a room in a prison where prisoners *are kept*.
People in rich countries normally have better *living conditions* than people in poor countries.

Bilde Verben!
Durch Hinzufügen der Silben "-ate" oder "-ise" bzw. "-ize" an den Wortstamm lassen sich Verben bilden, z.B.

organize / organise
recognize / recognise
illustrate
integrate

Blättere durch ein Lexikon und finde noch mehr Beispiele!

(no pl) bedeutet: Dieses Wort hat keine Mehrzahl.

(only plural) bedeutet: Dieses Wort wird nur oder gewöhnlich in der Mehrzahl genutzt.

(pl) weist auf eine unregelmäßige Mehrzahlform hin.

(informal) bedeutet: Dieses Wort ist umgangssprachlich.

Zu dieser Aufgabe gehören die folgenden Wörter.

Kleine Bilder und Beispielsätze helfen dabei, dir Wörter besser einzuprägen.

Hier findest du wichtige Tipps zur Wortbildung.

(AE) bedeutet: Dies ist die amerikanische Schreibweise bzw. ein Wort aus dem amerikanischen Englisch.

(BE) bedeutet: Dies ist das englische Wort oder die englische Schreibweise eines Wortes, das im Text im amerikanischen Englisch vorkommt.

The English alphabet

[eɪ]	[biː]	[siː]	[diː]	[iː]	[ef]	[dʒiː]	[eɪtʃ]	[aɪ]
a	b	c	d	e	f	g	h	i

[dʒeɪ]	[keɪ]	[el]	[em]	[en]	[əʊ]	[piː]	[kjuː]	[ɑː]
j	k	l	m	n	o	p	q	r

[es]	[tiː]	[juː]	[viː]	['dʌbljuː]	[eks]	[waɪ]	[zed]
s	t	u	v	w	x	y	z

English sounds

Im Englischen spricht man Wörter oft anders aus, als man sie schreibt. Die Aussprache der Wörter wird mit Hilfe der Lautschrift in jedem Wörterbuch angegeben. Man kann so auch neue Wörter richtig aussprechen, ohne sie vorher gehört zu haben.
Die Lautschrift ist eine Schrift, deren Symbole jeden Laut genau bezeichnen.
Hier ist eine Liste mit den Symbolen dieser Lautschrift zusammen mit Beispielwörtern, in denen der entsprechende Laut vorkommt.

Vokale
- [ɑː] arm
- [ʌ] but
- [e] desk
- [ə] a, an
- [ɜː] girl, bird
- [æ] apple
- [ɪ] in, it
- [i] happy
- [iː] easy, eat
- [ɒ] orange, sorry
- [ɔː] all, call
- [ʊ] look
- [u] January
- [uː] boot

Doppellaute
- [aɪ] eye, by, buy
- [aʊ] our
- [eə] air, there
- [eɪ] take, they
- [ɪə] here
- [ɔɪ] boy
- [əʊ] go, old
- [ʊə] tourist

Konsonanten
- [b] bag, club
- [d] duck, card
- [f] fish, laugh
- [g] get, dog
- [h] hot
- [j] you
- [k] can, duck
- [l] lot, small
- [m] more, mum
- [n] now, sun
- [ŋ] song, long
- [p] present, top
- [r] red, around
- [s] sister, class (stimmlos)
- [z] nose, dogs (stimmhaft)
- [t] time, cat
- [ʒ] television
- [dʒ] sausage
- [ʃ] fresh
- [tʃ] child, cheese
- [ð] these, mother (stimmhaft)
- [θ] bathroom, think (stimmlos)
- [v] very, have
- [w] what, word

- ['] Betonungszeichen für die folgende Silbe (Hauptbetonung)
- [ˌ] Betonungszeichen für die folgende Silbe (Nebenbetonung)

Words

Es gibt auch …
… eine Menge Wörter, die im Englischen wie im Deutschen gleich sind (– außer, dass die meisten von ihnen auf Deutsch groß geschrieben werden). Viele von ihnen sprechen wir auch gleich aus.
Du findest viele dieser Wörter auf dieser Seite. Sie sind nicht in den Wortlisten der einzelnen Kapitel, weil sie dir ja nicht neu sind. Bei denen, die ein bisschen anders ausgesprochen werden als im Deutschen, haben wir die Lautschrift farbig hervorgehoben.

action [ækʃn]
air bag [ˈeəbæg]
album [ˈælbəm]
anti- [ˈænti]
aroma [əˈrəʊmə]
arrogant [ˈærəgənt]
astronaut [ˈæstrənɔːt]
audio [ˈɔːdiəʊ]
baby [ˈbeɪbi]
baseball [ˈbeɪsˌbɔːl]
basketball [ˈbɑːskɪtˌbɔːl]
bitter [ˈbɪtə]
blind [blaɪnd]
blockade [blɒˈkeɪd]
bungee [ˈbʌndʒi]
button [bʌtn]
café [ˈkæfeɪ]
cartoon [kɑːˈtuːn]
chat room [ˈtʃætruːm]
collage [ˈkɒlɑːʒ]
college [ˈkɒlɪdʒ]
comic (strip) [ˈkɒmɪk (ˌstrɪp)]
computer [kəmˈpjuːtə]
container [kənˈteɪnə]
cool [kuːl]
demonstration [ˌdemənˈstreɪʃn]
deodorant [diˈəʊdərənt]
design [dɪˈzaɪn]
diabetes [ˌdaɪəˈbiːtiːz]
diesel [ˈdiːzl]
digital [ˈdɪdʒɪtl]
e-mail [ˈiːmeɪl]
extra [ˈekstrə]
fair, unfair [feə, ʌnˈfeə]
fan [fæn]
film [fɪlm]
fit, fitness [fɪt, ˈfɪtnəs]
folklore [ˈfəʊklɔː]
football [ˈfʊtˌbɔːl]
form [fɔːm]
gangster [ˈgæŋstə]

gas [gæs]
global player [ˌgləʊbl ˈpleɪə]
handball [ˈhændbɔːl]
hobby [ˈhɒbi]
home page [ˈhəʊmpeɪdʒ]
hotel [həʊˈtel]
ideal [aɪˈdɪəl]
idiot [ˈɪdɪət]
info, information [ˈɪnfəʊ, ˌɪnfəˈmeɪʃn]
initiative [ɪˈnɪʃətɪv]
installation [ˌɪnstəˈleɪʃn]
interface [ˈɪntəˌfeɪs]
international [ˌɪntəˈnæʃnəl]
Internet [ˈɪntəˌnet]
interview [ˈɪntəˌvjuː]
jeans [dʒiːnz]
karate [kəˈrɑːti]
laptop [ˈlæpˌtɒp]
leopard [ˈlepəd]
live [laɪv]
mama [məˈmɑː]
massage [ˈmæsɑːʒ]
militant [ˈmɪlɪtənt]
million [ˈmɪljən]
mission [mɪʃn]
model [mɒdl]
modern [ˈmɒdən]
moment [ˈməʊmənt]
motor [ˈməʊtə]
multinational [ˌmʌltiˈnæʃnəl]
musical [ˈmjuːzɪkəl]
national [ˈnæʃnəl]
neutral [ˈnjuːtrəl]
normal [nɔːml]
online [ˈɒnlaɪn]
operation [ˌɒpəˈreɪʃn]
park [pɑːk]
party [ˈpɑːti]
patchwork [ˈpætʃwɜːk]
pizza [ˈpiːtsə]
plan [plæn]

planet [ˈplænɪt]
platform [ˈplætfɔːm]
poster [ˈpəʊstə]
propaganda [ˌprɒpəˈgændə]
protest [ˈprəʊtest]
radio [ˈreɪdiəʊ]
reform [rɪˈfɔːm]
rest [rest]
ring [rɪŋ]
routine [ˌruːˈtiːn]
rugby [ˈrʌgbi]
sack [sæk]
saloon [səˈluːn]
science fiction [ˌsaɪəns ˈfɪkʃn]
screenshot [ˈskriːnʃɒt]
sexy [ˈseksi]
shampoo [ʃæmˈpuː]
show [ʃəʊ]
single [sɪŋgl]
slogan [ˈsləʊgən]
snack [snæk]
spandex [ˈspændeks]
star [stɑː]
studio [ˈstjuːdiəʊ]
supermodel [ˈsuːpəˌmɒdl]
symbol [sɪmbl]
system [ˈsɪstəm]
T-shirt [ˈtiːʃɜːt]
team [tiːm]
teenager [ˈtiːneɪdʒə]
tennis [ˈtenɪs]
text [tekst]
toast [təʊst]
tonne [tʌn]
tour [tʊə]
tourist [ˈtʊərɪst]
ultra [ˈʌltrə]
video (clip) [ˈvɪdiəʊ (ˌklɪp)]
villa [ˈvɪlə]
vitamin [ˈvɪtəmɪn]
volleyball [ˈvɒlibɔːl]
website [ˈwebˌsaɪt]

Theme 1 ● Figure, food and famine

I
figure [ˈfɪgə]	Gestalt, Figur	
famine [ˈfæmɪn]	Hungersnot	If many people in a country don't have enough to eat for a long time, you talk about a *famine*.

A1
influence [ˈɪnfluəns]	Einfluss	
celebrity [səˈlebrəti]	Berühmtheit, Star	
peer [pɪə]	Gleichaltrige/r	
nobody else [ˌnəʊbədi‿ˈels]	niemand anderes	The girl is looking at herself in the *mirror*.
but [bʌt]	außer	
mirror [ˈmɪrə]	Spiegel	
spot [spɒt]	Fleck; *hier:* Pickel	
corner [ˈkɔːnə]	Ecke	
sb doesn't care [ˌsʌmbədi ˌdʌzənt ˈkeə]	jdm ist es egal	
be out [ˌbi‿ˈaʊt]	*hier:* ausgehen, weggehen	A *reaction* is the way that you feel or behave as a result of something that happens.
reaction [riˈækʃn]	Reaktion	
avoid [əˈvɔɪd]	meiden, aus dem Weg gehen	to *avoid* = to keep away from somebody or something
go wrong [ˌgəʊ ˈrɒŋ]	schiefgehen	
disappointed [ˌdɪsəˈpɔɪntɪd]	enttäuscht	
next time [ˈnekst‿ˌtaɪm]	nächstes Mal	
expect [ɪkˈspekt]	erwarten, mit etwas rechnen	If you *expect* something you think that it will happen.
fine [faɪn]	in Ordnung, gut	
pick [pɪk]	aussuchen	
last [lɑːst]	*hier:* als Letzte(r, s)	
add up [ˌæd‿ˈʌp]	addieren, zusammenzählen	A change that is produced in a person or thing by another is an *effect*.

A2
effect [ɪˈfekt]	Wirkung, Auswirkung, Effekt	
skincare [ˈskɪnkeə]	Hautpflege	
clear [klɪə]	klar; rein	
range [reɪndʒ]	*hier:* Angebot, Sortiment	
skin [skɪn]	Haut	
sort out [ˌsɔːt‿ˈaʊt]	*hier:* klären	
drop-dead gorgeous *(informal)* [ˌdrɒpded ˈgɔːdʒəs]	wahnsinnig gut aussehend	
achieve [əˈtʃiːv]	erreichen	
visible [ˈvɪzəbl]	sichtbar	
guaranteed [ˌgærnˈtiːd]	garantiert	
cause [kɔːz]	verursachen, hervorrufen	His new *skincare* product *caused* a lot of *spots*.
truth [truːθ]	Wahrheit	
uncover [ʌnˈkʌvə]	aufdecken	uncover ≠ cover
breeze [briːz]	Brise	
get ready [ˌget ˈredi]	sich fertig machen	
goddess [ˈgɒdes]	Göttin	
silky-smooth [ˌsɪlki ˈsmuːð]	seidenweich	*Soap* is a product that you use with water to wash your body.
shaving cream [ˈʃeɪvɪŋ kriːm]	Rasiercreme	
soap [səʊp]	Seife	
twist [twɪst]	drehen	To open a locked door, you have to *turn* the key in the lock.
volume [ˈvɒljuːm]	Volumen	
turn [tɜːn]	drehen	

Theme 1

	rotate [rəʊˈteɪt]	rotieren
	stain [steɪn]	Verfärbung, Fleck
	gain [geɪn]	Erfolg
	leave [liːv]	*hier:* hinterlassen
	mark [mɑːk]	Fleck
	rock *(informal)* [rɒk]	es bringen, ein Supertyp sein
	protection [prəˈtekʃn]	Schutz
	invisible [ɪnˈvɪzəbl]	unsichtbar; verborgen
	confident [ˈkɒnfɪdnt]	selbstsicher, selbstbewusst
A3	have got the looks [ˌhæv gɒt ðə ˈlʊks]	gut aussehen
	looks *(only plural)* [lʊks]	Aussehen
	slim [slɪm]	schlank, schmal, dünn
	shadow [ˈʃædəʊ]	Schatten
	clip [klɪp]	Ausschnitt, Clip
	print out [ˌprɪntˈaʊt]	ausdrucken
	freeze [friːz]	Standbild
	shot [ʃɒt]	Aufnahme, Einstellung
	subtitle [ˈsʌbˌtaɪtl]	Untertitel; *hier:* Bildunterschrift
	especially [əˈspeʃli]	besonders
	have sth done [ˌhæv ˌsʌmθɪŋ ˈdʌn]	etw machen lassen
	retouch [ˌriːˈtʌtʃ]	retuschieren
	fat [fæt]	dick
	stressed [strest]	gestresst
	pressure [ˈpreʃə]	Druck
	keep up [ˌkiːpˈʌp]	aufrechterhalten
	image [ˈɪmɪdʒ]	*hier:* Bild
	bright [braɪt]	hell; strahlend; glänzend
A4	according to [əˈkɔːdɪŋ tʊ]	nach, zufolge
	advertising [ˈædvəˌtaɪzɪŋ]	Werbung, Reklame
	beauty [ˈbjuːti]	Schönheit
	skinny [ˈskɪni]	dünn, mager
	flawless [ˈflɔːləs]	fehlerlos, makellos
	unrealistic [ˌʌnrɪəˈlɪstɪk]	unrealistisch, wirklichkeitsfremd
	respond to [rɪˈspɒnd tʊ]	reagieren auf
	ideal [aɪˈdɪəl]	Idealvorstellung
	change [tʃeɪndʒ]	sich ändern
	point [pɔɪnt]	*hier:* Standpunkt
A5	**eating disorder** [ˈiːtɪŋ dɪsˌɔːdə]	Essstörung
	announcer [əˈnaʊnsə]	Sprecher/in
	program *(AE)* (= **programme** *BE*) [ˈprəʊgræm]	Programm, Plan
	be about [ˌbiˈəˈbaʊt]	handeln von
	listener [ˈlɪsənə]	Zuhörer/in
	grade *(AE)* [greɪd]	Note

You've got the looks!

slim = thin

A *shadow* is an area of darkness you see when something blocks the light.

The man *has* his shoes *cleaned*.

fat ≠ thin

An *image* is an opinion that people have about someone or something.

The girl is *skinny*.

respond to = react

This book *is about* ghosts.

grade (AE) = *mark (BE)*

Theme 1

Words Theme 1

guess [ges]	denken; vermuten	
average [ˈævrɪdʒ]	durchschnittlich	
by the time [ˌbaɪ ðə ˈtaɪm]	bis	
fall (AE) [fɔːl]	Herbst	
burned-out [ˌbɜːndˈaʊt]	ausgebrannt, völlig erschöpft	
plus [plʌs]	hier: überdies	
mom (AE = mum BE) [mɒm]	Mama	
fight [faɪt]	(sich) streiten; (be)kämpfen	
run around [ˌrʌn əˈraʊnd]	herumrennen	
lose weight [ˌluːz ˈweɪt]	abnehmen	
all the time [ˌɔːl ðə ˈtaɪm]	die ganze Zeit	
take control of sth [ˌteɪk kənˈtrəʊl əv ˌsʌmθɪŋ]	hier: Kontrolle über etw gewinnen	
weight [weɪt]	Gewicht	He's got to lose *weight*.
weigh [weɪ]	wiegen	There's a big difference between saying you'll do something and *actually* doing it.
actually [ˈæktʃuəli]	eigentlich, wirklich; tatsächlich	
around [əˈraʊnd]	in der Nähe	
nothing else [ˌnʌθɪŋ ˈels]	nichts weiter	
diet [ˈdaɪət]	Diät halten	
at that stage [ət ˌðæt ˈsteɪdʒ]	zu diesem Zeitpunkt, in dieser Phase	
exhausted [egˈzɔːstɪd]	erschöpft	
energy [ˈenədʒi]	Energie, Kraft	
freezing cold [ˌfriːzɪŋ ˈkəʊld]	eiskalt	
keep [kiːp]	hier: halten	
one day [ˈwʌn ˌdeɪ]	eines Tages	
sick [sɪk]	krank	He is *sick*. He has to *see a doctor*.
see a doctor [ˌsiː ə ˈdɒktə]	eine/n Arzt/Ärztin aufsuchen	
suffer from [ˈsʌfə frɒm]	leiden an	
anorexia [ˌænəˈreksiə]	Magersucht	*Anorexia* is an illness.
take a break [ˌteɪk ə ˈbreɪk]	eine Pause machen	
so that [səʊ ðæt]	sodass, hier: damit	
feel cold [ˌfiːl ˈkəʊld]	frieren	
A6 bulimia [bjuːˈlɪmiə]	Bulimie	If you *go on a diet* and can't stop, you are *suffering from anorexia*.
go on a diet [ˌgəʊ ɒn ə ˈdaɪət]	eine Diät machen	
be obsessed with [ˌbi əbˈsest wɪð]	besessen sein von; verrückt sein nach	
average [ˈævrɪdʒ]	Durchschnitt	
malnutrition [ˌmælnjuˈtrɪʃn]	Unterernährung	
infection [ɪnˈfekʃn]	Infektion, Ansteckung	lose weight ≠ gain weight
gain weight [ˌgeɪn ˈweɪt]	zunehmen	
obsessive [əbˈsesɪv]	zwanghaft	
pale [peɪl]	blass, bleich	
eating binge [ˈiːtɪŋ ˌbɪndʒ]	Essattacke	
induce [ɪnˈdjuːs]	hervorrufen, herbeiführen	
vomit [ˈvɒmɪt]	(sich) erbrechen, sich übergeben	The poor man is seasick and needs to *vomit*.
surprise [səˈpraɪz]	überraschen	

I *guess* I'm lost. Would you please show me the way to my hotel?

Theme 1

A7	approximately [əˈprɒksɪmətli]	ungefähr, etwa	An *estimated* amount is an amount you guess and are not sure of.
	estimated [ˈestɪmeɪtɪd]	geschätzt	
	male [meɪl]	Mann	
	anorexic [ˌænəˈreksɪk]	Magersüchtige/r; magersüchtig	
	within [wɪðˈɪn]	innerhalb	*within* a week = in seven days or less
	contract [kənˈtrækt]	bekommen, sich zuziehen	
	female [ˈfiːmeɪl]	Frau	*female* ≠ *male*
	recover [rɪˈkʌvə]	sich erholen, genesen	
	completely [kəmˈpliːtli]	völlig	
	graphical [ˈgræfɪkl]	grafisch	
	representation [ˌreprɪzenˈteɪʃn]	Darstellung	

	graphics *(only plural)* [ˈgræfɪks]	Grafik	His grandfather *developed* an illness. He is now in a wheelchair.
A8	develop [dɪˈveləp]	*hier:* bekommen	
	at the age of [æt ðiˈeɪdʒ əv]	im Alter von	*at the age of* = aged
	drop [drɒp]	fallen, sinken	
	BBC [ˌbiː biː ˈsiː]	*brit.* Sender	
	fairly [ˈfeəli]	ziemlich, recht	*fairly* = quite
	chunky [ˈtʃʌŋki]	stämmig, untersetzt	
	fat [fæt]	Fett	
	carbohydrate [ˌkɑːbəʊˈhaɪdreɪt]	Kohlenhydrat	
	level [levl]	Niveau; Ebene	
	zilch *(informal)* [zɪltʃ]	null	
	at all [ætˈɔːl]	überhaupt	His *physical* form is not very good.
	physical [ˈfɪzɪkl]	körperlich	
	trainer [ˈtreɪnə]	Trainer/in	
	for a while [fərəˈwaɪl]	eine Weile	
	performance [pəˈfɔːməns]	*hier:* Leistung	
	sponsor [ˈspɒnsə]	Sponsor/in	
	shocked [ʃɒkt]	schockiert, entsetzt	
	put on weight [ˌpʊt ɒn ˈweɪt]	zunehmen	

	gain [geɪn]	bekommen, erlangen	He trained hard to *gain muscles*.
	muscle [ˈmʌsl]	Muskel	
	work out [ˌwɜːkˈaʊt]	ausarbeiten	
A9	go through [ˌgəʊ ˈθruː]	durchgehen	
A10	be missing [ˌbiː ˈmɪsɪŋ]	fehlen	
	score [skɔː]	Punktestand, *hier:* Endergebnis	

	hurt [hɜːt]	verletzt, verwundet	She is *hurt*. Her arm is bleeding.
	New Zealand [njuːˈziːlənd]	Neuseeland	
A11	graphics software [ˈgræfɪks ˌsɒfweə]	Grafiksoftware	
	design [dɪˈzaɪn]	entwerfen, gestalten	She *is designing* a dress.
	ad (= advertisement) [æd, ədˈvɜːtɪsmənt]	Anzeige	

Theme 1

	draw up [ˌdrɔːˈʌp]	aufsetzen; erstellen; abfassen	
	unfit [ʌnˈfɪt]	nicht fit, in schlechter Form	
B1	photographer [fəˈtɒgrəfə]	Fotograf/in	*writer* = author
	writer [ˈraɪtə]	Autor/in	A *chapter* is one of the parts
	chapter [ˈtʃæptə]	Kapitel	that a book is divided into.
	item [ˈaɪtəm]	Artikel; Gegenstand	An *item* is an article.
	unfamiliar [ˌʌnfəˈmɪliə]	unbekannt, nicht vertraut	
	surprise [səˈpraɪz]	überraschen	
	packaged [ˈpækɪdʒd]	abgepackt	
	sack [sæk]	Beutel; Sack	
	frozen [ˈfrəʊzn]	tiefgekühlt	
	similarity [ˌsɪməˈlærəti]	Ähnlichkeit, Parallele	
	be used to [ˌbi: ˈjuːstˌtʊ]	gewohnt sein	
	column [ˈkɒləm]	Spalte	

B2	**plenty** [ˈplenti]	Reichtum, Überfluss	At the bus stop, the people
	queue [kjuː]	Schlange, Reihe	are waiting in a *queue*.
	only [ˈəʊnli]	einzige(r, s)	A *weekday* is a day of the
	night [naɪt]	Abend	week that is not Saturday and
	weekday [ˈwiːkdeɪ]	Wochentag	Sunday.
	bill [bɪl]	Rechnung	
	basic [ˈbeɪsɪk]	grundlegend	
	therapist [ˈθerəpɪst]	Therapeut/in	
	the poor [ðə ˈpɔː]	die Armen	
	fight off [ˌfaɪtˌˈɒf]	ankämpfen gegen	
	throw away [ˌθrəʊˌəˈweɪ]	wegwerfen	The boy is going to *throw*
	throw out [ˌθrəʊˌˈaʊt]	hinauswerfen, wegwerfen	*away* his rubbish.
	billion [ˈbɪljən]	Milliarde	
	yet [jet]	und doch, und trotzdem	
	low-income [ˌləʊ ˈɪnkʌm]	einkommensschwach	A rich person can *afford* to
	afford [əˈfɔːd]	sich leisten	buy expensive things.
	volunteer [ˌvɒlənˈtɪə]	ehrenamtlich	*volunteer* = voluntary
	act [ækt]	handeln; sich benehmen	
	surplus [ˈsɜːpləs]	überschüssig	
	the hungry [ðə ˈhʌŋgri]	die Hungernden	
	food bank [ˈfuːd ˌbæŋk]	Tafel *(Lebensmittelhilfe für sozial Schwache)*	
	unwanted [ʌnˈwɒntɪd]	unerwünscht; *hier:* nicht benötigt	*unwanted* = not wanted
	food outlet [ˈfuːdˌaʊtlet]	Restaurant, Imbiss	
	corporate kitchen [ˌkɔːprət ˈkɪtʃən]	Firmenküche	
	founder [ˈfaʊndə]	Gründer/in	
	organizer [ˈɔːgəˌnaɪzə]	Organisator/in	
	set up [ˌsetˌˈʌp]	*hier:* gründen	
	organization [ˌɔːgənaɪˈzeɪʃn]	Organisation	
	deliver [dɪˈlɪvə]	liefern, ausliefern	The boy *is delivering* pizza.
	need [niːd]	Not	
	across [əˈkrɒs]	*hier:* in	*support* = help that you give
	run [rʌn]	*hier:* betreiben	to someone who is having a
	support [səˈpɔːt]	Unterstützung	difficult time

177

Theme 1

	statement ['steɪtmənt]	Stellungnahme	
	hero (*pl* heroes) ['hɪərəʊ, 'hɪərəʊz]	Held	An *award* is a prize that is given to someone who has achieved something.
	award [əˈwɔːd]	Preis, Auszeichnung	
	findings (*only plural*) ['faɪndɪŋz]	Ergebnisse	*findings* = result
B3	Canadian [kəˈneɪdiən]	Kanadier/in; kanadisch	
	chain [tʃeɪn]	Kette	
	sum up [ˌsʌmˈʌp]	zusammenfassen	*sum up* = make a summary
	production [prəˈdʌkʃn]	Produktion	*Oil* is used for making fuels. Another sort of *oil* is used to make a salad dressing.
	link [lɪŋk]	Verbindung; Link	
	oil [ɔɪl]	Öl	
	natural [ˈnætʃrəl]	natürlich	
	fuel [ˈfjuːəl]	Kraftstoff, Treibstoff	
	fertilizer [ˈfɜːtəlaɪzə]	Dünger	
	chemical [ˈkemɪkl]	chemisch, Chemie-	
	pesticide [ˈpestɪsaɪd]	Schädlingsbekämpfungs- mittel	
	machinery [məˈʃiːnəri]	Maschinen, technische Geräte	
	(farming) seed [siːd]	Saatgut	
	bank [bæŋk]	Bank (Geldinstitut)	
	produce [ˈprɒdjuːs]	Erzeugnisse, Produkte	
	the railway(s) [ðə ˈreɪlweɪ]	die (Eisen)bahn	*the railways* 
	process [ˈprəʊses]	bearbeiten	
	pack [pæk]	(ein)packen	
	corporation [ˌkɔːpəˈreɪʃn]	Unternehmen	*Profit* is the money that you make by selling something after you have paid your costs.
	make up [meɪkˈʌp]	*hier:* bestehen aus	
	turnover [ˈtɜːnˌəʊvə]	Umsatz	
	profit [ˈprɒfɪt]	Gewinn, Profit	
	tractor [ˈtræktə]	Traktor	
	shortage [ˈʃɔːtɪdʒ]	Knappheit, Mangel	
	unfairly [ˌʌnˈfeəli]	unfair, ungerecht	
	chart [tʃɑːt]	Diagramm, Grafik	A *diagram* is a drawing that explains something.
	diagram [ˈdaɪəgræm]	Schaubild	
	visualize [ˈvɪʒuəlaɪz]	sich vorstellen, visualisieren	
B4	gonna (= going to) (*informal*) [ˈgʌnə]	werden	
	pray [preɪ]	beten	
	lean [liːn]	mager	
	wolf (*pl* wolves) [wʊlf, wʊlvz]	Wolf	
	howl [haʊl]	heulen	
	face [feɪs]	sich etw gegenübersehen, konfrontiert sein mit	
	weakness [ˈwiːknəs]	Schwäche	His *stomach* is empty. He wants to eat something.
	stomach [ˈstʌmək]	Magen	
	Lord [lɔːd]	Herr	
	make sb feel [ˌmeɪk sʌmbədi ˈfiːl]	jdm das Gefühl geben, dass ...	If you are *helpless*, you are not able to do anything without help.
	helpless [ˈhelpləs]	hilflos, machtlos	

Theme 1

	be over [ˌbiˈəʊvə]	vorbei sein, aus sein
	prayer [preə]	Gebet
	go together [ˌgəʊ təˈgeðə]	zusammenpassen
B5	campaign [kæmˈpeɪn]	Kampagne, Aktion
	end [end]	beenden
	the United Nations [ðə juːˌnaɪtɪd ˈneɪʃnz]	die Vereinten Nationen
	fight [faɪt]	Kampf, Streit
	annual [ˈænjuəl]	jährlich
	sponsor [ˈspɒnsə]	sponsern
	barefoot [ˈbeəfʊt]	barfuß
	mental [mentl]	geistig; psychisch
	potential [pəˈtenʃl]	Potenzial
	join in [ˌdʒɔɪnˈɪn]	mitmachen bei
B6	sketch (*pl* sketches) [sketʃ, ˈsketʃɪz]	Skizze
	economic [ˌiːkəˈnɒmɪk]	wirtschaftlich, Wirtschafts-
	trade [treɪd]	Handel
	donate [dəʊˈneɪt]	spenden
	politician [ˌpɒləˈtɪʃn]	Politiker/in
	distribute [dɪˈstrɪbjuːt]	verteilen
P2	form [fɔːm]	Form, Art
	all year [ˌɔːl ˈjɪə]	das ganze Jahr (über)
P3	bracket [ˈbrækɪt]	Klammer
	past progressive [ˌpɑːst prəʊˈgresɪv]	Verlaufsform der Vergangenheit
P4	opposite [ˈɒpəzɪt]	Gegenteil
	opposite [ˈɒpəzɪt]	gegensätzlich
	familiar [fəˈmɪliə]	vertraut
P5	How are things? (*informal*) [ˌhaʊ ə ˈθɪŋz]	Wie geht's?
	move [muːv]	umziehen
	honey [ˈhʌni]	Honig
	olive [ˈɒlɪv]	Olive
	bad [bæd]	*hier:* verdorben
	band [bænd]	Band; Gruppe
P6	silent letter [ˌsaɪlənt ˈletə]	stummer Laut
Test results	self-esteem [ˌselfɪˈstiːm]	Selbstwertgefühl
	doubt [daʊt]	*hier:* in Frage stellen
A1	be hard on oneself [ˌbiː ˈhɑːd ɒn wʌnˌself]	hart mit sich ins Gericht gehen

A *campaign* is a series of actions that a person or a group of people do to try and change or stop something.
end ≠ *start*

A *fight* is a situation in which people hit each other.
annual = every year
If you don't have any shoes, you have to walk *barefoot*.

Bilde Hauptwörter!
Durch Hinzufügen der Silben "-hood" an ein Hauptwort oder "-ence" bzw. "-ance" oder "-ness" an den Stamm eines Wortes kannst du weitere Wörter bilden. Schau dir die Beispiele an. Vielleicht fallen dir ja noch mehr Wörter ein?

neighbour	*neighbour**hood***
child	*child**hood***
different	*differ**ence***
ugly	*ugli**ness***
busy	*busi**ness***

This fish is *bad*. It stinks!

If you are *hard on yourself* you expect too much of yourself.

Die Vokabeln aus den OPTIONAL-Teilen findest du im englisch-deutschen Dictionary auf den Seiten 198–241.

Theme 2 ● Pages from America's past

1	Thanksgiving [ˈθæŋksˌɡɪvɪŋ]	Thanksgiving, amerik. Erntedankfest	Americans usually eat turkey at *Thanksgiving*.
	move sb [ˈmuːv ˌsʌmbədi]	*hier:* jdn umsiedeln, vertreiben	

Native American [ˌneɪtɪv əˈmerɪkən] — amerikanische/r Ureinwohner/in
native [ˈneɪtɪv] — einheimisch, eingeboren
buffalo (*pl* buffalo *or* buffaloes) [ˈbʌfələʊ] — Büffel
slave [sleɪv] — Sklave/Sklavin
president [ˈprezɪdənt] — Präsident/in
nuclear bomb [ˌnjuːkliə ˈbɒm] — Atombombe
the Cold War [ðə ˌkəʊld ˈwɔː] — der Kalte Krieg
weapon [ˈwepən] — Waffe
think of [ˈθɪŋk əv] — denken an, sich ausdenken
once [wʌns] — früher, einst
religious [rɪˈlɪdʒəs] — religiös
hunted [ˈhʌntɪd] — gejagt, gehetzt
weary [ˈwɪəri] — müde, erschöpft
chase [tʃeɪs] — verfolgen; nachjagen
promise [ˈprɒmɪs] — Versprechen
vision [ˈvɪʒn] — Vorstellung, Vision
reach [riːtʃ] — erreichen
kingdom [ˈkɪŋdəm] — Königreich
pope [pəʊp] — Papst/Päpstin
manager [ˈmænɪdʒə] — Geschäftsführer/in, Leiter/in

A *president* is the political leader of a democratic country.
the Cold War = the unfriendly relations between the USA and the Soviet Union after the second World War

weary = very, very tired

rival [ˈraɪvl] — Konkurrent/in
originate [əˈrɪdʒəneɪt] — hervorbringen, erfinden
paint [peɪnt] — malen, streichen
dear [dɪə] — Schatz
accent [ˈæksnt] — Akzent
Englishman (*pl* Englishmen) [ˈɪŋɡlɪʃmən, ˈɪŋɡlɪʃmən] — Engländer
alien [ˈeɪliən] — Ausländer/in
legal [ˈliːɡl] — *hier:* mit Aufenthaltsgenehmigung

The girl *is painting* her cupboard.
If the way you pronounce words shows that you come from another place, you have an *accent*.

legal ≠ illegal

glimpse [ɡlɪmps] — (kurzer/flüchtiger) Blick
research [rɪˈsɜːtʃ] — (er)forschen, untersuchen
scene [siːn] — Szene
listening sequence [ˈlɪsnɪŋ ˌsiːkwəns] — Hörsequenz
gallery walk [ˈɡæləri wɔːk] — *Galeriegang*
reading session [ˈriːdɪŋ ˌseʃn] — Lesestunde
onto [ˈɒntə] — auf
sheet of paper [ˌʃiːt əv ˈpeɪpə] — Blatt Papier

She is thinking of a new design and drawing it on a *sheet of paper*.

Theme 2

	display [dɪˈspleɪ]	ausstellen	*individual* = existing separately from other people or things
	individual [ˌɪndɪˈvɪdʒuəl]	einzeln, individuell	
	appropriate [əˈprəʊprieɪt]	entsprechend	
	orientation [ˌɔːriənˈteɪʃn]	Orientierung; Einweisung, Einführung	The guide is showing the *visitors* around.
	visitor [ˈvɪzɪtə]	Besucher/in, Gast	
	Siberia [saɪˈbɪəriə]	Sibirien	
	course [kɔːs]	*hier:* Verlauf	
	further [ˈfɜːðə]	weiter, (noch) mehr	
	south [saʊθ]	nach Süden	
G1	comparison [kəmˈpærɪsn]	Vergleich	
	launch [lɔːntʃ]	Start	
	satellite [ˈsætəlaɪt]	Satellit	
	protest [ˈprəʊtest]	Protest	
	stock market [ˈstɒk ˌmɑːkɪt]	Börse, Aktienmarkt	
	be based [ˌbiː ˈbeɪst]	seinen Sitz haben	
G2	give [ɡɪv]	*hier:* halten	He *is giving* a speech.
	inaugural speech [ɪˌnɔːɡjʊrəl ˈspiːtʃ]	Antrittsrede	
	stock price [ˈstɒk praɪs]	Aktienkurs	
	right up until [ˌraɪt ˌʌp ən ˈtɪl]	noch bis (zu)	They are dressed in a *Wild West* style.
	pub [pʌb]	Kneipe	
	perform [pəˈfɔːm]	vorführen, aufführen	
	Wild West [ˌwaɪld ˈwest]	Wilder Westen; Wildwest-	
G3	form [fɔːm]	Form, Art	
	start a business [stɑːt ə ˈbɪznəs]	ein Unternehmen gründen	
	garage [ˈɡærɑːʒ]	Garage	A *garage* is a building you keep your car in.
	Cherokee [ˈtʃerəkiː]	Cherokee/der Cherokee	
	move [muːv]	*hier:* ziehen	
	west [west]	westwärts, nach Westen	*west* ≠ east
G4	appropriate [əˈprəʊprieɪt]	angemessen; *hier:* passend	
G5	form [fɔːm]	formen; bilden	*Tobacco* is a plant that people smoke in cigarettes or pipes.
	tobacco [təˈbækəʊ]	Tabak	
	the English *(only plural)* [ðiˈɪŋglɪʃ]	die Engländer	
	Japanese [ˌdʒæpəˈniːz]	Japaner/in; japanisch	A *bomber* is a plane that drops bombs.
	bomber [ˈbɒmə]	Bombenflugzeug	
	pilgrim [ˈpɪlɡrɪm]	Pilger/in	
	land [lænd]	landen	
G6	modal verb [ˌməʊd(ə)l ˈvɜːb]	Modalverb	The *government* are the people who control a country and make decisions about its laws.
G7	rewrite [ˌriːˈraɪt]	neu schreiben, umschreiben	
	government [ˈɡʌvənmənt]	Regierung	
	independence [ˌɪndɪˈpendəns]	Unabhängigkeit	A *tax* is an amount of money that you have to pay to the government.
	tax [tæks]	Steuer, Abgabe	
	defeat [dɪˈfiːt]	besiegen	
	elect [iˈlekt]	wählen	
	black [blæk]	Schwarze/r	If you have *the vote* you have the right to elect somebody.
	the vote *(no pl)* [ðə ˈvəʊt]	Wahlrecht, Stimmrecht	

Theme 2/3

G8	past perfect [ˌpɑːst ˈpɜːfɪkt]	Plusquamperfekt, Vorvergangenheit	"Had gone" is the *past perfect* form of "go".
	southern [ˈsʌðən]	südlich, Süd-	
	declare [dɪˈkleə]	verkünden; erklären	
	superpower [ˈsuːpəˌpaʊə]	Supermacht	A *civil war* is a war between different groups of people within the same country.
	by the time [ˌbaɪ ðə ˈtaɪm]	*hier:* als	
	civil war [ˌsɪvl ˈwɔː]	Bürgerkrieg	
	once [wʌns]	sobald; als	
	arms race [ˈɑːmz reɪs]	Wettrüsten	
	come to an end [ˌkʌm tʊ ən ˈend]	zu Ende gehen	*come to an end* ≠ begin
G9	set sail [ˌset ˈseɪl]	in See stechen, auslaufen	
	descend [dɪˈsend]	hinabsteigen	A *lunar module* is a small vehicle used in space which lands on the moon.
	ladder [ˈlædə]	Leiter	
	lunar module [ˌluːnə ˈmɒdjuːl]	Mondlandefähre	
	arrest [əˈrest]	verhaften	

Die Vokabeln aus den einzelnen Projekten sowie aus dem OPTIONAL-Teil findest du im englisch-deutschen Dictionary auf den Seiten 198–241.

Theme 3 ● Human rights and wrongs

I	wrong [rɒŋ]	Unrecht	
A1	right [raɪt]	Recht	*right* ≠ *wrong*
	protest [prəˈtest]	protestieren	
	injustice [ɪnˈdʒʌstɪs]	Ungerechtigkeit	*injustice* ≠ justice
A2	connect [kəˈnekt]	*hier:* in Zusammenhang stehen	
A3	representative [ˌreprɪˈzentətɪv]	(Stell)vertreter/in	
	match [mætʃ]	passen zu; zusammenpassen	His tie and his shirt don't *match*.
	violation [ˌvaɪəˈleɪʃn]	Verletzung, Verstoß	
	around the world [əˌraʊnd ðə ˈwɜːld]	in der ganzen Welt	
	honour killing [ˈɒnə ˌkɪlɪŋ]	Ehrenmord	
	kidnap [ˈkɪdnæp]	entführen	
	murder [ˈmɜːdə]	ermorden	
	caste [kɑːst]	Kaste	
	religion *(no pl)* [rɪˈlɪdʒən]	Religion; Glaube	
	motive [ˈməʊtɪv]	Motiv, Beweggrund	
	by [baɪ]	*hier:* indem	
	honour [ˈɒnə]	Ehre	

By learning the vocabulary you will be well prepared for the test!

involve [ɪnˈvɒlv]	beinhalten, mit sich bringen; betreffen	*involve* = include something as a necessary part
consequence [ˈkɒnsɪkwəns]	Folge, Konsequenz	
case [keɪs]	Fall	
a week [ə ˈwiːk]	in der Woche	
proper [ˈprɒpə]	echt, richtig; *hier:* gut	
recently [ˈriːsntli]	kürzlich, vor kurzem	*recently* = not long ago
government [ˈgʌvənmənt]	Regierung	
criticize [ˈkrɪtɪsaɪz]	kritisieren	
keep [kiːp]	*hier:* unterbringen	
African [ˈæfrɪkən]	Afrikaner/in; afrikanisch	
migrant [ˈmaɪgrnt]	Zuwanderer/Zuwanderin	
emergency [ɪˈmɜːdʒnsi]	Notfall; *hier:* Notaufnahme	
set up [ˌsetˈʌp]	aufbauen	
Canary Islands [kəˈneəriˌaɪləndz]	Kanarische Inseln, Kanaren	
as long as [æz ˈlɒŋ æz]	solang(e)	
violate [ˈvaɪəleɪt]	verletzen	They *are campaigning* for animal rights.
campaign [kæmˈpeɪn]	kämpfen, sich engagieren	
outrageous [aʊtˈreɪdʒəs]	empörend; schockierend	
victim [ˈvɪktɪm]	Opfer	
summarize (= summarise) [ˈsʌməraɪz]	zusammenfassen	
feel [fiːl]	*hier:* halten von	A *declaration* is an official written statement.
declaration [ˌdekləˈreɪʃn]	Erklärung	
in order to [ɪnˈɔːdə tʊ]	um zu	
set out [ˌsetˈaʊt]	*hier:* darlegen	
apply [əˈplaɪ]	gelten; betreffen	A *race* is a group of people who are similar because they have for example the same skin colour.
whatever [wɒtˈevə]	was (auch immer)	
race [reɪs]	Rasse	
sex [seks]	Geschlecht	*sex*: male or female
cultural [ˈkʌltʃrəl]	kulturell	
background [ˈbækˌgraʊnd]	Herkunft, Verhältnisse	
by law [ˌbaɪ ˈlɔː]	gesetzlich	
participate in [pɑːˈtɪsɪpeɪtˌɪn]	teilnehmen an	
by means of [ˌbaɪ ˈmiːnzˌəv]	durch, mit Hilfe von	
election [ɪˈlekʃn]	Wahl	
secret ballot [ˌsiːkrət ˈbælət]	geheime Wahl	
start a family [ˌstɑːtˌə ˈfæmli]	eine Familie gründen	They *are attending* a meeting.
entitled [ɪnˈtaɪtld]	berechtigt	*secure* = guarantee or make sure
attend [əˈtend]	besuchen	
secure [sɪˈkjʊə]	sichern, garantieren	Your *origin* is the country, race or social situation that you come from.
convention [kənˈvenʃn]	Abkommen	
political [pəˈlɪtɪkl]	politisch	
conviction [kənˈvɪkʃn]	Überzeugung	The *freedom of the press* is the right of newspapers and magazines to publish articles without the control of the government.
origin [ˈɒrɪdʒɪn]	Herkunft	
impart [ɪmˈpɑːt]	vermitteln; (mit)geben	
include [ɪnˈkluːd]	beinhalten, einschließen	
freedom of the press [ˌfriːdəmˌəv ðə ˈpres]	Pressefreiheit	

A4 applies to the "victim" row.

Theme 3

	freedom of thought [ˌfriːdəm əv ˈθɔːt]	Gedankenfreiheit	
	freedom of conscience [ˌfriːdəm əv ˈkɒnʃns]	Gewissensfreiheit	The *freedom of religion* means you have the right to believe in any god you want to believe in.
	freedom of religion [ˌfriːdəm əv rɪˈlɪdʒən]	Religionsfreiheit	
	respect [rɪˈspekt]	Respekt, Achtung	You should treat everybody with *respect*.
	correspondence [ˌkɒrəˈspɒndəns]	Beziehung; Korrespondenz, Schriftverkehr	
	no one [ˈnəʊ ˌwʌn]	niemand	People who live in *slavery* are not free.
	slavery [ˈsleɪvəri]	Sklaverei	
	servitude [ˈsɜːvɪtjuːd]	Sklaverei, Knechtschaft	When you *are subjected to* something you are in a situation you don't want to be in.
	be subjected to [bɪ səbˈdʒektɪd tə]	ausgesetzt sein	
	torture *(no pl)* [ˈtɔːtʃə]	Folter	
	inhuman [ɪnˈhjuːmən]	unmenschlich	*inhuman* = not having any pity for someone and being very cruel to them
	degrading [dɪˈgreɪdɪŋ]	erniedrigend, entwürdigend	
	punishment [ˈpʌnɪʃmənt]	Bestrafung, Strafe	The *death penalty* is legal punishment by death.
	death penalty [ˈdeθ ˌpenlti]	Todesstrafe	
	abolish [əˈbɒlɪʃ]	abschaffen	
	condemn [kənˈdem]	verurteilen	*execute* = kill someone as a punishment for a crime
	execute [ˈeksɪkjuːt]	hinrichten	
A5	watch [wɒtʃ]	Wache	
	non- [nɒn]	nicht-	
	governmental [ˌgʌvənˈmentl]	staatlich	*Moscow* is the capital of Russia.
	Moscow [ˈmɒskəʊ]	Moskau	
	activist [ˈæktɪvɪst]	Aktivist/in	
	discrimination [dɪˌskrɪmɪˈneɪʃn]	Diskriminierung, Benachteiligung	
	support [səˈpɔːt]	unterstützen	
	cruelty [ˈkruːəlti]	Grausamkeit	
	wartime [ˈwɔːtaɪm]	Kriegszeit(en)	*wartime* ≠ peacetime
	Council of Europe [ˌkaʊnsl əv ˈjʊərəp]	Europarat	In a *democracy*, people have the right to vote for who runs the country.
	democracy [dɪˈmɒkrəsi]	Demokratie	
	the rule of law [ðə ˌruːl əv ˈlɔː]	die Rechtsstaatlichkeit	He cannot find the *solutions* to the questions.
	promote [prəˈməʊt]	*hier:* fördern	
	solution [səˈluːʃn]	Lösung	
	human trafficking [ˌhjuːmən ˈtræfɪkɪŋ]	Menschenhandel	*Racism* is a way of thinking that shows that you don't respect people who belong to races different from yours.
	racism [ˈreɪsɪzm]	Rassismus	
	violence [ˈvaɪələns]	Gewalt	
	abuse [əˈbjuːs]	Missbrauch	A *refugee* is someone who leaves their country, often because of war, and looks for safety in a different country.
	ensure [ɪnˈʃɔː]	sicherstellen, garantieren	
	movement [ˈmuːvmənt]	Bewegung	
	refugee [ˌrefjʊˈdʒiː]	Flüchtling	
	aim [eɪm]	Ziel, Absicht	
	active [ˈæktɪv]	aktiv	*active* ≠ passive
A6	workshop [ˈwɜːkˌʃɒp]	*hier:* Workshop, Seminar	

	university [ˌjuːnɪˈvɜːsəti]	Universität	The man *is being interrogated*.
	interrogate [ɪnˈterəgeɪt]	verhören, vernehmen	
	force [fɔːs]	zwingen	
	opening [ˈəʊpnɪŋ]	Eröffnung	
	ceremony [ˈserəməni]	Zeremonie, Feier	
	Beijing [ˌbeɪˈdʒɪŋ]	Peking	
	account [əˈkaʊnt]	Bericht	An *account* is a written or spoken report.
	Chinese [ˌtʃaɪˈniːz]	Chinese/Chinesin; chinesisch	
A7	UN (= United Nations) [ˌjuːˈen]	UNO	A *commission* is a group of people that is officially put in charge of something.
	commission [kəˈmɪʃn]	Kommission	
	after all [ˌɑːftərˈɔːl]	*hier:* letzten Endes	
	close [kləʊs]	nah(e)	
	college [ˈkɒlɪdʒ]	Gymnasium, College	
	seek [siːk]	suchen	
	justice [ˈdʒʌstɪs]	Gerechtigkeit	
	dignity [ˈdɪgnəti]	Würde	
	unless [ənˈles]	*hier:* wenn nicht	
	take seriously [ˌteɪk ˈsɪəriəsli]	ernst nehmen	
A8	action [ˈækʃn]	*hier:* Maßnahme, Aktion	
	be involved in [ˌbi ɪnˈvɒlvd ɪn]	beteiligt sein an	Many workers *are involved in* this protest.
	badge [bædʒ]	Abzeichen	
	flyer [ˈflaɪə]	Broschüre	
B1	**aspect** [ˈæspekt]	Aspekt, Gesichtspunkt	
	use [juːz]	*hier:* anwenden	
	carry out [ˌkæriˈaʊt]	ausführen	If you buy three CDs and each one costs five pounds, the *total* is 15 pounds.
	execution [ˌeksɪˈkjuːʃn]	Hinrichtung, Exekution	
	total [ˈtəʊtl]	Gesamtsumme; Anzahl	
	likely [ˈlaɪkli]	wahrscheinlich	
	refuse [rɪˈfjuːz]	ablehnen, sich weigern	
	use [juːs]	*hier:* Durchführung	
	calculate [ˈkælkjʊleɪt]	berechnen	
	minimum [ˈmɪnɪməm]	Mindest-	*minimum* ≠ maximum
	Saudi Arabia [ˌsaʊdi əˈreɪbiə]	Saudi-Arabien	
	Yemen [ˈjemən]	Jemen	
	Belarus [ˌbeləˈruːs]	Weißrussland	
	contain [kənˈteɪn]	enthalten	
B2	front [frʌnt]	*hier:* vorderer Buchdeckel	The judge *sentenced* the woman to nine years in prison.
B3	**death row** [ˌdeθ ˈrəʊ]	Todestrakt	
	sentence [ˈsentəns]	verurteilen	
	murder [ˈmɜːdə]	Mord	
	await [əˈweɪt]	erwarten; warten auf	*await* = wait for
B4	pen friend [ˈpen ˌfrend]	Brieffreund/in	
	extract [ˈekstrækt]	Auszug, Exzerpt	
	create [kriˈeɪt]	erschaffen, erzeugen	*create* = make, produce
	later on [ˌleɪtərˈɒn]	später	If you have a good *relationship* with someone, then you are close and get on well together.
	jealous [ˈdʒeləs]	eifersüchtig	
	relationship [rɪˈleɪʃnʃɪp]	Beziehung	
	ex-husband [ˌeks ˈhʌzbənd]	Ex-Mann	

violent ['vaɪələnt]	gewalttätig	
rage [reɪdʒ]	Wut, Zorn	*rage* = a strong feeling of anger
be high on drugs [ˌbiː ˌhaɪ ɒn 'drʌgz]	mit Drogen vollgepumpt sein	
alcohol ['ælkəhɒl]	Alkohol	
happen to do sth [ˌhæpən tə 'duː ˌsʌmθɪŋ]	zufällig etw tun	
heated ['hiːtɪd]	hitzig, erregt	
fierce [fɪəs]	heftig; stark	It looks like he is going to *shoot* someone.
shoot [ʃuːt]	(er)schießen	
sister-in-law ['sɪstər ɪn ˌlɔː]	Schwägerin	
miraculously [məˈrækjʊləsli]	wie durch ein Wunder	
live through [ˌlɪv 'θruː]	überstehen; *hier:* überleben	
sadly ['sædli]	leider	*sadly* = unfortunately
raging ['reɪdʒɪŋ]	*hier:* rasend	*Jealousy* is a feeling of anger or sadness that you feel towards someone who you think has something better than you do.
jealousy ['dʒeləsi]	Eifersucht	
inability [ˌɪnəˈbɪləti]	Unfähigkeit, Unvermögen	
control [kənˈtrəʊl]	*hier:* beherrschen	
anger ['æŋgə]	Ärger	
crime [kraɪm]	Verbrechen	
take a life [ˌteɪk ə 'laɪf]	jdn umbringen	
change back [ˌtʃeɪndʒ 'bæk]	*hier:* rückgängig machen	
raise [reɪz]	aufziehen; (an)heben; hochziehen	
helper ['helpə]	Helfer/in; *hier:* Unterstützung	
paying ['peɪɪŋ]	rentabel, einträglich	
unhappy [ʌnˈhæpi]	unglücklich	*unhappy* ≠ happy
manage ['mænɪdʒ]	es schaffen	If you *depend on* your friends for your *happiness*, then without your friends you would not be happy.
happiness ['hæpinəs]	Glück, Zufriedenheit	
depend on [dɪˈpend ɒn]	abhängen von	
particular [pəˈtɪkjʊlə]	bestimmt	
lift [lɪft]	(hoch)heben, anheben	
fenced-in [ˌfenstˈɪn]	eingezäunt	
yard [jɑːd]	Hof	
inmate ['ɪnmeɪt]	Insasse/Insassin; Häftling	*inmate* = prisoner
church service ['tʃɜːtʃ ˌsɜːvɪs]	Gottesdienst	
cell [sel]	Zelle	
headset ['hedset]	Kopfhörer	
access ['ækses]	Zugang	
rarely ['reəli]	selten, nicht oft	*rarely* = not often
nowadays ['naʊədeɪz]	heutzutage	
avoid [əˈvɔɪd]	vermeiden	
boredom ['bɔːdəm]	Langeweile	
cooking ['kʊkɪŋ]	Kochen	
dancing ['dɑːnsɪŋ]	Tanzen	They love *dancing*.
daily life [ˌdeɪli 'laɪf]	Alltagsleben	
the most [ˌðə 'məʊst]	*hier:* das Beste	
totally ['təʊtli]	völlig, total	*totally* = completely
partying ['pɑːtiɪŋ]	Feiern	
bet [bet]	wetten	

Theme 3

	guys *(only plural, AE)* [gaɪz]	Leute	
	folk [fəʊk]	Leute	A *lawn* is an area of grass that is cut short.
	lawn [lɔ:n]	Rasen	
	purpose [ˈpɜ:pəs]	Grund; Absicht, Ziel; Zweck	Something that is *lethal* is very dangerous and able to kill you.
	lethal [ˈli:θl]	tödlich	
	injection [ɪnˈdʒekʃn]	Spritze	
	despite [dɪˈspaɪt]	trotz	
	plea [pli:]	Appell	
	spare [speə]	verschonen	
	passage [ˈpæsɪdʒ]	Passage	If you *back* something *up* you find reasons for your opinion.
	back up [ˌbækˈʌp]	unterstützen, bestätigen	
	optimistic [ˌɒptɪˈmɪstɪk]	optimistisch	
	a great deal [əˈgreɪt di:l]	eine Menge, ziemlich viel	*a great deal* = a lot
B5	present participle [ˌpreznt ˈpɑ:tɪsɪpl]	Partizip Präsens	
B6	teenage [ˈti:neɪdʒ]	jugendlich	Your *nephew* is the son of your brother or sister.
	nephew [ˈnefju:]	Neffe	
	debate [dɪˈbeɪt]	Debatte, Diskussion	
	rather than [ˈrɑ:ðə ðæn]	anstatt	*rather than* = instead of
	regulation [ˌregjuˈleɪʃn]	Vorschrift, Bestimmung	The child *is screaming* at his mother.
	within [wɪˈðɪn]	innerhalb	
	scream [skri:m]	schreien	
	run over [ˌrʌnˈəʊvə]	überfahren	
	determined [dɪˈtɜ:mɪnd]	entschlossen	
	Geneva [dʒəˈni:və]	Genf	A *congress* is a kind of meeting.
	congress [ˈkɒŋgres]	Kongress, Tagung	
	participant [pɑ:ˈtɪsɪpənt]	Teilnehmer/in	
	sentence [ˈsentəns]	Urteil; Strafe	A *murderer* is someone who has killed another person.
	murderer [ˈmɜ:dərə]	Mörder/in	
	allow for [əˈlaʊ fɔ:]	einkalkulieren	
	innocent [ˈɪnəsnt]	unschuldig	
	form [fɔ:m]	Form, Art	
	deterrent [dɪˈterənt]	Abschreckung(smittel)	
	plural [ˈplʊərəl]	Plural, Mehrzahl	
	although [ɔ:lˈðəʊ]	obwohl	
	singular [ˈsɪŋgjʊlə]	Singular, Einzahl	
	introduction [ˌɪntrəˈdʌkʃn]	Vorstellung; Einführung	
	talk [tɔ:k]	Gespräch, Unterhaltung; Vortrag	The woman is giving a *talk*.
B7	symptom [ˈsɪmptəm]	Symptom, Zeichen	
	affront [əˈfrʌnt]	Beleidigung, Affront	
	human [ˈhju:mən]	menschlich; Menschen-	
	revenge [rɪˈvendʒ]	Rache	If you *trust* someone, you are sure that they are an honest, good and reliable person.
	save [seɪv]	retten; schützen	
	trust [trʌst]	vertrauen	
	bureaucrat [ˈbjʊərəkræt]	Bürokrat/in	
	collect [kəˈlekt]	*hier:* eintreiben	
	equitably [ˈekwɪtəbli]	gerecht, fair	*equitably* = fair
	pothole [ˈpɒthəʊl]	Schlagloch	A *citizen* is someone who has the right to live permanently in a particular country.
	decide [dɪˈsaɪd]	entscheiden, bestimmen	
	citizen [ˈsɪtɪzn]	(Staats)bürger/in	

Theme 3

author [ˈɔːθə]	Verfasser/in, Autor/in	*author* = writer
prior to [ˈpraɪə tʊ]	vor	*commit* = do something illegal or morally wrong
commit [kəˈmɪt]	begehen	
police lieutenant [pəˌliːs lefˈtenənt]	Polizeihauptwachtmeister/in	
firm [fɜːm]	*hier:* überzeugt	
believer [bɪˈliːvə]	Anhänger/in	If you are a *firm believer* in something then you think that it is the correct or right thing to do.
term [tɜːm]	Amtszeit	
governor [ˈgʌvnə]	Gouverneur	
frustration [frʌˈstreɪʃn]	Frustration	
concern [kənˈsɜːn]	Sorge, Besorgnis	
administration [ədˌmɪnɪˈstreɪʃn]	Verwaltung	A *penalty* is a punishment for breaking a rule or law.
penalty [ˈpenlti]	Strafe	
capital system [ˌkæpɪtl ˈsɪstəm]	System der Todesstrafe	
haunt [hɔːnt]	verfolgen	
demon [ˈdiːmən]	Dämon, Besessene/r	
error [ˈerə]	Fehler, Irrtum	*error* = mistake
determine [dɪˈtɜːmɪn]	ermitteln, feststellen	
among [əˈmʌŋ]	unter; inmitten von	
the guilty [ðə ˈgɪlti]	Schuldige/r	
deserve [dɪˈzɜːv]	verdienen	The girl is happy *because of* the snow.
because of [bɪˈkɒz ɒv]	wegen	
commute a sentence [kəˌmjuːt ə ˈsentəns]	ein Strafmaß herabsetzen	
former [ˈfɔːmə]	ehemalige(r, s), frühere(r, s)	
be supposed to [ˌbiː səˈpəʊst tə]	*hier:* sollen	to *place* something on the table = to put something on the table
place [pleɪs]	legen, stellen	
ahead of [əˈhed əv]	vor	
the gist [ðə ˈdʒɪst]	das Wesentliche; Hauptpunkte	*the gist* = the most important aspect
quote [kwəʊt]	zitieren	
B8 order [ˈɔːdə]	anordnen; ordnen	If you are *racist* then you behave badly towards or dislike people of a race different from your own.
text block [ˈtekst ˌblɒk]	Textbaustein	
sexist [ˈseksɪst]	sexistisch	
racist [ˈreɪsɪst]	rassistisch	
feel sorry [ˌfiːl ˈsɒri]	bedauern	
final [ˈfaɪnl]	letzte(r, s)	
appeal [əˈpiːl]	Einspruch, Berufung	The boy *is taking responsibility* for his dog and taking him for a walk.
forgive [fəˈgɪv]	vergeben, verzeihen	
redemption [rɪˈdempʃn]	Wiedergutmachung	
take responsibility [ˌteɪk rɪˌspɒnsəˈbɪləti]	Verantwortung übernehmen	
couple [kʌpl]	Paar	
application [ˌæplɪˈkeɪʃn]	*hier:* Antrag	
pardon [ˈpɑːdn]	Begnadigung	
decline [dɪˈklaɪn]	*hier:* ablehnen	to *decline* = not to accept
spiritual advisor [ˌspɪrɪtʃuəl ədˈvaɪzə]	*hier:* geistl. Beistand	

	admit [əd'mɪt]	zugeben	*admit* = agree that something is true
	rape [reɪp]	vergewaltigen	
	pardon board ['pɑːdn ˌbɔːd]	Begnadigungskommission	
	hearing ['hɪərɪŋ]	Anhörung; Gerichtsverhandlung	Someone who is given a *life sentence* has to spend the rest of their life in prison.
	life sentence ['laɪf ˌsentəns]	lebenslängliche Haftstrafe	
	life imprisonment [ˌlaɪf ɪm'prɪznmənt]	lebenslängliche Haftstrafe	A *jury* is a group of people who judge a court case.
	jury ['dʒʊəri]	Geschworene	
	lawyer ['lɔːjə]	Rechtsanwalt/-anwältin	
	burial ['beriəl]	Beerdigung	
	bubble [bʌbl]	Blase	
	Roman Catholic [ˌrəʊmən 'kæθlɪk]	römisch-katholisch	"To be or not to be" is a famous Shakespeare *quotation*.
B9	quotation [kwəʊ'teɪʃn]	Zitat	
	pick on sb ['pɪk ɒn ˌsʌmbədi]	auf jdm herumhacken	
	'em (= them) *(informal)* [əm]	sie, ihnen	
	beat up [ˌbiːt 'ʌp]	verprügeln	
	figure out sth *(informal)* [ˌfɪɡər 'aʊt ˌsʌmθɪŋ]	etw herausfinden	If you move your head up and down to show that you agree with something then you *nod*.
	nod [nɒd]	nicken	
	scum [skʌm]	Abschaum; Mistkerl	
	god [ɡɒd]	Gott	
	human being [ˌhjuːmən 'biːɪŋ]	Mensch	
B10	unit ['juːnɪt]	Einheit, Abteilung	
	pay attention to [ˌpeɪ ə'tenʃn tə]	achten auf	
	banner ['bænə]	Transparent, Spruchband	
	think of ['θɪŋk əv]	*hier:* halten von	
P1	be based [ˌbi 'beɪst]	seinen Sitz haben	
P4	Spain ['speɪn]	Spanien	
	Greece [ɡriːs]	Griechenland	
P5	shorten ['ʃɔːtn]	(ver)kürzen	
P6	look forward to doing sth [ˌlʊk 'fɔːwəd tə ˌduːɪŋ sʌmθɪŋ]	sich darauf freuen, etw zu tun	
P7	power ['paʊə]	Macht, Einfluss	
	check in [ˌtʃek 'ɪn]	einchecken; sich (an der Rezeption) anmelden	

Bilde Adjektive!
Durch Hinzufügen der Silben "-ble", "-ic(al)", "-y" oder "-ist" an den Stamm eines Wortes kannst du Adjektive bilden.

terri**ble**	happ**y**
relia**ble**	guilt**y**
spiritu**al**	sex**ist**
feder**al**	rac**ist**

Das funktioniert auch mit anderen Silben, z.B. "-ive", "-less", "-ous" oder "-ful". Finde Beispiele!

Die Vokabeln aus den OPTIONAL-Teilen findest du im englisch-deutschen Dictionary auf den Seiten 198–241.

Theme 4 ● Living together

I	role [rəʊl]	Rolle	
	arranged [əˈreɪndʒd]	arrangiert	When someone is laughing, you hear *laughter*.
	laughter [ˈlɑːftə]	Gelächter, Lachen	
	model [ˈmɒdl]	Modell	to *represent* = to be an example of something
	represent [ˌrepriˈzent]	repräsentieren; darstellen	
	remaining [rɪˈmeɪnɪŋ]	übrig, restlich	
	granddaughter [ˈɡrænˌdɔːtə]	Enkelin	
	single [ˈsɪŋɡl]	allein erziehend	
	blended [ˈblendɪd]	hier: Patchwork-	A *nightmare* is a very frightening or bad dream.
	nightmare [ˈnaɪtˌmeə]	Albtraum	
	adopted [əˈdɒptɪd]	adoptiert	
	traditional [trəˈdɪʃnəl]	traditionell	This is the *traditional type* of clothing for Scottish men.
	type [taɪp]	Art	
	extended [ɪkˈstendɪd]	erweitert	
	co-housing [kəʊ ˈhaʊzɪŋ]	gemeinschaftliches Wohnen	
	presentation [ˌpreznˈteɪʃn]	Präsentation, Vortrag	
	literary [ˈlɪtrəri]	Literatur-	
	open day [ˈəʊpən deɪ]	Tag der offenen Tür	
G1	stress [stres]	Betonung, Akzent	
	syllable [ˈsɪləbəl]	Silbe	
G2	future [ˈfjuːtʃə]	zukünftig	If a couple are *well-suited*, then they are likely to have a good relationship.
	well-suited [ˌwelˈsuːt ɪd]	gut zusammenpassend	
G3	exchange [ɪksˈtʃeɪndʒ]	austauschen	
	tense [tens]	Zeitform, Tempus	
	shift [ʃɪft]	Verschiebung	A *millionaire* has got lots of money.
G4	millionaire [ˌmɪljəˈneə]	Millionär/in	
G5	burger bar [ˈbɜːɡə bɑː]	Schnellimbiss	
	hopefully [ˈhəʊpfli]	hoffentlich	
G8	participle [ˈpɑːtɪsɪpl]	Partizip	
	princess [ˌprɪnˈses]	Prinzessin	A *pond* is an area of water similar to a lake but smaller.
	pond [pɒnd]	Teich	
	frog [frɒɡ]	Frosch	
	bottom [ˈbɒtəm]	Boden	
	cast a spell on sb [ˌkɑːst ə ˈspel ɒn ˌsʌmbədi]	jdn verzaubern	A *chat-up line* is something you can say to a boy or girl you like to start a conversation and show that you like them.
	frog's leg [ˈfrɒɡz ˌleɡ]	Froschschenkel	
G9	present [ˈpreznt]	jetzig, gegenwärtig	
G10	chat-up line [ˈtʃætʌp ˌlaɪn]	Anmache, Anmachspruch	
G11	be out of breath [bi ˌaʊt əʊ ˈbreθ]	außer Atem sein	
	jog [dʒɒɡ]	joggen	
	snow [snəʊ]	schneien	It *is snowing*.
	voice [vɔɪs]	Stimme	
G12	ending [ˈendɪŋ]	hier: Endung	
	resistance [rɪˈzɪstəns]	Widerstand	

Die Vokabeln aus den Projekten findest du im englisch-deutschen Dictionary auf den Seiten 198–241.

Theme 5 ● Global Player

I	sweatshop [ˈswetʃɒp]	Ausbeuterbetrieb	
A1	sound [saʊnd]	Geräusch, Klang	
	caption [ˈkæpʃn]	Bildunterschrift	If something is *sacred* then it is considered connected to God in a special way or holy.
	auto rickshaw [ˈɔːtəʊ ˌrɪkʃɔː]	Autoriksha	
	cricket [ˈkrɪkɪt]	Kricket	
	sacred [ˈseɪkrɪd]	heilig	
	Calcutta [kælˈkʌtə]	Kalkutta	*Calcutta* is a city in India.
	industry [ˈɪndəstri]	Industrie	*Courage* is being able to do something that you know is right or good although it is dangerous or very difficult.
A2	**flag** [flæg]	Fahne, Flagge	
	stand for [ˈstænd fɔː]	bedeuten, stehen für	
	courage [ˈkʌrɪdʒ]	Mut, Tapferkeit	
	faith [feɪθ]	Vertrauen; Glaube	
	yearly [ˈjɪəli]	jährlich	If you measure the *yearly rainfall* you measure the amount of rain that has fallen in a year.
	rainfall [ˈreɪnfɔːl]	Niederschlag	
	colony [ˈkɒləni]	Kolonie	
	independent [ˌɪndɪˈpendənt]	unabhängig, selbständig	A *colony* is a country that is controlled by another country.
	Hinduism [ˈhɪnduˌɪzm]	Hinduismus	
	Hindu [ˌhɪnˈduː]	Hindu; hinduistisch, Hindu-	
	eternal [ɪˈtɜːnl]	ewig, immer während	
	leader [ˈliːdə]	*hier:* Führer/in	A *leader* is responsible for a group, organization or country.
	nationalist [ˈnæʃnəlɪst]	nationalistisch	
	rule [ruːl]	Herrschaft	
	not only ... but also [ˌnɒt ˌəʊnli ˌbʌt ˌɔːlsəʊ]	nicht nur ..., sondern auch ...	
	producer [prəˈdjuːsə]	Produzent/in	
	Diwali [dɪˈwɑːli]	*Lichterfest*	
	official [əˈfɪʃl]	offiziell	
	pyjamas *(only plural)* [pəˈdʒɑːməz]	Schlafanzug	He is wearing his *pyjamas*.
	outdoors [ˌaʊtˈdɔːz]	im Freien, draußen	
	import [ɪmˈpɔːt]	importieren	*import* ≠ export
	sleepwear [ˈsliːpweə]	Schlafkleidung	
	garment [ˈgɑːmənt]	Kleidungsstück	*garment* = item of clothing
	string instrument [ˌstrɪŋ ˈɪnstrʊmənt]	Saiteninstrument	
	well-known [ˌwelˈnəʊn]	(allgemein) bekannt; berühmt	*well-known* = known by many people
	Asian [ˈeɪʒn]	Asiate/Asiatin; asiatisch	
	Bengal [ˌbenˈgɔːl]	Bengale/Bengalin; bengalisch	
	rhinoceros (*pl* rhinoceros *or* rhinoceroses) [raɪˈnɒsərəs, raɪˈnɒsərəs, raɪˈnɒsərəsɪz]	Nashorn	
	industry [ˈɪndəstri]	Industrie	
	be left [biː ˈleft]	übrig bleiben	
A3	**civilization** [ˌsɪvlaɪˈzeɪʃn]	Zivilisation, Kultur	The cake *has been divided into* three pieces.
	brick [brɪk]	Ziegel, Backstein	
	divide into [dɪˈvaɪd ˌɪntʊ]	(auf)teilen in	
	period [ˈpɪəriəd]	Zeitspanne, Zeitraum	

Theme 5

wealth [welθ]	Reichtum	wealth ≠ poverty
Macedonia [ˌmæsɪˈdəʊnɪə]	Makedonien, Mazedonien	
battle [ˈbætl]	Kampf; Schlacht	
conquer [ˈkɒŋkə]	erobern, besiegen	Hamburg and Kiel are cities in *northern* Germany.
northern [ˈnɔːðən]	Nord-, nördlich	
the Roman Empire [ðə ˌrəʊmənˈempaɪə]	das Römische Reich	

Roman [ˈrəʊmən]	Römer/in; römisch
empire [ˈempaɪə]	Imperium, Reich
silver [ˈsɪlvə]	Silber
pearl [pɜːl]	Perle
spice [spaɪs]	Gewürz
silk [sɪlk]	Seide
ivory [ˈaɪvəri]	Elfenbein

An elephant's tusk is made of a type of bone called *ivory*.

major [ˈmeɪdʒə]	bedeutend, wichtig; hier: Haupt-
reincarnation [ˌriːˌɪnkɑːˈneɪʃn]	Reinkarnation, Wiedergeburt
appear [əˈpɪə]	(er)scheinen; auftauchen

If someone *appears* somewhere you see them suddenly for the first time.

golden [ˈgəʊldən]	aus Gold, golden
age [eɪdʒ]	Zeitalter, Ära
literature [ˈlɪtrətʃə]	Literatur
Muslim [ˈmʊzlɪm]	Moslem/in; moslemisch
practise [ˈpræktɪs]	hier: ausüben
severe [sɪˈvɪə]	schwer, schlimm; heftig

A *severe* problem is very serious.

conflict [ˈkɒnflɪkt]	Konflikt
Portuguese [ˌpɔːtʃʊˈgiːz]	Portugiese/Portugiesin; portugiesisch
sailor [ˈseɪlə]	Matrose, Seemann

A *sailor* works on a boat or a ship.

colonist [ˈkɒlənɪst]	Kolonist/in; Siedler/in
Denmark [ˈdenmɑːk]	Dänemark
the Netherlands [ðə ˈneðələndz]	die Niederlande
take [teɪk]	hier: übernehmen
control [kənˈtrəʊl]	Kontrolle
empress [ˈemprəs]	Kaiserin
salt [sɔːlt]	Salz
march [mɑːtʃ]	Marsch
tax [tæks]	Steuer, Abgabe
independence [ˌɪndɪˈpendəns]	Unabhängigkeit
fort [fɔːt]	Fort, Festung
military [ˈmɪlɪtəri]	Militär-
camp [kæmp]	(Zelt)lager
republic [rɪˈpʌblɪk]	Republik
single [ˈsɪŋgl]	einzige(r, s)
unified [ˈjuːnɪfaɪd]	einheitlich, vereint
warn [wɔːn]	warnen, ermahnen
integrate [ˈɪntɪgreɪt]	integrieren
perish [ˈperɪʃ]	sterben; untergehen; hier: verschwinden

Bilde Verben!
Durch Hinzufügen der Silben "-ate" oder "-ise" bzw. "-ize" an den Wortstamm lassen sich Verben bilden, z.B.

organize / *organise*
recognize / *recognise*
illustrate
integrate

Blättere durch ein Lexikon und finde noch mehr Beispiele!

perish = die

Theme 5

	permanent ['pɜːmənənt]	permanent, ständig	
	Kashmir [ˌkæʃˈmɪə]	Kaschmir	
	underground [ˌʌndəˈɡraʊnd]	unterirdisch	*underground* = below the surface of the ground
	nuclear [ˈnjuːklɪə]	Atom-	
	so-called [ˈsəʊ kɔːld]	so genannt	
	populous [ˈpɒpjʊləs]	bevölkerungsreich	If you live in *poverty* then you do not have enough money to pay for your day-to-day needs.
	power [ˈpaʊə]	Macht, Einfluss	
	South Asia [ˌsaʊθ ˈeɪʒə]	Südasien	
	poverty [ˈpɒvəti]	Armut	
	illiteracy [ɪˈlɪtərəsi]	Analphabetentum	
	corruption [kəˈrʌpʃn]	Korruption, Bestechung	
	public health [ˌpʌblɪk ˈhelθ]	Volksgesundheit	
A5	**guide** [ɡaɪd]	Fremdenführer/in	
	reality [riˈæləti]	Realität, Wirklichkeit	If you go on an *exchange* you stay with a family in a foreign country, and your exchange partner comes to your country to stay with you, too. If you notice something happening you *observe* it.
	travel [ˈtrævl]	Reisen	
	extensive [ɪkˈstensɪv]	weit; *hier:* umfangreich	
	contact [ˈkɒntækt]	Kontakt, Verbindung	
	exchange [ɪksˈtʃeɪndʒ]	Austausch	
	observe [əbˈzɜːv]	beobachten	
	encourage [ɪnˈkʌrɪdʒ]	Mut machen, ermutigen	
	milk [mɪlk]	melken	
	plough [plaʊ]	pflügen	
	fish [fɪʃ]	fischen, angeln	
	gain experience [ˌɡeɪn ɪkˈspɪəriəns]	Erfahrungen sammeln	
	abroad [əˈbrɔːd]	(im/ins) Ausland	When you successfully finish your studies at university you *graduate*.
	graduate [ˈɡrædʒueɪt]	seinen Abschluss machen	
	intern [ˈɪntɜːn]	Praktikant/in	
	set [set]	*hier:* Drehort	
	dirt [dɜːt]	Schmutz, Dreck	
	damaged [ˈdæmɪdʒd]	beschädigt	He wishes that he had a more exciting method of *transport*.
	transport [ˈtrænspɔːt]	Transport; Verkehrsmittel	
	packed [pækt]	voll	
	joke [dʒəʊk]	Spaß, Witz	
	be used to [ˌbi ˈjuːst tʊ]	gewohnt sein	
	otherwise [ˈʌðəwaɪz]	sonst, ansonsten	
	in terms of … [ɪn ˈtɜːmz əv]	was … angeht	
	while [waɪl]	Weile	
	get used to [ˌɡet ˈjuːst tʊ]	sich gewöhnen an	
	call centre [ˈkɔːlsentər]	Callcenter	
	remind sb [rɪˈmaɪnd ˌsʌmbədi]	jdn erinnern	If you do not have any money in your purse, you can make your *payment* with a *credit card*.
	credit card [ˈkredɪt kɑːd]	Kreditkarte	
	payment [ˈpeɪmənt]	Zahlung	
	client [ˈklaɪənt]	Kunde/Kundin	
	lately [ˈleɪtli]	kürzlich, in letzter Zeit	*lately* = not long ago
	suffer [ˈsʌfə]	erleiden, ertragen	
	recent [ˈriːsnt]	kürzlich; neueste; jüngste	
	financial [faɪˈnænʃl]	finanziell	*financial* = involving money

Theme 5

	crisis (*pl* crises) ['kraɪsɪs, 'kraɪsiːz]	Krise
	colleague ['kɒliːg]	Kollege/Kollegin
	educated ['edjukeɪtɪd]	(gut) ausgebildet
	downside ['daʊnsaɪd]	Kehrseite, Schattenseite
	paradise ['pærədaɪs]	Paradies
	high-paying [ˌhaɪ'peɪɪŋ]	hochbezahlt
	be scared of [ˌbiː 'skeəd ˌɒv]	Angst haben vor
	empathy ['empəθi]	Einfühlungsvermögen
	patience ['peɪʃns]	Geduld
	business ['bɪznəs]	Geschäft
	everyday ['evrideɪ]	alltäglich
A6	leave out [ˌliːv ˈaʊt]	auslassen, weglassen
A7	divide up [dɪˌvaɪd ˈʌp]	aufteilen
	globalization [ˌgləʊbəlaɪˈzeɪʃn]	Globalisierung
B1	label ['leɪbl]	Etikett; Marke
	Cambodia [kæmˈbəʊdiə]	Kambodscha
	cotton ['kɒtn]	Baumwolle
	sleeve [sliːv]	Ärmel
B2	group [gruːp]	gruppieren
	heading ['hedɪŋ]	Überschrift
	else [els]	sonst
	shopping ['ʃɒpɪŋ]	Einkaufen
	up to date [ˌʌp tʊ 'deɪt]	auf dem neuesten Stand
	awesome ['ɔːsm]	spitze, super
	elsewhere [ˌelsˈweə]	woanders, anderswo
	get sth done [ˌget ˌsʌmθɪŋ 'dʌn]	etw machen lassen
	refugee camp [ˌrefjʊˈdʒiː kæmp]	Flüchtlingslager
	textile factory ['tekstaɪl ˌfæktri]	Textilfabrik
	by candlelight [baɪ 'kændllaɪt]	bei Kerzenlicht
	poor [pɔː]	*hier:* unzureichend, mangelhaft; schlecht
	bead [biːd]	Perle
	sew [səʊ]	nähen
B3	textile company ['tekstaɪl ˌkʌmpni]	Textilunternehmen
	manager ['mænɪdʒə]	Geschäftsführer/in, Leiter/in
	US [juːˈes]	die USA
	cotton farming ['kɒtn ˌfɑːmɪŋ]	Baumwollanbau
	fabric ['fæbrɪk]	Stoff
	mainly ['meɪnli]	hauptsächlich, in erster Linie
	Asia ['eɪʒə]	Asien
	low [ləʊ]	niedrig

An *educated* person has had a good education and knows a lot.

If you want to catch a fish you need a lot of *patience* because it can take hours!

The *label* tells you the size of the shirt.

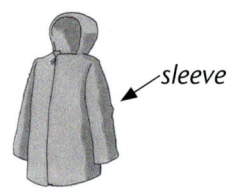

elsewhere = somewhere else

If you do something *by candlelight* then you have lit a candle.

Most clothes are made in *textile companies* using machines.

Another word for "*fabric*" is "cloth".

low ≠ *high*

	down [daʊn]	unten
	cut out [ˌkʌt ˈaʊt]	ausschneiden
	buyer [ˈbaɪə]	Käufer/in
	ship [ʃɪp]	verschiffen, transportieren
	load [ləʊd]	(auf)laden
	cost [kɒst]	Preis, Kosten
	consider [kənˈsɪdə]	*hier:* bedenken, berücksichtigen
B4	**child labour** [ˈtʃaɪld ˌleɪbə]	Kinderarbeit
	retailer [ˈriːteɪlə]	Einzelhändler/in
	turnaround [ˈtɜːnəˌraʊnd]	Bearbeitungszeit, Lieferzeit
	ethical [ˈeθɪkl]	ethisch
	shop [ʃɒp]	einkaufen
	benefit [ˈbenɪfɪt]	profitieren
	developing world *(no pl)* [dɪˈveləpɪŋ ˌwɜːld]	Entwicklungsländer
	standard of living [ˌstændəd əv ˈlɪvɪŋ]	Lebensstandard
	official [əˈfɪʃl]	Amtsperson
	developing country [dɪˈveləpɪŋ ˌkʌntri]	Entwicklungsland
	proper [ˈprɒpə]	echt, richtig; *hier:* gut
	working conditions [ˈwɜːkɪŋ kənˌdɪʃnz]	Arbeitsbedingungen
	properly [ˈprɒpəli]	anständig
	root [ruːt]	Wurzel
	flexible [ˈfleksəbl]	flexibel, anpassungsfähig
	direct [daɪˈrekt]	direkt
	comparison [kəmˈpærɪsn]	Vergleich
	claim [kleɪm]	behaupten
B5	agree with [əˈɡriː wɪð]	einer Meinung sein mit
	argue [ˈɑːɡjuː]	*hier:* argumentieren
	certain [ˈsɜːtn]	gewiss, bestimmt
B6	**pay** [peɪ]	Lohn, Gehalt
	rely on [rɪˈlaɪ ɒn]	*hier:* angewiesen sein auf
	extra [ˈekstrə]	zusätzlich
	common [ˈkɒmən]	üblich, gewöhnlich
	bonded labour [ˌbɒndɪd ˈleɪbə]	Knechtschaft
	slavery [ˈsleɪvəri]	Sklaverei
	be in practice [ˌbiː ɪn ˈpræktɪs]	praktizieren
	ban [bæn]	verbieten; ausschließen
	income [ˈɪnkʌm]	Einkommen, Lohn
	escape [ɪˈskeɪp]	fliehen; entkommen
B7	e.g. [ˌiː ˈdʒiː]	z.B.
P5	**relative pronoun** [ˌrelətɪv ˈprəʊnaʊn]	Relativpronomen

analyse (= analyze) [ˈænəlaɪz]
analysieren, untersuchen

When young children are made to work long hours for little money we talk of *child labour*.

The *standard of living* is often lower in the *developing world* than in the Western world because they often do not have as much money there.

The *root* of a plant is the part that grows under the ground.
If you make a *comparison*, you compare two or more things or people.
agree with = be of the same opinion

Your *pay* is how much money you get for doing your job.

Someone who lives in *slavery* is not free.

escape = get away from a place where you are in danger
e.g. = for example

Theme 5/6

P6	preposition [ˌprepəˈzɪʃn]	Verhältniswort, Präposition	"Gone" is the *past participle* of "go".
P7	past participle [ˌpɑːst ˈpɑːtɪsɪpl]	Partizip Perfekt	

> Die Vokabeln aus den OPTIONAL-Teilen findest du im englisch-deutschen Dictionary auf den Seiten 198–241.

Theme 6 ● Hopes and dreams

I	bit [bɪt]	Stück; Teil	Your *starting point* is the point from where you begin to do something.
	contribution [ˌkɒntrɪˈbjuːʃn]	Beitrag	
	starting point [ˈstɑːtɪŋ ˌpɔɪnt]	Ausgangspunkt	
	various [ˈveərɪəs]	verschieden	to *aim* = to hope to achieve something
	aim [eɪm]	zielen; anstreben	
	artistic [ɑːˈtɪstɪk]	kreativ, künstlerisch	
	display [dɪˈspleɪ]	Ausstellung	
	sculpture [ˈskʌlptʃə]	Bildhauerei, Skulptur	
	sound [saʊnd]	Geräusch, Klang	Someone who is *creative* has a lot of new ideas and imagination.
	land art [ˈlænd ˌɑːt]	Kunstform	
	creative [kriˈeɪtɪv]	kreativ, schöpferisch	
G1	complain [kəmˈpleɪn]	klagen, sich beklagen	
	text [tekst]	(jdm) eine SMS senden	
	pay a compliment [ˌpeɪ ə ˈkɒmplɪmənt]	ein Kompliment machen	If you *pay* someone *a compliment*, you say something nice to them.
G3	reduce [rɪˈdjuːs]	verringern, reduzieren	
	carbon footprint [ˈkɑːbən ˌfʊtprɪnt]	CO_2-Fußabdruck	*Global warming* is the slow increase in the temperature of the Earth.
	global warming [ˌɡləʊbl ˈwɔːmɪŋ]	Erwärmung der Erdatmosphäre	
	eco- [iːkəʊ]	Öko-	
	impact [ˈɪmpækt]	Auswirkung, Einfluss	*impact* = effect or influence
	calculator [ˈkælkjʊˌleɪtə]	Rechner	
	heat [hiːt]	heizen	
	fossil fuel [ˈfɒsəl ˌfjuːəl]	fossiler Brennstoff	Coal and oil are *fossil fuels*.
G4	conditional clause [kənˌdɪʃnəl ˈklɔːz]	Bedingungssatz	
G7	along [əˈlɒŋ]	entlang	*The Great Wall of China* is a tourist attraction.
	the Great Wall of China [ðə ˌɡreɪt ˌwɔːl əv ˈtʃaɪnə]	Chinesische Mauer	
	the Czech Republic [ðə ˌtʃek rɪˈpʌblɪk]	Tschechische Republik	
	Poland [ˈpəʊlənd]	Polen	*Poland* and *the Czech Republic* are countries in the *European Union*.
	EU (= European Union) [ˌiː ˈjuː, ˌjʊərəˌpiːən ˈjuːnɪən]	EU (= Europäische Union)	

Theme 6

	the Atlantic (Ocean) [ðɪ‿ətˈlæntɪk]	der Atlantik	
	the North Sea [ðə ˌnɔːθ ˈsiː]	die Nordsee	There are lots of trains at a *station*.
	station [ˈsteɪʃn]	Bahnhof	
	the Thames [ðə ˈtemz]	Themse	
G8	get married [ˌget ˈmærid]	heiraten	
	eventually [ɪˈventʃuəli]	schließlich; irgendwann	
G9	ecological [ˌiːkəˈlɒdʒɪkl]	ökologisch	
	low-energy [ˌləʊ ˈenədʒi]	energiesparend	
	fuel-efficient [ˈfjuːəliˌfɪʃnt]	Benzin sparend	
	solar [ˈsəʊlər]	Solar-	
	heating [ˈhiːtɪŋ]	Heizung	*Solar* energy is a type of *renewable* energy.
	renewable [rɪˈnjuːəbl]	erneuerbar	
	power [ˈpaʊə]	*hier:* Strom, Elektrizität	
	energy-efficient [ˈenədʒiiˌfɪʃnt]	energiesparend	*recycle* = change waste materials so that they can be used again
	recycle [riːˈsaɪkl]	recyceln, wiederverwenden	

Die Vokabeln aus den Projekten findest du im englisch-deutschen Dictionary auf den Seiten 198–241.

Dictionary English – German

A

a / an [ə, ən] ein(e) I/W
(twice) a (week) [ˌtwaɪs ə ˈwiːk] (zweimal) pro (Woche) III/2A1
abolish [əˈbɒlɪʃ] abschaffen VI/3A4
Aboriginal [ˌæbəˈrɪdʒnəl] der Aboriginals (nachgestellt); austral. Ureinwohner/in V/4A3
Aborigine [ˌæbəˈrɪdʒəni] austral. Ureinwohner/in V/4I
abortion [əˈbɔːʃn] Abtreibung VI/4 Project 6
about [əˈbaʊt] über I/1A4; ungefähr III/5A1
be about [ˌbi əˈbaʊt] handeln von VI/1A5
above [əˈbʌv] oberhalb; *hier:* oben II/4A5; über II/3C1
abroad [əˈbrɔːd] (im/ins) Ausland VI/5A5
°**absolutely** [ˈæbsəluːtli] absolut, völlig VI/BS 3
°**abundant** [əˈbʌndənt] reichlich VI/BS 2
abuse [əˈbjuːs] Missbrauch VI/3A5
accent [ˈæksnt] Akzent VI/2I
accept [əkˈsept] annehmen, akzeptieren IV/2B2
access [ˈækses] Zugang VI/3B4
accident [ˈæksɪdnt] Unfall III/3B1
accommodation [əˌkɒməˈdeɪʃn] Unterkunft V/2A2
°**accord** [əˈkɔːd] gewähren VI/BS 8
according to [əˈkɔːdɪŋ tʊ] nach, zufolge VI/5B4
account [əˈkaʊnt] Bericht VI/3A6
accusation [ˌækjuˈzeɪʃn] Beschuldigung VI/4 Project 4
°**accuse** [əˈkjuːz] anklagen VI/BS 3
achieve [əˈtʃiːv] erreichen VI/1A2
°**acknowledge** [əkˈnɒlɪdʒ] zugeben VI/BS 6
across [əˈkrɒs] über II/2C1
across [əˈkrɒs] *hier:* in VI/1B2
°**from across** [frəm əˈkrɒs] quer durch VI/BS 6
act [ækt] handeln; sich benehmen VI/1B2
act [ækt] *hier:* Gesetz VI/2 Project 1
act out [ˌækt ˈaʊt] nachspielen II/2A3
action [ˈækʃn] Handlung, Tat IV/5B3
action [ˈækʃn] *hier:* Maßnahme, Aktion VI/3A8
active [ˈæktɪv] aktiv VI/3A5
activist [ˈæktɪvɪst] Aktivist/in VI/2 Project 3

activity [ækˈtɪvəti] Aktivität, Unternehmung V/1A2
actor/actress [ˈæktə/ˈæktrəs] Schauspieler/in III/7A2
actually [ˈæktʃuəli] eigentlich, wirklich; tatsächlich VI/1A5
ad (= advertisement) [æd, ədˈvɜːtɪsmənt] Anzeige VI/1A11
AD (= Anno Domini) [ˌeɪˈdiː] n. Chr., nach Christus V/5A8
add [æd] hinzufügen I/5C3
add up [ˌæd ˈʌp] addieren, zusammenzählen VI/1A1
additional [əˈdɪʃnəl] zusätzlich V/1B9
address [əˈdres] Adresse, Anschrift V/2A3
°**adhesive** [ədˈhiːsɪv] Klebstoff VI/5O
adjective [ˈædʒɪktɪv] Adjektiv II/1A3
adjust [əˈdʒʌst] *hier:* anpassen VI/6 Project 5
administration [ədˌmɪnɪˈstreɪʃn] Verwaltung VI/3B7
admit [ədˈmɪt] zugeben VI/3B8
adopt [əˈdɒpt] annehmen, übernehmen VI/2 Project 1
adopted [əˈdɒptɪd] adoptiert VI/4I
adoptive [əˈdɒptɪv] Adoptiv- VI/4 Project 6
adult [ˈædʌlt] Erwachsene/r III/7B1
advantage [ədˈvɑːntɪdʒ] Vorteil VI/6 Project 4
adventure [ədˈventʃə] Abenteuer, Erlebnis II/1B6
adventurous [ədˈventʃərəs] abenteuerlustig, risikofreudig V/1A3
advert (= advertisement) [ˈædvɜːt, ədˈvɜːtɪsmənt] Anzeige, Inserat III/7B1
advertising [ˈædvəˌtaɪzɪŋ] Werbung, Reklame VI/6 Project 1
(piece of) advice [ədˈvaɪs] Rat(schlag) IV/2B2
advice columnist [ədˈvaɪs ˌkɒləmnɪst] Briefkastenonkel/-tante VI/4 Project 6
advise sb (to do sth) [ədˈvaɪz sʌmbədi] jdm raten(, etw zu tun) IV/5B3
spiritual advisor [ˌspɪrɪtʃuəl ədˈvaɪzə] *hier:* geistl. Beistand VI/3B8
aeroplane (= plane) [ˈeərəˌpleɪn] Flugzeug III/5A2
°**affair** [əˈfeə] Angelegenheit VI/BS 3
affect [əˈfekt] auswirken auf, beeinflussen VI/6 Project 4

affection [əˈfekʃn] Zuneigung, Liebe VI/4 Project 4
afford [əˈfɔːd] sich leisten VI/1B2
affront [əˈfrʌnt] Beleidigung, Affront VI/3B7
Africa [ˈæfrɪkə] Afrika VI/2 Project 3
African [ˈæfrɪkən] Afrikaner/in; afrikanisch VI/2 Project 3
African American [ˈæfrɪkən əˈmerɪkən] Afroamerikaner/in; afroamerikanisch VI/2 Project 3
after [ˈɑːftə] danach; nachher IV/4A2; nach I/2C6; nachdem IV/8B4
after all [ˌɑːftər ˈɔːl] schließlich IV/5A3
after all [ˌɑːftər ˈɔːl] *hier:* letzten Endes VI/3A7
after that [ˈɑːftə ðæt] danach IV/1B3
afternoon [ˌɑːftəˈnuːn] Nachmittag I/2C1
afterwards [ˈɑːftəwədz] später; danach, anschließend II/2C3
again [əˈgen] wieder; noch (ein)mal I/1C2
against [əˈgenst] gegen I/3A3
age [eɪdʒ] Alter II/4C3
age [eɪdʒ] Zeitalter, Ära VI/5A3
at the age of [æt ði ˈeɪdʒ əv] im Alter von VI/1A8
aged [eɪdʒd] im Alter von III/7B1
agree [əˈgriː] zustimmen II/5C3
agree on [əˈgriː ɒn] sich einigen auf IV/5A3
agree with [əˈgriː wɪð] einer Meinung sein mit VI/5B5
agricultural [ˌægrɪˈkʌltʃrəl] landwirtschaftlich VI/2 Project 3
ahead of [əˈhed əv] vor VI/3B7
aim [eɪm] zielen; anstreben VI/6I
aim [eɪm] Ziel, Absicht VI/3A5
ain't (= do I not / am I not) [eɪnt] tue ich nicht / bin ich nicht VI/4 Project 1
air [eə] Luft III/5B1
°**air conditioning** [ˈeə kənˌdɪʃnɪŋ] Klimaanlage VI/5O
aircraft [ˈeəkrɑːft] Flugzeug VI/2 Project 4
airlift [ˈeəlɪft] Luftbrücke VI/2 Project 5
airport [ˈeəpɔːt] Flughafen II/2C1
air travel [ˈeəˌtrævl] Flug, Flugreise VI/2 Project 4
°**aisle** [aɪl] Gang VI/BS 3
alcohol [ˈælkəhɒl] Alkohol VI/2 Project 4

Dictionary English – German

°Algonkin (= Algonquin) [ˈælɡɒŋkɪn] Algonkier/in; algonkisch VI/BS 4
alien [ˈeɪliən] Ausländer/in VI/2I; fremd; seltsam VI/BS 2; *hier:* Außerirdische/r VI/BS 3
alive [əˈlaɪv] *hier:* am Leben VI/2 Project 1; lebendig VI/6 Project 5
°be all about [ˌbiˈɔːlˌəbaʊt] *hier:* sich nur drehen um VI/BS 1
°all around [ɔːl əˈraʊnd] darum herum VI/1O
all day [ɔːl ˈdeɪ] den ganzen Tag II/6A4
all in all [ˌɔːl ɪn ˈɔːl] alles in allem V/4A5
°all of a sudden [ˌɔːl əv ə ˈsʌdn] ganz plötzlich VI/BS 3
all over the world [ɔːlˌəʊvə ðə ˈwɜːld] auf der ganzen Welt IV/2A8
all (the) [ɔːl] alle(s); der/die/das ganze I/1A3
All the best! [ɔːl ðə ˈbest] Alles Gute! II/4B9
all the time [ˌɔːl ðə ˈtaɪm] die ganze Zeit VI/1A5
all year [ˌɔːl ˈjɪə] das ganze Jahr (über) VI/1P2
all-black movie [ˌɔːlblæk ˈmuːvi] Film, in dem nur Schwarze als (Haupt)darsteller vorkommen VI/2 Project 4
°all-time [ˈɔːl taɪm] unübertroffen VI/BS 3
°allergic [əˈlɜːdʒɪk] allergisch VI/BS 3
alliance [əˈlaɪəns] Allianz, Bündnis VI/2 Project 5
Allied [ˈælaɪd] alliiert, verbündet VI/2 Project 5
allow [əˈlaʊ] erlauben, gestatten V/1B5
allow for [əˈlaʊ fɔː] einkalkulieren VI/3B6
ally [ˈælaɪ] Verbündete/r; Alliierte/r VI/2 Project 5
almost [ˈɔːlməʊst] fast, beinahe III/3B1
°alms-seeker [ˈɑːmzˌsiːkə] Almosensammler/in, Bettler/in VI/BS 2
alone [əˈləʊn] allein II/3C1
along [əˈlɒŋ] entlang VI/6G7
already [ɔːlˈredi] schon, bereits II/3A1
alright (= all right) [ˌɔːl ˈraɪt] in Ordnung VI/4 Project 4

also [ˈɔːlsəʊ] auch, außerdem I/5A1
alternative [ɔːlˈtɜːnətɪv] alternativ VI/4 Project 6
although [ɔːlˈðəʊ] obwohl VI/3B6
always [ˈɔːlweɪz] immer I/1C1
am (= ante meridiem) [ˌeɪˈem, ˌænti məˈrɪdiəm] morgens, vormittags *(nur hinter Uhrzeit zwischen Mitternacht und 12 Uhr mittags)* I/2B7
amazing [əˈmeɪzɪŋ] erstaunlich, toll V/5B2
ambition [æmˈbɪʃn] Ehrgeiz VI/6 Project 1
America [əˈmerɪkə] Amerika IV/3A2
American [əˈmerɪkən] Amerikaner/in; amerikanisch IV/1A4
amnesia [æmˈniːziə] Amnesie, Gedächtnisschwund VI/6 Project 5
among [əˈmʌŋ] unter; inmitten von VI/2 Project 5
amount [əˈmaʊnt] Menge, Betrag V/5A4
analyse (= analyze) [ˈænəlaɪz] analysieren, untersuchen VI/5B3
°anatomy [əˈnætəmi] Anatomie VI/BS 2
and [ænd] und I/1A2
anew [əˈnjuː] noch einmal, von neuem VI/6 Project 2
anger [ˈæŋɡə] Ärger VI/3B4
angry [ˈæŋɡri] verärgert; zornig; wütend II/3B2
°angular [ˈæŋɡjʊlə] kantig, knochig VI/BS 2
animal [ˈænɪml] Tier I/1A4
°ankle [ˈæŋkl] (Fuß)knöchel VI/BS 2
announce [əˈnaʊns] verkünden, bekannt geben IV/8B2
announcer [əˈnaʊnsə] Sprecher/in VI/1A5
annual [ˈænjuəl] jährlich VI/1B5
anorexia [ˌænəˈreksiə] Magersucht VI/1A5
anorexic [ˌænəˈreksɪk] Magersüchtige/r; magersüchtig VI/1A7
another [əˈnʌðə] noch eine(r, s) I/3C2; *hier:* ein(e) andere(r, s) II/3C1
answer [ˈɑːnsə] (be)antworten I/2A7; Antwort II/1B5
any [ˈeni] (irgend)ein(e); jede(r, s) III/3A1
anybody [ˈeniˌbɒdi] jede(r); jemand I/5C4

anyone [ˈeniˌwʌn] jede(r, s) VI/2 Project 4; (irgend)jemand VI/BS 1
anything [ˈeniˌθɪŋ] (irgend)etwas III/6A7
anything else [ˌeniθɪŋ ˈels] (irgend)etwas anderes II/5C3
anyway [ˈeniˌweɪ] sowieso, überhaupt; jedenfalls IV/2A5
anywhere [ˈeniˌweə] überall IV/3A5
°anywhere [ˈeniˌweə] irgendwo VI/BS 3
anywhere else [ˌeniweərˈels] irgendwo anders IV/3A3
°apart from [əˈpɑːt frəm] abgesehen von VI/BS 2
apartment *(AE)* [əˈpɑːtmənt] Wohnung IV/3A3
apologize (= apologise) [əˈpɒlədʒaɪz] sich entschuldigen V/4A3
°apparently [əˈpærəntli] offensichtlich VI/BS 3
appeal [əˈpiːl] Einspruch, Berufung VI/3B8; *hier:* bitten um VI/3B8
appear [əˈpɪə] (er)scheinen; auftauchen VI/5A3
apple [ˈæpl] Apfel I/1C1
application [ˌæplɪˈkeɪʃn] *hier:* Antrag VI/3B8
letter of application [ˌletər əvˌæplɪˈkeɪʃn] Bewerbungsschreiben V/2A5
apply [əˈplaɪ] gelten; betreffen VI/3A4
apply (for) [əˈplaɪ] sich bewerben (um) V/2A5
appreciate [əˈpriːʃieɪt] schätzen, zu schätzen wissen V/3I
apprenticeship [əˈprentɪsʃɪp] Ausbildung, Lehre V/2B5
°approach [əˈprəʊtʃ] sich nähern VI/BS 5
appropriate [əˈprəʊprieɪt] angemessen; *hier:* passend VI/2G4; entsprechend VI/2I
approximately [əˈprɒksɪmətli] ungefähr, etwa VI/1A7
April [ˈeɪprəl] April I/5C2
architecture [ˈɑːkɪtektʃə] Architektur VI/6 Project 4
Are you ready to order? [ɑː juː ˌredi tʊˈɔːdə] Möchten Sie schon bestellen? III/1A3
area [ˈeəriə] Gebiet, Region; *hier:* Viertel, Gegend II/6B6
argue [ˈɑːɡjuː] *hier:* argumentieren IV/5B5

argument ['ɑ:gjʊmənt] Auseinandersetzung; Argument IV/5A3
arm [ɑ:m] Arm I/2A4
arms race ['ɑ:mz reɪs] Wettrüsten VI/2G8
around [ə'raʊnd] um (... herum) I/1B1; ungefähr V/2A6
around [ə'raʊnd] in der Nähe VI/1A5; *hier:* draußen VI/BS 1
around the world [ə‚raʊnd ðə 'wɜ:ld] in der ganzen Welt VI/2 Project 5
arrange [ə'reɪndʒ] arrangieren; vereinbaren VI/2 Project 1
arranged [ə'reɪndʒd] arrangiert VI/4I
arrest [ə'rest] verhaften VI/2 Project 3
arrival [ə'raɪvl] Ankunft IV/8B2
arrive [ə'raɪv] ankommen II/5B1
art [ɑ:t] (bildende) Kunst I/5A1
piece of art [‚pi:s əv 'ɑ:t] Kunstwerk IV/7B1
article ['ɑ:tɪkl] Artikel IV/2A8
artist ['ɑ:tɪst] Künstler/in IV/7B4
artistic [ɑ:'tɪstɪk] kreativ, künstlerisch VI/6I
as [æz] als; wie; da II/6B3
as ... as [əz əz] (genau)so ... wie ... II/4B2
as if [əz ‚ɪf] als ob V/4B6
as long as [æz 'lɒŋ‿æz] solang(e) VI/3A3
as well [əz 'wel] auch V/2A6
as well as [əz 'wel‿əz] *hier:* sowie VI/2 Project 3
be ashamed [‚bi‿ə'ʃeɪmd] sich schämen VI/2 Project 3
Asia ['eɪʒə] Asien VI/5B3
Asian ['eɪʒn] Asiate/Asiatin; asiatisch VI/2 Project 3
ask [ɑ:sk] fragen; bitten I/2A7
ask for directions [‚ɑ:sk fə dɪ'rekʃnz] nach dem Weg fragen III/8A4
ask for help [‚ɑ:sk fə 'help] um Hilfe bitten III/8A4
ask questions [‚ɑ:sk ‚'kwestʃnz] Fragen stellen I/2A7
ask sb out [‚ɑ:sk ‚sʌmbədi‿'aʊt] fragen, ob jd mit einem ausgehen will VI/4 Project 1
be asleep [‚bi‿ə'sli:p] schlafen IV/4B1
fall asleep [‚fɔ:l‿ə'sli:p] einschlafen IV/6B1
aspect ['æspekt] Aspekt, Gesichtspunkt VI/3B1
°**ass** *(informal)* [æs] Arsch VI/BS 3

be assassinated [‚bi‿ə'sæsɪneɪtɪd] *hier:* Opfer eines Attentats werden VI/2 Project 3
°**assign** [ə'saɪn] zuweisen VI/BS 3
association [ə‚səʊsi'eɪʃn] Assoziation VI/6 Project 3
°**assume** [ə'sju:m] annehmen VI/BS 8
°**astronomer** [ə'strɒnəmə] Astronom/in VI/BS 3
astronomical [‚æstrə'nɒmɪkl] astronomisch VI/6 Project 1
at [æt] auf, an, in, bei I/1C1; *hier:* um I/3A1
at all [æt‿'ɔ:l] überhaupt VI/1A8
at first [ət 'fɜ:st] zuerst II/5C2
at Gillian's [æt 'dʒɪliənz] bei Gillian (zu Hause) I/3C2
at last [ət 'lɑ:st] endlich, schließlich II/6A2
at least [ət 'li:st] mindestens, zumindest II/2A6
at night [ət 'naɪt] nachts I/3B1
at once [ət 'wʌns] sofort V/5A7
at sb's house [‚æt sʌmbədiz 'haʊs] bei jdm zu Hause II/3A1
at that stage [ət ‚ðæt 'steɪdʒ] zu diesem Zeitpunkt, in dieser Phase VI/1A5
at the back (of) [‚æt ðə 'bæk] hinten II/1C5
at the beginning [‚ət ðə bɪ'gɪnɪŋ] am Anfang, zu Beginn III/3A3
(at the) corner ['kɔ:nə] (an der) Ecke II/2B4
at the doctor's [‚ət ðə 'dɒktəz] beim Arzt/bei der Ärztin III/2B2
at the front (of) [‚æt ðə 'frʌnt] vorne II/1C5
at the moment [‚æt ðə 'məʊmənt] im Augenblick, momentan II/2A5
at the same time [ət ðə ‚seɪm 'taɪm] gleichzeitig, zur gleichen Zeit IV/5A2
at the time [æt ðə 'taɪm] zu diesem Zeitpunkt VI/2 Project 4
at the weekend [ət ðə wi:k'end] am Wochenende II/6A1
(at) what time [wɒt‚'taɪm] (um) wie viel Uhr II/1B8
Atlantic [ət'læntɪk] Atlantik(-) VI/2 Project 4
the Atlantic (Ocean) [ði‿ət'læntɪk] der Atlantik VI/2 Project 1
atmosphere ['ætməsfɪə] Atmosphäre, Stimmung VI/6 Project 4
attach [ə'tætʃ] befestigen; beilegen; *hier:* anhängen IV/3A2

attack [ə'tæk] angreifen V/4B6
attend [ə'tend] besuchen VI/3A4
pay attention to [‚peɪ‿ə'tenʃn tə] achten auf VI/3B10
°**pay attention to sb** [‚peɪ‿ə'tenʃn tə ‚sʌmbədi] jdm Aufmerksamkeit schenken VI/BS 3
attitude ['ætɪtju:d] Haltung, Einstellung V/3I
°**attract** [ə'trækt] anziehen VI/BS 8
attractive [ə'træktɪv] attraktiv, verlockend V/2A2
audience ['ɔ:diəns] Publikum VI/4 Project 2
audition [ɔ:'dɪʃn] Vorsprechen, Vorsingen, Vortanzen IV/7A2
August ['ɔ:gəst] August I/5C2
aunt [ɑ:nt] Tante I/W
Australia [ɒ'streɪliə] Australien V/4A2
Australian [ɒ'streɪliən] Australier/in; australisch V/4A2
author ['ɔ:θə] Verfasser/in, Autor/in VI/3B7
auto rickshaw ['ɔ:təʊ ‚rɪkʃɔ:] Autoriksha VI/5A1
°**automobile** ['ɔ:təməʊ‚bi:l] Auto, Kraftfahrzeug VI/5O
autoworker ['ɔ:təʊwɜ:kə] *Arbeiter/in in der Automobilindustrie* VI/2 Project 4
autumn ['ɔ:təm] Herbst I/4C8
available [ə'veɪləbl] verfügbar, zur Verfügung stehend V/2A3
average ['ævrɪdʒ] Durchschnitt VI/1A6; durchschnittlich VI/1A5
aviation *(no pl)* [‚eɪvi'eɪʃn] Fliegerei, Luftfahrt VI/2 Project 4
avoid [ə'vɔɪd] vermeiden VI/3B4
avoid [ə'vɔɪd] meiden, aus dem Weg gehen VI/1A1
await [ə'weɪt] erwarten; warten auf VI/3B3
award [ə'wɔ:d] Preis, Auszeichnung VI/1B2
aware [ə'weə] bewusst, *hier:* wachsam, vorsichtig V/5A6
°**away** [ə'weɪ] weg VI/BS 1
°**get away with sth** [‚get‿ə'weɪ wɪð ‚sʌmθɪŋ] mit etw ungestraft davonkommen VI/BS 3
awesome ['ɔ:sm] spitze, super VI/5B2
awful ['ɔ:fl] furchtbar, schrecklich III/1A10
°**awkward** ['ɔ:kwəd] unbehaglich VI/BS 6

Dictionary English – German

B

B&B (= **bed and breakfast**) [ˌbiˑən ˈbiː] Übernachtung mit Frühstück, Frühstückspension V/2A2
babe (= **baby**) *(informal) (AE)* [beɪb, ˈbeɪbi] Baby, Schatz, Liebling VI/4 Project 1
babysit [ˈbeɪbiˌsɪt] babysitten III/6A2
back [bæk] Rücken; Rückseite I/2A4; zurück I/4C5
back [bæk] *hier:* der hintere Teil VI/2 Project 3
change back [ˌtʃeɪndʒ ˈbæk] *hier:* rückgängig machen VI/3B4
in back *(AE)* [ɪn ˈbæk] im Hintergrund VI/4 Project 5
back up [ˌbækˈʌp] unterstützen, bestätigen VI/3B4
background [ˈbækˌɡraʊnd] Herkunft, Verhältnisse VI/3A4
background [ˈbækˌɡraʊnd] Hintergrund VI/4 Project 4
°**backpack** [ˈbækpæk] Rucksack VI/BS 3
bacon [ˈbeɪkən] (Schinken)speck VI/4 Project 1
bad [bæd] schlecht; schlimm III/1B1
bad [bæd] *hier:* verdorben VI/1P5
feel bad [ˌfiːl ˈbæd] sich schlecht fühlen III/2B1
(bad) cold [kəʊld] (starke) Erkältung III/2B1
bad luck [bæd ˈlʌk] Pech IV/2A1
badge [bædʒ] Abzeichen VI/3A8
bag [bæɡ] Tasche II/1C1
straw bale [strɔː ˈbeɪl] Strohballen VI/6 Project 4
ball [bɔːl] Ball I/3B7
secret ballot [ˌsiːkrət ˈbælət] geheime Wahl VI/3A4
ban [bæn] verbieten; ausschließen VI/5B6
banana [bəˈnɑːnə] Banane I/2C2
band [bænd] Band; Gruppe VI/1P5
bandage [ˈbændɪdʒ] Verband III/2B2
°**bang** [bæŋ] Krach machen VI/BS 6
bank [bæŋk] Bank *(Geldinstitut)* VI/1B3
banner [ˈbænə] Transparent, Spruchband VI/3B10
°**bar** [bɑː] Lokal, Bar VI/BS 3; Stange, Gitterstab VI/BS 5
bar chart [ˈbɑːˌtʃɑːt] Säulendiagramm V/1B1
barefoot [ˈbeəfʊt] barfuß VI/1B5
°**barely** [ˈbeəli] kaum VI/BS 1

barren [ˈbærən] karg, öde VI/6 Project 2
be based [ˌbiː ˈbeɪst] seinen Sitz haben VI/2 Project 5
be based on [ˌbiː ˈbeɪst ɒn] basieren auf, beruhen auf V/6I
°**basement** [ˈbeɪsmənt] Untergeschoss; *hier:* Keller VI/BS 1
basic [ˈbeɪsɪk] grundlegend VI/1B2
°**basically** [ˈbeɪsɪkli] im Wesentlichen, im Grunde VI/5O
basket [ˈbɑːskɪt] Korb I/3B4
bath [bɑːθ] Bad(ewanne) I/W
bathroom [ˈbɑːθˌruːm] Bad(ezimmer) I/2A2
battle [ˈbætl] Kampf; Schlacht VI/2 Project 2
BBC [ˌbiː biː ˈsiː] *brit. Sender* VI/1A8
BC (= **before Christ**) [ˌbiːˈsiː] v. Chr., vor Christus V/5A8
be [biː] sein I/W
be able to do sth [biːˌeɪbl tə ˌduː ˈsʌmθɪŋ] etw tun können II/5C2
be afraid (of) [ˌbɪ əˈfreɪd] Angst haben (vor) II/5C2
be alive [biˌəˈlaɪv] leben, am Leben sein II/6B2
be allowed to do sth [biˌəˌlaʊd tə ˈduː ˌsʌmθɪŋ] etw tun dürfen II/5A3
be angry about [biːˌæŋɡri əˌbaʊt] sich ärgern über II/5A3
be lucky [bi ˈlʌki] Glück haben II/3C1
be on holiday [ˌbi ɒn ˈhɒlɪdeɪ] Urlaub/Ferien haben I/6A3
be right [ˌbiː ˈraɪt] Recht haben III/1B1
be up to sb [ˌbiːˌʌp tʊ ˌsʌmbədi] von jdm abhängen, jdm überlassen sein IV/7B4
beach [biːtʃ] Strand II/1A1
°**sandy beach** [ˌsændi ˈbiːtʃ] Sandstrand VI/BS 1
bead [biːd] Perle VI/5B2
beam [biːm] strahlen VI/6 Project 5
bean [biːn] Bohne VI/4 Project 1
°**bear** [beə] Bär VI/BS 3
polar bear [ˈpəʊlə beə] Eisbär VI/4 Project 3
beat [biːt] schlagen; *hier.* besiegen II/5C4
beat [biːt] Takt VI/6 Project 5
beat up [ˌbiːtˈʌp] verprügeln VI/3B9
beating [ˈbiːtɪŋ] Schlagen VI/6 Project 5
beautiful [ˈbjuːtəfl] schön II/2B1

beauty [ˈbjuːti] Schönheit VI/1A4
because [bɪˈkɒz] weil, da I/4B1
because of [bɪˈkɒz ɒv] wegen VI/3B7
become [bɪˈkʌm] werden II/6B2
bed [bed] Bett I/W
bedroom [ˈbedruːm] Schlafzimmer I/4C2
before [bɪˈfɔː] bevor I/4C4; vor I/2B2; zuvor, vorher II/6A2
begin [bɪˈɡɪn] anfangen, beginnen II/1B3
beginning [bɪˈɡɪnɪŋ] Anfang; Beginn II/3C2
at the beginning [ˌæt ðə bɪˈɡɪnɪŋ] am Anfang, zu Beginn III/3A3
behave [bɪˈheɪv] sich benehmen V/5A6
behind [bɪˈhaɪnd] hinter I/2A2
behold [bɪˈhəʊld] erblicken, anzuschauen VI/6 Project 2
Beijing [ˌbeɪˈdʒɪŋ] Peking VI/3A6
believe [bɪˈliːv] glauben II/1C4
believer [bɪˈliːvə] Anhänger/in VI/3B7
belong (to) [bɪˈlɒŋ tʊ] gehören (zu) IV/8A6
°**feel a sense of belonging** [ˌfiːl ə ˌsens əv bɪˈlɒŋɪŋ] sich dazugehörig fühlen VI/BS 6
°**beloved** [bɪˈlʌvɪd] Geliebte/r VI/BS 8
below [bɪˈləʊ] unten, darunter I/4B1; unter I/2C2
°**bend over** [ˌbendˈəʊvə] sich vorbeugen VI/BS 6
benefit [ˈbenɪfɪt] profitieren VI/5B4; nützen VI/BS 6
Bengal [ˌbenˈɡɔːl] Bengale/Bengalin; bengalisch VI/5A2
beside [bɪˈsaɪd] neben VI/4 Project 1
besides [bɪˈsaɪdz] außerdem, überdies VI/2 Project 3; abgesehen von VI/BS 1
best [best] beste(r, s) II/L
best man [ˌbest ˈmæn] Trauzeuge VI/4 Project 6
bet [bet] wetten VI/3B4
°**betray** [bɪˈtreɪ] verraten VI/BS 3
better [ˈbetə] besser I/1A5
between [bɪˈtwiːn] zwischen I/2C4
between [bɪˈtwiːn] dazwischen VI/2 Project 3
°**bible** [ˈbaɪbl] Bibel VI/BS 5
bicycle [ˈbaɪsɪkl] Fahrrad II/6C2
big [bɪɡ] groß I/W
bike [baɪk] (Fahr)rad I/1A5

bill [bɪl] Rechnung VI/1B2
Could we have the bill, please? [kʊd wi: hæv ðə 'bɪl ˌpli:z] Wir möchten bitte zahlen!, Die Rechnung, bitte! III/1A3
billion [ˈbɪljən] Milliarde VI/1B2
bin [bɪn] Mülleimer, Mülltonne I/1C1
eating binge [ˈi:tɪŋ ˌbɪndʒ] Essattacke VI/1A6
°**biofuel** [ˈbaɪəʊˌfju:əl] Biotreibstoff VI/6 Project 4
biography [baɪˈɒgrəfi] Biografie VI/2 Project 2
°**biology** [baɪˈɒlədʒi] Biologie VI/BS 1
bird [bɜ:d] Vogel II/2B3
°**birth** [bɜ:θ] Geburt VI/BS 5
date of birth [ˌdeɪt əv ˈbɜ:θ] Geburtsdatum V/2A3
place of birth [ˌpleɪs əv ˈbɜ:θ] Geburtsort V/2A3
give birth to [ˌgɪv ˈbɜ:θ tʊ] zur Welt bringen VI/4 Project 1
birthday [ˈbɜ:θdeɪ] Geburtstag I/5B4
bit [bɪt] Stück; Teil VI/6I
a bit [ə ˈbɪt] ein bisschen II/1A4
°**bite** [baɪt] Biss VI/1O
black [blæk] schwarz I/W
black [blæk] Schwarze/r VI/2 Project 3
°**black eye** [ˌblæk ˈaɪ] blaues Auge VI/BS 3
blackboard [ˈblækˌbɔ:d] Tafel I/1C1
°**shoulder blade** [ˈʃəʊldə ˌbleɪd] Schulterblatt VI/BS 9
°**blame** [bleɪm] jdm die Schuld geben VI/BS 6
°**blast** [blɑ:st] sprengen; hier: schießen VI/BS 3
°**bleed** [bli:d] bluten VI/BS 3
°**blemish** [ˈblemɪʃ] Makel, Schönheitsfehler VI/BS 8
blend into [ˌblend ˈɪntʊ] verschmelzen mit VI/6 Project 4
blended [ˈblendɪd] hier: Patchwork- VI/4I
text block [ˈtekst ˌblɒk] Textbaustein VI/3B8
°**blond(e)** [blɒnd] blond VI/BS 3
blood [blʌd] Blut VI/6 Project 5
bloody [ˈblʌdi] blutig VI/2 Project 4; hier: blutig schlagen VI/BS 3
bloody (informal) [ˈblʌdi] verdammt VI/4 Project 4
blouse [blaʊz] Bluse II/5B5

blow [bləʊ] Schlag VI/4 Project 1
blue [blu:] blau I/2A5
board [bɔ:d] Brett; Tafel I/3C3
°**censor board** [ˈsensə ˌbɔ:d] Zensurbehörde VI/BS 8
on board [ˌɒn ˈbɔ:d] an Bord VI/6 Project 3
pardon board [ˈpɑ:dn ˌbɔ:d] Begnadigungskommission VI/3B8
boarding school [ˈbɔ:dɪŋ sku:l] Internat V/4B6
boat [bəʊt] Boot; Schiff II/2C1
body [ˈbɒdi] Körper I/6C1
°**bodywork** [ˈbɒdiwɜ:k] Karosserie VI/5O
boil up [ˌbɔɪl ˈʌp] aufkochen VI/4 Project 1
°**Bollywood** [ˈbɒliwʊd] in Mumbai angesiedelte Filmindustrie VI/BS 8
bomb [bɒm] Bombe V/6I
bomb [bɒm] bombardieren VI/2 Project 5
nuclear bomb [ˌnju:kliə ˈbɒm] Atombombe VI/2I
bomber [ˈbɒmə] Bombenflugzeug VI/2 Project 5
bombing [ˈbɒmɪŋ] Bombardierung, Bombenanschlag VI/2 Project 5
bonded labour [ˌbɒndɪd ˈleɪbə] Knechtschaft VI/5B6
°**bone** [bəʊn] Knochen VI/BS 2
book [bʊk] Buch I/1A8
bookshop [ˈbʊkˌʃɒp] Buchladen III/7B1
boot [bu:t] Stiefel III/6A7
°**boot** [bu:t] Kofferraum VI/5O
bootleg [ˈbu:tˌleg] illegal herstellen; hier: brennen VI/2 Project 4
bored [bɔ:d] gelangweilt IV/4A2
boredom [ˈbɔ:dəm] Langeweile VI/3B4
boring [ˈbɔ:rɪŋ] langweilig II/1A2
be born [ˌbi: ˈbɔ:n] geboren werden III/7A2
borough [ˈbʌrə] Verwaltungsbezirk; Stadtteil IV/3LL3
boss [bɒs] Chef/in IV/6B1
the Boston Tea Party [ðə ˌbɒstən ˈti: ˌpɑ:ti] Widerstandsakt gegen die britische Kolonialpolitik VI/2 Project 1
both [bəʊθ] beide IV/7A3
°**both** [bəʊθ] hier: beides VI/BS 3
both ... and ... [ˈbəʊθ ænd] sowohl ... als auch ... V/5B3
bottle [ˈbɒtl] Flasche I/2C2
bottom [ˈbɒtəm] Boden VI/2I

°**boundary** [ˈbaʊndəri] Grenze VI/BS 1
box [bɒks] Kiste; Schachtel; Kasten I/2P3
boy [bɔɪ] Junge I/1A2
boyfriend [ˈbɔɪˌfrend] Freund (Partner) III/4B2
bracket [ˈbrækɪt] Klammer VI/1P3
°**brand** [brænd] hier: Brandmal VI/BS 2
°**brave** [breɪv] mutig; tapfer VI/BS 3
bread [bred] Brot I/2C2
break [breɪk] (sich) brechen III/2B2; Pause I/5A1
break [breɪk] hier: Umbruch VI/6 Project 2
take a break [ˌteɪk ə ˈbreɪk] eine Pause machen VI/1A5
break away [ˌbreɪk əˈweɪ] sich losreißen von, sich absetzen VI/6 Project 3
break of day [ˌbreɪk əv ˈdeɪ] Tagesanbruch VI/6 Project 2
break up [ˌbreɪk ˈʌp] sich trennen, Schluss machen III/4B1
breakaway [ˈbreɪkəˌweɪ] Lossagung, Absplitterung VI/6 Project 3
breakfast [ˈbrekfəst] Frühstück I/1A4
breath [breθ] Atem(zug), Luft V/1B1
be out of breath [bi: ˌaʊt əv ˈbreθ] außer Atem sein VI/4G11
hold one's breath [ˌhəʊld wʌnz ˈbreθ] die Luft anhalten VI/4 Project 3
breathe [bri:ð] atmen V/1B5
breeze [bri:z] Brise VI/1A2
brick [brɪk] Ziegel, Backstein VI/5A3
°**bride** [braɪd] Braut VI/BS 8
bridge [brɪdʒ] Brücke II/2C1
brief [bri:f] kurz VI/2 Project 5
bright [braɪt] hell; strahlend; glänzend VI/1A3
brilliant (informal) [ˈbrɪljənt] toll, klasse I/3A1
brilliant [ˈbrɪljənt] hier: hervorragend VI/2 Project 3
bring [brɪŋ] (mit)bringen I/1B4
British [ˈbrɪtɪʃ] britisch IV/1B3
°**in broad daylight** [ɪn ˌbrɔ:d ˈdeɪlaɪt] am hellichten Tag VI/BS 2
brochure [ˈbrəʊʃə] Broschüre III/5A2
broken [ˈbrəʊkən] gebrochen V/1B3; hier: kaputt V/2B7

Dictionary English – German

broken-winged [ˌbrəʊkən ˈwɪŋd] mit gebrochenen Flügeln VI/6 Project 2
brother [ˈbrʌðə] Bruder I/1A4
brothers and sisters [ˈbrʌðəz ənd ˌsɪstəz] Geschwister I/1A6
brown [braʊn] braun I/2A5
brush one's teeth [ˌbrʌʃ wʌnz ˈtiːθ] sich die Zähne putzen III/4A3
brutally [ˈbruːtli] brutal VI/2 Project 3
bubble [bʌbl] Blase VI/3B8
buffalo (pl buffalo or buffaloes) [ˈbʌfələʊ] Büffel VI/2I
build [bɪld] bauen II/6A1
building [ˈbɪldɪŋ] Gebäude, Bau II/5B1
light bulb [ˈlaɪt ˌbʌlb] Glühbirne VI/6 Project 4
bulimia [bjuːˈlɪmɪə] Bulimie VI/1A6
°bully [ˈbʊli] Kerl, Schläger VI/BS 3
bullying [ˈbʊliɪŋ] Mobbing II/5I
°bureau [ˈbjʊərəʊ] Amt, Behörde VI/BS 3
bureaucrat [ˈbjʊərəkræt] Bürokrat/in VI/3B7
burger bar [ˈbɜːgə baː] Schnellimbiss VI/4G5
burial [ˈberiəl] Beerdigung VI/3B8
burn [bɜːn] (ver)brennen II/3C1
burned-out [ˌbɜːndˈaʊt] ausgebrannt, völlig erschöpft VI/1A5
bus [bʌs] Bus I/2B7
bus stop [ˈbʌs ˌstɒp] Bushaltestelle II/5C1
business [ˈbɪznəs] Geschäft VI/5A5
start a business [ˌstaːtə ˈbɪznəs] ein Unternehmen gründen VI/2 Project 5
busy [ˈbɪzi] beschäftigt; arbeitsreich IV/1A2
busy [ˈbɪzi] *hier:* voll; viel befahren VI/6 Project 1
but [bʌt] aber I/1A3
but [bʌt] außer VI/1A1
not only ... but also [ˌnɒt ˌəʊnli ˌbʌt ˈɔːlsəʊ] nicht nur ..., sondern auch ... VI/5A2
butcher's [ˈbʊtʃəz] Metzgerei V/4B6
butter [ˈbʌtə] Butter I/2B1
button [ˈbʌtn] Knopf; *hier:* Taste V/5A4
buy [baɪ] kaufen I/2C1
buyer [ˈbaɪə] Käufer/in VI/5B3
by [baɪ] *hier:* indem VI/3A3; *hier:* von II/6A4
by [baɪ] *hier:* im VI/2 Project 1; *hier:* im Jahr; bis zum Jahr VI/2 Project 3

°by [baɪ] *hier:* in der Nähe von VI/BS 3; *hier:* nach VI/BS 3
by (+ *Verkehrsmittel*) [baɪ] mit II/6C2
by (+ *Zeitpunkt*) [baɪ] (spätestens) bis II/5A2
by heart [baɪ ˈhɑːt] auswendig II/4C2
by now [baɪ ˈnaʊ] mittlerweile VI/2 Project 2
by the time [ˌbaɪ ðə ˈtaɪm] *hier:* als VI/2G8
Bye. (*informal*) [baɪ] Tschüss. I/6C6

C

°cactus (*pl* cactuses *or* cacti) [ˈkæktəs, ˈkæktəsɪz, ˈkæktaɪ] Kaktus VI/BS 2
cage [keɪdʒ] Käfig I/3B4
cake [keɪk] Kuchen; Torte II/4B6
calculate [ˈkælkjʊleɪt] berechnen VI/3B1
calculator [ˈkælkjʊˌleɪtə] Rechner VI/6 Project 4
Calcutta [kælˈkʌtə] Kalkutta VI/5A1
calendar [ˈkælɪndə] Kalender II/4A5
Californian [ˌkæləˈfɔːniən] Kalifornier/in; kalifornisch VI/2 Project 2
call [kɔːl] (an)rufen; nennen I/2B3; (Telefon)anruf III/2B1
call centre [ˈkɔːlsentə] Callcenter VI/5A5
call sb names [ˌkɔːl sʌmbədi ˈneɪmz] jdn beschimpfen II/5C3
called [kɔːld] *hier:* genannt III/5B1
be called [ˌbiː ˈkɔːld] heißen IV/7B4
°calm [ˈkɑːm] ruhig, gelassen VI/BS 6
Cambodia [kæmˈbəʊdiə] Kambodscha VI/5B1
camera [ˈkæmrə] Kamera, Fotoapparat IV/5A1
camp [kæmp] (Zelt)lager VI/5A3
refugee camp [ˌrefjʊˈdʒiː kæmp] Flüchtlingslager VI/5B2
campaign [kæmˈpeɪn] Kampagne, Aktion V/1B9; kämpfen, sich engagieren VI/3A3
campsite [ˈkæmpˌsaɪt] Zeltplatz VI/6 Project 4
can [kæn] können I/1A4
°can [kæn] Dose, Büchse VI/BS 5
Canadian [kəˈneɪdiən] Kanadier/in; kanadisch VI/1B3
Canary Islands [kəˈneəriˌaɪləndz] Kanarische Inseln, Kanaren VI/3A3

°cancer [ˈkænsə] Krebs VI/BS 3
candidate [ˈkændɪdeɪt] Kandidat/in V/2A5
by candlelight [baɪ ˈkændllaɪt] bei Kerzenlicht VI/5B2
°canoe [kəˈnuː] Kanu, Paddelboot VI/BS 4
°canvas [ˈkænvəs] Segeltuch VI/BS 3
cap [kæp] Mütze, Kappe IV/7B4
capital [ˈkæpɪtl] Hauptstadt V/4A2
capital system [ˌkæpɪtl ˈsɪstəm] *System der Todesstrafe* VI/3B7
captain [ˈkæptɪn] Kapitän/in; Mannschaftsführer/in V/4A3
caption [ˈkæpʃn] Bildunterschrift VI/5A1
capture [ˈkæptʃə] *hier:* einfangen, festhalten VI/6 Project 2
car [kɑː] Auto I/1B5
(car) technician [ˈkɑː tekˌnɪʃn] Mechatroniker/in V/2A8
carbohydrate [ˌkɑːbəʊˈhaɪdreɪt] Kohlenhydrat VI/1A8
carbon [ˈkɑːbən] Kohlenstoff VI/6 Project 4
carbon dioxide [ˌkɑːbən daɪˈɒksaɪd] Kohlendioxid VI/6 Project 4
carbon footprint [ˈkɑːbən ˌfʊtprɪnt] CO_2-Fußabdruck VI/6 Project 4
card [kɑːd] Pappe, Karton; Karte I/1C4
credit card [ˈkredɪt kɑːd] Kreditkarte VI/5A5
sb doesn't care [ˌsʌmbədi ˌdʌzənt ˈkeə] jdm ist es egal VI/1A1
care (about) [ˈkeərəˌbaʊt] sich etw machen (aus) VI/2 Project 2
career [kəˈrɪə] Beruf; Karriere V/2A2
careful [ˈkeəfl] vorsichtig II/3C2
°carefully [ˈkeəfli] sorgfältig, gründlich VI/BS 2
carnival [ˈkɑːnɪvl] Karneval, Volksfest III/3I
°(plastic) carrier bag [ˌplæstɪk ˈkæriə ˌbæg] Plastiktüte VI/BS 2
carrot [ˈkærət] Möhre, Karotte, Mohrrübe I/1A4
carry [ˈkæri] tragen I/6C5
carry out [ˌkæriˈaʊt] ausführen VI/3B1
cartridge [ˈkɑːtrɪdʒ] Patrone I/1C4
case [keɪs] Fall VI/3A3
individual case [ˌɪndɪˌvɪdʒuəl ˈkeɪs] Einzelfall VI/2 Project 4
°in case ... [ɪn ˈkeɪs] für den Fall, dass ... VI/BS 6

Dictionary English – German

cash [kæʃ] Bargeld III/6I
cash desk [ˈkæʃ ˌdesk] Kasse IV/6B1
cast [kɑːst] *hier:* werfen über, verteilen VI/6 Project 5
cast a spell on sb [ˌkɑːst ə ˈspel ɒn ˌsʌmbədi] jdn verzaubern VI/4 Project 1
cast aside [ˌkɑːst əˈsaɪd] sich befreien von VI/4 Project 2
caste [kɑːst] Kaste VI/3A3
castle [ˈkɑːsl] Burg, Schloss III/4A9
cat [kæt] Katze I/1A6
catch [kætʃ] fangen I/6A3
°**catch one's eye** [ˌkætʃ wʌnz ˈaɪ] *hier:* den Blick fangen VI/BS 6
category [ˈkætəgəri] Kategorie VI/4 Project 6
cattle [ˈkætl] Rinder; Vieh V/4B6
cause [kɔːz] verursachen, hervorrufen VI/1A2
'**cause** (= because) [kɒz] weil, da VI/6 Project 5
celebrate [ˈseləˌbreɪt] feiern II/4A1
celebration [ˌseləˈbreɪʃn] Feier II/4I
celebrity [səˈlebrəti] Berühmtheit, Star VI/1A1
cell [sel] Zelle VI/3B4
cellphone (AE) [ˈselˌfəʊn] Handy IV/3A3
°**censor board** [ˈsensə ˌbɔːd] Zensurbehörde VI/BS 8
center (AE = **centre** BE) [ˈsentə] Zentrum, Mitte II/6B6
century [ˈsentʃəri] Jahrhundert III/5B2
ceremony [ˈserəməni] Zeremonie, Feier VI/3A6
certain [ˈsɜːtn] gewiss, bestimmt IV/5B5
certainly [ˈsɜːtnli] sicherlich, bestimmt IV/1A8
chain [tʃeɪn] Kette VI/1B3
chair [tʃeə] Stuhl I/W
challenge [ˈtʃælɪndʒ] Herausforderung, schwierige Aufgabe VI/2 Project 5
challenging [ˈtʃælɪndʒɪŋ] (heraus)fordernd V/1A3
chance [tʃɑːns] Möglichkeit, Gelegenheit; Chance IV/5A3
take a chance [ˌteɪk ə ˈtʃɑːns] etw riskieren VI/6 Project 3
change [tʃeɪndʒ] (ver)ändern; austauschen I/3B6; (Ver)änderung IV/8B4; Wechselgeld I/5B6; *hier:* umsteigen I/4B1
change [tʃeɪndʒ] sich ändern VI/1A4

make a change [ˌmeɪk ə ˈtʃeɪndʒ] eine Änderung vornehmen VI/6 Project 3
change back [ˌtʃeɪndʒ ˈbæk] *hier:* rückgängig machen VI/3B4
°**change clothes** [ˌtʃeɪndʒ ˈkləʊðz] sich umziehen VI/BS 1
°**change one's mind** [ˌtʃeɪndʒ wʌnz ˈmaɪnd] seine Meinung ändern VI/BS 3
°**changing room** [ˈtʃeɪndʒɪŋ ˌruːm] Umkleidekabine VI/BS 1
chapter [ˈtʃæptə] Kapitel VI/1B1
character [ˈkærɪktə] Charakter; *hier:* Figur IV/4B3
°**charge** [tʃɑːdʒ] angreifen VI/BS 3
charity [ˈtʃærəti] Wohltätigkeitsorganisation III/6B1
°**charity** [ˈtʃærəti] Barmherzigkeit VI/BS 3
charming [ˈtʃɑːmɪŋ] bezaubernd, reizend VI/4 Project 1
chart [tʃɑːt] Diagramm, Grafik VI/1B3
chase [tʃeɪs] verfolgen; nachjagen VI/2I
chat with/to [ˈtʃæt wɪð/ ˌtʊ] plaudern mit, chatten mit IV/1B2
chat-up line [ˈtʃætʌp ˌlaɪn] Anmache, Anmachspruch VI/4 Project 1
cheap [tʃiːp] billig, preiswert II/4B2
°**cheat** [tʃiːt] betrügen VI/BS 2
check [tʃek] überprüfen, kontrollieren III/1B4
check in [ˌtʃek ˈɪn] einchecken; sich (an der Rezeption) anmelden VI/3P7
checklist [ˈtʃeklɪst] Checkliste, Kontrollliste V/5A6
cheek [tʃiːk] Wange VI/4 Project 2
cheese [tʃiːz] Käse I/2B1
chemical [ˈkemɪkl] chemisch, Chemie- VI/1B3
Cherokee [ˈtʃerəkiː] Cherokee/der Cherokee VI/2 Project 2
chest of drawers [ˌtʃest əv ˈdrɔːz] Kommode I/4A1
chew [tʃuː] kauen II/5A5
(chewing) gum [(ˈtʃuːɪŋ) gʌm] Kaugummi II/5B1
chicken [ˈtʃɪkɪn] Huhn I/2C2
chief [tʃiːf] Leiter/in; Führer/in; *hier:* Häuptling VI/2 Project 1
child labour [ˈtʃaɪld ˌleɪbə] Kinderarbeit VI/5B4
child (*pl* **children**) [tʃaɪld, ˈtʃɪldrən] Kind I/1A6

childhood [ˈtʃaɪldˌhʊd] Kindheit IV/7B4
Chinese [ˌtʃaɪˈniːz] Chinese/Chinesin; chinesisch VI/3A6
fish and chip shop [ˌfɪʃ ən ˈtʃɪp ʃɒp] Fischimbiss VI/4 Project 6
chips (only plural) [tʃɪps] Pommes frites III/1A2
chocolate [ˈtʃɒklət] Schokolade I/2C1
°**choice** [tʃɔɪs] Wahl VI/BS 8
°**choke** [tʃəʊk] *hier:* ersticken VI/1O
choose [tʃuːz] wählen; sich entscheiden II/1A3
chorus (*pl* **choruses**) [ˈkɔːrəs, ˈkɔːrəsɪz] Refrain VI/4 Project 4
Christmas [ˈkrɪsməs] Weihnachten I/6P7
Christmas Day [ˌkrɪsməs ˈdeɪ] erster Weihnachtsfeiertag II/4A4
Christmas Eve [ˌkrɪsməs ˈiːv] Heiligabend II/4A4
chuckle [ˈtʃʌkl] in sich hineinlachen VI/4 Project 1
chunky [ˈtʃʌŋki] stämmig, untersetzt VI/1A8
church [tʃɜːtʃ] Kirche II/4A4
church service [ˈtʃɜːtʃ ˌsɜːvɪs] Gottesdienst VI/3B4
°**cigarette** [ˌsɪgəˈret] Zigarette VI/BS 5
cinema [ˈsɪnəmə] Kino II/1A4
citizen [ˈsɪtɪzn] (Staats)bürger/in VI/3B7
city [ˈsɪti] (Groß)stadt I/6B1
civil rights (only plural) [ˌsɪvl ˈraɪts] Bürgerrechte VI/2 Project 3
civil war [ˌsɪvl ˈwɔː] Bürgerkrieg VI/2 Project 2
civilian [səˈvɪliən] Zivilist/in VI/2 Project 5
civilization [ˌsɪvlaɪˈzeɪʃn] Zivilisation, Kultur VI/5A3
claim [kleɪm] behaupten VI/5B4
class [klɑːs] (Schul)klasse I/1A6; *hier:* Unterricht(sstunde) II/5B1
classmate [ˈklɑːsˌmeɪt] Klassenkamerad/in, Mitschüler/in II/2A1
classroom [ˈklɑːsˌruːm] Klassenzimmer I/1C2
conditional clause [kənˌdɪʃnəl ˈklɔːz] Bedingungssatz VI/6G4
clay [kleɪ] Lehm; *hier:* Sand VI/6 Project 4
clean [kliːn] sauber I/3B4; sauber machen I/4B2
°**cleaning-up** [ˌkliːnɪŋ ˈʌp] Säuberung VI/BS 2

Dictionary English – German

clear [klɪə] klar; rein VI/1A2
°**keep clear of** [ˌkiːp ˈklɪər ˌəv] sich fern halten von VI/BS 4
clergyman [ˈklɜːdʒɪmən] Geistliche/r VI/2 Project 3
clever [ˈklevə] klug, schlau III/2A7
client [ˈklaɪənt] Kunde/Kundin VI/5A5
climb (up) [ˈklaɪm] (hinauf)steigen; klettern (auf) II/2C1
clip [klɪp] Ausschnitt, Clip VI/1A3; (Fahrrad)klammer VI/BS 2; stutzen VI/BS 9
clock [klɒk] Uhr I/2B6
close [kləʊs] schließen, zumachen IV/5B2
close [kləʊs] nah(e) VI/3A7; *hier:* fest VI/BS 3; nah(e), eng VI/BS 1
closed [kləʊzd] geschlossen, zu; *hier:* gesperrt III/6B1
clothes *(only plural)* [ˈkləʊðz] Kleider, Kleidung I/1A8
clothing [ˈkləʊðɪŋ] Kleidung III/2A3
°**cloud** [klaʊd] (sich) verfinstern VI/BS 1; Wolke VI/BS 1
club [klʌb] Klub, Verein; Schul-AG I/3A1
°**clunk** [klʌŋk] dumpfes Geräusch VI/BS 5
co-housing [kəʊ ˈhaʊzɪŋ] *gemeinschaftliches Wohnen* VI/4I
coach [kəʊtʃ] Trainer/in IV/2A1
coast [kəʊst] Küste V/4A3
coat [kəʊt] Mantel II/4C3
cob [kɒb] Strohlehm VI/6 Project 4
°**moral code** [ˌmɒrəl ˈkəʊd] Sittenkodex VI/BS 3
°**code of honour** [ˌkəʊd ˌəv ˌˈɒnə] Ehrenkodex VI/BS 2
coffee [ˈkɒfi] Kaffee V/2A8
coin [kɔɪn] Münze, Geldstück IV/6B1
cold [kəʊld] kalt I/1C1
(bad) cold [kəʊld] (starke) Erkältung III/2B1
feel cold [ˌfiːl ˈkəʊld] frieren VI/1A5
the Cold War [ðə ˌkəʊld ˈwɔː] der Kalte Krieg VI/2I
collapse [kəˈlæps] zusammenbrechen VI/2 Project 4
colleague [ˈkɒliːg] Kollege/Kollegin VI/5A5
collect [kəˈlekt] sammeln I/3A1
collect [kəˈlekt] *hier:* eintreiben VI/3B7
collection [kəˈlekʃn] Sammlung I/3A1

college [ˈkɒlɪdʒ] Gymnasium, College VI/3A7
collide [kəˈlaɪd] zusammenstoßen VI/6 Project 5
colonial [kəˈləʊniəl] Kolonist/in VI/2 Project 1
colonist [ˈkɒlənɪst] Kolonist/in; Siedler/in VI/2 Project 1
colony [ˈkɒləni] Kolonie VI/5A2
colour [ˈkʌlə] Farbe I/1A8
colourful [ˈkʌləfl] farbenfroh, bunt IV/7B1
column [ˈkɒləm] Spalte VI/1B1
advice columnist [ədˈvaɪs ˌkɒləmnɪst] Briefkastenonkel/-tante VI/4 Project 6
combination [ˌkɒmbɪˈneɪʃn] Kombination, Zusammenstellung VI/6 Project 4
combine [kəmˈbaɪn] verbinden, kombinieren V/1A8
come [kʌm] kommen I/1A6
come about [ˌkʌm ˌəˈbaʊt] passieren VI/2 Project 2; passieren; *hier:* dazu kommen VI/2 Project 1
°**come around** [ˌkʌm ˌəˈraʊnd] vorbeikommen VI/BS 2
come back [ˌkʌm ˈbæk] zurückkommen III/7A6
come in [ˌkʌm ˌˈɪn] hereinkommen I/5C4
Come on! [ˌkʌm ˌˈɒn] Komm(t) schon!; Mach(t) jetzt! III/1B1; *hier:* Jetzt hör aber auf! II/1A4
°**come over** [ˌkʌm ˌˈəʊvə] herüberkommen VI/BS 7
come to an end [ˌkʌm tʊ ˌən ˌˈend] zu Ende gehen VI/2G8
come to sb's mind [ˌkʌm tuː ˌsʌmbədiz ˈmaɪnd] jdm einfallen IV/1A1
comedy [ˈkɒmədi] Komödie VI/2 Project 4
°**comfortable** [ˈkʌmftəbl] behaglich, bequem VI/BS 6
comment [ˈkɒment] Kommentar, Bemerkung V/1B4; sich äußern, einen Kommentar abgeben V/5A2
commission [kəˈmɪʃn] Kommission VI/3A5
commit [kəˈmɪt] begehen VI/3B7
common [ˈkɒmən] üblich, gewöhnlich VI/5B6
have in common [ˌhæv ˌɪn ˈkɒmən] gemeinsam haben VI/4 Project 1
commonly [ˈkɒmənli] häufig, gemeinhin VI/4 Project 2

°**communal** [ˈkɒmjʊnl] gemeinsam, Gemeinschafts- VI/BS 6
communicate [kəˈmjuːnɪkeɪt] kommunizieren, sich verständigen V/2A5
communication [kəˌmjuːnɪˈkeɪʃn] Kommunikation, Verständigung V/5I
communication skills [kəˌmjuːnɪˈkeɪʃn ˌskɪlz] Kommunikationsfähigkeit V/2B1
communist [ˈkɒmjʊnɪst] Kommunist/in; kommunistisch VI/2 Project 5
community [kəˈmjuːnəti] Gemeinde, Gemeinschaft V/4A2
commute a sentence [kəˌmjuːt ˌə ˈsentəns] ein Strafmaß herabsetzen VI/3B7
company [ˈkʌmpni] Firma, Unternehmen IV/1B2
company [ˈkʌmpni] *hier:* Besuch, Gäste VI/2 Project 3
textile company [ˈtekstaɪl ˌkʌmpni] Textilunternehmen VI/5B3
compare [kəmˈpeə] vergleichen II/4B2
comparison [kəmˈpærɪsn] Vergleich VI/5B4
competition [ˌkɒmpəˈtɪʃn] Wettbewerb IV/2A8
complain [kəmˈpleɪn] klagen, sich beklagen VI/6G1
complete [kəmˈpliːt] vervollständigen II/1A4
complete [kəmˈpliːt] *hier:* fertigstellen VI/2 Project 2
completely [kəmˈpliːtli] völlig VI/1A7
complication [ˌkɒmplɪˈkeɪʃn] Komplikation VI/6 Project 5
pay a compliment [ˌpeɪ ˌə ˈkɒmplɪmənt] ein Kompliment machen VI/6G1
compost [ˈkɒmpɒst] Kompost- VI/6 Project 4; kompostieren VI/6 Project 4
compost heap [ˈkɒmpɒst ˌhiːp] Komposthaufen VI/6 Project 4
con [kɒn] Kontra, Wider IV/5A3
concentrate (on) [ˈkɒnsnˌtreɪt] sich konzentrieren (auf) V/5B3
concept [ˈkɒnsept] Vorstellung, Idee VI/6 Project 5
concern [kənˈsɜːn] Sorge, Besorgnis VI/3B7
concert [ˈkɒnsət] Konzert III/7A6
condemn [kənˈdem] verurteilen VI/5B4

205

Dictionary English – German

condition [kənˈdɪʃn] Zustand VI/6 Project 5
conditional clause [kənˌdɪʃnəl ˈklɔːz] Bedingungssatz VI/6G4
working conditions [ˈwɜːkɪŋ kənˌdɪʃnz] Arbeitsbedingungen VI/5B4
conditions (only plural) [kənˈdɪʃnz] Bedingungen, Verhältnisse V/1A6
the Confederacy [ðə kənˈfedərəsi] die Konföderierten Staaten von Amerika VI/2 Project 3
conference [ˈkɒnfrəns] Konferenz, Tagung VI/2 Project 5
confident [ˈkɒnfɪdnt] selbstsicher, selbstbewusst VI/1A2
conflict [ˈkɒnflɪkt] Konflikt VI/5A3
confused [kənˈfjuːzd] verwirrt, durcheinander VI/4 Project 1
confusion [kənˈfjuːʒn] Verwirrung VI/4 Project 4
congress [ˈkɒŋgres] Kongress, Tagung VI/3B6
Congress [ˈkɒŋgres] der (amerikanische) Kongress VI/2 Project 1
conjunction [kənˈdʒʌŋkʃn] Konjunktion, Bindewort IV/7A4
connect [kəˈnekt] hier: in Zusammenhang stehen VI/3A2; hier: miteinander verbunden sein VI/4 Project 6; verbinden, anschließen VI/6 Project 5
get connected [ˌget kəˈnektɪd] verbunden werden V/5I
connection [kəˈnekʃn] Verbindung; Anschluss V/5A2
conquer [ˈkɒŋkə] erobern, besiegen VI/5A3
°conscience [ˈkɒnʃns] Gewissen VI/BS 2
freedom of conscience [ˌfriːdəm əv ˈkɒnʃns] Gewissensfreiheit VI/3A4
consequence [ˈkɒnsɪkwəns] Folge, Konsequenz VI/3A3
consider [kənˈsɪdə] hier: bedenken, berücksichtigen VI/5B3; halten für, betrachten VI/BS 8; hier: in Betracht ziehen VI/BS 4
°considerable [kənˈsɪdrəbl] erheblich, beträchtlich VI/BS 8
°school constitution [ˈskuːl kɒnstɪˌtjuːʃn] Schulordnung VI/BS 3
consumer [kənˈsjuːmə] Verbraucher/in V/1B5
contact [ˈkɒntækt] sich in Verbindung setzen mit V/2A2

contact [ˈkɒntækt] Kontakt, Verbindung VI/5A5
contain [kənˈteɪn] enthalten VI/3B1
°content [ˈkɒntent] Inhalt, Gehalt VI/BS 2
continent [ˈkɒntɪnənt] Kontinent, Erdteil VI/6 Project 5
continue [kənˈtɪnjuː] weitermachen mit IV/8B2
contract [kənˈtrækt] bekommen, sich zuziehen VI/1A7
contribute [kənˈtrɪbjuːt] beisteuern, spenden V/3I
contribution [ˌkɒntrɪˈbjuːʃn] Beitrag VI/6I
control [kənˈtrəʊl] kontrollieren, steuern V/2B1
control [kənˈtrəʊl] hier: beherrschen VI/3B4; Kontrolle VI/5A3
take control of sth [ˌteɪk kənˈtrəʊl əv ˌsʌmθɪŋ] hier: Kontrolle über etw gewinnen VI/1A5
controversial [ˌkɒntrəˈvɜːʃl] umstritten, kontrovers VI/2 Project 5
convention [kənˈvenʃn] Abkommen VI/3A4
conversation [ˌkɒnvəˈseɪʃn] Gespräch, Unterhaltung IV/1A7
conviction [kənˈvɪkʃn] Überzeugung VI/3A4
cook [kʊk] Koch/Köchin II/3A4; kochen; braten II/3A4
cooking [ˈkʊkɪŋ] Kochen VI/3B4
do the cooking [ˌduː ðə ˈkʊkɪŋ] kochen III/4B2
°cool [kuːl] Ruhe, Gelassenheit VI/BS 5
stay cool [ˌsteɪ ˈkuːl] ruhig bleiben III/4B1
copy [ˈkɒpi] abschreiben II/1A4
°copy [ˈkɒpi] Kopie VI/BS 3
corner [ˈkɔːnə] Ecke VI/1A1
corporate kitchen [ˌkɔːprət ˈkɪtʃən] Firmenküche VI/1B2
corporation [ˌkɔːpəˈreɪʃn] Unternehmen VI/1B3
correct [kəˈrekt] korrigieren IV/1B3; richtig, korrekt I/5B5
correspondence [ˌkɒrəˈspɒndəns] Beziehung; Korrespondenz, Schriftverkehr VI/3A4
corruption [kəˈrʌpʃn] Korruption, Bestechung VI/5A3
cost [kɒst] kosten II/6A4
cost [kɒst] Preis, Kosten VI/5B3
costume [ˈkɒstjuːm] Kostüm III/3A1

cotton [ˈkɒtn] Baumwolle VI/5B1
cotton farming [ˈkɒtn ˌfɑːmɪŋ] Baumwollanbau VI/5B3
could [kʊd] könnte(n/st/t) II/4B7
Could we have the bill, please? [kʊd wiː ˌhæv ðə ˈbɪl ˌpliːz] Wir möchten bitte zahlen!, Die Rechnung, bitte! III/1A3
Council of Europe [ˌkaʊnsl əv ˈjʊərəp] Europarat VI/3A5
°counsel [ˈkaʊnsl] (be)raten VI/BS 5
count [kaʊnt] zählen V/2A6
country [ˈkʌntri] Land I/3A1
developing country [dɪˈveləpɪŋ ˌkʌntri] Entwicklungsland VI/5B4
countryside [ˈkʌntriˌsaɪd] Land IV/8A5
couple [ˈkʌpl] Paar VI/3B8
a couple of [ə ˈkʌpl əv] einige, ein paar IV/6B1
courage [ˈkʌrɪdʒ] Mut, Tapferkeit VI/5A2
course [kɔːs] Kurs; hier: Fach V/2A2
course [kɔːs] hier: Verlauf VI/2I
cousin [ˈkʌzn] Cousin/e I/5C7
cover [ˈkʌvə] bedecken, abdecken V/4A2
cow [kaʊ] Kuh I/6B1
°cram [kræm] stopfen VI/BS 6
°crap (informal) [kræp] Scheiß(e) VI/BS 1
crash [kræʃ] hier: Zusammenbruch VI/2 Project 4
crazy [ˈkreɪzi] verrückt, wahnsinnig IV/4B1
cream [kriːm] Sahne VI/4 Project 1; cremefarben VI/BS 6
create [kriˈeɪt] erschaffen, erzeugen VI/3B4
creative [kriˈeɪtɪv] kreativ, schöpferisch VI/6I
opening credit [ˌəʊpənɪŋ ˈkredɪt] einleitende Danksagung VI/4 Project 6
credit card [ˈkredɪt kɑːd] Kreditkarte VI/5A5
°give sb the creeps [ˌgɪv ˌsʌmbədi ðə ˈkriːps] jdm nicht geheuer sein VI/BS 1
cricket [ˈkrɪkɪt] Kricket VI/5A1
crime [kraɪm] Verbrechen VI/3B4
crisis (pl crises) [ˈkraɪsɪs, ˈkraɪsiːz] Krise VI/5A5
crisps (only plural) [krɪsps] Chips II/4C4
critic [ˈkrɪtɪk] Kritiker/in IV/7A3
critical [ˈkrɪtɪkl] kritisch, missbilligend IV/7B5

206

Dictionary English – German

criticize [ˈkrɪtɪsaɪz] kritisieren VI/3A3
cross [krɒs] überqueren VI/2 Project 1
crossing [ˈkrɒsɪŋ] Überfahrt, *hier:* Überquerung VI/2 Project 4
°crucify [ˈkruːsɪfaɪ] kreuzigen, lynchen VI/BS 3
cruel [ˈkruːəl] grausam, gemein V/1B5
cruelty [ˈkruːəlti] Grausamkeit VI/3A5
°crush [krʌʃ] zusammendrücken, zerdrücken VI/BS 3
crusty [ˈkrʌsti] *Kuchensorte* VI/4 Project 1
cry [kraɪ] weinen; schreien II/3C3
Cuba [ˈkjuːbə] Kuba VI/2 Project 5
Cuban [ˈkjuːbən] Kubaner/in; kubanisch VI/2 Project 5
°cuffed [kʌft] mit Handschellen gefesselt VI/BS 5
cultivate [ˈkʌltɪveɪt] anbauen VI/2 Project 1
cultural [ˈkʌltʃrəl] kulturell VI/3A4
culture [ˈkʌltʃə] Kultur V/4A4
cup [kʌp] Tasse I/2B3
cupboard [ˈkʌbəd] Schrank II/3A1
°curious [ˈkjʊəriəs] neugierig VI/BS 2
°current [ˈkʌrənt] Strom VI/BS 5
°curse [kɜːs] fluchen VI/1O
curtain [ˈkɜːtn] Vorhang VI/6 Project 2
customer [ˈkʌstəmə] Kunde/Kundin III/6A6
cut [kʌt] schneiden II/3A4
cut out [ˌkʌt ˈaʊt] ausschneiden VI/5B3
CV (= curriculum vitae) [ˌsiːˈviː] Lebenslauf V/2A2
cycle [ˈsaɪkl] Rad fahren II/5A5
cycle [ˈsaɪkl] Zyklus, Kreislauf VI/6 Project 5
°cylinder [ˈsɪlɪndə] Zylinder VI/5O
the Czech Republic [ðə ˌtʃek rɪˈpʌblɪk] Tschechische Republik VI/6G7

D

dad *(informal)* [dæd] Papa, Vati I/1A3
daddy [ˈdædi] Vati, Papi VI/4 Project 5
daily [ˈdeɪli] jeden Tag, täglich III/7B1
daily life [ˌdeɪli ˈlaɪf] Alltagsleben VI/3B4
damaged [ˈdæmɪdʒd] beschädigt VI/5A5
dance [dɑːns] Tanz IV/7A2; tanzen I/4C5

dancing [ˈdɑːnsɪŋ] Tanzen VI/3B4
dangerous [ˈdeɪndʒərəs] gefährlich II/2B5
dare [deə] sich trauen VI/2 Project 3
dark [dɑːk] dunkel II/3A1
darkness [ˈdɑːknəs] Dunkelheit, Finsternis VI/6 Project 3
date [deɪt] Datum III/3A3
date [deɪt] ausgehen (mit) VI/4 Project 2
up to date [ˌʌp tʊ ˈdeɪt] auf dem neuesten Stand VI/5B2
date of birth [ˌdeɪt əv ˈbɜːθ] Geburtsdatum V/2A3
daughter [ˈdɔːtə] Tochter I/5C7
dawn [dɔːn] anbrechen, dämmern VI/6 Project 5
day [deɪ] Tag I/4I
break of day [ˌbreɪk əv ˈdeɪ] Tagesanbruch VI/6 Project 2
one day [ˈwʌn ˌdeɪ] eines Tages VI/1A5
°in broad daylight [ɪn ˌbrɔːd ˈdeɪlaɪt] am hellichten Tag VI/BS 2
°daytime [ˈdeɪtaɪm] tagsüber VI/BS 3
dead [ded] tot IV/4B1
°in the dead of night [ɪn ðə ˌded əv ˈnaɪt] mitten in der Nacht VI/BS 2
deal [diːl] Geschäft, Abkommen VI/4 Project 2
a great deal [ə ˌɡreɪt ˈdiːl] eine Menge, ziemlich viel VI/3B4
°no big deal [ˌnəʊ ˌbɪɡ ˈdiːl] nichts Besonderes VI/BS 1
deal with [ˈdiːl wɪð] sich befassen mit; *hier:* umgehen mit V/2B1
dear [dɪə] Sehr geehrte(r) …, *hier:* Liebe(r, s) … II/5A3
dear [dɪə] lieb, teuer VI/2 Project 2; Schatz VI/2I
Dear Sir or Madam, (…) [ˌdɪə ˈsɜːr ɔː ˈmædəm] Sehr geehrte Damen und Herren! (…) V/2A5
death [deθ] Tod IV/7B4
death penalty [ˈdeθ ˌpenlti] Todesstrafe VI/3A4
death row [ˌdeθ ˈrəʊ] Todestrakt VI/3B3
debate [dɪˈbeɪt] Debatte, Diskussion VI/3B6
°decay [dɪˈkeɪ] *hier:* Fäulnis VI/BS 2
December [dɪˈsembə] Dezember I/5C2
decide [dɪˈsaɪd] sich entscheiden; beschließen III/5A2

decide [dɪˈsaɪd] entscheiden, bestimmen VI/3B7
decision [dɪˈsɪʒn] Entscheidung V/1B3
declaration [ˌdekləˈreɪʃn] Erklärung VI/3A4
Declaration of Independence [ˌdekləˌreɪʃn əv ˌɪndɪˈpendəns] *Unabhängigkeitserklärung* VI/2 Project 1
declare [dɪˈkleə] verkünden; erklären VI/2 Project 3
decline [dɪˈklaɪn] *hier:* ablehnen VI/3B8
deep [diːp] tief III/5B1
°by default [baɪ dɪˈfɔːlt] automatisch VI/BS 6
defeat [dɪˈfiːt] besiegen VI/2 Project 2
defend [dɪˈfend] verteidigen V/1B5
°defend oneself [dɪˈfend wʌnˌself] sich verteidigen VI/BS 3
°deficiency [dɪˈfɪʃənsi] Mangel VI/BS 2
definitely [ˈdefnətli] eindeutig, definitiv V/5B3
definition [ˌdefəˈnɪʃn] Definition, Erklärung V/6I
degrading [dɪˈɡreɪdɪŋ] erniedrigend, entwürdigend VI/3A4
°delay [dɪˈleɪ] verschieben, aufschieben VI/5O
delegate [ˈdeləɡət] Delegierte/r VI/2 Project 1
°deliberately [dɪˈlɪbərətli] absichtlich VI/BS 6
°delicate [ˈdelɪkət] *hier:* zart VI/1O
delicious [dɪˈlɪʃəs] köstlich, lecker III/1B1
deliver [dɪˈlɪvə] liefern, ausliefern VI/1B2
democracy [dɪˈmɒkrəsi] Demokratie VI/3A5
democratic [ˌdeməˈkrætɪk] demokratisch VI/2 Project 5
demon [ˈdiːmən] Dämon, Besessene/r VI/3B7
°go into denial [ˌɡəʊ ˌɪntʊ dɪˈnaɪəl] *hier:* die Augen vor der Wahrheit verschließen wollen VI/BS 2
°denim [ˈdenɪm] blauer Jeansstoff VI/BS 5
Denmark [ˈdenmɑːk] Dänemark VI/5A3
department store [dɪˈpɑːtmənt ˌstɔː] Kaufhaus II/4B2
departure [dɪˈpɑːtʃə] Abreise, Abfahrt IV/8B2

D

Dictionary English – German

depend on [dɪˈpend ɒn] abhängen von VI/3B4
°**dependency** [diˈpendənsi] Abhängigkeit VI/BS 2
°**dependent** [diˈpendənt] abhängig VI/BS 2
depict [dɪˈpɪkt] darstellen; zeigen VI/6 Project 5
Great Depression [ˌgreɪt dɪˈpreʃn] Weltwirtschaftskrise VI/2 Project 4
descend [diˈsend] hinabsteigen VI/2G9
describe [dɪˈskraɪb] beschreiben II/3C2
description [dɪˈskrɪpʃn] Beschreibung V/1B5
deserve [dɪˈzɜːv] verdienen VI/3B7
design [dɪˈzaɪn] entwerfen, gestalten VI/1A11
°**desirable** [diˈzaɪərəbl] erstrebenswert VI/5O
desk [desk] Schreibtisch I/1C1
°**despair** [dɪˈspeə] Verzweiflung VI/BS 2
be desperate to do sth [ˌbi: ˈdesprət tə ˌduː ˈsʌmθɪŋ] etw unbedingt tun wollen VI/4 Project 3
despite [diˈspaɪt] trotz VI/3B4
dessert [dɪˈzɜːt] Nachtisch III/1A2
destruction [diˈstrʌkʃn] Zerstörung, *hier:* Vernichtung VI/2 Project 5
detach [diˈtætʃ] abnehmen, abtrennen VI/6 Project 2
detail [ˈdiːteɪl] Detail, Einzelheit V/2A2
determine [diˈtɜːmɪn] ermitteln, feststellen VI/3B7
determined [diˈtɜːmɪnd] entschlossen VI/3B6
deterrent [diˈterənt] Abschreckung(smittel) VI/3B6
be devastated [ˌbi: ˈdevəsteɪtɪd] völlig am Boden zerstört sein VI/4 Project 1
develop [dɪˈveləp] entwickeln; erarbeiten V/5A8; *hier:* bekommen VI/1A8
develop [dɪˈveləp] sich entwickeln VI/2 Project 4
developing country [dɪˈveləpɪŋ ˌkʌntri] Entwicklungsland VI/5B4
developing world *(no pl)* [dɪˈveləpɪŋ ˌwɜːld] Entwicklungsländer VI/5B4
development [dɪˈveləpmənt] Entwicklung VI/2 Project 4
diagram [ˈdaɪəgræm] Schaubild V/4A5

dialogue [ˈdaɪəˌlɒg] Gespräch, Dialog II/1A1
°**diaper** [ˈdaɪəpə] Windel VI/BS 5
diary [ˈdaɪəri] Tagebuch V/2A6
dictionary [ˈdɪkʃənri] Wörterbuch III/1B6
die [daɪ] sterben V/6I
diet [ˈdaɪət] Nahrung, Ernährung VI/BS 2; Diät halten VI/1A5
go on a diet [ˌgəʊ ɒn ə ˈdaɪət] eine Diät machen VI/1A6
°**differ** [ˈdɪfə] sich unterscheiden VI/BS 8
difference [ˈdɪfrəns] Unterschied II/5B6
difference [ˈdɪfrəns] *hier:* (Meinungs)verschiedenheit VI/2 Project 3
different [ˈdɪfrənt] anders, andere(r, s); unterschiedlich, verschieden I/4A5
difficult [ˈdɪfɪklt] schwierig, schwer II/1B5
°**digger** [ˈdɪgə] (Gold)gräber/in VI/BS 3
°**dignified** [ˈdɪgnɪfaɪd] würdig, würdevoll VI/BS 2
dignity [ˈdɪgnəti] Würde VI/3A7
diligent [ˈdɪlɪdʒənt] sorgfältig, gewissenhaft VI/6 Project 2
°**dim** [dɪm] abdunkeln, verdunkeln VI/BS 5
dinner [ˈdɪnə] Abendessen; Mittagessen I/4A4
dinosaur [ˈdaɪnəˌsɔː] Dinosaurier II/6B1
carbon dioxide [ˌkɑːbən daɪˈɒksaɪd] Kohlendioxid VI/6 Project 4
diplomatic [ˌdɪpləˈmætɪk] diplomatisch VI/2 Project 1
direct [daɪˈrekt] direkt VI/5B4
°**direction** [daɪˈrekʃn] Richtung VI/BS 2
ask for directions [ˌɑːsk fə dɪˈrekʃnz] nach dem Weg fragen III/8A4
give (sb) directions [ˌgɪv dɪˈrekʃnz] (jdm) den Weg beschreiben III/8A4
dirt [dɜːt] Schmutz, Dreck VI/5A5
dirty [ˈdɜːti] dreckig, schmutzig II/2A2
°**the disabled** [ðə dɪsˈeɪbld] die Behinderten VI/BS 2
disadvantage [ˌdɪsədˈvɑːntɪdʒ] Nachteil VI/6 Project 4
disagree [ˌdɪsəˈgriː] nicht einverstanden sein IV/5A3

°**disappear** [ˌdɪsəˈpɪə] verschwinden VI/BS 3
disappointed [ˌdɪsəˈpɔɪntɪd] enttäuscht VI/1A1
°**disappointing** [ˌdɪsəˈpɔɪntɪŋ] enttäuschend VI/BS 6
disaster [dɪˈzɑːstə] Katastrophe, Unglück VI/6 Project 1
discover [dɪˈskʌvə] herausfinden, entdecken, finden V/4A3
discrimination [dɪˌskrɪmɪˈneɪʃn] Diskriminierung, Benachteiligung VI/3A5
discuss [dɪˈskʌs] besprechen, diskutieren II/4B5
discussion [dɪˈskʌʃn] Diskussion, Erörterung II/5B6
disease [dɪˈziːz] Krankheit V/1B5
disguise [dɪsˈgaɪz] verkleiden VI/2 Project 1; Verkleidung, Maske VI/6 Project 2
dish (*pl* **dishes**) [dɪʃ, ˈdɪʃɪz] Schale, Schüssel; Gericht IV/1A4
°**dismount** [dɪsˈmaʊnt] absteigen VI/BS 2
eating disorder [ˈiːtɪŋ dɪsˌɔːdə] Essstörung VI/1A5
display [dɪˈspleɪ] Ausstellung VI/6I
display [dɪˈspleɪ] ausstellen VI/2I
disprove [dɪsˈpruːv] widerlegen VI/4 Project 6
°**distance** [ˈdɪstəns] *hier:* Distanz VI/BS 2
distant [ˈdɪstənt] fern; entfernt VI/4 Project 2
°**distort** [dɪˈstɔːt] verzerren VI/BS 2
distribute [dɪˈstrɪbjuːt] verteilen VI/1B6
°**diverse** [daɪˈvɜːs] vielfältig, breit gefächert VI/BS 8
divide [dɪˈvaɪd] teilen VI/2 Project 5
divide into [dɪˈvaɪd ˌɪntʊ] (auf)teilen in VI/5A3
divide up [dɪˌvaɪd ˈʌp] aufteilen VI/5A7
get divorced [ˌget dɪˈvɔːst] sich scheiden lassen VI/4 Project 2
Diwali [dɪˈwɑːli] Lichterfest VI/5A2
do [duː] tun, machen I/1B5
°**do away with** [duˌəˈweɪ wɪð] loswerden, abschaffen VI/5O
do research [ˌduː rɪˈsɜːtʃ] forschen; *hier:* recherchieren VI/2 Project 3
do sport [ˌduː ˈspɔːt] Sport treiben III/2A1
make sb do sth [ˌmeɪk sʌmbədi ˈduː ˌsʌmθɪŋ] jdn dazu bringen, etw zu tun IV/7A3

208

Dictionary English – German

do the shopping [ˌduː ðə ˈʃɒpɪŋ] einkaufen (gehen) I/4B3
do the washing up [ˌduː ðə ˌwɒʃɪŋ ˈʌp] abspülen I/4B6
do without sth [ˌduː wɪðˈaʊt ˌsʌmθɪŋ] ohne etw auskommen, auf etw verzichten V/1B1
How do you do? [ˌhaʊ duː juː ˈduː] Guten Tag! V/2B7
doctor [ˈdɒktə] Arzt/Ärztin II/3C1
see a doctor [ˌsiː ə ˈdɒktə] einen Arzt/Ärztin aufsuchen VI/1A5
dog [dɒg] Hund I/1A6
°**doll** [dɒl] Puppe VI/BS 1
°**domestic** [dəˈmestɪk] häuslich VI/BS 6
donate [dəʊˈneɪt] spenden VI/1B6
get sth done [ˌget ˌsʌmθɪŋ ˈdʌn] etw machen lassen VI/5B2
have sth done [ˌhæv ˌsʌmθɪŋ ˈdʌn] etw machen lassen VI/1A3
door [dɔː] Tür I/W
°**dormitory** [ˈdɔːmətri] Schlafsaal VI/BS 1
dos and don'ts [ˌduːz ənd ˈdəʊnts] was man tun und was man nicht tun sollte II/5I
dossier [ˈdɒsieɪ] Dossier, Akte II/2B1
°**dot** [dɒt] Punkt, Tupfen VI/BS 8
°**double** [ˈdʌbl] doppelt VI/BS 2
doubt [daʊt] *hier:* bezweifeln VI/1Test results 1A2
down [daʊn] hinunter, hinab I/5B4
down [daʊn] unten VI/5B3
down under (*informal*) [ˌdaʊn ˈʌndə] (in / nach) Australien V/4I
download [ˌdaʊnˈləʊd] herunterladen V/5A6
downside [ˈdaʊnsaɪd] Kehrseite, Schattenseite VI/5A5
dozen [ˈdʌzn] Dutzend VI/2 Project 1
drama [ˈdrɑːmə] Theater(kurs); Schauspielerei I/5A2
°**drama** [ˈdrɑːmə] *hier:* Dramatik VI/BS 8
draw [drɔː] zeichnen I/1B6
draw [drɔː] *hier:* hineinziehen, verwickeln VI/4 Project 6
draw up [ˌdrɔː ˈʌp] aufsetzen; erstellen; abfassen VI/1A11
drawing [ˈdrɔːɪŋ] Zeichnung, Skizze IV/7B4
dream [driːm] Traum I/1B5; träumen II/3B1
dress [dres] Kleid I/2C7; sich anziehen I/4C4

°**dress** [dres] anziehen VI/BS 2
dress up [ˌdres ˈʌp] sich verkleiden III/3A1
drink [drɪŋk] Getränk II/5A4; trinken I/2B1
have a drink [ˌhæv ə ˈdrɪŋk] etw trinken III/3B2
drive [draɪv] fahren II/3A4
drive [draɪv] *hier:* vertreiben VI/2 Project 3; *hier:* Einfahrt VI/BS 2
driver [ˈdraɪvə] Fahrer/in VI/2 Project 2
driving licence [ˈdraɪvɪŋ ˌlaɪsns] Führerschein V/2A2
drop [drɒp] fallen lassen VI/4 Project 3; fallen, sinken VI/1A8; *hier:* abwerfen VI/2 Project 5
°**drop out of school** [ˌdrɒp ˌaʊt əv ˈskuːl] die Schule abbrechen VI/BS 3
drop-dead gorgeous (*informal*) [ˌdrɒpded ˈgɔːdʒəs] wahnsinnig gut aussehend VI/1A2
drug [drʌg] Medikament, Droge V/1B5
be high on drugs [ˌbiː ˌhaɪ ɒn ˈdrʌgz] mit Drogen vollgepumpt sein VI/3B4
drum [drʌm] Trommel VI/6 Project 5
°**dude** [duːd] Typ VI/BS 3
°**due to** [ˈdjuː tʊ] wegen VI/BS 8
the dumb [ðə ˈdʌm] *hier:* die Dummen, die Blöden VI/6 Project 5
during [ˈdjʊərɪŋ] während IV/3B1
dustbin man (*pl* **dustbin men**) [ˈdʌsbɪn mæn, ˈdʌsbɪn men] Müllmann IV/6A1
Dutch [dʌtʃ] niederländisch, holländisch VI/2 Project 2

E

e.g. [ˌiː ˈdʒiː] z.B. VI/5B7
each [iːtʃ] jede(r, s) III/6B1
each other [ˌiːtʃ ˈʌðə] einander III/3B4
ear [ɪə] Ohr I/2A2
early [ˈɜːli] früh II/4A3
earn [ɜːn] verdienen III/6A2
earring [ˈɪərɪŋ] Ohrring IV/4A2
earth [ɜːθ] Erde, Boden IV/5B1
earthquake [ˈɜːθkweɪk] Erdbeben VI/4 Project 3
east [iːst] Osten III/4A9
easy [ˈiːzi] leicht, einfach I/4C1
eat [iːt] essen I/1A4

eat out [ˌiːt ˈaʊt] essen gehen III/1I
°**eating** [ˈiːtɪŋ] Essen VI/BS 2
eating binge [ˈiːtɪŋ ˌbɪndʒ] Essattacke VI/1A6
eating disorder [ˈiːtɪŋ dɪsˌɔːdə] Essstörung VI/1A5
eco- [iːkəʊ] Öko- VI/6 Project 4
ecological [ˌiːkəˈlɒdʒɪkl] ökologisch VI/6G9
economic [ˌiːkəˈnɒmɪk] wirtschaftlich, Wirtschafts- VI/1B6
economy [ɪˈkɒnəmi] Wirtschaft V/5B3
educated [ˈedjukeɪtɪd] (gut) ausgebildet VI/5A5
education [ˌedjuˈkeɪʃn] Bildung; Ausbildung V/2A3
effect [ɪˈfekt] Wirkung, Auswirkung, Effekt VI/1A2
effort [ˈefət] Mühe, Anstrengung VI/2 Project 5
egg [eg] Ei I/2B1
eight [eɪt] acht I/2A2
(eight) o'clock [əˈklɒk] (acht) Uhr I/2A2
°**not ... either** [nɒt ˈaɪðə/ˈiːðr] auch nicht VI/BS 6
either ... or ... [ˌaɪðə ... ˈɔː] entweder ... oder ... IV/3B4
°**either of you** [ˈaɪðər/ˈiːðr əv ˌjuː] eine/r von euch beiden VI/BS 7
°**elder** [ˈeldə] Ältere/r VI/BS 8
°**elderly** [ˈeldəl] ältere(r,s) VI/BS 2
°**the elderly** [ðɪ ˈeldəli] ältere Menschen, Senioren VI/BS 2
eldest [ˈeldɪst] älteste(r,s) VI/4 Project 6
elect [ɪˈlekt] wählen VI/2 Project 2
election [ɪˈlekʃn] Wahl VI/3A4
°**electric** [ɪˈlektrɪk] elektrisch; elektrisierend VI/BS 5
electricity [ɪˌlekˈtrɪsəti] Elektrizität, Strom III/5A5
elephant [ˈelɪfənt] Elefant I/3B4
elephant grass [ˈelɪfənt ˌgrɑːs] Elefantengras VI/6 Project 4
elevator (*AE*) [ˈelɪveɪtə] Aufzug, Fahrstuhl IV/3A3
eleven [ɪˈlevn] elf I/1A4
else [els] sonst VI/5B2
no one else [ˌnəʊwʌn ˈels] niemand anderes IV/4A2
nobody else [ˌnəʊbədi ˈels] niemand anderes VI/1A2
nothing else [ˌnʌθɪŋ ˈels] nichts weiter VI/1A5
something else [ˌsʌmθɪŋ ˈels] etwas anderes IV/3A2

Dictionary English – German

What else ...? [ˌwɒt ˈels] Was sonst ...? V/2B8
elsewhere [ˌelsˈweə] woanders, anderswo VI/5B2
'em (= them) (informal) [əm] sie, ihnen VI/3B9
°**emaciated** [ɪˈmeɪʃieɪtɪd] abgemagert, ausgezehrt VI/BS 2
embarrassed [ɪmˈbærəst] verlegen VI/4 Project 3
emergency [ɪˈmɜːdʒnsi] Notfall; *hier:* Notaufnahme VI/3A3
emigrant [ˈemɪgrənt] Auswanderer/Auswanderin VI/2 Project 1
emigrate [ˈemɪgreɪt] auswandern, emigrieren IV/8A6
emigration [ˌemɪˈgreɪʃn] Auswanderung, Emigration IV/8A2
emission [ɪˈmɪʃn] Emission, Abgabe; Ausstoß VI/6 Project 4
°**emotional** [ɪˈməʊʃnəl] emotional, gefühlsmäßig VI/BS 3
°**empathise with sb** [ˈempəθaɪz wɪð ˌsʌmbədi] sich in jdn einfühlen VI/BS 6
empathy [ˈempəθi] Einfühlungsvermögen VI/5A5
empire [ˈempaɪə] Imperium, Reich VI/5A3
the Roman Empire [ðə ˌrəʊmən ˈempaɪə] das Römische Reich VI/5A3
employ [ɪmˈplɔɪ] beschäftigen, einstellen V/2B1
employee [ɪmˈplɔɪiː] Angestellte/r; Mitarbeiter/in V/2A8
employer [ɪmˈplɔɪə] Arbeitgeber/in V/2B1
empress [ˈemprəs] Kaiserin VI/5A3
empty [ˈempti] leer II/3C2
°**empty-headed** [ˌemptiˈhedɪd] hohlköpfig, strohdumm VI/BS 1
enclose [ɪnˈkləʊz] beilegen, beifügen V/2A5
encounter [ɪnˈkaʊntə] begegnen VI/6 Project 2
encourage [ɪnˈkʌrɪdʒ] Mut machen, ermutigen VI/5A5
end [end] beenden V/1B5; Ende II/1A4
end [end] enden, aufhören VI/2 Project 4
come to an end [ˌkʌm tʊ ən ˈend] zu Ende gehen VI/2G8
in the end [ˌɪn ði ˈend] letzten Endes; schließlich IV/2B2
end up [ˌend ˈʌp] enden VI/4 Project 2

ending [ˈendɪŋ] Ende, Schluss II/3C2
ending [ˈendɪŋ] *hier:* Endung VI/4G12
enemy [ˈenəmi] Feind/in VI/6 Project 5
energy [ˈenədʒi] Energie, Kraft VI/1A5
energy-efficient [ˈenədʒiiˌfɪʃnt] energiesparend VI/6G9
energy-saving [ˈenədʒiˌseɪvɪŋ] energiesparend VI/6 Project 4
engine [ˈendʒɪn] Maschine, Motor III/5B1
England [ˈɪŋglənd] England II/LL1
English [ˈɪŋglɪʃ] englisch; Englisch I/1C4
the English (only plural) [ði ˈɪŋglɪʃ] die Engländer VI/2G5
English-speaking [ˈɪŋglɪʃˌspiːkɪŋ] englischsprachig III/7B3
Englishman (pl Englishmen) [ˈɪŋglɪʃmən, ˈɪŋglɪʃmən] Engländer VI/2I
enjoy [ɪnˈdʒɔɪ] genießen II/1B2
enjoy oneself [ɪnˈdʒɔɪ wʌnˌself] sich amüsieren IV/2A1
enough [ɪˈnʌf] genug I/5C5
fair enough [ˌfeər ɪˈnʌf] in Ordnung, schön und gut VI/6 Project 1
ensure [ɪnˈʃɔː] sicherstellen, garantieren VI/3A5
enter [ˈentə] hineingehen, eintreten; betreten VI/4 Project 1
°**entertainment** [ˌentəˈteɪnmənt] Unterhaltung VI/BS 8
entitled [ɪnˈtaɪtld] berechtigt VI/3A4
entry [ˈentri] *hier:* Eintrag V/1B3
environment [ɪnˈvaɪrənmənt] Umwelt IV/5B1
environmental [ɪnˌvaɪrənˈmentl] Umwelt- VI/6 Project 1
envy [ˈenvi] Neid VI/6 Project 2
equal [ˈiːkwəl] gleich V/4A3
equal [ˈiːkwəl] an etw herankommen, gleichkommen VI/6 Project 5
°**equally** [ˈiːkwəli] ebenso, gleichermaßen VI/BS 2
°**equate** [ɪˈkweɪt] gleichsetzen mit VI/BS 8
equitably [ˈekwɪtəbli] gerecht, fair VI/3B7
era [ˈɪərə] Ära, Epoche VI/2 Project 4
eraser [ɪˈreɪzə] Radiergummi II/1C1
°**erect** [ɪˈrekt] *hier:* erigiert VI/BS 3

°**ergonomic** [ˌɜːgəˈnɒmɪk] ergonomisch VI/BS 3
error [ˈerə] Fehler, Irrtum VI/3B7
escape [ɪˈskeɪp] fliehen; entkommen VI/2 Project 3
especially [əˈspeʃli, ɪˈspeʃli] besonders VI/1A3
essential [ɪˈsenʃl] unbedingt erforderlich VI/2 Project 1
establish [ɪˈstæblɪʃ] gründen VI/2 Project 1; *hier:* einführen VI/2 Project 4
estimate [ˈestɪmət] Schätzung VI/6 Project 4
°**estimate** [ˈestɪmeɪt] (ein)schätzen VI/BS 2
estimated [ˈestɪmeɪtɪd] geschätzt VI/1A7
eternal [ɪˈtɜːnl] ewig, immer während VI/5A2
°**eternity** [ɪˈtɜːnəti] Ewigkeit VI/1O
ethical [ˈeθɪkl] ethisch VI/5B4
°**ethics** [ˈeθɪks] Ethik VI/BS 2
EU (= European Union) [ˌiː ˈjuː, ˌjʊərəˌpiːən ˈjuːniən] EU (= Europäische Union) VI/6G7
Europe [ˈjʊərəp] Europa II/6C2
European [ˌjʊərəˈpiːən] Europäer/in; europäisch V/4A3
even [ˈiːvn] selbst; sogar III/2A3
not even [ˌnɒt ˈiːvn] noch nicht einmal IV/4A2
°**even if** [ˌiːvən ˈɪf] selbst wenn VI/BS 6
even though [ˌiːvən ˈðəʊ] selbst wenn; obwohl IV/8B2
evening [ˈiːvnɪŋ] Abend I/4B3
event [ɪˈvent] Ereignis, Veranstaltung III/3A3
eventually [ɪˈventʃuəli] schließlich; irgendwann VI/2 Project 1
ever [ˈevə] jemals, schon einmal III/1A10
not ever [ˌnɒt ˈevə] nie VI/4 Project 3
every [ˈevri] jede(r, s) I/4A6
everybody [ˈevriˌbɒdi] jede(r); alle I/1A4
everyday [ˈevrideɪ] alltäglich VI/5A5
everyone [ˈevriwʌn] jede(r); alle I/4B2
everything [ˈevriθɪŋ] alles II/4B6
everywhere [ˈevriˌweə] überall IV/6B1
evil [ˈiːvl] böse VI/4 Project 1; Übel, das Böse VI/6 Project 5
ex-husband [ˌeks ˈhʌzbənd] Ex-Mann VI/3B4

Dictionary English – German

exactly [ɪɡˈzækli] genau VI/2 Project 4
exam [ɪɡˈzæm] Prüfung III/7A6
take an exam [ˌteɪk ən ɪɡˈzæm] eine Prüfung ablegen IV/2B2
example [ɪɡˈzɑːmpl] Beispiel II/2B4
except (for) [ɪkˈsept] außer VI/2 Project 1
excerpt [ˈeksɜːpt] (Text)auszug V/4B5
exchange [ɪksˈtʃeɪndʒ] Austausch VI/5A5
exchange [ɪksˈtʃeɪndʒ] austauschen VI/4 Project 1
excited [ɪkˈsaɪtɪd] aufgeregt, begeistert V/2A6
exciting [ɪkˈsaɪtɪŋ] aufregend, spannend III/2A3
°exclusively [ɪkˈskluːsɪvli] ausschließlich, exklusiv VI/BS 6
°excuse [ɪkˈskjuːz] Entschuldigung; Ausrede VI/BS 1
Excuse me! [ɪkˈskjuːz mi] Entschuldigen Sie bitte!, Entschuldigung! I/5B6
execute [ˈeksɪkjuːt] hinrichten VI/3B1
execution [ˌeksɪˈkjuːʃn] Hinrichtung, Exekution VI/3B1
exercise [ˈeksəsaɪz] Bewegung, Übung III/5B2
exercise book [ˈeksəsaɪz ˌbʊk] Heft I/1A4
exhausted [eɡˈzɔːstɪd, ɪɡˈzɔːstɪd] erschöpft VI/1A5
exhibit [ɪɡˈzɪbɪt] ausstellen VI/6 Project 4
exhibition [ˌeksɪˈbɪʃn] Ausstellung IV/7B4
exist [ɪɡˈzɪst] existieren, bestehen V/1B5
°expand [ɪkˈspænd] erweitern, ausbauen VI/5O
expect [ɪkˈspekt] erwarten, mit etwas rechnen VI/1A1
expectation [ˌekspekˈteɪʃn] Erwartung VI/4 Project 2
°expedition [ˌekspəˈdɪʃn] (Forschungs)reise, Expedition VI/BS 4
expensive [ɪkˈspensɪv] teuer II/2B2
experience [ɪkˈspɪəriəns] Erfahrung; Erlebnis IV/6A3
experiment [ɪkˈsperɪmənt] Experiment, Versuch VI/6 Project 4
expert [ˈekspɜːt] Experte/Expertin V/5B2

explain [ɪkˈspleɪn] erklären III/5A2
explode [ɪkˈspləʊd] explodieren VI/2 Project 4
°explore [ɪkˈsplɔː] erforschen, untersuchen VI/BS 1
export [ˈekspɔːt] Export(artikel) VI/2 Project 1
express [ɪkˈspres] ausdrücken V/2B1
expression [ɪkˈspreʃn] Ausdruck IV/2B2
extended [ɪkˈstendɪd] erweitert VI/4I
extensive [ɪkˈstensɪv] weit; hier: umfangreich VI/5A5
extra [ˈekstrə] zusätzlich VI/5B6
extract [ˈekstrækt] Auszug, Exzerpt VI/3B4
extreme sport(s) [ɪkˈstriːm spɔːts] Extremsport(art) V/1A2
extremely [ɪkˈstriːmli] äußerst, höchst IV/1A6
eye [aɪ] Auge I/2A2
°black eye [ˌblæk ˈaɪ] blaues Auge VI/BS 3
°catch one's eye [ˌkætʃ wʌnz ˈaɪ] hier: den Blick fangen VI/BS 6
eye-catching [ˈaɪˌkætʃɪŋ] auffallend, ins Auge springend VI/6 Project 2
°eyebrow [ˈaɪbraʊ] Augenbraue VI/BS 1

F

fabric [ˈfæbrɪk] Stoff VI/5B3
face [feɪs] Gesicht I/2A2
face [feɪs] sich etw gegenübersehen, konfrontiert sein mit VI/1B4
°let's face it [ˌlets ˈfeɪs ɪt] machen wir uns doch nichts vor VI/BS 3
fact [fækt] Tatsache IV/2A9
°in fact [ɪn ˈfækt] tatsächlich; genau genommen VI/BS 3
fact file [ˈfækt faɪl] Steckbrief VI/2 Project 5
factory [ˈfæktri] Fabrik, Werk V/1B5
factory farming [ˈfæktri ˌfɑːmɪŋ] automatisierte Viehhaltung V/1B5
°faded [ˈfeɪdɪd] ausgeblichen VI/BS 2
fair [feə] hier: angemessen VI/6 Project 1
fair enough [ˌfeər ɪˈnʌf] in Ordnung, schön und gut VI/6 Project 1
fairly [ˈfeəli] ziemlich, recht VI/1A8

faith [feɪθ] Vertrauen; Glaube VI/5A2
yours faithfully [ˌjɔːz ˈfeɪθfli] mit freundlichen Grüßen V/2A5
°fake [feɪk] Fälschung, Attrappe VI/BS 3
fall [fɔːl] fallen I/4C9
fall (AE) [fɔːl] Herbst VI/1A5
fall asleep [ˌfɔːl əˈsliːp] einschlafen IV/6B1
fall for sb [ˈfɔːl fə ˌsʌmbədi] sich in jdn verlieben VI/4 Project 3
fall in love (with) [ˌfɔːl ɪn ˈlʌv] sich verlieben (in) II/3A8
false [fɔːls] falsch VI/4 Project 4
familiar [fəˈmɪliə] vertraut VI/1P4
family [ˈfæmli] Familie I/5C2
family tree [ˈfæmli ˌtriː] Familienstammbaum IV/8A4
famine [ˈfæmɪn] Hungersnot VI/1I
famous [ˈfeɪməs] berühmt III/5A2
fancy sb [ˈfænsi ˌsʌmbədi] jdn attraktiv finden, auf jdn stehen VI/4 Project 1
fantasize [ˈfæntəsaɪz] fantasieren, sich vorstellen VI/6 Project 2
fantastic [fænˈtæstɪk] fantastisch, super V/2A8
FAQ (= frequently asked questions) [ˌef eɪ ˈkjuː] oft gestellte Fragen VI/4 Project 1
far [fɑː] weit III/5A1
°take sth too far [ˌteɪk ˌsʌmθɪŋ tuː ˈfɑː] es zu weit treiben VI/BS 3
far away [ˌfɑːr əˈweɪ] fern; weit entfernt VI/6 Project 3
farm [fɑːm] Bauernhof I/3B8
°farm [fɑːm] bebauen; hier: anbauen VI/BS 4
farmer [ˈfɑːmə] Bauer/Bäuerin IV/3B2
farmhouse [ˈfɑːmhaʊs] Bauernhaus VI/6 Project 4
farming [ˈfɑːmɪŋ] Ackerbau und Viehzucht VI/2 Project 1
cotton farming [ˈkɒtn ˌfɑːmɪŋ] Baumwollanbau VI/5B3
fashion [ˈfæʃn] Mode V/3I
fast [fɑːst] schnell II/1B2
fast [fɑːst] hier: fest VI/6 Project 2
fat [fæt] dick VI/1A3; Fett VI/1A8
father [ˈfɑːðə] Vater I/1B2
the Pilgrim Fathers (only plural) [ðə ˌpɪlɡrɪm ˈfɑːðəz] die Pilgerväter VI/2 Project 1
°favour [ˈfeɪvə] Gefallen VI/BS 5
favourite [ˈfeɪvrət] Liebling; Favorit/in III/2A7

favourite [ˈfeɪv(ə)rət] Lieblings- I/W
fear [fɪə] fürchten, befürchten VI/6 Project 5
feast [fiːst] Festmahl, Festessen VI/2 Project 1
feature [ˈfiːtʃə] Merkmal, Eigenschaft IV/5A1
February [ˈfebruəri] Februar I/3A1
feed [fiːd] satt machen, ernähren IV/3B2; zu essen geben, füttern I/3B8
feedback [ˈfiːdbæk] Feedback, Rückmeldung V/2A4
feel [fiːl] (sich) fühlen I/4B5
feel [fiːl] hier: halten von VI/3A4
feel bad [ˌfiːl ˈbæd] sich schlecht fühlen III/2B1
feel cold [ˌfiːl ˈkəʊld] frieren VI/1A5
feel safe [fiːl ˈseɪf] sich sicher fühlen II/5C4
feel sorry [ˌfiːl ˈsɒri] bedauern VI/3B8
feel trapped [ˌfiːl ˈtræpt] sich gefangen fühlen VI/4 Project 5
feeling [ˈfiːlɪŋ] Gefühl III/2A4
felt-tip [ˌfelt ˈtɪp] Filzstift II/1C1
female [ˈfiːmeɪl] weiblich III/3A3
female [ˈfiːmeɪl] Frau VI/1A7
feminine [ˈfemənɪn] feminin, weiblich VI/4 Project 1
fenced-in [ˌfenst ˈɪn] eingezäunt VI/3B4
ferry [ˈferi] Fähre IV/3A2
fertilizer [ˈfɜːtəlaɪzə] Dünger VI/1B3
festival [ˈfestɪvl] Fest, Festival III/2A4
fetch [fetʃ] holen VI/4 Project 1
a few [ə ˈfjuː] einige; wenige II/3C1
field [fiːld] Feld VI/2 Project 3
fierce [fɪəs] heftig; stark VI/3B4
fight [faɪt] (sich) streiten; (be)kämpfen VI/1A5
fight [faɪt] hier: austragen VI/2 Project 4; Kampf, Streit VI/1B5
°**pick a fight** [ˌpɪk ə ˈfaɪt] einen Streit anzetteln VI/BS 3
fight off [ˌfaɪt ˈɒf] ankämpfen gegen VI/1B2
°**fighter** [ˈfaɪtə] Kämpfer/in VI/BS 3
figure [ˈfɪɡə] Gestalt, Figur VI/1I; hier: Zahl V/4A5
°**figure** (AE) [ˈfɪɡə] schätzen VI/BS 3
figure out sth (informal) [ˌfɪɡər ˈaʊt ˌsʌmθɪŋ] etw herausfinden VI/3B9
fill [fɪl] füllen I/6A2
fill in [ˌfɪl ˈɪn] ausfüllen I/2A4; eintragen I/5A1
fill out [ˌfɪl ˈaʊt] ausfüllen V/5A6

film [fɪlm] filmen, drehen VI/2 Project 1
film guide [ˈfɪlm ˌɡaɪd] Filmführer VI/4 Project 6
°**film-maker** [ˈfɪlm ˌmeɪkə] Filmemacher/in VI/BS 8
final [ˈfaɪnl] letzte(r, s) VI/3B8; endgültig VI/BS 9
finally [ˈfaɪnli] schließlich, endlich V/2A6
financial [faɪˈnænʃl] finanziell VI/5A5
find [faɪnd] finden I/1A4
find out [ˌfaɪnd ˈaʊt] herausfinden I/1B1
find out about [ˌfaɪnd ˈaʊt əˌbaʊt] sich informieren über I/3B4
findings (only plural) [ˈfaɪndɪŋz] Ergebnisse VI/1B2
fine [faɪn] in Ordnung, gut I/2B4
°**fine** [faɪn] gut; edel VI/BS 4
finger [ˈfɪŋɡə] Finger I/2A4
finish [ˈfɪnɪʃ] (be)enden, aufhören IV/1A4
fire [ˈfaɪə] Feuer; Brand II/3C1
fire [ˈfaɪə] hier: Kamin, Ofen VI/4 Project 1
firefly [ˈfaɪəflaɪ] Glühwürmchen VI/6 Project 2
firework [ˈfaɪəwɜːk] Feuerwerkskörper II/4C3
°**fireworks** (pl) [ˈfaɪəˌwɜːks] Feuerwerk VI/BS 1
firm [fɜːm] hier: überzeugt VI/3B7
first [fɜːst] erste(r, s) I/3A1; zuerst, als Erstes I/4B1
fish (pl fish or fishes) [fɪʃ, fɪʃ, ˈfɪʃɪz] Fisch I/4A6
fish [fɪʃ] fischen, angeln VI/2 Project 1
fish and chip shop [ˌfɪʃ ən ˈtʃɪp ʃɒp] Fischimbiss VI/4 Project 6
°**fistfight** [ˈfɪstfaɪt] Schlägerei VI/BS 3; sich prügeln VI/BS 3
°**fisticuffs** (only plural) [ˈfɪstɪkʌfs] Handgreiflichkeiten VI/BS 3
fit in [ˌfɪt ˈɪn] sich einfügen V/2A2
five [faɪv] fünf I/1A4
fix [fɪks] festmachen; hier: reparieren IV/6A1
flag [flæɡ] Fahne, Flagge VI/5A2
°**flank** [flæŋk] flankieren VI/BS 5
flat [flæt] (Etagen)wohnung, Mietwohnung III/4B1
flawless [ˈflɔːləs] fehlerlos, makellos VI/1A4
flexible [ˈfleksəbl] flexibel, anpassungsfähig VI/5B4
°**flick** [flɪk] wegschnippen VI/BS 6
°**flicker** [ˈflɪkə] aufflackern VI/BS 5

flight [flaɪt] Flug, Fliegen III/8B1
°**float** [fləʊt] schwimmen; treiben, schweben VI/BS 1
°**flood** [flʌd] Überschwemmung, Hochwasser VI/BS 5
floor [flɔː] (Fuß)boden I/4A1; Stock, Stockwerk IV/3A2
flower [ˈflaʊə] Blume I/4B2
°**flush** [flʌʃ] Spülung VI/BS 5
fly [flaɪ] fliegen I/6A3
flyer [ˈflaɪə] Broschüre VI/3A8
focus on [ˈfəʊkəs ˌɒn] sich konzentrieren auf VI/2 Project 1
folded [ˈfəʊldɪd] zusammengefaltet VI/4 Project 3
folder [ˈfəʊldə] Mappe, Ordner IV/8A5
folk [fəʊk] Leute VI/3B4
follow [ˈfɒləʊ] folgen II/1B5
°**follow** [ˈfɒləʊ] hier: befolgen VI/BS 3
following [ˈfɒləʊɪŋ] folgende(r, s) IV/1B3
font [fɒnt] Schriftart VI/6 Project 2
food [fuːd] Essen I/5C4
food bank [ˈfuːd ˌbæŋk] Tafel (Lebensmittelausgabe für sozial Schwache) VI/1B2
food outlet [ˈfuːd ˌaʊtlet] Restaurant, Imbiss VI/1B2
food technology [ˌfuːd tekˈnɒlədʒi] Ernährungslehre I/5A2
on foot [ɒn ˈfʊt] zu Fuß IV/5B2
foot (pl **feet**) [fʊt, fiːt] Fuß I/2A2
football [ˈfʊtbɔːl] Fußball I/1A4
°**football** (AE) [ˈfʊtˌbɔːl] (American) Football VI/BS 3
footprint [ˈfʊtprɪnt] Fußabdruck VI/6 Project 4
carbon footprint [ˈkɑːbən ˌfʊtprɪnt] CO_2-Fußabdruck VI/6 Project 4
for [fɔː] für I/1A4
for [fɔː] denn VI/6 Project 2
for ... (+ Zeitraum) [fə] für ..., ... lang II/1A4
for an hour [ˌfɔːr ən ˈaʊə] eine Stunde lang II/5A2
for example [ˌfər ɪɡˈzɑːmpl] zum Beispiel II/2B8
°**for real** [fə ˈrɪəl] hier: wirklich VI/BS 2
for sale [fə ˈseɪl] zu verkaufen I/3A1
forbid [fəˈbɪd] verbieten VI/2 Project 4
force [fɔːs] Truppe VI/2 Project 2; zwingen VI/2 Project 2
force-feed [ˌfɔːsˈfiːd] zwangsernähren; hier: mästen VI/6 Project 5

Dictionary English – German

forced marriage [ˌfɔːst ˈmærɪdʒ] Zwangsehe VI/4 Project 2
°forefathers (only plural) [ˈfɔːˌfɑːðəz] Ahnen, Vorfahren VI/BS 4
°forehead [ˈfɔːhed] Stirn VI/BS 8
foreign [ˈfɒrɪn] ausländisch, fremd III/8A4
forest [ˈfɒrɪst] Wald II/3B1
forever [fərˈevə] ewig; für immer VI/2 Project 2
forget [fəˈget] vergessen I/1C5
forgive [fəˈgɪv] vergeben, verzeihen VI/3B8
forgiveness [fəˈgɪvnəs] Vergebung VI/3B8
fork [fɔːk] Gabel I/2B3
form [fɔːm] Form, Art VI/3B6; Klasse; Jahrgangsstufe IV/2A1
form [fɔːm] formen; bilden VI/2G5
registration form [ˌredʒɪˈstreɪʃn ˌfɔːm] Anmeldeformular V/5A6
formally [ˈfɔːməli] offiziell VI/2 Project 1
former [ˈfɔːmə] ehemalige(r, s), frühere(r, s) VI/3B7
fort [fɔːt] Fort, Festung VI/5A3
fortune [ˈfɔːtʃən] Vermögen VI/2 Project 4
I look forward to hearing from you. [aɪ ˌlʊk ˌfɔːwəd tə ˈhɪərɪŋ frəm juː] Ich hoffe, von Ihnen zu hören. V/2A5
fossil fuel [ˈfɒsəl ˌfjuːəl] fossiler Brennstoff VI/6 Project 4
found [faʊnd] gründen V/4A3
founder [ˈfaʊndə] Gründer/in VI/1B2
four [fɔː] vier I/1B1
frame [freɪm] einrahmen, umrahmen VI/6 Project 2; Rahmen; Gerüst VI/6 Project 4
France [frɑːns] Frankreich IV/1B3
frank [fræŋk] aufrichtig, ehrlich VI/4 Project 1
°freak [friːk] Missgeburt; Monster VI/BS 1
°freak (informal) [friːk] jdn durchdrehen lassen VI/BS 3
°freaky [ˈfriːki] irre VI/BS 3
free [friː] frei V/2A2
(for) free [friː] gratis, umsonst III/5A1
free time [ˌfriː ˈtaɪm] Freizeit III/2A1
freedom [ˈfriːdəm] Freiheit IV/7B5
freedom of conscience [ˌfriːdəm əv ˈkɒnʃns] Gewissensfreiheit VI/3A4
freedom of religion [ˌfriːdəm əv rɪˈlɪdʒən] Religionsfreiheit VI/3A4

freedom of the press [ˌfriːdəm əv ðə ˈpres] Pressefreiheit VI/3A4
freedom of thought [ˌfriːdəm əv ˈθɔːt] Gedankenfreiheit VI/3A4
freeze [friːz] Standbild VI/1A3
freezing cold [ˌfriːzɪŋ ˈkəʊld] eiskalt VI/1A5
French [frentʃ] Franzose/Französin; französisch; hier: Französisch I/5A2
fresh [freʃ] frisch III/1A2
Friday [ˈfraɪdeɪ] Freitag I/2B7
fridge (informal) [frɪdʒ] Kühlschrank II/4B6
friend [frend] Freund/in I/1I
friendly [ˈfrendli] freundlich I/1B2
make friends [ˌmeɪk ˈfrendz] sich anfreunden, Freundschaften schließen V/5A2
friendship [ˈfrendʃɪp] Freundschaft IV/4A2
frightened [ˈfraɪtnd] verängstigt VI/4 Project 4
frog [frɒg] Frosch VI/4 Project 1
frog's leg [ˈfrɒgz ˌleg] Froschschenkel VI/4 Project 1
from [frəm] von, aus I/W
°from across [frəm əˈkrɒs] quer durch VI/BS 6
front [frʌnt] hier: vorderer Buchdeckel VI/3B2; Vorderseite VI/BS 5; vorderste(r, s); hier: Vorder- VI/BS 3
frozen [ˈfrəʊzn] tiefgekühlt VI/1B1
frozen [ˈfrəʊzn] hier: überfroren VI/6 Project 2
fruit [fruːt] Frucht; Obst I/2B1
°fruitful [ˈfruːtfl] ertragreich; fruchtbar VI/BS 6
°fruitfully [ˈfruːtfli] nützlich VI/BS 6
frustration [frʌˈstreɪʃn] Frustration VI/3B7
°fuck (informal) [fʌk] vögeln VI/BS 3
fuel [ˈfjuːəl] Kraftstoff, Treibstoff VI/1B3
fossil fuel [ˈfɒsəl ˌfjuːəl] fossiler Brennstoff VI/6 Project 4
fuel-efficient [ˈfjuːəliˌfɪʃnt] Benzin sparend VI/6G9
full [fʊl] voll I/4B1
full [fʊl] vollständig VI/6 Project 5
full-time [fʊl ˈtaɪm] Ganztags-, Vollzeit- IV/6A5
fun [fʌn] Spaß II/4A6
°be fun [ˌbi ˈfʌn] Spaß machen VI/BS 1
good fun [ˌgʊd ˈfʌn] lustig V/2A2

have fun [ˌhæv ˈfʌn] Spaß haben IV/2A3
funeral [ˈfjuːnrəl] Begräbnis, Beerdigung VI/4 Project 6
funny [ˈfʌni] lustig, witzig, komisch I/6B3
furious [ˈfjʊəriəs] wütend VI/4 Project 3
further [ˈfɜːðə] weiter, (noch) mehr VI/2I
future [ˈfjuːtʃə] Zukunft II/3A1
future [ˈfjuːtʃə] zukünftig VI/4G2

G

gain [geɪn] bekommen, erlangen VI/1A8
gain [geɪn] Erfolg VI/1A2
gain experience [ˌgeɪn ɪkˈspɪəriəns] Erfahrungen sammeln VI/5A5
gain weight [ˌgeɪn ˈweɪt] zunehmen VI/1A6
gallery walk [ˈgæləri wɔːk] Galeriegang VI/2I
game [geɪm] Spiel II/1B8
gang [gæŋ] Gruppe, Bande, Clique VI/2 Project 4
°gap [gæp] Lücke VI/BS 6
garage [ˈgærɑːʒ] (Kfz-)Werkstatt V/2A8
garage [ˈgærɑːʒ] Garage VI/2 Project 5
garbage (AE) [ˈgɑːbɪdʒ] Müll, Abfall IV/1A2
garden [ˈgɑːdn] Garten I/1B2
°gardener [ˈgɑːdnə] Gärtner/in VI/BS 4
garment [ˈgɑːmənt] Kleidungsstück VI/5A2
gate [geɪt] Tor; Flugsteig, Gate IV/3A1
°geeky (informal) [ˈgiːki] dämlich VI/BS 3
°generous [ˈdʒenrəs] großzügig; hier: wohlwollend VI/BS 6
Geneva [dʒəˈniːvə] Genf VI/3B6
geography [dʒiˈɒgrəfi] Erdkunde, Geografie I/5A2
German [ˈdʒɜːmən] Deutsche/r; deutsch II/1C6
Germany [ˈdʒɜːməni] Deutschland I/1A8
°gesture [ˈdʒestʃə] Handbewegung, Geste VI/BS 8
get [get] erhalten, bekommen I/2C1; werden II/3C1; hier: holen, kaufen I/2C7
get around [ˌget əˈraʊnd] herumkommen II/2B2

Dictionary English – German

°get away with sth [ˌget ə'weɪ wɪð ˌsʌmθɪŋ] mit etw ungestraft davonkommen VI/BS 3
get divorced [ˌget dɪ'vɔːst] sich scheiden lassen VI/4 Project 2
get in touch [ˌget ɪn 'tʌtʃ] in Kontakt treten IV/5A3
get involved [ˌget ɪn'vɒlvd] hier: beteiligt sein VI/2 Project 5; hier: sich engagieren VI/6 Project 4
get married [ˌget 'mærɪd] heiraten VI/4 Project 1
get on [ˌget 'ɒn] einsteigen IV/3B2
get ready [ˌget 'redi] sich fertig machen VI/1A2
get started [ˌget 'stɑːtɪd] beginnen V/5B3
get sth done [ˌget ˌsʌmθɪŋ 'dʌn] etw machen lassen VI/5B2
°get sth straight [ˌget sʌmθɪŋ 'streɪt] etw klarstellen VI/BS 3
get there ['get ðeə] hinkommen IV/3A3
get to know sb [ˌget tuː 'nəʊ ˌsʌmbədi] jdn kennen lernen IV/4B1
get together [ˌget tə'geðə] zusammenkommen V/6I
get up [ˌget 'ʌp] aufstehen I/4C4
get well card [get 'wel ˌkɑːd] Genesungskarte II/6A5
get-together ['getə,geðə] Treffen VI/4 Project 6
giant ['dʒaɪənt] riesig VI/2 Project 5; Riese VI/BS 3
gift [gɪft] Geschenk IV/8B2
giggle ['gɪgl] kichern VI/4 Project 1
giraffe [dʒə'rɑːf] Giraffe II/2B3
girl [gɜːl] Mädchen I/1A6
girlfriend ['gɜːl,frend] Freundin; Partnerin III/4B1
the gist [ðə 'dʒɪst] das Wesentliche; Hauptpunkte VI/3B7
give [gɪv] geben I/2B4; hier: nennen, angeben V/1B3
give [gɪv] hier: halten VI/2 Project 2
give a talk [ˌgɪv ə 'tɔːk] einen Vortrag halten VI/2 Project 2
give birth to [ˌgɪv 'bɜːθ tʊ] zur Welt bringen VI/4 Project 1
give (sb) directions [ˌgɪv dɪ'rekʃnz] (jdm) den Weg beschreiben III/8A4
°give sb the creeps [ˌgɪv ˌsʌmbədi ðə 'kriːps] jdm nicht geheuer sein VI/BS 1
give up [ˌgɪv 'ʌp] aufgeben III/4B2
°giver ['gɪvə] Spender/in VI/BS 2

°do the giving [ˌduː ðə 'gɪvɪŋ] hier: einlenken VI/BS 6
°glare (at) [gleə] (an)starren VI/BS 6
glass [glɑːs] Glas I/1A4
(pair of) glasses (only plural) [ˌpeər əv 'glɑːsɪz] Brille III/2B4
°gleam [gliːm] schimmern VI/BS 5
glimpse [glɪmps] (kurzer/flüchtiger) Blick VI/2I
global warming [ˌgləʊbl 'wɔːmɪŋ] Erwärmung der Erdatmosphäre VI/6G3
globalization [ˌgləʊbəlaɪ'zeɪʃn] Globalisierung VI/5A7
glove [glʌv] Handschuh I/4C7
glue (no pl) [gluː] Klebstoff II/1C1
go [gəʊ] gehen I/1A2; hier: fahren I/5A3
go away [ˌgəʊ ə'weɪ] weggehen, fortgehen IV/8A1
°go hungry [ˌgəʊ 'hʌŋgri] hungern VI/BS 2
°go into denial [ˌgəʊ ɪntʊ dɪ'naɪəl] hier: die Augen vor der Wahrheit verschließen wollen VI/BS 2
go on [ˌgəʊ 'ɒn] hier: passieren IV/1B3; weitergehen V/5A4
°go on [ˌgəʊ 'ɒn] hier: weiterreden VI/1O
go on a diet [ˌgəʊ ɒn ə 'daɪət] eine Diät machen VI/1A6
go on holiday [ˌgəʊ ɒn 'hɒlɪdeɪ] in Urlaub gehen/fahren II/1A1
go out [gəʊ 'aʊt] ausgehen; weggehen II/3A1
go out with sb (informal) [ˌgəʊ 'aʊt wɪð ˌsʌmbədi] mit jdm gehen III/4B1
go shopping [ˌgəʊ 'ʃɒpɪŋ] einkaufen gehen I/2C1
go swimming [gəʊ 'swɪmɪŋ] schwimmen gehen II/6A2
go through [ˌgəʊ 'θruː] durchgehen VI/1A9
go together [ˌgəʊ tə'geðə] zusammenpassen VI/1B4
go vegetarian [ˌgəʊ vedʒə'teərɪən] Vegetarier/in werden V/1B4
go with [ˌgəʊ 'wɪð] passen zu II/4A4
go wrong [ˌgəʊ 'rɒŋ] schiefgehen VI/1A1
goal [gəʊl] Ziel; Tor I/3A5
god [gɒd] Gott VI/3B9
goddess ['gɒdes] Göttin VI/1A2
°keep sb going [ˌkiːp ˌsʌmbədi 'gəʊɪŋ] hier: jdn am Leben erhalten VI/BS 2

gold [gəʊld] Gold V/4A3
gold prospector ['gəʊld prə,spektə] Goldsucher/in VI/2 Project 2
gold rush ['gəʊld rʌʃ] Goldrausch VI/2 Project 2
golden ['gəʊldən] aus Gold, golden VI/5A3
gonna (= going to) (informal) ['gʌnə] werden VI/1B4
good [gʊd] gut I/1A4; Gut, Ware VI/5B4
be good at sth [biː 'gʊd ət ˌsʌmθɪŋ] etw gut können IV/1B3
Good evening. [gʊd 'iːvnɪŋ] Guten Abend. III/1A3
good luck [gʊd 'lʌk] viel Glück II/4A3
°good-bye [ˌgʊd'baɪ] Auf Wiedersehen. VI/BS 3
°good-looking [ˌgʊd'lʊkɪŋ] gut aussehend VI/BS 1
Goodbye. [ˌgʊd'baɪ] Auf Wiedersehen. III/2B1
°goofy ['guːfi] doof, blöd VI/BS 1
°gorgeous ['gɔːdʒəs] großartig VI/BS 1
drop-dead gorgeous (informal) [ˌdrɒpded 'gɔːdʒəs] wahnsinnig gut aussehend VI/1A1
gotta (= have got to) (informal) ['gɒtə] müssen VI/6 Project 3
government ['gʌvənmənt] Regierung VI/2 Project 1
governmental [ˌgʌvən'mentl] staatlich VI/3A5
governor ['gʌvnə] Gouverneur VI/3B7
grade (AE) [greɪd] Note VI/1A5
graduate ['grædʒʊeɪt] Absolvent/in VI/2 Project 5; seinen Abschluss machen VI/5A5
gram (= gramme) [græm] Gramm VI/4 Project 5
grammar ['græmə] Grammatik II/4B2
on a grand scale [ɒn ə ˌgrænd 'skeɪl] im großen Stil VI/2 Project 4
granddaughter ['græn,dɔːtə] Enkelin VI/4I
grandfather ['græn,fɑːðə] Großvater IV/4B1
grandma (informal) ['græn,mɑː] Oma, Omi I/W
grandmother ['græn,mʌðə] Großmutter III/1B1
grandpa (informal) ['græn,pɑː] Opa, Opi I/5C5

214

Dictionary English – German

grandparents *(only plural)* [ˈɡrænˌpeərənts] Großeltern II/1A1
graphical [ˈɡræfɪkl] grafisch VI/1A7
graphics software [ˈɡræfɪksˌsɒftweə] Grafiksoftware VI/1A11
grass [ɡrɑːs] Gras I/6A2
grateful [ˈɡreɪtfl] dankbar VI/4 Project 1
°**gratitude** [ˈɡrætɪtjuːd] Dankbarkeit VI/BS 2
°**grease** [ɡriːs] Fett; *hier:* Kettenöl VI/BS 2
great [ɡreɪt] groß, riesig; großartig I/1A3
Great Barrier Reef [ˌɡreɪt ˈbæriə riːf] Großes Barriereriff V/4A2
(Great) Britain [ˌɡreɪt ˈbrɪtn] Großbritannien II/LL1
a great deal [ə ˈɡreɪt ˌdiːl] eine Menge, ziemlich viel VI/3B4
Great Depression [ˌɡreɪt dɪˈpreʃn] Weltwirtschaftskrise *(1929)* VI/2 Project 4
the Great Wall of China [ðə ˌɡreɪt ˌwɔːl əv ˈtʃaɪnə] Chinesische Mauer VI/6G7
°**greatly** [ˈɡreɪtli] sehr VI/BS 8
Greece [ɡriːs] Griechenland VI/3P4
greed [ɡriːd] Gier VI/6 Project 5
green [ɡriːn] grün I/2A4; *hier:* umweltfreundlich, ökologisch IV/5B2
grey [ɡreɪ] grau I/2A7
grid [ɡrɪd] Gitter; *hier:* Tabelle II/1A4
°**grieve** [ɡriːv] bekümmert sein; trauern VI/BS 6
groceries *(only plural)* [ˈɡrəʊsəriz] Lebensmittel V/4B6
°**groom** [ɡruːm] Bräutigam VI/BS 8
ground [ɡraʊnd] (Erd)boden; Erde V/4A3
ground floor [ˈɡraʊnd flɔː] Erdgeschoss, Parterre IV/6B1
group [ɡruːp] Gruppe I/4B4; (Musik)gruppe III/7A1
group [ɡruːp] gruppieren VI/5B2
grow [ɡrəʊ] wachsen, größer werden V/1B5
grow [ɡrəʊ] *hier:* werden VI/2 Project 3
grow up [ˌɡrəʊ ˈʌp] erwachsen werden II/3A4; aufwachsen VI/6 Project 3
°**guarantee** [ˌɡærnˈtiː] garantieren VI/BS 2

guaranteed [ˌɡærnˈtiːd] garantiert VI/1A2
°**guard** [ɡɑːd] schützen VI/BS 2; Wache VI/BS 5
guess [ɡes] (er)raten III/3A4; denken; vermuten VI/1A5
°**guess** [ɡes] Vermutung VI/1O
Guess what! [ˌɡes ˈwɒt] Rate mal!; Stell dir vor! V/2A6
guest [ɡest] Gast V/2A2
guide [ɡaɪd] Fremdenführer/in VI/5A5
film guide [ˈfɪlm ˌɡaɪd] Filmführer VI/4 Project 6
°**guilt** [ɡɪlt] Schuld(gefühl) VI/BS 2
the guilty [ðə ˈɡɪlti] Schuldige/r VI/3B7
guitar [ɡɪˈtɑː] Gitarre III/7A2
°**guy** [ɡaɪ] Kerl, Typ VI/BS 1
guys *(only plural, AE)* [ɡaɪz] Leute VI/3B4
gym (= gymnastics) [dʒɪm] Turnen III/7B1

H

hair *(no pl)* [heə] Haar(e) I/2A2
°**half** [hɑːf] halb VI/BS 3
half an hour [ˌhɑːf ən ˈaʊə] eine halbe Stunde II/2B1
half past ten [ˌhɑːf pɑːst ˈten] halb elf I/2B6
half *(pl* **halves***)* [hɑːf, hɑːvz] Hälfte III/7A6
°**half-eaten** [ˌhɑːf ˈiːtn] halb gegessen VI/BS 2
°**hallway** [ˈhɔːlweɪ] Korridor, Gang VI/BS 3
ham [hæm] Schinken III/1A2
hamster [ˈhæmstə] Hamster I/3B4
hand [hænd] Hand I/2A2
°**hand** [hænd] (über)geben, (über)reichen VI/BS 3
on the one hand ..., on the other hand ... [ɒn ðə ˈwʌn ˌhænd ..., ɒn ðiˌˈʌðə ˌhænd] einerseits ... andererseits ... IV/5A3
°**handcuffs** *(only plural)* [ˈhændkʌfs] Handschellen VI/BS 5
°**handful** [ˈhændfʊl] Handvoll VI/BS 1
°**handle** [ˈhændl] Griff, Henkel; *hier:* Stiel VI/1O; *hier:* bewältigen VI/BS 3
°**handshake** [ˈhændʃeɪk] Händeschütteln, Händedruck VI/BS 8
handsome [ˈhænsəm] gut aussehend VI/4 Project 1
handy [ˈhændi] praktisch, nützlich V/5B2

°**hang** [hæŋ] hängen; fallen VI/BS 2
°**hang out** [ˌhæŋ ˈaʊt] Zeit verbringen VI/BS 7
hang (up) [hæŋ] aufhängen IV/7B4
happen [ˈhæpən] geschehen, passieren II/3A6
happen to do sth [ˌhæpən tə ˈduː ˌsʌmθɪŋ] zufällig etw tun VI/3B4
happiness [ˈhæpinəs] Glück, Zufriedenheit VI/3B4
happy [ˈhæpi] glücklich; zufrieden; fröhlich I/3B3
Happy birthday (to you)! [ˌhæpi ˈbɜːθdeɪ] Alles Gute zum Geburtstag! I/3C4
Happy New Year! [ˌhæpi njuː ˈjɪə] Gutes/Frohes neues Jahr! II/4A2
harbour [ˈhɑːbə] Hafen IV/8B2
hard [hɑːd] hart; schwer II/3B1; *hier:* anstrengend II/2A1; *hier:* schwierig III/5B1
°**hard** [hɑːd] *hier:* fest VI/1O
be hard on oneself [ˌbiː ˈhɑːd ɒn wʌnˌself] hart mit sich ins Gericht gehen VI/1Test results 1A2
hard skill [ˈhɑːd skɪl] Fachkompetenz V/2B1
harmony [ˈhɑːməni] Harmonie VI/6 Project 1
harsh [hɑːʃ] rau; hart VI/4 Project 1
harvest [ˈhɑːvɪst] Ernte VI/2 Project 1
hat [hæt] Hut; Mütze I/4C7
hate [heɪt] hassen, nicht ausstehen können I/1A5
haunt [hɔːnt] verfolgen VI/3B7
have [hæv] haben I/W; *hier:* essen, trinken I/2B1
have a drink [ˌhæv ə ˈdrɪŋk] etw trinken III/3B2
have a good time [ˌhæv ə ɡʊd ˈtaɪm] sich amüsieren I/6A6
have a look at [ˌhæv ə ˈlʊk ət] sich ansehen II/2C1
have a party [ˌhæv ə ˈpɑːti] eine Party machen II/4A2
have a temperature [ˌhæv ə ˈtemprɪtʃə] Fieber haben III/2B1
have breakfast [hæv ˈbrekfəst] frühstücken I/2B2
have fun [ˌhæv ˈfʌn] Spaß haben IV/2A3
have got [ˌhæv ˈɡɒt] haben I/W
have got the looks [ˌhæv ɡɒt ðə ˈlʊks] gut aussehen VI/1A3
have in common [ˌhæv ɪn ˈkɒmən] gemeinsam haben VI/4 Project 1

Dictionary English – German

have sth done [ˌhæv ˌsʌmθɪŋ ˈdʌn] etw machen lassen VI/1A3
have tea [ˌhæv ˈtiː] Tee trinken II/2C1
have to do sth [ˌhæv tə ˈduː ˌsʌmθɪŋ] etw tun müssen III/2A7
he [hi] er I/1A4
head [hed] Kopf I/2A4
heading [ˈhedɪŋ] Überschrift VI/5B2
headline [ˈhedˌlaɪn] Schlagzeile; *hier:* Überschrift IV/8B2
headset [ˈhedset] Kopfhörer VI/3B4
°**heal** [hiːl] heilen VI/BS 5
health [helθ] Gesundheit III/2A4
healthy [ˈhelθi] gesund III/2A1
compost heap [ˈkɒmpɒst ˌhiːp] Komposthaufen VI/6 Project 4
hear [hɪə] hören I/1A1
hearing [ˈhɪərɪŋ] Anhörung; Gerichtsverhandlung VI/3B8
heart [hɑːt] Herz V/1A6
°**heartland** [ˈhɑːtlænd] Kerngebiet, Herz VI/BS 2
heat [hiːt] Hitze V/4B6
heat [hiːt] erhitzen; aufwärmen VI/6 Project 4; heizen VI/6G3; *hier:* Wärme VI/BS 1
heated [ˈhiːtɪd] hitzig, erregt VI/3B4
heating [ˈhiːtɪŋ] Heizung VI/6G9
heating fuel [ˈhiːtɪŋ ˌfjuːəl] Brennmaterial VI/6 Project 4
°**heaven** [ˈhevn] Himmel VI/1O
heavy [ˈhevi] schwer; stark I/4C10
hedgehog [ˈhedʒˌhɒg] Igel I/3B2
height [haɪt] Höhe; Höhepunkt VI/2 Project 3
°**hell** [hel] Hölle VI/1O
Hello. [həˈləʊ] Hallo. I/1A2
help [help] helfen I/1B2
help [help] Hilfe VI/2 Project 1
ask for help [ˌɑːsk fə ˈhelp] um Hilfe bitten III/8A4
help out [ˌhelp ˈaʊt] (aus)helfen, unterstützen II/2B8
Help! [help] (Zu) Hilfe! II/3B2
helper [ˈhelpə] Helfer/in; *hier:* Unterstützung VI/3B4
helpful [ˈhelpfl] hilfreich, nützlich; hilfsbereit III/4B1
helpless [ˈhelpləs] hilflos, machtlos VI/1B4
her [hɜː] sie; ihr(e, n) I/1A4
here [hɪə] hier(her) I/1B2
Here you are! [ˌhɪə juːˈɑː] Hier, bitte!, Bitte schön! III/5A1

°**hermit** [ˈhɜːmɪt] Eremit/in, Einsiedler/in VI/BS 3
hero *(pl* heroes*)* [ˈhɪərəʊ, ˈhɪərəʊz] Held VI/1B2
hers [hɜːz] ihre (r, s) IV/8A6
herself [həˈself] sich; selbst IV/2A2
hide [haɪd] verstecken II/4A6
hideous [ˈhɪdiəs] grässlich, scheußlich VI/4 Project 4
high [haɪ] hoch I/6C1
be high on drugs [ˌbi ˌhaɪ ɒn ˈdrʌgz] mit Drogen vollgepumpt sein VI/3B4
high school *(AE)* [ˈhaɪ ˌskuːl] Highschool (weiterführende Schule) IV/1B2
high technology [ˌhaɪ tekˈnɒlədʒi] Hightech, Hochtechnologie VI/2 Project 5
high-paying [ˌhaɪˈpeɪɪŋ] hochbezahlt VI/5A5
highway *(AE)* [ˈhaɪˌweɪ] Hauptstraße, Schnellstraße VI/6 Project 2
hijack [ˈhaɪdʒæk] entführen VI/2 Project 5
hill [hɪl] Hügel V/1A6
him [hɪm] ihm, ihn I/3B4
himself [hɪmˈself] sich; selbst IV/2A2
Hindu [ˌhɪnˈduː] Hindu; hinduistisch, Hindu- VI/4 Project 2
Hinduism [ˈhɪnduˌɪzm] Hinduismus VI/5A2
his [hɪs] sein(e, r) I/1A2
history [ˈhɪst(ə)ri] Geschichte I/5A1
hit [hɪt] schlagen; treffen; stoßen (gegen) III/3A3
hold [həʊld] halten III/1B1
hold [həʊld] *hier:* der Meinung sein VI/5B4
hold on [ˌhəʊldˈɒn] warten V/5A4
hold on tight [ˌhəʊldˌɒn ˈtaɪt] sich festhalten, sich festklammern V/1A6
hold one's breath [ˌhəʊld wʌnz ˈbreθ] die Luft anhalten VI/4 Project 3
hold up [ˌhəʊldˈʌp] hochhalten, heben VI/6 Project 5; aushalten, durchhalten VI/BS 5
hole [həʊl] Loch III/5B2
holiday [ˈhɒlɪdeɪ] Urlaub, Ferien I/6A1
holiday [ˈhɒlɪdeɪ] *hier:* Feiertag VI/4 Project 6
home [həʊm] *hier:* Heimat III/4I; Zuhause I/3A1; zuhause; *hier:* nach Hause I/5A3

°**homeroom** *(AE)* [ˈhəʊmruːm] erste Stunde VI/BS 3
homework *(no pl)* [ˈhəʊmˈwɜːk] Hausaufgaben I/1C1
honest [ˈɒnɪst] ehrlich V/2A2
honey [ˈhʌni] Honig VI/1P5
honour [ˈɒnə] Ehre VI/3A3; ehren VI/BS 8
°**code of honour** [ˌkəʊdˌəvˈɒnə] Ehrenkodex VI/BS 2
honour killing [ˈɒnəˌkɪlɪŋ] Ehrenmord VI/3A3
hop [hɒp] hüpfen VI/4 Project 1
hope [həʊp] hoffen I/3A4; Hoffnung V/6I
hopefully [ˈhəʊpfli] hoffentlich VI/4G5
°**hopelessness** [ˈhəʊpləsnəs] Hoffnungslosigkeit VI/BS 3
horrible [ˈhɒrəbl] schrecklich V/1B3
°**horrified** [ˈhɒrɪfaɪd] entsetzt VI/BS 9
horse [hɔːs] Pferd I/3A7
°**hospital** [ˈhɒspɪtl] Krankenhaus VI/BS 6
hot [hɒt] heiß I/4A6; *hier:* scharf III/1B1
hour [ˈaʊə] Stunde I/6A6
house [haʊs] Haus I/W
house husband [ˈhaʊsˌhʌzbənd] Hausmann VI/4 Project 5
housework [ˈhaʊsˌwɜːk] Hausarbeit VI/4 Project 5
housing [ˈhaʊzɪŋ] Wohnungen VI/6 Project 4
how [haʊ] wie I/W
How are things? *(informal)* [ˌhaʊ ə ˈθɪŋz] Wie geht's? VI/1P5
How are you? [ˌhaʊˈɑːˌjʊː] Wie geht es dir/Ihnen/euch? I/4B5
How do you do? [ˌhaʊ du juːˈduː] Guten Tag! V/2B7
how many [haʊ ˈmeni] wie viele II/1B8
How much is/are …? [ˌhaʊ mʌtʃˌɪzˌɑː] Was kostet/ kosten …? I/2C5
How old are you? [haʊˌəʊldəˌjʊː] Wie alt bist du/seid ihr? I/W
how to [ˈhaʊ tə] wie man II/1A1
however [haʊˈevə] *hier:* jedoch IV/7B5
howl [haʊl] heulen VI/1B4
hug [hʌg] Umarmung VI/4 Project 2; umarmen VI/BS 3
huge [hjuːdʒ] riesig, riesengroß III/5B1

Dictionary English – German

hum [hʌm] Summen, Brummen VI/6 Project 5
human [ˈhjuːmən] menschlich; Menschen- VI/3B7
human being [ˌhjuːmən ˈbiːɪŋ] Mensch VI/3B9
°human race [ˌhjuːmən ˈreɪs] menschliche Rasse; *hier:* Menschen VI/BS 6
human rights *(only plural)* [ˌhjuːmən ˈraɪts] Menschenrechte V/6I
human trafficking [ˌhjuːmən ˈtræfɪkɪŋ] Menschenhandel VI/3A5
°humiliation [hjuːˌmɪliˈeɪʃn] Demütigung, Erniedrigung VI/BS 2
humorous [ˈhjuːmərəs] lustig, komisch VI/4G4
hundreds [ˈhʌndrədz] Hunderte VI/2 Project 3
hunger [ˈhʌŋɡə] Hunger IV/8A2
hungry [ˈhʌŋɡri] hungrig I/1A3
°go hungry [ˌɡəʊ ˈhʌŋɡri] hungern VI/BS 2
the hungry [ðə ˈhʌŋɡri] die Hungernden VI/1B2
hunt [hʌnt] jagen VI/2 Project 1
hunted [ˈhʌntɪd] gejagt, gehetzt VI/2I
hurry up [ˌhʌriˈʌp] sich beeilen II/3B2
hurt [hɜːt] verletzt, verwundet VI/1A10; wehtun, schmerzen III/2B1
hurt [hɜːt] Schmerz, Verletzung VI/4 Project 4
husband [ˈhʌzbənd] Ehemann I/5C7
°hustle [ˈhʌsl] *hier:* sich beeilen VI/BS 3
hut [hʌt] Hütte V/4B6
°hyped-up [ˌhaɪptˈʌp] überdreht; *hier:* herausgeputzt VI/BS 1

I

I [aɪ] ich I/W
I don't think so. [aɪ ˌdəʊnt ˈθɪŋk səʊ] Ich glaube nicht. II/1C4
I see. [aɪ ˈsiː] Ich verstehe. V/2B7
I'd like (to) ... [aɪd ˈlaɪk] Ich hätte/würde gern ... I/5B6
I'll have ... [ˈaɪl hæv] Ich werde ... nehmen/essen. III/1A3
I'm fine. [aɪm ˈfaɪn] Es geht mir gut. I/4B5

I'm (from ...) [aɪm] Ich bin/komme (aus ...) I/W
ice [aɪs] Eis VI/4 Project 3
ice cream [ˌaɪs ˈkriːm] Eiskrem, Eis I/2C1
ice-skating [ˈaɪsˌskeɪtɪŋ] Schlittschuhlaufen, Eislaufen V/1A4
°ID (= I.D. = identification card) [ˌaɪˈdiː] Ausweis VI/BS 3
idea [aɪˈdɪə] Idee I/1A3; Vorstellung II/3A1
ideal [aɪˈdɪəl] Idealvorstellung VI/1A4
if [ɪf] wenn, falls; ob I/5A3
°if [ɪf] wenn auch VI/BS 2
°ignore [ɪɡˈnɔː] ignorieren, nicht beachten VI/BS 3
ill [ɪl] krank II/3A4
illegal [ɪˈliːɡl] ungesetzlich, illegal V/5A6
illiteracy [ɪˈlɪtərəsi] Analphabetentum VI/5A3
°illiterate [ɪˈlɪtərət] analphabetisch; *hier:* ungebildet, unkultiviert VI/BS 8
illness [ˈɪlnəs] Krankheit, Erkrankung V/1B5
illustrate [ˈɪləstreɪt] illustrieren, veranschaulichen V/4A3
illustration [ˌɪləˈstreɪʃn] Illustration, Abbildung VI/6 Project 2
image [ˈɪmɪdʒ] *hier:* Bild VI/1A3
°imagination [ɪˌmædʒɪˈneɪʃn] Fantasie, Vorstellungskraft VI/BS 1
imagine [ɪˈmædʒɪn] sich vorstellen III/5A5
°immature [ˌɪməˈtjʊə] unreif, kindisch VI/BS 3
immediately [ɪˈmiːdiətli] sofort VI/4 Project 6
°immense [ɪˈmens] riesig, enorm VI/BS 8
immigrant [ˈɪmɪɡrənt] Einwanderer/in IV/3A2
immigration [ˌɪmɪˈɡreɪʃn] Einwanderung, Immigration V/4A5
impact [ˈɪmpækt] Auswirkung, Einfluss VI/6 Project 4
impart [ɪmˈpɑːt] vermitteln; (mit) geben VI/3A4
imperative [ɪmˈperətɪv] Imperativ, Befehlsform V/5B3
import [ɪmˈpɔːt] importieren VI/5A2
important [ɪmˈpɔːtnt] wichtig IV/2A5

impress [ɪmˈpres] beeindrucken, imponieren VI/4 Project 1
°impressive [ɪmˈpresɪv] beeindruckend VI/3O
imprison [ɪmˈprɪzn] inhaftieren VI/2 Project 4
life imprisonment [ˌlaɪf ɪmˈprɪznmənt] lebenslängliche Haftstrafe VI/3B8
improve [ɪmˈpruːv] verbessern IV/7A4
in [ɪn] in I/W
in English [ɪn ˈɪŋɡlɪʃ] auf Englisch II/1A1
in front of [ɪn ˈfrʌnt əv] vor I/2C2
in German [ɪn ˈdʒɜːmən] auf Deutsch II/1B6
in groups [ɪn ˈɡruːps] in Gruppen, gruppenweise II/1B6
in the afternoon [ɪn ðiː ˌɑːftəˈnuːn] am Nachmittag I/6A3
in the end [ɪn ðiː ˈend] letzten Endes; schließlich IV/2B2
in the evening [ɪn ðiː ˈiːvnɪŋ] am Abend I/4B4
in the middle [ɪn ðə ˈmɪdl] in der Mitte; mitten in/auf II/1C5
in the morning [ɪn ðə ˈmɔːnɪŋ] am Morgen I/4C4
in the street [ɪn ðə ˈstriːt] auf der Straße II/2A1
°in vain [ɪn ˈveɪn] vergeblich, umsonst VI/BS 6
inability [ˌɪnəˈbɪləti] Unfähigkeit, Unvermögen VI/3B4
inaugural speech [ɪˌnɔːɡjʊrəl ˈspiːtʃ] Antrittsrede VI/2 Project 3
incident [ˈɪnsɪdnt] Vorfall, Ereignis VI/2 Project 5
include [ɪnˈkluːd] beinhalten, einschließen VI/3A4
including [ɪnˈkluːdɪŋ] einschließlich VI/4 Project 2
income [ˈɪnkʌm] Einkommen, Lohn VI/5B6
°increase [ɪnˈkriːs] ansteigen, zunehmen VI/5O
increasingly [ɪnˈkriːsɪŋli] zunehmend VI/2 Project 1
independence [ˌɪndɪˈpendəns] Unabhängigkeit VI/5A3
Declaration of Independence [ˌdekləˌreɪʃn əv ˌɪndɪˈpendəns] *Unabhängigkeitserklärung* VI/2 Project 1
War of Independence [ˌwɔːr əv ˌɪndɪˈpendəns] *Unabhängigkeitskrieg* VI/2 Project 1

217

Dictionary English – German

independent [ˌɪndɪˈpendənt] unabhängig, selbständig VI/5A2
India [ˈɪndiə] Indien II/L
Indian [ˈɪndiən] Inder/in; indisch III/1B1
Indian [ˈɪndiən] Indianer/in; indianisch VI/2 Project 1
indigenous [ɪnˈdɪdʒənəs] (ein)heimisch VI/2 Project 2
individual [ˌɪndɪˈvɪdʒuəl] einzeln, individuell VI/2I
individual [ˌɪndɪˈvɪdʒuəl] Einzelperson VI/4 Project 2
individual case [ˌɪndɪˌvɪdʒuəl ˈkeɪs] Einzelfall VI/2 Project 4
induce [ɪnˈdjuːs] hervorrufen, herbeiführen VI/1A6
industrialization [ɪnˌdʌstriəlaɪˈzeɪʃn] Industrialisierung VI/2 Project 4
industry [ˈɪndəstri] Industrie VI/5A2
industry [ˈɪndəstri] hier: Branche VI/2 Project 4
inefficient [ˌɪnəˈfɪʃnt] ineffizient, unwirtschaftlich VI/6 Project 2
infection [ɪnˈfekʃn] Infektion, Ansteckung VI/1A6
influence [ˈɪnfluəns] beeinflussen VI/2 Project 1; Einfluss VI/1A1
°**inform** [ɪnˈfɔːm] informieren VI/BS 9
information (no pl) [ˌɪnfəˈmeɪʃn] Information I/3A1
information technology [ɪnfəˈmeɪʃn tekˌnɒlədʒi] Informationstechnologie; hier: Informatik I/5A2
informed [ɪnˈfɔːmd] informiert VI/2 Project 2
inhabitant [ɪnˈhæbɪtənt] Einwohner/in V/4A3
inhuman [ɪnˈhjuːmən] unmenschlich VI/3A4
inhumane [ˌɪnhjuˈmeɪn] inhuman, barbarisch VI/2 Project 2
injection [ɪnˈdʒekʃn] Spritze VI/3B4
injury [ˈɪndʒəri] Verletzung VI/2 Project 5
injustice [ɪnˈdʒʌstɪs] Ungerechtigkeit VI/3A1
inmate [ˈɪnmeɪt] Insasse/Insassin; Häftling VI/3B4
innocent [ˈɪnəsnt] unschuldig VI/3B6
innovation [ˌɪnəʊˈveɪʃn] Neuerung, Reform VI/6 Project 4
°**insert** [ɪnˈsɜːt] (hinein)stecken VI/BS 5

inside [ˌɪnˈsaɪd] innen, drinnen III/1A6
°inside [ˌɪnˈsaɪd] hinein VI/BS 3
°**insist** [ɪnˈsɪst] bestehen VI/BS 1
°**inspect** [ɪnˈspekt] untersuchen, kontrollieren VI/BS 2
instead [ɪnˈsted] stattdessen VI/4 Project 1
instead of [ɪnˈsted əv] statt IV/2A1
instruction [ɪnˈstrʌkʃn] Anweisung, Instruktion V/5B2
insult [ɪnˈsʌlt] beleidigen VI/BS 3
insulting [ɪnˈsʌltɪŋ] beleidigend V/5A6
integrate [ˈɪntɪɡreɪt] integrieren VI/5A3
integration [ˌɪntɪˈɡreɪʃn] Integration VI/2 Project 3
°**intelligence** [ɪnˈtelɪdʒəns] Intelligenz VI/BS 6
intelligent [ɪnˈtelɪdʒnt] klug, intelligent VI/4 Project 1
intend [ɪnˈtend] beabsichtigen, planen VI/4 Project 1
interest [ˈɪntrəst] Interesse V/2A3
be interested in [ˌbiˈɪntrəstɪd ɪn] sich interessieren für III/5A2
interesting [ˈɪntrəstɪŋ] interessant I/5A2
intern [ˈɪntɜːn] Praktikant/in VI/5A5
°**interpreter** [ɪnˈtɜːprɪtə] Dolmetscher/in VI/BS 4
interrogate [ɪnˈterəɡeɪt] verhören, vernehmen VI/3A6
interrupt [ˌɪntəˈrʌpt] unterbrechen V/2B9
intervention [ˌɪntəˈvenʃn] Eingreifen VI/2 Project 5
interview [ˈɪntəˌvjuː] interviewen, befragen III/4A3; Vorstellungsgespräch V/2A2
into [ˈɪntʊ] in I/2A4
intolerable [ɪnˈtɒlərəbl] unerträglich, untolerierbar VI/2 Project 1
introduce [ˌɪntrəˈdjuːs] vorstellen V/2B7
introduce [ˌɪntrəˈdjuːs] hier: einführen VI/2 Project 1
introduction [ˌɪntrəˈdʌkʃn] Vorstellung; Einführung VI/3B6
invade [ɪnˈveɪd] einfallen, einmarschieren VI/2 Project 5
invasion [ɪnˈveɪʒn] Invasion, Einmarsch VI/2 Project 5
invent [ɪnˈvent] erfinden III/5B2
invention [ɪnˈvenʃn] Erfindung III/5A2

inventor [ɪnˈventə] Erfinder/in III/5B2
invisible [ɪnˈvɪzəbl] unsichtbar; verborgen VI/1A2
invite [ɪnˈvaɪt] einladen II/4B9
involve [ɪnˈvɒlv] beinhalten, mit sich bringen; betreffen VI/3A3
be involved in [ˌbiˈɪnˈvɒlvdˈɪn] beteiligt sein an VI/3A8
get involved [ˌɡetˈɪnˈvɒlvd] hier: beteiligt sein VI/2 Project 5; hier: sich engagieren VI/6 Project 4
Iraq [ɪˈrɑːk] Irak VI/2 Project 5
Irish [ˈaɪrɪʃ] irisch IV/8A4
°**irresistible** [ˌɪrɪˈzɪstəbl] unwiderstehlich VI/BS 6
island [ˈaɪlənd] Insel III/4I
issue [ˈɪʃuː] Thema, Frage, Angelegenheit V/1B5
it [ɪt] es I/1A4
It's ... £ (pounds). [ɪts ... ˈpaʊndz] Es kostet ... Pfund. III/6A7
Italian [ɪˈtæljən] Italiener/in; italienisch III/1A2
Italy [ˈɪtəli] Italien IV/4B1
item [ˈaɪtəm] Artikel; Gegenstand VI/1B1
its [ɪts] sein(e), ihr(e) I/3B2
ivory [ˈaɪvəri] Elfenbein VI/5A3

J

°**jabber** [ˈdʒæbə] plappern, quasseln VI/1O
jacket [ˈdʒækɪt] Jacke I/4C7
traffic jam [ˈtræfɪk dʒæm] Stau V/1B3
°**janitor** [ˈdʒænɪtə] Hausmeister/in VI/BS 3
January [ˈdʒænjuəri] Januar I/5C2
Japanese [ˌdʒæpəˈniːz] Japaner/in; japanisch VI/2 Project 5
jealous [ˈdʒeləs] eifersüchtig VI/3B4
jealousy [ˈdʒeləsi] Eifersucht VI/3B4
jet plane [ˈdʒet ˌpleɪn] Düsenflugzeug VI/2 Project 5
Jewish [ˈdʒuːɪʃ] jüdisch VI/2 Project 4
°**jibber** [ˈdʒɪbə] plappern, quasseln VI/1O
job [dʒɒb] Arbeit, Stelle, Aufgabe I/4C1
°**jock** (AE) [dʒɒk] Sportfanatiker/in (abwertend) VI/BS 3
join [dʒɔɪn] hier: beitreten, Mitglied werden V/5A2; hier: mitmachen bei IV/2A8
join in [ˌdʒɔɪnˈɪn] mitmachen bei VI/1B5

Dictionary English – German

°join [dʒɔɪn] *hier:* sich gesellen zu VI/BS 6
joint [dʒɔɪnt] gemeinsam; *hier:* verbündet VI/2 Project 2
joke [dʒəʊk] Spaß, Witz VI/5A5
You must be joking! [jʊ ˌmʌst bi ˈdʒəʊkɪŋ] Das meinst du doch nicht im Ernst!, Das soll wohl ein Witz sein! II/3A1
journalist [ˈdʒɜːnəlɪst] Journalist/in V/4A4
journey [ˈdʒɜːni] Reise; Fahrt III/5A1
joy [dʒɔɪ] Freude, Vergnügen VI/4 Project 5
juice [dʒuːs] Saft I/1A4
July [dʒʊˈlaɪ] Juli I/5C2
jump [dʒʌmp] springen II/1B2
°jump [dʒʌmp] Sprung VI/BS 1
°jumper [ˈdʒʌmpə] Pullover VI/BS 6
June [dʒuːn] Juni I/2P3
junk food [ˈdʒʌŋk ˌfuːd] Schnellgerichte, ungesundes Essen IV/1B3
jury [ˈdʒʊəri] Geschworene VI/3B8
just [dʒʌst] *hier:* gerade (eben) III/7A6; nur, bloß, einfach III/7A6
°just as [ˈdʒʌst ˌəz] genauso (wie) VI/BS 2
justice [ˈdʒʌstɪs] Gerechtigkeit VI/3A7

K

kangaroo [ˌkæŋɡəˈruː] Känguru V/4A2
Kashmir [ˌkæʃˈmɪə] Kaschmir VI/5A3
keep [kiːp] aufbewahren; behalten I/4A6; *hier:* halten VI/1A5
keep [kiːp] *hier:* (ein)halten VI/2 Project 2; *hier:* unterbringen VI/3A3
°keep clear of [ˌkiːp ˈklɪər ˌəv] sich fern halten von VI/BS 4
keep in touch [ˌkiːp ɪn ˈtʌtʃ] in Kontakt bleiben V/5A2
keep on doing sth [ˌkiːp ˌɒn ˈduːɪŋ ˌsʌmθɪŋ] etw weiter(hin) tun IV/2A1
keep sb down [ˌkiːp ˌsʌmbədi ˈdaʊn] jdn unterdrücken, klein halten VI/4 Project 4
°keep sb going [ˌkiːp ˌsʌmbədi ˈɡəʊɪŋ] *hier:* jdn am Leben erhalten VI/BS 2
keep up [ˌkiːp ˈʌp] aufrechterhalten VI/1A3
keyword [ˈkiːwɜːd] Schlüsselwort V/1A2

°khaki [ˈkɑːki] Khakihose VI/BS 3
kick [kɪk] treten, schießen III/2B2
kid [kɪd] Kind, Jugendliche(r) IV/1A2
You're kidding! *(informal)* [jɔː ˈkɪdɪŋ] Das ist doch nicht dein Ernst! III/7A6
kidnap [ˈkɪdnæp] entführen VI/3A3
°kidnapper [ˈkɪdnæpə] Entführer/in VI/BS 8
kill [kɪl] töten V/1B1
°killer [ˈkɪlə] Mörder/in VI/BS 3
°serial killer [ˈsɪəriəl ˌkɪlə] Serienmörder/in VI/BS 3
honour killing [ˈɒnə ˌkɪlɪŋ] Ehrenmord VI/3A3
kilo [ˈkiːləʊ] Kilo I/5B1
kilometre [kɪˈlɒmɪtə] Kilometer III/6B2
kind [kaɪnd] Art, Sorte I/3C2
°kind of [ˈkaɪnd ˌəv] irgendwie VI/BS 3
all kinds of [ˌɔːl ˈkaɪndz ˌəv] alle möglichen V/2A6
king [kɪŋ] König II/4C1
kingdom [ˈkɪŋdəm] Königreich VI/2I
kiss [kɪs] küssen II/5A5
kiss [kɪs] Kuss VI/4 Project 1
kitchen [ˈkɪtʃən] Küche I/2B3
corporate kitchen [ˌkɔːprət ˈkɪtʃən] Firmenküche VI/1B2
°Kiwi *(informal)* [ˈkiːwiː] Neuseeländer/in VI/3O
knee [niː] Knie I/2A4
knife (*pl* knives) [naɪf, naɪvz] Messer I/2B3
know [nəʊ] wissen; kennen I/1A6
get to know sb [ˌɡet tuː ˈnəʊ ˌsʌmbədi] jdn kennen lernen IV/4B1
°knowing [ˈnəʊɪŋ] wissend, vielsagend VI/BS 6
knowledge [ˈnɒlɪdʒ] Kenntnisse, Wissen V/2A3
known [nəʊn] bekannt VI/2 Project 1
°kohl [kəʊl] Kajal VI/BS 8
Korean [kəˈrɪən] Koreaner/in; koreanisch; *hier:* Korea- VI/2 Project 5
kph (= kilometres per hour) [ˌkeɪ piːˈeɪtʃ (= kɪˌlɒmɪtəz pɜːˈaʊə)] km/h III/5B2

L

label [ˈleɪbl] Etikett; Marke VI/5B1
°labour [ˈleɪbə] Arbeit VI/5O
bonded labour [ˌbɒndɪd ˈleɪbə] Knechtschaft VI/5B6

child labour [ˈtʃaɪld ˌleɪbə] Kinderarbeit VI/5B4
°lad [læd] Junge VI/BS 3
ladder [ˈlædə] Leiter VI/2G9
lady [ˈleɪdi] Frau; Dame VI/2 Project 2
lake [leɪk] See II/2C1
°lakh *(ind. Englisch)* [lɑːk] einhunderttausend VI/5O
land [lænd] Land III/5B2
land [lænd] landen VI/2 Project 1
land art [ˈlænd ˌɑːt] Kunstform VI/6I
landing permission [ˈlændɪŋ pəˌmɪʃn] Erlaubnis zum Anlegen VI/2 Project 4
landscape [ˈlændskeɪp] Landschaft VI/6 Project 4
language [ˈlæŋɡwɪdʒ] Sprache II/4A1
lap [læp] Schoß VI/4 Project 1
large [lɑːdʒ] groß II/2C1
last [lɑːst] letzte(r, s) I/5A1
last [lɑːst] (an)dauern VI/4 Project 2; *hier:* als Letzte(r, s) VI/1A1
late [leɪt] jüngste(r, s); letzte(r, s); neueste(r, s) IV/3A3
(too) late [leɪt] (zu) spät II/1B5
lately [ˈleɪtli] kürzlich, in letzter Zeit VI/5A5
later [ˈleɪtə] später II/1A4
later on [ˌleɪtər ˈɒn] später VI/3B4
laugh [lɑːf] lachen I/6C5
laughter [ˈlɑːftə] Gelächter, Lachen VI/4I
launch [lɔːntʃ] Start VI/2G1
launch a satellite [ˌlɔːntʃ ə ˈsætəlaɪt] einen Satelliten in den Weltraum schießen VI/2 Project 5
by law [ˌbaɪ ˈlɔː] gesetzlich VI/3A4
the rule of law [ðə ˌruːl əv ˈlɔː] die Rechtsstaatlichkeit VI/3A5
lawn [lɔːn] Rasen VI/3B4
lawyer [ˈlɔːjə] Rechtsanwalt/-anwältin VI/3B8
layout [ˈleɪaʊt] Layout, Aufmachung V/2A4
lead [liːd] führen III/2A1
leader [ˈliːdə] *hier:* Führer/in VI/5A2
leaf (*pl* leaves) [liːf, liːvz] Blatt II/2B3
lean [liːn] mager VI/1B4
°lean over [ˌliːn ˈəʊvə] sich herüberbeugen VI/BS 3
leap [liːp] Sprung, Satz VI/2 Project 5
learn [lɜːn] *hier:* erfahren V/2A5; lernen I/1C6

D

Dictionary English – German

least [liːst] am wenigsten II/5B1
leave [liːv] (weg)gehen; abfahren II/5A2; verlassen II/5B1
leave [liːv] *hier:* hinterlassen VI/1A2
leave behind [ˌliːv bɪˈhaɪnd] zurücklassen V/4B5
leave out [ˌliːv ˈaʊt] auslassen, weglassen VI/5A6
Lebanon [ˈlebənən] Libanon VI/2 Project 5
left [left] linke(r, s) I/2A4
be left [bi ˈleft] übrig bleiben VI/5A2
leg [leg] Bein I/2A4
legal [ˈliːgl] *hier:* mit Aufenthaltsgenehmigung VI/2I
°**legend** [ˈledʒnd] Sage, Legende VI/BS 8
lemon [ˈlemən] Zitrone I/5B1
lend [lend] leihen IV/7B7
°**length** [leŋθ] Länge VI/5O
less [les] weniger III/2A3
lesson [ˈlesn] Stunde I/3C4
let [let] lassen I/1A2
°**let sb down** [ˌlet ˌsʌmbədi ˈdaʊn] jdn enttäuschen VI/BS 6
let's (= let us) … [lets, ˈlet əs] lass(t) uns … I/1A2
°**let's face it** [ˌlets ˈfeɪs ɪt] machen wir uns doch nichts vor VI/BS 3
lethal [ˈliːθl] tödlich VI/3B4
letter [ˈletə] Brief; Buchstabe I/3C3
letter of application [ˌletər əv ˌæplɪˈkeɪʃn] Bewerbungsschreiben V/2A5
level [levl] Niveau; Ebene VI/1A8
library [ˈlaɪbrəri] Bibliothek, Bücherei II/6B4
lie [laɪ] liegen; sich hinlegen II/3C1
lie [laɪ] Lüge VI/6 Project 2
lie down [ˌlaɪ ˈdaʊn] sich hinlegen V/1B5
police lieutenant [pəˌliːs lefˈtenənt] Polizeihauptwachtmeister/in VI/3B7
life (*pl* **lives**) [laɪf, laɪvz] Leben I/4C1
take a life [ˌteɪk ə ˈlaɪf] jdn umbringen VI/3B4
life imprisonment [ˌlaɪf ɪmˈprɪznmənt] lebenslängliche Haftstrafe VI/3B8
life sentence [ˈlaɪf ˌsentəns] lebenslängliche Haftstrafe VI/3B8
life vest [ˈlaɪf ˌvest] Rettungsweste V/1A6
lifestyle [ˈlaɪfstaɪl] Lebensstil V/3I
°**lifetime** [ˈlaɪftaɪm] Leben(szeit) VI/BS 4

lift [lɪft] (hoch)heben, anheben VI/3B4
light [laɪt] Licht I/4A4
°**light** [laɪt] leicht VI/5O
light bulb [ˈlaɪt ˌbʌlb] Glühbirne VI/6 Project 4
like [laɪk] mögen I/W; wie I/4A6
°**like** [laɪk] *hier:* als ob VI/BS 3
like best [ˈlaɪk ˌbest] am liebsten mögen II/4A4
like this/that [laɪk ˈðɪs] so; auf diese Weise II/1B1
likely [ˈlaɪkli] wahrscheinlich VI/3B1
°**lime** [laɪm] Limette VI/BS 3
°**limited** [ˈlɪmɪtɪd] *mit beschränkter Haftung* VI/5O
line [laɪn] Linie; Zeile IV/5B1
chat-up line [ˈtʃætʌp ˌlaɪn] Anmache, Anmachspruch VI/4 Project 1
stand in line [ˌstænd ɪn ˈlaɪn] anstehen IV/8B2
liner [ˈlaɪnə] Passagierschiff VI/2 Project 4
°**lingo** (*informal*) [ˈlɪŋgəʊ] Sprache, Kauderwelsch VI/BS 4
link [lɪŋk] Verbindung; Link VI/1B3; verbinden VI/BS 2
lion [ˈlaɪən] Löwe II/2B3
lip [lɪp] Lippe VI/4 Project 2
°**lisp** [lɪsp] Lispeln VI/BS 3
list [lɪst] Liste III/1A1
listen (to) [ˈlɪsn] (zu)hören I/1A1
listener [ˈlɪsənə] Zuhörer/in VI/1A5
listening sequence [ˈlɪsnɪŋ ˌsiːkwəns] Hörsequenz VI/2I
literary [ˈlɪtrəri] Literatur- VI/4I
literature [ˈlɪtrətʃə] Literatur VI/5A3
little [ˈlɪtl] klein I/4C6; wenig V/1B5
a little [ə ˈlɪtl] ein wenig, ein bisschen III/2A2
live [lɪv] leben, wohnen I/W
live through [ˌlɪv ˈθruː] überstehen; *hier:* überleben VI/3B4
°**living** [ˈlɪvɪŋ] lebend VI/BS 3
make a living [ˌmeɪk ə ˈlɪvɪŋ] seinen Lebensunterhalt verdienen IV/6I
standard of living [ˌstændəd əv ˈlɪvɪŋ] Lebensstandard V/5B4
living room [ˈlɪvɪŋ ˌruːm] Wohnzimmer I/4B2
load [ləʊd] (auf)laden V/5B3
loads [ləʊdz] jede Menge VI/4 Project 5

°**lobby** [ˈlɒbi] Eingangshalle, Vorhalle VI/BS 5
local [ˈləʊkəl] hiesig, örtlich V/2A8
°**be located** [ˌbi ləʊˈkeɪtɪd] liegen, gelegen sein VI/BS 8
location [ləʊˈkeɪʃn] Lage, (Stand)ort V/2A2
°**lock** [lɒk] abschließen VI/BS 2
log [lɒg] Holzklotz, Holzscheit VI/4 Project 1
°**loincloth** [ˈlɔɪnklɒθ] Lendenschurz VI/BS 2
Londoner [ˈlʌndənə] Londoner/in VI/4 Project 6
lonely [ˈləʊnli] einsam V/4B6
long [lɒŋ] lang I/2A5
(long) ago [əˈgəʊ] vor (langer Zeit) I/5A1
as long as [æz ˈlɒŋ æz] solang(e) VI/3A3
°**in the long run** [ˌɪn ðə ˈlɒŋ ˌrʌn] langfristig gesehen VI/BS 6
look [lʊk] Aussehen V/3I; Blick IV/4A4; sehen, schauen I/1A2; *hier:* aussehen I/3B8
look after [lʊk ˈɑːftə] sich kümmern um II/1A4
look at [ˈlʊk ət] betrachten, sehen I/1C1
look back [ˌlʊk ˈbæk] zurückblicken IV/8A5
look for [ˈlʊk fə] suchen nach II/2A1
look forward to doing sth [ˌlʊk ˈfɔːwəd tə ˌduːɪŋ sʌmθɪŋ] sich darauf freuen, etw zu tun VI/3P6
I look forward to hearing from you. [aɪ ˌlʊk ˌfɔːwəd tə ˈhɪərɪŋ frəm juː] Ich hoffe, von Ihnen zu hören. V/2A5
look through [ˌlʊk ˈθruː] durchsehen V/3I
look up [ˌlʊk ˈʌp] nachschlagen III/2A7
°**look up** [ˌlʊk ˈʌp] nach oben sehen VI/BS 1
have got the looks [ˌhæv gɒt ðə ˈlʊks] gut aussehen VI/1A3
looks (*only plural*) [lʊks] Aussehen VI/1A3
Lord [lɔːd] Herr VI/1B4
lorry [ˈlɒri] Lastwagen V/2B7
lose [luːz] verlieren II/3C1
lose one's way [ˌluːz wʌnz ˈweɪ] sich verirren II/6A8
lose weight [ˌluːz ˈweɪt] abnehmen VI/1A5

Dictionary English – German

°loser [ˈluːzə] Verlierer/in VI/BS 1
°loss [lɒs] Verlust VI/BS 5; *hier:* Niederlage VI/BS 3
be lost [bi ˈlɒst] sich verirrt haben VI/4 Project 3
a lot (of) [ə ˈlɒt (əv)] viel(e) I/1A1
lots *(informal)* [lɒt] viel, jede Menge II/1A4
lots of [ˈlɒts‿əv] viel, jede Menge I/3A6
loud [laʊd] laut I/1C5
love [lʌv] Liebe III/4B1; lieben; sehr gern mögen I/1A4
love [lʌv] Liebling, Schatz VI/4 Project 4
love *(in Briefen)* [lʌv] alles Liebe, viele Grüße II/6C6
be in love (with) [ˌbiː ɪn ˈlʌv] verliebt sein (in) IV/4B6
lovely [ˈlʌvli] nett, liebenswürdig IV/4A2; schön, hübsch; *hier:* herrlich I/4C5
°**loving** [ˈlʌvɪŋ] liebend, liebevoll VI/BS 5
low [ləʊ] niedrig VI/2 Project 4
low-energy [ˌləʊ ˈenədʒi] energiesparend VI/6G9
low impact [ˌləʊ ˈɪmpækt] schadstoffreduziert, wenig belastend VI/6 Project 4
low-income [ˌləʊ ˈɪnkʌm] einkommensschwach VI/1B2
°**lower** [ˈləʊə] senken VI/5O
loyalty [ˈlɔɪəlti] Treue VI/4 Project 5
luckily [ˈlʌkɪli] glücklicherweise VI/4 Project 2
lunar module [ˌluːnə ˈmɒdjuːl] Mondlandefähre VI/2G9
lunch [lʌntʃ] Mittagessen I/5A1
°**lunchtime** [ˈlʌntʃtaɪm] Mittagszeit VI/BS 3
lyrics *(only plural)* [ˈlɪrɪks] (Lied)text IV/5B1

M

Macedonia [ˌmæsɪˈdəʊniə] Makedonien, Mazedonien VI/5A3
machinery [məˈʃiːnəri] Maschinen, technische Geräte VI/1B3
mad [mæd] *hier:* wie verrückt VI/4 Project 4; *hier:* böse, wütend VI/BS 3
Dear Sir or Madam, (…) [ˌdɪə ˈsɜːr‿ɔː ˈmædəm] Sehr geehrte Damen und Herren! (…) V/2A5
magazine [ˌmæɡəˈziːn] Zeitschrift, Magazin II/3B1

°**magician** [məˈdʒɪʃn] Zauberer/Zauberin VI/BS 3
°**magnificently** [mæɡˈnɪfɪsntli] hervorragend, beeindruckend VI/1O
mail [meɪl] Post V/4B6
main [meɪn] Haupt- V/1B5
main course [ˈmeɪn ˌkɔːs] Hauptgericht III/1A2
main idea [ˌmeɪn aɪˈdɪə] Grundidee VI/6 Project 5
mainly [ˈmeɪnli] hauptsächlich, in erster Linie VI/5B3
mains *(only plural)* [meɪnz] Versorgungsnetz VI/6 Project 4
maize [meɪz] Mais VI/2 Project 1
major [ˈmeɪdʒə] bedeutend, wichtig; *hier:* Haupt- VI/5A3
make [meɪk] machen I/1A8
make a call [ˌmeɪk ə ˌkɔːl] telefonieren II/5B1
make a change [ˌmeɪk ə ˈtʃeɪndʒ] eine Änderung vornehmen VI/6 Project 3
make a living [ˌmeɪk ə ˈlɪvɪŋ] seinen Lebensunterhalt verdienen IV/6I
°**make a point** [ˌmeɪk ə ˈpɔɪnt] seinen Standpunkt deutlich machen VI/BS 8
make a wish [ˌmeɪk ə ˈwɪʃ] sich etwas wünschen VI/6 Project 3
make friends [ˌmeɪk ˈfrendz] sich anfreunden, Freundschaften schließen V/5A2
°**make it** [ˈmeɪk‿ɪt] es schaffen VI/BS 7
make money [meɪk ˈmʌni] Geld verdienen II/3B1
°**make one's way** [ˌmeɪk wʌnz ˈweɪ] sich auf den Weg machen VI/BS 3
make sb do sth [ˌmeɪk sʌmbədi ˈduː ˌsʌmθɪŋ] jdn dazu bringen, etw zu tun IV/7A3
make sb feel [ˌmeɪk sʌmbədi ˈfiːl] jdm das Gefühl geben, dass … VI/1B4
make sure [ˌmeɪk ˈʃɔː] achten auf V/2A8
make up [meɪk‿ˈʌp] erfinden, (sich) ausdenken II/6B2
make up [meɪk‿ˈʌp] *hier:* bestehen aus VI/1B3
°**makeshift** [ˈmeɪkʃɪft] behelfsmäßig VI/BS 8
peace making [ˈpiːs ˌmeɪkɪŋ] Befriedung VI/2 Project 1

male [meɪl] männlich III/3A3
male [meɪl] Mann VI/1A7
mall [mɔːl] (große) Einkaufspassage IV/2B4
malnutrition [ˌmælnjuˈtrɪʃn] Unterernährung VI/1A6
man *(pl* **men)** [mæn, men] Mann I/2A7; Mensch II/3B1
best man [ˌbest ˈmæn] Trauzeuge VI/4 Project 6
manage [ˈmænɪdʒ] es schaffen VI/3B4
manager [ˈmænɪdʒə] Geschäftsführer/in, Leiter/in VI/2I
mankind [mænˈkaɪnd] Menschheit VI/2 Project 5
manners *(only plural)* [ˈmænəz] Manieren V/2B1
°**manual** [ˈmænjuəl] manuell, Hand- VI/5O
manufacture [ˌmænjuˈfæktʃə] Herstellung, Erzeugung VI/6 Project 4; herstellen VI/5O
many [ˈmeni] viele I/3B1
map [mæp] (Land)karte III/6B2
March [mɑːtʃ] März I/3B7
march [mɑːtʃ] Marsch VI/2 Project 4
mark [mɑːk] markieren, kennzeichnen IV/1A1; Note, Zensur V/2B1
mark [mɑːk] Fleck VI/1A2
market [ˈmɑːkɪt] Markt I/1B1
stock market [ˈstɒk ˌmɑːkɪt] Börse, Aktienmarkt VI/2 Project 4
marriage [ˈmærɪdʒ] Heirat; Ehe IV/4B6
married [ˈmærɪd] verheiratet I/5C7
get married [ˌget ˈmærɪd] heiraten VI/4 Project 1
marry [ˈmæri] heiraten; verheiraten IV/4B1
°**Martian** [ˈmɑːʃn] Marsmensch VI/BS 2
°**mascot** [ˈmæskət] Maskottchen VI/BS 3
mass [mæs] Masse; *hier:* Massen- VI/2 Project 5
massacre [ˈmæsəkə] Massaker, Blutbad VI/2 Project 1
match [mætʃ] passen zu; zusammenpassen VI/3A3; Spiel I/3A3
match (with/to) [mætʃ] zuordnen I/3B3
matching [ˈmætʃɪŋ] passend V/2A2
mate [meɪt] Freund/in, Kumpel VI/4 Project 5
material [məˈtɪəriəl] Material, Stoff V/6I

Dictionary English – German

maths [mɑːθs] Mathe I/5A1
matter ['mætə] von Bedeutung sein VI/6 Project 4; Angelegenheit, Sache VI/BS 8
°no matter how [nəʊ 'mætə ˌhaʊ] ganz gleich, wie ..., egal, wie ... VI/BS 3
°maximum ['mæksɪməm] maximal, Höchst- VI/5O
may [meɪ] können, mögen IV/5B1
May [meɪ] Mai I/5C2
maybe ['meɪbi] vielleicht, möglicherweise I/4B3
me [miː] mir, mich; hier: ich I/1A3
meadow ['medəʊ] Wiese VI/6 Project 4
meal [miːl] Mahlzeit, Essen III/1B1
mean [miːn] bedeuten; meinen I/4B5
mean [miːn] gemein VI/4 Project 4
meaning ['miːnɪŋ] Bedeutung III/2A7
by means of [ˌbaɪ 'miːnz ˌəv] durch, mit Hilfe von VI/3A4
°meant to be ['ment ˌtə ˌbiː] sein sollen VI/BS 2
measure ['meʒə] (ab)messen VI/6 Project 4
meat [miːt] Fleisch II/2B3
the media [ðə 'miːdiə] die Medien V/6I
mediate ['miːdieɪt] hier: sprachmitteln V/1A5
medicine ['medsn] Medizin, Medikamente III/4A1
meet [miːt] (sich) treffen I/1B5
member ['membə] Angehörige/r, Mitglied IV/2A8
memorial [məˈmɔːriəl] Denkmal, Ehrenmal VI/2 Project 5
°memorize ['meməraɪz] sich einprägen VI/BS 3
memory ['meməri] Gedächtnis; Erinnerung IV/7B4
mental [mentl] geistig; psychisch VI/1B5
mention ['menʃn] erwähnen IV/8A5
menu ['menjuː] Speisekarte III/1A2
mess [mes] Unordnung, Chaos; Dreck VI/4 Project 4
°mess up [ˌmesˈʌp] etw in Unordnung bringen VI/BS 1
message ['mesɪdʒ] Nachricht, Botschaft IV/5I; Nachrichten schicken V/5A4
°metaphor ['metəfə] Metapher, bildhafte Sprache VI/BS 3

metre ['miːtə] Meter III/5B2
Middle East [ˌmɪdl ˈiːst] Naher Osten VI/4 Project 2
°midnight ['mɪdˌnaɪt] Mitternacht VI/BS 5
might [maɪt] könnte(st, n) II/2A4
migrant ['maɪgrnt] Zuwanderer/Zuwanderin VI/3A3
mile [maɪl] Meile (= 1,609 km) III/6B1
military ['mɪlɪtəri] Militär- VI/2 Project 5
milk [mɪlk] Milch I/2B1
milk [mɪlk] melken VI/5A5
°mill around [ˌmɪl əˈraʊnd] umherlaufen VI/BS 5
millionaire [ˌmɪljəˈneə] Millionär/in VI/4G4
mind [maɪnd] Geist, Verstand VI/6 Project 1; hier: Kopf VI/4 Project 3; jdm etw ausmachen, jdn stören VI/4 Project 1; hier: an etw denken VI/BS 4; hier: Gedanken, Erinnerung VI/BS 2
°change one's mind [ˌtʃeɪndʒ wʌnz ˈmaɪnd] seine Meinung ändern VI/BS 3
come to sb's mind [ˌkʌm tuː ˌsʌmbədiz ˈmaɪnd] jdm einfallen IV/1A1
mindless ['maɪndləs] sinnlos; hier: gedankenlos VI/4 Project 4
mine [maɪn] meine(r, s) IV/8A6
°mineral ['mɪnrəl] Mineral VI/BS 2
minimum ['mɪnɪməm] Mindest- VI/3B1
minute ['mɪnɪt] Minute II/2B1
miraculously [məˈrækjʊləsli] wie durch ein Wunder VI/3B4
mirror ['mɪrə] Spiegel VI/1A1
miss [mɪs] vermissen; verpassen II/6A5
Miss [mɪs] Miss; Fräulein; Frau Lehrerin VI/4 Project 3
missile ['mɪsaɪl] Rakete VI/2 Project 5
be missing [ˌbiː ˈmɪsɪŋ] fehlen VI/5B1
mistake [mɪˈsteɪk] Fehler IV/6B1
mistreat [mɪsˈtriːt] misshandeln; schlecht behandeln VI/2 Project 2
mix in [ˌmɪksˈɪn] untermischen VI/4 Project 5
mobile (phone) ['məʊbaɪl (fəʊn)] Mobiltelefon, Handy II/5B1
°mobility [məʊˈbɪlət i] Beweglichkeit VI/5O

modal verb [ˌməʊdl ˈvɜːb] Modalverb VI/2G6
model ['mɒdl] Modell VI/4I
model (text) ['mɒdl] Mustertext II/1C6
lunar module [ˌluːnə ˈmɒdjuːl] Mondlandefähre VI/2G9
mom (AE = mum BE) [mɒm] Mama VI/1A5
°moment ['məʊmənt] Moment, Augenblick VI/BS 3
Monday ['mʌndeɪ] Montag I/2B7
money ['mʌni] Geld II/2B8
be short of money (informal) [biː ʃɔːt ˌəv ˈmʌni] knapp bei Kasse sein III/6A2
monkey ['mʌŋki] Affe I/6C1
monopoly [məˈnɒpəli] Monopol VI/2 Project 1
month [mʌnθ] Monat I/5C1
°mood [muːd] Laune, Stimmung VI/BS 8
moon [muːn] Mond II/3A1
°mop [mɒp] Mopp, Wischer VI/1O
°moral code [ˌmɒrəl ˈkəʊd] Sittenkodex VI/BS 3
°morality [məˈræləti] moralische Grundsätze VI/BS 8
more [mɔː] mehr I/1C4; noch mehr; weitere(r, s) II/6A7
morning ['mɔːnɪŋ] Morgen, Vormittag I/2A2
Moscow ['mɒskəʊ] Moskau VI/3A5
most [məʊst] am meisten II/5B1; die meisten III/6B1
the most [ˌðə ˈməʊst] hier: das Beste VI/3B4
°most [məʊst] hier: fast VI/BS 3
mostly ['məʊsli] meistens, hauptsächlich V/1B5
mother ['mʌðə] Mutter I/2B3
°mother ['mʌðə] bemuttern VI/BS 6
°mother tongue [ˌmʌðə ˈtʌŋ] Muttersprache VI/BS 4
°mothering ['mʌðərɪŋ] Muttersein VI/BS 6
motivate ['məʊtɪveɪt] anspornen, motivieren VI/6 Project 4
motive ['məʊtɪv] Motiv, Beweggrund VI/3A3
mountain ['maʊntɪn] Berg II/1A4
mouse (pl mice) [maʊs, maɪs] Maus I/3B1
mouth [maʊθ] Mund I/2A2
mouth [maʊθ] lautlos sagen VI/4 Project 3

Dictionary English – German

°mouthwash [ˈmaʊθwɒʃ] Mundwasser VI/BS 3
move [muːv] (sich) bewegen II/3C1
move [muːv] Bewegung; *hier:* Schritt VI/4 Project 1; *hier:* ziehen VI/2 Project 2; umziehen VI/1P5
°move in [ˌmuːv ˈɪn] einziehen VI/BS 6
move on [ˌmuːv ˈɒn] weitergehen VI/6 Project 3; *hier:* weitermachen mit VI/BS 3
move sb [ˈmuːv ˌsʌmbədi] *hier:* jdn umsiedeln, vertreiben VI/2I
movement [ˈmuːvmənt] Bewegung VI/2 Project 3
movie [ˈmuːvi] Film VI/2 Project 4
all-black movie [ˌɔːlblæk ˈmuːvi] Film, in dem nur Schwarze als (Haupt)darsteller vorkommen VI/2 Project 4
Mr [ˈmɪstə] Herr *(Anrede)* I/W
Mrs [ˈmɪsɪz] Frau *(Anrede)* I/W
much [mʌtʃ] viel; sehr I/1A5; *hier:* häufig, oft II/5A5
multicultural [ˌmʌltiˈkʌltʃərəl] multikulturell VI/4 Project 2
mum *(informal)* [mʌm] Mama, Mutti I/1A3
murder [ˈmɜːdə] Mord VI/3B3
murder [ˈmɜːdə] ermorden VI/2 Project 3
murderer [ˈmɜːdərə] Mörder/in VI/3B6
muscle [ˈmʌsl] Muskel VI/1A8
muscular [ˈmʌskjʊlə] muskulös VI/4 Project 1
museum [mjuːˈziːəm] Museum II/2C5
music [ˈmjuːzɪk] Musik I/6C6
musician [mjuːˈzɪʃn] Musiker/in III/7A2
Muslim [ˈmʊzlɪm] Moslem/in; moslemisch VI/4 Project 6
must [mʌst] müssen I/4A4
must not [ˌmʌst ˈnɒt] nicht dürfen II/5A3
°mute [mjuːt] stumm VI/BS 3
°mutilate [ˈmjuːtɪleɪt] verstümmeln VI/BS 3
°mutter [ˈmʌtə] murmeln VI/BS 6
my [maɪ] mein(e) I/W
myself [maɪˈself] mir, mich; selbst IV/2A2
°mysterious [mɪˈstɪəriəs] geheimnisvoll, rätselhaft VI/BS 3

N

°Namaste [nʌmʌsˈteː] *Begrüßung* VI/BS 8
name [neɪm] (be)nennen V/1A2; Name I/W
narrow [ˈnærəʊ] eng; knapp III/3B1
nation [ˈneɪʃn] Nation, Land V/4A3
nationalist [ˈnæʃnəlɪst] nationalistisch VI/5A2
nationality [ˌnæʃəˈnæləti] Nationalität V/2A3
native [ˈneɪtɪv] einheimisch, eingeboren VI/2I; Einheimische/r VI/BS 4
Native American [ˌneɪtɪv əˈmerɪkən] amerikanische/r Ureinwohner/in VI/2I
natural [ˈnætʃrəl] natürlich VI/1B3
nature [ˈneɪtʃə] Natur V/1A6
near [nɪə] nahe (bei) I/1B1
°near [nɪə] sich nähern, näher kommen VI/BS 6
nearly [ˈnɪəli] fast, beinahe II/3A8
°neatly [ˈniːtli] sauber, ordentlich VI/BS 2
necessary [ˈnesəseri] nötig, notwendig V/2B1
neck [nek] Hals; Nacken I/2A2
need [niːd] brauchen II/1B5
°need [niːd] Not VI/BS 4
need to [ˈniːd tʊ] müssen IV/1A2
negative [ˈnegətɪv] negativ IV/8A1
negro [ˈniːgrəʊ] Neger *(abwertend)* VI/2 Project 3
neighborhood (AE = **neighbourhood** BE) [ˈneɪbəhʊd] Viertel; Umgebung IV/3A3
neighbour [ˈneɪbə] Nachbar/in II/4A2
neither [ˈnaɪðə] auch nicht IV/3B5
neither ... nor ... [ˌnaɪðə ˈnɔː] weder ... noch ... V/1B5
nephew [ˈnefjuː] Neffe VI/3B6
nervous [ˈnɜːvəs] nervös IV/6B2
Net [net] Internet, Netz V/5B2
the Netherlands [ðə ˈneðələndz] die Niederlande V/5A3
network [ˈnetwɜːk] Netz(werk) V/5A2
never [ˈnevə] nie(mals) I/4C1
°nevertheless [ˌnevəðəˈles] trotzdem, dennoch VI/5O
new [njuː] neu I/1A2
New Year [ˌnjuː ˈjɪə] Neujahr II/4A3
New Zealand [njuː ˈziːlənd] Neuseeland VI/1A10

news *(no pl)* [njuːz] Neuigkeit; Nachrichten II/1B4
newspaper [ˈnjuːzˌpeɪpə] Zeitung I/4C10
next [nekst] nächste(r, s) I/2B7
next time [ˈnekstˌtaɪm] nächstes Mal VI/1A1
next to [ˈnekst tə] neben I/2C2
nice [naɪs] schön; nett I/1B2
Nice to meet you. [ˌnaɪs tə ˈmiːt jə] Es freut mich, Sie/dich kennen zu lernen. I/4B5
°nick [nɪk] mitgehen lassen VI/BS 6
nickname [ˈnɪkneɪm] Spitzname, Kosename VI/2 Project 2
night [naɪt] Abend VI/1B2; Nacht II/3C2
°in the dead of night [ɪn ðə ˌded əv ˈnaɪt] mitten in der Nacht VI/BS 2
nightmare [ˈnaɪtˌmeə] Albtraum VI/4I
nine [naɪn] neun I/2B4
no [nəʊ] kein(e) I/1A6; nein I/W
°no matter how [nəʊ ˈmætə ˌhaʊ] ganz gleich, wie ..., egal, wie ... VI/BS 3
no one [ˈnəʊˌwʌn] niemand VI/3A4
no one else [ˌnəʊwʌn ˈels] niemand anderes IV/4A2
°in no time at all [ɪn ˌnəʊ ˌtaɪm ət əˈɔːl] im Nu, in null Komma nichts VI/BS 9
°no way [ˌnəʊ ˈweɪ] keinesfalls VI/BS 3
Nobel Peace Prize [nəʊˌbel ˈpiːs praɪz] Friedensnobelpreis VI/2 Project 3
nobody [ˈnəʊˌbɒdi] niemand I/5C4
nobody else [ˌnəʊbədi ˈels] niemand anderes VI/1A1
nod [nɒd] nicken VI/3B9
noise [nɔɪz] Lärm, Geräusch III/3A3
noisy [ˈnɔɪzi] laut IV/1A8
non- [nɒn] nicht- VI/3A5
non-stop [ˌnɒnˈstɒp] nonstop, ununterbrochen VI/2 Project 4
non-violent [ˌnɒn ˈvaɪələnt] gewaltfrei VI/2 Project 3
nonsense [ˈnɒnsns] Unsinn, Quatsch VI/2 Project 4
nor [nɔː] und auch nicht, noch IV/3B5
normally [ˈnɔːmli] normalerweise III/4B2
north [nɔːθ] *hier:* in nördliche Richtung III/5A1; Norden I/4C10

223

°north [nɔːθ] nördlich VI/BS 3
North America [ˌnɔːθ ə'merɪkə] Nordamerika VI/4 Project 4
the North Sea [ðə ˌnɔːθ 'siː] die Nordsee VI/6G7
northern ['nɔːðən] Nord-, nördlich VI/5A3
Northern California [ˌnɔːðn ˌkælə'fɔːniə] Nordkalifornien VI/2 Project 5
Northern Ireland [ˌnɔːð(ə)n ˈaɪələnd] Nordirland II/LL1
nose [nəʊz] Nase I/2A2
not [nɒt] nicht I/1A4
not ... any [nɒt ˈeni] keine(r, s) II/6A4
not ... anywhere [ˌnɒt ˈeniweə] nirgendwo(hin) II/6A2
not ... either [ˌnɒt ˈaɪðə] auch nicht IV/3A2
not any [nɒt ˈæni] kein(e) II/3A9
not anymore [ˌnɒt ˌeniˈmɔː] nicht mehr II/5C2
not anyone [ˌnɒt ˈeniwʌn] niemand II/3A1
not anything [nɒt ˈeniθɪŋ] nichts II/3C5
not only ... but also [ˌnɒt ˌəʊnli ˌbʌt ˈɔːlsəʊ] nicht nur ..., sondern auch ... VI/5A2
note [nəʊt] Notiz IV/6B1
nothing [ˈnʌθɪŋ] nichts II/6B2
nothing else [ˌnʌθɪŋ ˈels] nichts weiter VI/1A5
notice [ˈnəʊtɪs] bemerken IV/1B3
°take notice [ˌteɪk ˈnəʊtɪs] Notiz nehmen VI/BS 6
°notion [ˈnəʊʃn] Vorstellung VI/BS 6
°notoriously [nəʊˈtɔːriəsli] notorisch, bekanntlich VI/BS 8
noun [naʊn] Hauptwort, Substantiv II/1A3
novel [ˈnɒvl] Roman VI/4 Project 1
November [nəʊˈvembə] November I/3B7
now [naʊ] jetzt I/1B2
by now [baɪ ˈnaʊ] mittlerweile VI/2 Project 2
now that [ˈnaʊ ðæt] jetzt, wo ... VI/2 Project 2
nowadays [ˈnaʊədeɪz] heutzutage VI/3B4
nowhere [ˈnəʊweə] nirgends, nirgendwo VI/6 Project 1
nuclear [ˈnjuːkliə] Atom- VI/5A3; nuklear, Atom- VI/2 Project 5
nuclear bomb [ˌnjuːkliə ˈbɒm] Atombombe VI/2I

number [ˈnʌmbə] Zahl; Ziffer, Nummer I/1A6
°nun [nʌn] Nonne VI/BS 5
nurse [nɜːs] (Kranken)schwester, (Kranken)pfleger II/3A4

O

obey [əˈbeɪ] gehorchen; hier: (be) folgen VI/2 Project 3
object [ˈɒbdʒekt] Objekt, Satzgegenstand IV/7B7
observe [əbˈzɜːv] beobachten VI/5A5
be obsessed with [ˌbi əbˈsest wɪð] besessen sein von; verrückt sein nach VI/1A6
°obsession [əbˈseʃn] Besessenheit VI/BS 1
obsessive [əbˈsesɪv] zwanghaft VI/1A6
obsolete [ˈɒbsəliːt] veraltet, überholt VI/2 Project 2
°obvious [ˈɒbviəs] deutlich, offensichtlich VI/BS 2
obviously [ˈɒbviəsli] offensichtlich V/1B5
°occasion [əˈkeɪʒn] Gelegenheit VI/BS 9
°occasionally [əˈkeɪʒnəli] gelegentlich VI/BS 8
occur [əˈkɜː] geschehen; stattfinden VI/6 Project 5
ocean [ˈəʊʃn] Ozean, Meer V/5B3
October [ɒkˈtəʊbə] Oktober I/3A1
of [ɒf] von II/1A2
of course [əv ˈkɔːs] natürlich II/1A4
of one's own [ˌəv wʌnz ˈəʊn] eigene(r, s) (nachgestellt) VI/4 Project 5
°offend [əˈfend] beleidigen, kränken VI/BS 8
offer [ˈɒfə] anbieten, bieten V/2A2
office [ˈɒfɪs] Büro V/2B6
office worker [ˈɒfɪs ˌwɜːkə] Büroangestellte/r IV/6A1
official [əˈfɪʃl] offiziell VI/5A2
official [əˈfɪʃl] Amtsperson VI/5B4
often [ˈɒfn] oft, häufig I/1A7
oil [ɔɪl] Öl VI/1B3
old [əʊld] alt I/W
old-fashioned [ˌəʊld ˈfæʃnd] altmodisch VI/4 Project 2
olive [ˈɒlɪv] Olive VI/1P5
Olympic Games [əˌlɪmpɪk ˈgeɪmz] Olympische Spiele V/4A3
on [ɒn] auf, an, in I/1A8

on foot [ɒn ˈfʊt] zu Fuß IV/5B2
(on) Sundays [ˈsʌndeɪz] sonntags II/2C1
on the Internet [ˌɒn ði ˈɪntənet] im Internet II/1B7
on the left [ˌɒn ðə ˈleft] links, auf der linken Seite II/1C5
on the one hand ..., on the other hand ... [ɒn ðə ˈwʌn ˌhænd ..., ɒn ði ˌʌðə ˌhænd] einerseits ... andererseits ... IV/5A3
(on the) phone [fəʊn] (am) Telefon II/4C3
on the right [ˌɒn ðə ˈraɪt] rechts, auf der rechten Seite II/1C5
on time [ɒn ˈtaɪm] pünktlich V/2A6
once [wʌns] einmal II/1A4
once [wʌns] früher, einst VI/2I; sobald; als VI/2G8
at once [ət ˈwʌns] sofort V/5A7
once a year [ˌwʌns ə ˈjɪə] einmal im/pro Jahr III/6B1
once more [wʌns ˈmɔː] noch einmal V/5B3
once upon a time [ˌwʌns əˌpɒn ə ˈtaɪm] es war einmal; vor langer Zeit VI/4 Project 1
one [wʌn] eins; ein(e) I/1P7
the one [ðə ˈwʌn] derjenige/diejenige/dasjenige IV/3A2
one day [ˈwʌn ˌdeɪ] eines Tages VI/1A5
°one-way [ˌwʌnˈweɪ] in einer Richtung; einseitig VI/BS 3
onion [ˈʌnjən] Zwiebel III/1A2
only [ˈəʊnli] einzige(r, s) VI/1B2; nur I/6A3
onto [ˈɒntə] auf VI/2I
open [ˈəʊpən] aufmachen, öffnen I/1C1; offen, geöffnet I/6B1; sich öffnen, aufgehen II/2C1
open day [ˈəʊpən deɪ] Tag der offenen Tür VI/4I
opening [ˈəʊpnɪŋ] Eröffnung VI/3A6
opening credit [ˌəʊpənɪŋ ˈkredɪt] einleitende Danksagung VI/4 Project 6
operation [ˌɒpəˈreɪʃn] Unternehmung, Einsatz VI/2 Project 5
opinion [əˈpɪnjən] Meinung, Ansicht IV/1B3
in my opinion [ɪn ˌmaɪ əˈpɪnjən] meiner Meinung nach IV/1B3
opportunity [ˌɒpəˈtjuːnəti] Gelegenheit V/2A2
opposite [ˈɒpəzɪt] gegenüber I/2C2

Dictionary English – German

opposite [ˈɒpəzɪt] gegensätzlich VI/1P4; Gegenteil VI/1P4
optimistic [ˌɒptɪˈmɪstɪk] optimistisch VI/3B4
or [ɔː] oder I/1A2
oral [ˈɔːrəl] mündlich (überliefert) VI/2 Project 5
orange [ˈɒrɪndʒ] orange I/5C5; Orange, Apfelsine I/1A4
orator [ˈɒrətə] Redner/in VI/2 Project 3
order [ˈɔːdə] bestellen V/5A6; Bestellung VI/5B2; Ordnung, Reihenfolge IV/4B2
order [ˈɔːdə] anordnen; ordnen VI/3B8; Befehl, Anordnung VI/2 Project 3
in order to [ɪnˈɔːdə tʊ] um zu VI/3A4
Are you ready to order? [ɑː juː ˌredi tʊ ˈɔːdə] Möchten Sie schon bestellen? III/1A3
ordinary [ˈɔːdnəri] gewöhnlich, normal VI/2 Project 4
organic [ɔːˈgænɪk] organisch; aus biologischem Anbau VI/6 Project 4
organization [ˌɔːgənaɪˈzeɪʃn] Organisation VI/1B2
organize [ˈɔːgənaɪz] organisieren; koordinieren; ordnen IV/5A1
organizer [ˈɔːgəˌnaɪzə] Organisator/in VI/1B2
orientation [ˌɔːriənˈteɪʃn] Orientierung; Einweisung, Einführung VI/2I
origin [ˈɒrɪdʒɪn] Herkunft VI/3A4
originally [əˈrɪdʒnəli] ursprünglich V/4A3
originate [əˈrɪdʒəneɪt] hervorbringen, erfinden VI/2I
other [ˈʌðə] andere(r, s) I/2A7
otherwise [ˈʌðəwaɪz] sonst, ansonsten VI/5A5
our [aʊə] unser(e) I/1A2
ours [aʊəz] unsere(r, s) IV/8A6
ourselves [aʊəˈselvz] uns; selbst IV/2A2
out [aʊt] außen, draußen VI/BS 1
be out [ˌbiˈaʊt] *hier:* ausgehen, weggehen VI/1A1
out of [ˈaʊt əv] aus VI/6 Project 3
be out of work [biˌaʊt əv ˈwɜːk] arbeitslos sein III/4B2
outback [ˈaʊtbæk] Hinterland (Australiens) V/4A2
outdoor [ˌaʊtˈdɔː] für draußen VI/5A2

outdoors [ˌaʊtˈdɔːz] im Freien, draußen VI/5P2
food outlet [ˈfuːdˌaʊtlet] Restaurant, Imbiss VI/1B2
outline [ˈaʊtlaɪn] Umriss, Kontur VI/4 Project 3
outrageous [aʊtˈreɪdʒəs] empörend; schockierend VI/3A3
outside [ˌaʊtˈsaɪd] außen, außerhalb; *hier:* draußen II/3C3
over [ˈəʊvə] über I/2C3
°**over** [ˈəʊvə] hinüber VI/BS 3
be over [ˌbiˈəʊvə] vorbei sein, aus sein VI/1B4
over and over [ˌəʊvərənˈəʊvə] immer wieder VI/2 Project 2
over there [ˌəʊvəˈðeə] dort drüben I/2C2
overcome [ˌəʊvəˈkʌm] bewältigen VI/6 Project 5
own [əʊn] besitzen IV/1B3; eigene(r, s) I/6A2
owner [ˈəʊnə] Besitzer/in V/2A5
Oxfam [ˈɒksfæm] *Hilfsorganisation* VI/5B4

P

p (= **penny;** *pl* **pennies** *or* **pence**) [ˈpeni, pens] Penny II/6A4
Pacific [pəˈsɪfɪk] Pazifik VI/2 Project 2
pack [pæk] (ein)packen VI/1B3
packaged [ˈpækɪdʒd] abgepackt VI/1B1
packed [pækt] voll VI/5A5
page [peɪdʒ] Seite I/2A7
pain [peɪn] Schmerz V/4B5
paint [peɪnt] malen, streichen VI/2I
painter [ˈpeɪntə] (Kunst)maler/in IV/7B4
painting [ˈpeɪntɪŋ] Bild, Gemälde IV/7B4
pair [peə] Paar I/6A6
a pair of trousers [əˌpeərəvˈtraʊzəz] eine Hose III/6A6
Pakistani [ˌpɑːkɪˈstɑːni] Pakistani, Pakistaner/in; pakistanisch VI/4 Project 6
pale [peɪl] blass, bleich VI/1A6
°**palm** [pɑːm] Handfläche, Handteller VI/BS 8
palm tree [ˈpɑːm triː] Palme VI/6 Project 3
paper [ˈpeɪpə] Papier I/4B7
sheet of paper [ˌʃiːt əvˈpeɪpə] Blatt Papier VI/2I
°**paperwork** [ˈpeɪpəwɜːk] *hier:* Papierkram VI/BS 3

parade [pəˈreɪd] Parade, Umzug III/3A1
paradise [ˈpærədaɪs] Paradies VI/4 Project 3
paragraph [ˈpærəˌgrɑːf] Absatz, Abschnitt IV/8B2
pardon [ˈpɑːdn] Begnadigung VI/3B8
pardon board [ˈpɑːdnˌbɔːd] Begnadigungskommission VI/3B8
parent [ˈpeərənt] Elternteil VI/4 Project 6
parents *(only plural)* [ˈpeərənts] Eltern I/1A6
parliament [ˈpɑːləmənt] Parlament VI/2 Project 1
part [pɑːt] Teil; Gegend; Rolle IV/2B4
part-time [ˌpɑːtˈtaɪm] Teilzeit V/2A2
participant [pɑːˈtɪsɪpənt] Teilnehmer/in VI/3B6
participate in [pɑːˈtɪsɪpeɪt ɪn] teilnehmen an VI/3A4
participle [ˈpɑːtɪsɪpl] Partizip VI/4G8
particular [pəˈtɪkjʊlə] bestimmt VI/3B4
°**parting** [ˈpɑːtɪŋ] Scheitel VI/BS 8
partner [ˈpɑːtnə] Partner/in I/1A6
partying [ˈpɑːtiɪŋ] Feiern VI/3B4
pass [pɑːs] *hier:* verabschieden VI/2 Project 2; *hier:* bestehen VI/BS 2
passage [ˈpæsɪdʒ] Passage VI/3B4
°**passer-by** (*pl* **passers-by**) [ˌpɑːsəˈbaɪ, ˌpɑːsəzˈbaɪ] Passant/in VI/BS 2
passion [ˈpæʃn] Leidenschaft VI/6 Project 5
°**passion fruit** [ˈpæʃnfruːt] Passionsfrucht VI/BS 6
passive [ˈpæsɪv] Passiv V/1B5
password [ˈpɑːswɜːd] Passwort V/5A6
past [pɑːst] vergangen, frühere(r, s) V/1B9; Vergangenheit II/2C1; vorbei an; hinter, nach I/2B6
past participle [ˌpɑːst ˈpɑːtɪsɪpl] Partizip Perfekt VI/5P7
past perfect [ˌpɑːst ˈpɜːfɪkt] Plusquamperfekt, Vorvergangenheit VI/2G8
past progressive [ˌpɑːst prəʊˈgresɪv] Verlaufsform der Vergangenheit VI/1P3
patience [ˈpeɪʃns] Geduld VI/5A5
patient [ˈpeɪʃnt] Patient/in III/2B3
°**pause** [pɔːz] innehalten VI/BS 3

225

Dictionary English – German

pay [peɪ] (be)zahlen III/5B1; Lohn, Gehalt VI/5B6
pay a compliment [ˌpeɪ ə ˈkɒmplɪmənt] ein Kompliment machen VI/6G1
pay attention to [ˌpeɪ əˈtenʃn tə] achten auf VI/3B10
°pay attention to sb [ˌpeɪ əˈtenʃn tə ˌsʌmbədi] jdm Aufmerksamkeit schenken VI/BS 3
paying [ˈpeɪɪŋ] rentabel, einträglich VI/3B4
payment [ˈpeɪmənt] Zahlung VI/5A5
PE (= physical education) [piːˈiː, ˌfɪzɪklˌedjʊˈkeɪʃn] Sport(unterricht) II/5B1
peace [piːs] Frieden, Ruhe IV/5B7
peace making [ˈpiːs ˌmeɪkɪŋ] Befriedung VI/2 Project 1
peaceful [ˈpiːsfl] friedlich IV/7B5
pearl [pɜːl] Perle VI/5A3
peer [pɪə] Gleichaltrige/r VI/1A1
pen [pen] Stift I/1A8
pen friend [ˈpen ˌfrend] Brieffreund/in VI/3B4
penalty [ˈpenlti] Strafe VI/3B7
death penalty [ˈdeθ ˌpenlti] Todesstrafe VI/3A4
pencil [ˈpensl] Bleistift I/1A8
pencil case [ˈpensl ˌkeɪs] Federmäppchen I/1C4
penguin [ˈpeŋgwɪn] Pinguin II/2B3
people [ˈpiːpl] hier: Volk V/4B5; Leute, Menschen I/1B6
per cent [pəˈsent] Prozent V/4A5
perfect [ˈpɜːfɪkt] vollkommen, perfekt II/2C1
°perfection [pəˈfekʃn] Perfektion, Vollkommenheit VI/BS 8
perform [pəˈfɔːm] vorführen, aufführen VI/2 Project 4
performance [pəˈfɔːməns] hier: Leistung VI/1A8; Vorführung, Aufführung IV/7B4
perhaps [pəˈhæps] vielleicht II/2A1
period [ˈpɪəriəd] Zeitspanne, Zeitraum VI/2 Project 2
perish [ˈperɪʃ] sterben; untergehen; hier: verschwinden VI/5A3
permanent [ˈpɜːmənənt] hier: dauerhaft VI/2 Project 1; permanent, ständig VI/5A3
landing permission [ˈlændɪŋ pəˌmɪʃn] Erlaubnis zum Anlegen VI/2 Project 4
person [ˈpɜːsn] Person, Mensch V/2B9

personal [ˈpɜːsnəl] persönlich V/2A3
persuade [pəˈsweɪd] überreden; überzeugen IV/2B4
pesticide [ˈpestɪsaɪd] Schädlingsbekämpfungsmittel VI/1B3
pet [pet] Haustier I/1A4
petunia [pəˈtjuːniə] Petunie VI/4 Project 5
phone [fəʊn] anrufen III/2B1
photo [ˈfəʊtəʊ] Foto I/1A8
photographer [fəˈtɒgrəfə] Fotograf/in VI/1B1
take photos [ˌteɪk ˈfəʊtəʊz] fotografieren III/3A2
phrase [freɪz] Satz; Ausdruck; (Rede)wendung III/3B1
physical [ˈfɪzɪkl] körperlich VI/1A8
physical education [ˌfɪzɪkl ˌedjʊˈkeɪʃn] Sport(unterricht) I/5A2
pick [pɪk] aussuchen VI/1A1
°pick a fight [ˌpɪk ə ˈfaɪt] einen Streit anzetteln VI/BS 3
pick on sb [ˈpɪk ɒn ˌsʌmbədi] auf jdm herumhacken VI/3B9
°pick out [ˌpɪk ˈaʊt] hier: herausnehmen VI/BS 2
pick up [ˌpɪk ˈʌp] aufheben; abholen VI/4 Project 3
°pick up sb [ˌpɪk ˈʌp ˌsʌmbədi] jdn. abholen VI/BS 7
pickpocket [ˈpɪkˌpɒkɪt] Taschendieb/in III/3A4
°picnic [ˈpɪknɪk] Picknick VI/BS 6
picture [ˈpɪktʃə] Bild I/1A7
pie chart [ˈpaɪ tʃɑːt] Tortendiagramm V/4A5
piece [piːs] Stück I/6C4; Stück, Werk; hier: Graffiti IV/7B4
(piece of) advice [ədˈvaɪs] Rat(schlag) IV/2B4
piece of art [ˌpiːs əv ˈɑːt] Kunstwerk IV/7B1
pig [pɪg] Schwein V/1B5
°pile [paɪl] Stapel, Haufen VI/BS 6
pilgrim [ˈpɪlgrɪm] Pilger/in VI/2 Project 1
the Pilgrim Fathers (only plural) [ðə ˌpɪlgrɪm ˈfɑːðəz] die Pilgerväter VI/2 Project 1
pillow [ˈpɪləʊ] (Kopf)kissen, Polster II/5A5
pinch [pɪntʃ] Prise VI/4 Project 5
pioneering [ˌpaɪəˈnɪərɪŋ] bahnbrechend VI/6 Project 4
pipe [paɪp] Pfeife VI/4 Project 1
place [pleɪs] Ort; Platz I/3A8

place [pleɪs] legen, stellen VI/3B7; hier: platzieren VI/BS 8; hier: Wohnung VI/BS 7
place of birth [ˌpleɪs əv ˈbɜːθ] Geburtsort V/2A3
placement [ˈpleɪsmənt] hier: Stelle V/2A2
°plain [pleɪn] einfach; klar VI/BS 6
plan [plæn] planen; vorbereiten II/2B4
plane [pleɪn] Flugzeug I/5B1
plant [plɑːnt] Pflanze II/2B3
°plant [plɑːnt] pflanzen VI/BS 4
plaster [ˈplɑːstə] Pflaster VI/4 Project 3
plastic [ˈplæstɪk] Plastik, Kunststoff IV/5B1
°plastic bag [ˌplæstɪk ˈbæg] Plastiktüte VI/BS 2
plate [pleɪt] Teller I/2B3
play [pleɪ] (Theater)stück I/3A1; spielen I/1A6
°play a trick on sb [ˌpleɪ ə ˈtrɪk ɒn ˌsʌmbədi] jdm einen Streich spielen VI/BS 1
player [ˈpleɪə] Spieler/in IV/2A5
plea [pliː] Appell VI/3B4
pleasant [ˈpleznt] angenehm VI/6 Project 1
please [pliːz] bitte I/1C1
be pleased with sb [ˌbi ˈpliːzd wɪð ˌsʌmbədi] mit jdm zufrieden sein IV/6B2
pleasure [ˈpleʒə] Freude, Vergnügen V/1B1
plenty [ˈplenti] Reichtum, Überfluss VI/1B2; viel VI/BS 3
plot [plɒt] Handlung VI/4 Project 6
plough [plaʊ] pflügen VI/5A5
plural [ˈplʊərəl] Plural, Mehrzahl VI/3B6
plus [plʌs] plus, zuzüglich V/2A2
plus [plʌs] hier: überdies VI/1A5
pm (= post meridiem) [ˌpiːˈem, ˌpəʊst məˈrɪdiəm] nachmittags, abends (nur hinter Uhrzeit zwischen 12 Uhr mittags und Mitternacht) I/2B7
pocket [ˈpɒkɪt] Tasche (an Kleidungsstücken) IV/4A2
pocket money [ˈpɒkɪt ˌmʌni] Taschengeld II/6A4
poem [ˈpəʊɪm] Gedicht V/6I
poet [ˈpəʊɪt] Dichter/in VI/4 Project 4
point [pɔɪnt] Punkt; hier: Komma III/6B2

Dictionary English – German

point [pɔɪnt] *hier:* Standpunkt VI/1A4; *hier:* Zeitpunkt VI/4 Project 2
°make a point [ˌmeɪk ə ˈpɔɪnt] seinen Standpunkt deutlich machen VI/BS 8
°(there's) no point in doing sth [ðeəz ˌnəʊ ˌpɔɪnt ɪn ˈduːɪŋ ˌsʌmθɪŋ] (es) hat keinen Zweck, etw zu tun VI/BS 1
point of view [ˌpɔɪnt əv ˈvjuː] Gesichtspunkt, Standpunkt IV/4A5
Poland [ˈpəʊlənd] Polen VI/2 Project 5
polar bear [ˈpəʊlə beə] Eisbär VI/4 Project 3
the police [ðə pəˈliːs] die Polizei II/2A1
police lieutenant [pəˌliːs lefˈtenənt] Polizeihauptwachtmeister/in VI/3B7
police officer [pəˈliːs ˌɒfɪsə] Polizeibeamter/-beamtin II/3A4
°polished [ˈpɒlɪʃt] glänzend VI/BS 5
polite [pəˈlaɪt] höflich II/4B6
political [pəˈlɪtɪkl] politisch VI/3A4
politician [ˌpɒləˈtɪʃn] Politiker/in VI/1B6
pollute [pəˈluːt] verschmutzen IV/5B1
pond [pɒnd] Teich VI/4 Project 1
poor [pɔː] arm II/1B2
poor [pɔː] *hier:* schlecht VI/5B6; *hier:* unzureichend, mangelhaft VI/5B2
the poor [ðə ˈpɔː] die Armen VI/1B2
pope [pəʊp] Papst/Päpstin VI/2I
popular [ˈpɒpjʊlə] beliebt, populär IV/1A2
population [ˌpɒpjʊˈleɪʃn] Bevölkerung V/4A2
populous [ˈpɒpjʊləs] bevölkerungsreich VI/5A3
porch (*pl* porches) [pɔːtʃ, ˈpɔːtʃɪz] Veranda VI/4 Project 5
portfolio [pɔːtˈfəʊliəʊ] (Akten)mappe II/1A2
Portuguese [ˌpɔːtʃʊˈgiːz] Portugiese/Portugiesin; portugiesisch VI/5A3
°pose [pəʊz] Haltung, Pose VI/BS 3; *hier:* darstellen VI/BS 8
°position [pəˈzɪʃn] Platz, Stelle VI/BS 5
positive [ˈpɒzətɪv] positiv IV/8A1
possibility [ˌpɒsəˈbɪləti] Möglichkeit V/5B2

possible [ˈpɒsəbəl] möglich IV/4A4
post [pəʊst] schicken; bekannt geben; einen Beitrag verfassen V/1B4
°trading post [ˈtreɪdɪŋ pəʊst] Laden VI/BS 3
pot [pɒt] Topf; Kanne VI/4 Project 1
potato (*pl* potatoes) [pəˈteɪtəʊ, pəˈteɪtəʊz] Kartoffel I/5B1
potential [pəˈtenʃl] Potenzial VI/1B5; potenziell, möglich VI/BS 3
pothole [ˈpɒthəʊl] Schlagloch VI/3B7
°potted [ˈpɒtɪd] Topf- VI/BS 2
pound [paʊnd] Pfund (engl. Währung) II/3B1
poverty [ˈpɒvəti] Armut VI/5A3
power [ˈpaʊə] *hier:* Kraft, Stärke IV/7A3; Macht, Einfluss VI/5A3
power [ˈpaʊə] *hier:* Strom, Elektrizität VI/6G9
°powerlessness [ˈpaʊələsnəs] Machtlosigkeit VI/BS 2
be in practice [ˌbiː ɪn ˈpræktɪs] praktizieren VI/5B6
Practice matters. [ˌpræktɪs ˈmætəz] *etwa:* Übung macht den Meister. III/1P1
practise [ˈpræktɪs] üben III/6A7
practise [ˈpræktɪs] *hier:* ausüben VI/5A3; praktizieren VI/4 Project 2
°prawn [prɔːn] Garnele, Krabbe VI/BS 6
pray [preɪ] beten VI/6 Project 3
prayer [preə] Gebet VI/1B4
preacher [ˈpriːtʃə] Geistliche/r; Pfarrer/in VI/6 Project 5
prefer [prɪˈfɜː] vorziehen, bevorzugen IV/1A4
pregnancy [ˈpregnənsi] Schwangerschaft VI/4 Project 6
pregnant [ˈpregnənt] schwanger VI/4 Project 6
racial prejudice (*no pl*) [ˌreɪʃl ˈpredʒʊdɪs] Rassenvorurteil VI/2 Project 3
prepare (for) [prɪˈpeə] (sich) vorbereiten (auf) IV/1B3
be prepared [ˌbiː prɪˈpeəd] bereit sein V/2B5
be prepared [ˌbiː prɪˈpeəd] *hier:* rechnen mit VI/6 Project 2
preposition [ˌprepəˈzɪʃn] Verhältniswort, Präposition VI/5P6
present [ˈpreznt] Geschenk I/5B4

present [prɪˈzent] präsentieren; *hier:* aufführen II/4A6
present [ˈpreznt] jetzig, gegenwärtig VI/4G9
present participle [ˌpreznt ˈpɑːtɪsɪpl] Partizip Präsens VI/3B5
presentation [ˌpreznˈteɪʃn] Präsentation, Vortrag VI/4I
president [ˈprezɪdənt] Präsident/in VI/2I
°press [pres] drücken; pressen VI/BS 8
freedom of the press [ˌfriːdəm əv ðə ˈpres] Pressefreiheit VI/3A4
°the press [ðə ˈpres] die Presse VI/BS 5
pressure [ˈpreʃə] Druck VI/1A3
°presumably [prɪˈzjuːməbli] vermutlich VI/BS 6
pretend [prɪˈtend] vorgeben V/5A6
pretty [ˈprɪti] hübsch I/6A3
°Pretty [ˈprɪti] *hier:* eine hübsche Person VI/BS 1
pretty (*informal*) [ˈprɪti] ziemlich IV/1A2
prevent [prɪˈvent] verhindern V/1B5
prevent [prɪˈvent] abhalten VI/2 Project 5
price [praɪs] Preis I/5B6
stock price [ˈstɒk praɪs] Aktienkurs VI/2 Project 4
°pride [praɪd] Stolz VI/5O
prime minister [ˌpraɪm ˈmɪnɪstə] Premierminister/in V/4A3
prince [prɪns] Prinz; Fürst VI/4 Project 1
princess [ˌprɪnˈses] Prinzessin VI/4 Project 1
print [prɪnt] Druck VI/6 Project 1
print out [ˌprɪnt ˈaʊt] ausdrucken VI/1A3
prior to [ˈpraɪə tʊ] vor VI/3B7
priority [praɪˈɒrəti] vorrangige Angelegenheit, Priorität VI/6 Project 1
prison [ˈprɪzn] Gefängnis V/4A3
prisoner [ˈprɪznə] Gefangene/r III/4A1
private [ˈpraɪvət] privat V/5A2
°privilege [ˈprɪvəlɪdʒ] Privileg, Vorrecht VI/BS 8
prize [praɪz] Preis, Auszeichnung VI/2 Project 3
Nobel Peace Prize [nəʊˌbel ˈpiːs praɪz] Friedensnobelpreis VI/2 Project 3
pro [prəʊ] Pro, Für IV/5A3

227

Dictionary English – German

probably [ˈprɒbəbli] wahrscheinlich V/5A2
problem [ˈprɒbləm] Problem I/3A4
proceed [prəˈsiːd] fortschreiten, vorangehen VI/6 Project 5
process [ˈprəʊses] bearbeiten VI/1B3
produce [prəˈdjuːs] herstellen, produzieren IV/1A2
produce [ˈprɒdjuːs] Erzeugnisse, Produkte VI/1B3
producer [prəˈdjuːsə] Produzent/in VI/5A2
product [ˈprɒdʌkt] Produkt, Erzeugnis V/1B5
production [prəˈdʌkʃn] Produktion VI/1B3
profile [ˈprəʊfaɪl] Profil, Porträt V/5A2
profit [ˈprɒfɪt] Gewinn, Profit VI/1B3
program *(AE)* (= **programme** *BE*) [ˈprəʊɡræm] Programm, Plan VI/1A5
°**programme** [ˈprəʊɡræm] programmieren VI/BS 1
°**programming** [ˈprəʊɡræmɪŋ] Programmierung VI/BS 1
past progressive [ˌpɑːst prəʊˈɡresɪv] *Verlaufsform der Vergangenheit* VI/1P3
prohibition [ˌprəʊɪˈbɪʃn] Verbot VI/2 Project 4
project [ˈprɒdʒekt] Projekt II/2B7
promise [ˈprɒmɪs] Versprechen VI/2I
promote [prəˈməʊt] *hier:* fördern VI/3A5
relative pronoun [ˌrelətɪv ˈprəʊnaʊn] Relativpronomen VI/5P5
°**proof** [pruːf] Beweis VI/BS 3
proper [ˈprɒpə] echt, richtig; *hier:* gut VI/5B4
properly [ˈprɒpəli] anständig VI/5B4
°**propose** [prəˈpəʊz] vorschlagen VI/BS 6
gold prospector [ˈɡəʊld prəˌspektə] Goldsucher/in VI/2 Project 2
protect [prəˈtekt] schützen V/5B3
protection [prəˈtekʃn] Schutz VI/1A2
protest [prəˈtest] protestieren VI/3A1
protest [ˈprəʊtest] Protest VI/2 Project 3
Protestant [ˈprɒtɪstənt] Protestant/in; protestantisch VI/2 Project 1
protester [prəˈtestə] Protestierende/r VI/2 Project 1
proud [praʊd] stolz IV/2B1

°**provide for oneself** [prəˌvaɪd fə wʌnˈself] für sich selbst sorgen VI/BS 2
provided [prəˈvaɪdɪd] vorausgesetzt VI/4 Project 2
°**provincial** [prəˈvɪnʃl] provinziell VI/BS 8
provocative [prəˈvɒkətɪv] provokativ VI/4 Project 1
°**prudish** [ˈpruːdɪʃ] prüde VI/1O
pub [pʌb] Kneipe VI/2 Project 4
public [ˈpʌblɪk] öffentlich IV/7B5
°**in public** [ɪn ˈpʌblɪk] in der Öffentlichkeit VI/BS 1
public health [ˌpʌblɪk ˈhelθ] Volksgesundheit VI/5A3
publish [ˈpʌblɪʃ] veröffentlichen IV/7B5
°**pull** [pʊl] ziehen VI/BS 5
°**pull off** [ˌpʊl ˈɒf] ausziehen; *hier:* abziehen VI/BS 1
°**pull oneself together** [ˌpʊl wʌnˌself təˈɡeðə] sich zusammennehmen VI/BS 6
°**pummel** [ˈpʌml] fertig machen VI/BS 3
°**punch** [pʌntʃ] (Faust)schlag VI/BS 3; (mit der Faust) schlagen VI/BS 3
°**throw a punch** [ˌθrəʊ ə ˈpʌntʃ] jdm einen Faustschlag versetzen VI/BS 3
°**punching bag** *(AE)* [ˈpʌntʃɪŋ bæɡ] Punchingball, Sandsack VI/BS 3
punctual [ˈpʌŋktʃuəl] pünktlich V/2B1
punishment [ˈpʌnɪʃmənt] Bestrafung, Strafe VI/3A4
pupil [ˈpjuːpl] Schüler/in I/1C2
°**purchase** [ˈpɜːtʃəs] kaufen, erwerben VI/BS 3
purple [ˈpɜːpl] violett, lila VI/4 Project 5
purpose [ˈpɜːpəs] Grund; Absicht, Ziel; Zweck VI/3B4
°**push** [pʊʃ] stoßen; schieben VI/BS 1
put [pʊt] setzen, legen, stellen I/2C5
°**put a stop to sth** [ˌpʊt ə ˈstɒp tə ˌsʌmθɪŋ] etw ein Ende setzen VI/BS 3
put in [ˌpʊt ˈɪn] hineinsetzen/-legen/-stellen I/6C4
be put off [ˌbiː ˌpʊt ˈɒf] abgeschreckt sein VI/4 Project 1
put on [ˌpʊt ˈɒn] anziehen II/5B4
put on [ˌpʊt ˈɒn] *hier:* erheben auf VI/2 Project 1

put on weight [ˌpʊt ɒn ˈweɪt] zunehmen VI/1A8
put up [ˌpʊt ˈʌp] *hier:* erhöhen VI/2 Project 1; bauen, errichten VI/BS 2
pyjamas *(only plural)* [pəˈdʒɑːməz] Schlafanzug VI/5A2

Q

qualification [ˌkwɒlɪfɪˈkeɪʃn] Qualifikation; Voraussetzung IV/6B4
quality [ˈkwɒləti] Qualität; Eigenschaft V/2B6
quarter of an hour [ˈkwɔːtər əv ən ˌaʊə] Viertelstunde IV/4A2
quarter (to/past) [ˈkwɔːtə] Viertel (vor/nach) I/2A2
queen [kwiːn] Königin III/3A3
question [ˈkwestʃn] Frage II/1B8
queue [kjuː] Schlange, Reihe VI/1B2
quick [kwɪk] schnell I/3B2
quiet [ˈkwaɪət] leise, ruhig II/3C1
quiet [ˈkwaɪət] Stille, Ruhe VI/6 Project 1
quit [kwɪt] aufhören (mit) IV/2B2
quite [kwaɪt] ziemlich IV/3A2
quotation [kwəʊˈteɪʃn] Zitat VI/3B9
quote [kwəʊt] Zitat V/2A9

R

race [reɪs] Rasse VI/3A4
arms race [ˈɑːmz reɪs] Wettrüsten VI/2 Project 5
°**human race** [ˌhjuːmən ˈreɪs] menschliche Rasse; *hier:* Menschen VI/BS 6
racial prejudice *(no pl)* [ˌreɪʃl ˈpredʒʊdɪs] Rassenvorurteil VI/2 Project 3
racism [ˈreɪsˌɪzm] Rassismus VI/3A5
racist [ˈreɪsɪst] rassistisch VI/3B8
radiation [ˌreɪdiˈeɪʃn] (Ver)strahlung VI/2 Project 5
rage [reɪdʒ] Wut, Zorn VI/3B4
raging [ˈreɪdʒɪŋ] *hier:* rasend VI/3B4
railroad [ˈreɪlrəʊd] Eisenbahn VI/2 Project 2
railroad worker [ˈreɪlrəʊd ˌwɜːkə] Bahnarbeiter/in VI/2 Project 2
(railway) station [ˈsteɪʃn] Bahnhof II/2C1
the railway(s) [ðə ˈreɪlweɪ] die (Eisen)bahn VI/1B3
rain [reɪn] Regen I/4C9; regnen II/3A1
rainbow [ˈreɪnˌbəʊ] Regenbogen I/3B8

rainfall ['reɪnfɔːl] Niederschlag VI/5A2
rainwater ['reɪnˌwɔːtə] Regenwasser VI/6 Project 4
rainy ['reɪni] regnerisch I/4C8
raise [reɪz] aufziehen; (an)heben; hochziehen VI/3B4
°**random** ['rændəm] zufällig, wahllos VI/BS 1
range [reɪndʒ] *hier:* Angebot, Sortiment VI/1A2; *hier:* Vielfalt, Spektrum VI/BS 8
rape [reɪp] vergewaltigen VI/3B8
°**rapidly** ['ræpɪdli] schnell, rasch VI/BS 9
°**rare** [reə] rar, selten VI/BS 8
rarely ['reəli] selten, nicht oft VI/3B4
rather than ['rɑːðə ðæn] anstatt VI/3B6
°**rating** ['reɪtɪŋ] Einschätzung, Einstufung VI/BS 8
re-elect [ˌriːɪ'lekt] wieder wählen VI/2 Project 4
reach [riːtʃ] erreichen VI/2I; langen, herankommen VI/1O
reach out [ˌriːtʃ'aʊt] greifen nach VI/6 Project 3
react [ri'ækt] reagieren VI/4 Project 6
reaction [ri'ækʃn] Reaktion VI/1A1
read [riːd] lesen I/1A4
read along [ˌriːd ə'lɒŋ] mitlesen I/1B2
read out [ˌriːd 'aʊt] laut vorlesen V/2B7
read up [ˌriːd 'ʌp] sich informieren VI/4 Project 2
reading session ['riːdɪŋ ˌseʃn] Lesestunde VI/2I
reading tour ['riːdɪŋ ˌtʊə] Lesereise VI/4 Project 4
ready ['redi] fertig, bereit III/6B2
get ready [ˌget 'redi] sich fertig machen VI/1A2
real [rɪəl] wirklich, echt III/5B1
realise (= realize) ['rɪəlaɪz] sich bewusst sein über, erkennen V/1B1
realistic [ˌrɪə'lɪstɪk] realistisch IV/1A6
reality [ri'æləti] Realität, Wirklichkeit VI/5A5
°**in reality** [ɪn ri'æləti] in Wirklichkeit, tatsächlich VI/BS 2
really ['rɪəli] wirklich I/6B2
rearrange [ˌriːə'reɪndʒ] umstellen VI/6 Project 5
reason ['riːzn] Grund IV/2B1

reassure [ˌriːə'ʃɔː] beruhigen VI/4 Project 2
receive [rɪ'siːv] erhalten, bekommen IV/5A1
recent ['riːsnt] kürzlich; neueste; jüngste VI/5A5
recently ['riːsntli] kürzlich, vor kurzem VI/3A3
recipe ['resəpi] Rezept V/1B9
recite [rɪ'saɪt] rezitieren, vortragen VI/6 Project 2
recognize ['rekəgnaɪz] erkennen IV/4B1
°**recognize** ['rekəgnaɪz] *hier:* anerkennen VI/BS 8
°**reconcile** ['rekənsaɪl] (sich) versöhnen VI/BS 6
record [rɪ'kɔːd] aufzeichnen; *hier:* aufnehmen II/3B4
record [rɪ'kɔːd] *hier:* niederschreiben VI/4 Project 1
°**record** ['rekɔːd] Rekord VI/BS 3
recording [rɪ'kɔːdɪŋ] Aufnahme V/6I
recover [rɪ'kʌvə] sich erholen, genesen VI/1A7
recovery [rɪ'kʌvri] Erholung VI/2 Project 4
recycle [ˌriː'saɪkl] recyceln, wiederverwenden VI/6G9
recycled [ˌriː'saɪkld] recycelt, wiederverwertet VI/6 Project 4
red [red] rot I/1A6
°**red-haired** [ˌred'heəd] rothaarig VI/BS 6
redemption [rɪ'dempʃn] Wiedergutmachung VI/3B8
reduce [rɪ'djuːs] verringern, reduzieren VI/6 Project 4
reference ['refrəns] Empfehlungsschreiben; Zeugnis V/2A3
refugee [ˌrefjʊ'dʒiː] Flüchtling VI/2 Project 4
refugee camp [ˌrefjʊ'dʒiː kæmp] Flüchtlingslager VI/5B2
refuse [rɪ'fjuːz] ablehnen, sich weigern VI/2 Project 4
registration form [ˌredʒɪ'streɪʃn ˌfɔːm] Anmeldeformular V/5A6
regulation [ˌregjuː'leɪʃn] Vorschrift, Bestimmung VI/3B6
reincarnation [ˌriːˌɪnkɑː'neɪʃn] Reinkarnation, Wiedergeburt VI/5A3
rejuvenate [rɪ'dʒuːvəneɪt] revitalisieren VI/6 Project 5
relationship [rɪ'leɪʃnʃɪp] Beziehung VI/3B4

relative ['relətɪv] Verwandte(r) III/8B1
relative pronoun [ˌrelətɪv 'prəʊnaʊn] Relativpronomen VI/5P5
°**relax** [rɪ'læks] sich entspannen VI/BS 7
release [rɪ'liːs] freilassen, freigeben VI/6 Project 4; herausbringen VI/2 Project 4; *hier:* Verkauf VI/5O
reliable [rɪ'laɪəbl] verlässlich, zuverlässig V/2A2
°**relief** [rɪ'liːf] Erleichterung VI/BS 2
freedom of religion [ˌfriːdəm əv rɪ'lɪdʒən] Religionsfreiheit VI/3A4
religion *(no pl)* [rɪ'lɪdʒən] Religion; Glaube VI/3A3
religious [rɪ'lɪdʒəs] religiös VI/2I
religious education [rɪˌlɪdʒəs ˌedjʊ'keɪʃn] Religionslehre I/5A2
rely on [rɪ'laɪ ɒn] *hier:* angewiesen sein auf VI/5B6; sich verlassen auf VI/6G9
remain [rɪ'meɪn] bleiben V/1B5
remaining [rɪ'meɪnɪŋ] übrig, restlich VI/4I
remember [rɪ'membə] *hier:* daran denken IV/1A2; sich erinnern (an) II/4C2
remind sb [rɪ'maɪnd ˌsʌmbədi] jdn erinnern VI/5A5
°**reminder** [rɪ'maɪndə] Mahnung; Erinnerung VI/BS 2
removal [rɪ'muːvl] Umzug; *hier:* Vertreibung VI/2 Project 2
renewable [rɪ'njuːəbl] erneuerbar VI/6G9; erneuerbare Energiequelle VI/6 Project 4
repair [rɪ'peə] Reparatur V/2A8; reparieren IV/6A5
repeat [rɪ'piːt] wiederholen II/6C2
°**replace** [rɪ'pleɪs] ersetzen VI/5O
reply [rɪ'plaɪ] Antwort IV/2A1; antworten, erwidern V/5A6
report [rɪ'pɔːt] Bericht III/5B1
report (to) [rɪ'pɔːt] berichten III/2A2
reported question [rɪˌpɔːtɪd 'kwestʃn] indirekte Frage V/4B7
reporter [rɪ'pɔːtə] Reporter/in III/5B3
represent [ˌreprɪ'zent] repräsentieren; darstellen VI/4I
representation [ˌreprɪzen'teɪʃn] Darstellung VI/1A7
representative [ˌreprɪ'zentətɪv] (Stell)vertreter/in VI/3A3
republic [rɪ'pʌblɪk] Republik VI/5A3

(Republic of) Ireland [ˈaɪələnd] (Republik) Irland II/LL1
°**requirement** [rɪˈkwaɪəmənt] Voraussetzung; Erfordernis VI/BS 6
research [rɪˈsɜːtʃ] (er)forschen, untersuchen VI/2I; Forschung; *hier:* Nachforschung V/2B6
do research [ˌduː rɪˈsɜːtʃ] forschen; *hier:* recherchieren VI/2 Project 3
°**resemble** [rɪˈzembl] ähneln VI/BS 4
reservation [ˌrezəˈveɪʃn] Reservat VI/2 Project 2
°**resist** [rɪˈzɪst] Widerstand leisten VI/BS 6
resistance [rɪˈzɪstəns] Widerstand VI/4G12
respect [rɪˈspekt] Respekt, Achtung VI/3A4; respektieren, anerkennen V/5A6
°**respectful** [rɪˈspektfl] respektvoll VI/BS 8
°**in all respects** [ɪnˌɔːl rɪˈspekts] in allen Punkten VI/BS 6
respond to [rɪˈspɒnd tʊ] reagieren auf VI/1A4
response [rɪˈspɒns] Antwort; Reaktion VI/2 Project 1
take responsibility [ˌteɪk rɪˌspɒnsəˈbɪləti] Verantwortung übernehmen VI/3B8
responsible [rɪˈspɒnsəbl] verantwortlich V/2A8
°**rest** [rest] ruhen; *hier:* liegen VI/BS 8
restaurant [ˈrestrɒnt] Restaurant, Gaststätte III/1A2
result [rɪˈzʌlt] Ergebnis V/1B1
as a result [æzˌə rɪˈzʌlt] als Folge VI/6 Project 4
result from [rɪˈzʌlt frəm] resultieren aus, sich ergeben aus VI/6 Project 4
resulting [rɪˈzʌltɪŋ] sich daraus ergebend VI/4 Project 3
retailer [ˈriːteɪlə] Einzelhändler/in VI/5B4
retouch [ˌriːˈtʌtʃ] retuschieren VI/1A3
return [rɪˈtɜːn] zurückkehren IV/8B2
°**in return** [ɪn rɪˈtɜːn] dafür VI/BS 4
°**in return for** [ɪn rɪˈtɜːn fɔː] als Gegenleistung VI/BS 4
revenge [rɪˈvendʒ] Rache VI/3B7
review [rɪˈvjuː] Kritik, Rezension IV/1A6

°**revisit** [ˌriːˈvɪzɪt] wieder besuchen VI/BS 6
revolving [rɪˈvɒlvɪŋ] rotierend, sich drehend VI/6 Project 3
rewarding [rɪˈwɔːdɪŋ] befriedigend, lohnend VI/6 Project 1
rewrite [ˌriːˈraɪt] neu schreiben, umschreiben VI/2G7
rhinoceros (*pl* rhinoceros or rhinoceroses) [raɪˈnɒsərəs, raɪˈnɒsərəs, raɪˈnɒsərəsɪz] Nashorn VI/5A2
rhyme (*no pl*) [raɪm] Reim II/4C2
rice [raɪs] Reis IV/3B2
rich [rɪtʃ] reich II/3A1
ride [raɪd] fahren (mit); reiten I/3A7; Fahrt III/5B1
°**ridiculous** [rɪˈdɪkjʊləs] lächerlich VI/1O
right [raɪt] Recht VI/3A1; rechte(r, s) I/2A4; richtig II/1B3; richtig, in Ordnung I/2B3
right [raɪt] *hier:* direkt, gleich VI/4 Project 2
be right [ˌbiː ˈraɪt] Recht haben III/1B1
right away [ˌraɪt əˈweɪ] sofort V/5B2
right up until [ˌraɪt ʌp ənˈtɪl] noch bis (zu) VI/2G2
human rights (*only plural*) [ˌhjuːmən ˈraɪts] Menschenrechte V/6I
rise [raɪz] steigen VI/2 Project 4
°**risk** [rɪsk] Risiko VI/BS 8; riskieren VI/BS 8
take a risk [ˌteɪk ə ˈrɪsk] etw riskieren VI/6 Project 3
rival [ˈraɪvl] Konkurrent/in VI/2I
river [ˈrɪvə] Fluss II/2C5
road [rəʊd] Straße I/5B4
rock [rɒk] Stein; Fels III/4A1
rock [rɒk] schaukeln; erschüttern VI/4 Project 3
rock (*informal*) [rɒk] es bringen, ein Supertyp sein VI/1A2
rocket [ˈrɒkɪt] Rakete VI/2 Project 5
role [rəʊl] Rolle VI/4I
°**role model** [ˈrəʊl ˌmɒdəl] Rollenbild VI/BS 3
°**roll** [rəʊl] *hier:* Namensliste, Verzeichnis VI/BS 3
°**rolled into one** [ˌrəʊld ˌɪntʊ ˈwʌn] *hier:* in einem VI/BS 2
Roman [ˈrəʊmən] Römer/in; römisch VI/5A3
Roman Catholic [ˌrəʊmən ˈkæθlɪk] römisch-katholisch VI/3B8

the Roman Empire [ðə ˌrəʊmən ˈempaɪə] das Römische Reich VI/5A3
roof (*pl* roofs *or* rooves) [ruːf, ruːfs, ruːvz] Dach; *hier:* Krone IV/1A6
rooftop [ˈruːftɒp] Dach VI/6 Project 4
room [ruːm] Platz, Raum; Zimmer I/1A5
root [ruːt] Wurzel VI/5B4
rose [rəʊz] Rose I/5B2
rotate [rəʊˈteɪt] rotieren VI/1A2
route [ruːt] Strecke, Route III/6B2
°**row** [rəʊ] Reihe VI/BS 3
death row [ˌdeθ ˈrəʊ] Todestrakt VI/3B3
royal [ˈrɔɪəl] königlich VI/4 Project 2
rubber [ˈrʌbə] Gummi; Radiergummi I/1A8
rubbish [ˈrʌbɪʃ] Müll IV/5B2
°**rude** [ruːd] unhöflich VI/BS 6
°**ruin** [ˈruːɪn] Ruine VI/BS 1
rule [ruːl] Regel II/4B4
rule [ruːl] Herrschaft VI/2 Project 1; regieren VI/6 Project 5
the rule of law [ðə ˌruːl əv ˈlɔː] die Rechtsstaatlichkeit VI/3A5
ruler [ˈruːlə] Lineal I/1A8
run [rʌn] *hier:* betreiben VI/1B2; laufen, rennen I/3A4
°**in the long run** [ɪn ðə ˈlɒŋ ˌrʌn] langfristig gesehen VI/BS 6
run around [ˌrʌn əˈraʊnd] herumrennen VI/1A5
run over [ˌrʌn ˈəʊvə] überfahren VI/3B6
runner [ˈrʌnə] Läufer/in III/6B1
rupee [ˌruːˈpiː] Rupie VI/5B2
rush [rʌʃ] *hier:* Schwall, Woge VI/6 Project 3

S

sack [sæk] Beutel; Sack VI/1B1
sacred [ˈseɪkrɪd] heilig VI/5A1
sad [sæd] traurig III/4B1
sadly [ˈsædli] leider VI/3B4
safe [seɪf] sicher II/6B2
sail [seɪl] segeln V/4A2
°**sail** [seɪl] Segel VI/BS 4
set sail [ˌset ˈseɪl] in See stechen, auslaufen VI/2G9
sailor [ˈseɪlə] Matrose, Seemann VI/5A3
salad [ˈsæləd] Salat II/4C3
salary [ˈsæləri] Gehalt V/2B5
°**sale** [seɪl] Verkauf, Absatz VI/5O
salt [sɔːlt] Salz VI/5A3

Dictionary English – German

the same [ðə ˈseɪm] der/die/das Gleiche III/2A2
°**the same** [ðə ˈseɪm] *hier:* gleich VI/BS 1
sand [sænd] Sand I/6A2
°**sandy beach** [ˌsændi ˈbiːtʃ] Sandstrand VI/BS 1
satellite [ˈsætəlaɪt] Satellit VI/2 Project 5
satisfied [ˈsætɪsfaɪd] zufrieden VI/4 Project 5
Saturday [ˈsætədeɪ] Samstag I/2B3
sauce [sɔːs] Soße, Sauce III/1A2
Saudi Arabia [ˌsaʊdi əˈreɪbiə] Saudi-Arabien VI/3B1
sausage [ˈsɒsɪdʒ] Wurst, Würstchen II/4C6
save [seɪv] *hier:* aufheben V/2A8; sparen IV/5B2
save [seɪv] retten; schützen VI/3B7
say [seɪ] sagen I/1A1
on a grand scale [ɒn ə ˌgrænd ˈskeɪl] im großen Stil VI/2 Project 4
scan [skæn] überfliegen; absuchen V/2A2
scandal [ˈskændl] Skandal VI/6 Project 1
°**scare away** [ˌskeər əˈweɪ] verscheuchen, abschrecken VI/BS 3
be scared of [bi ˈskeəd əv] Angst haben vor VI/5A5
scarf (*pl* **scarves**) [skɑːf, skɑːvz] Schal II/4B2
scene [siːn] Szene VI/2I
°**schedule** (*AE*) [ˈʃedjuːl, ˈskeˌdʒuːl] *hier:* Stundenplan VI/BS 3
school [skuːl] Schule I/1A6
°**drop out of school** [ˌdrɒp ˌaʊt əv ˈskuːl] die Schule abbrechen VI/BS 3
°**school constitution** [ˈskuːl kɒnstɪˌtjuːʃn] Schulordnung VI/BS 3
°**school yard** [ˈskuːljɑːd] Schulhof VI/BS 3
schoolbag [ˈskuːlbæg] Schultasche I/1A8
science [ˈsaɪəns] (Natur)wissenschaft I/5A1
score [skɔː] schießen (*Tor*) I/3A5
score [skɔː] Punktestand, *hier:* Endergebnis VI/1A10
Scotland [ˈskɒtlənd] Schottland II/1A4
scout [skaʊt] Kundschafter/in; Späher/in VI/2 Project 2

scout for [ˈskaʊt fɔː] Ausschau halten nach VI/4 Project 4
°**scrape** [skreɪp] schaben, kratzen VI/BS 5
scream [skriːm] schreien VI/3B6
°**scream** [skriːm] Schrei VI/BS 3
screenplay [ˈskriːnpleɪ] Drehbuch VI/4 Project 2
sculpture [ˈskʌlptʃə] Bildhauerei, Skulptur VI/6I
scum [skʌm] Abschaum; Mistkerl VI/3B9
sea [siː] Meer, (die) See I/2A2
°**sealed** [siːld] verschlossen VI/BS 6
search engine [ˈsɜːtʃ ˌendʒɪn] Suchmaschine V/5B2
search (for) [ˈsɜːtʃ] suchen (nach) V/2A2
search the Internet [ˌsɜːtʃ ði ˈɪntənet] im Internet suchen II/6B4
°**search through** [ˌsɜːtʃ ˈθruː] durchsuchen VI/BS 2
seasick [ˈsiːˌsɪk] seekrank IV/8B2
season [ˈsiːzn] Jahreszeit; *hier:* Saison IV/2A5
seat [siːt] (Sitz)platz VI/2 Project 3; setzen, einen Platz anweisen VI/BS 5
second [ˈsekənd] Sekunde II/3A1; zweite(r, s) I/4A4
secret [ˈsiːkrət] geheim VI/4 Project 1
secret ballot [ˌsiːkrət ˈbælət] geheime Wahl VI/3A4
°**secretary** [ˈsekrətəri] Sekretär/in VI/BS 3
secure [sɪˈkjʊə] sichern, garantieren VI/3A4
security [sɪˈkjʊərəti] Sicherheit VI/6 Project 1
see [siː] *hier:* treffen III/8B1; sehen I/1A1
see a doctor [ˌsiː ə ˈdɒktə] einen Arzt/Ärztin aufsuchen VI/1A5
°**see about** [ˌsiː əˈbaʊt] sich kümmern um VI/BS 5
°**see sb out** [ˌsiː ˌsʌmbədi ˈaʊt] jdn hinausbegleiten VI/BS 5
see you (later) [ˈsiː jʊ] bis bald II/6C6
See you soon! [ˌsiː jʊ ˈsuːn] Bis bald! I/3A4
I see. [ˌaɪ ˈsiː] Ich verstehe. V/2B7
seed [siːd] aussäen VI/6 Project 5; Same, Korn VI/BS 4
(farming) seed [siːd] Saatgut VI/1B3

seek [siːk] suchen VI/3A7
seem [siːm] scheinen I/3B1
°**seizure** [ˈsiːʒə] Anfall VI/BS 3
select [səˈlekt] aussuchen, auswählen VI/4 Project 6
°**self-absorption** [ˌself əbˈzɔːpʃn] Ichbezogenheit VI/BS 6
self-esteem [ˌselfɪˈstiːm] Selbstwertgefühl VI/1 Test results 1A2
self-sufficient [ˌself səˈfɪʃnt] selbstversorgend, autark VI/6 Project 4
selfish [ˈselfɪʃ] selbstsüchtig VI/4 Project 2
sell [sel] verkaufen I/4B3
seller [ˈselə] Verkäufer/in III/6A7
senator [ˈsenətə] Senator/in VI/2 Project 2
send [send] (zu)schicken II/1C4
senior [ˈsiːniə] vorgesetzt VI/5B4; Oberstufenschüler/in VI/BS 3
°**feel a sense of belonging** [ˌfiːl ə ˌsens əv bɪˈlɒŋɪŋ] sich dazugehörig fühlen VI/BS 6
sentence [ˈsentəns] Satz I/1A5; verurteilen VI/3B3
sentence [ˈsentəns] Urteil; Strafe VI/3B6
commute a sentence [kəˌmjuːt ə ˈsentəns] ein Strafmaß herabsetzen VI/3B7
life sentence [ˈlaɪf ˌsentəns] lebenslängliche Haftstrafe VI/3B8
separate [ˈseprət] getrennt, separat VI/2 Project 5
°**separate** [ˈsepəreɪt] trennen VI/BS 7
September [sepˈtembə] September I/5C2
listening sequence [ˈlɪsnɪŋ ˌsiːkwəns] Hörsequenz VI/2I
°**serial killer** [ˈsɪəriəl ˌkɪlə] Serienmörder/in VI/BS 3
series [ˈsɪəriːz] Serie VI/2 Project 4
serious [ˈsɪəriəs] ernst; schwer VI/4 Project 1
°**be serious** [bi ˈsɪəriəs] etw ernst meinen VI/BS 1
take seriously [ˌteɪk ˈsɪəriəsli] ernst nehmen VI/3A7
°**servant** [ˈsɜːvnt] Diener/in VI/BS 4
°**serve** [sɜːv] dienen VI/BS 8
service [ˈsɜːvɪs] Service, Dienst(leistung) VI/6 Project 4
servitude [ˈsɜːvɪtjuːd] Sklaverei, Knechtschaft VI/3A4
°**session** [ˈseʃn] Sitzung; Stunde VI/BS 6

231

Dictionary English – German

reading session [ˈriːdɪŋ ˌseʃn] Lesestunde VI/2I

set [set] *hier:* Drehort VI/5A5; *hier:* festgefahren VI/4 Project 2; Satz; Garnitur VI/BS 1

°**set about doing sth** [ˌset ə ˌbaʊt ˈduːɪŋ ˌsʌmθɪŋ] sich daran machen, etw zu tun VI/BS 2

°**set off** [ˌset ˈɒf] aufbrechen, sich auf den Weg machen VI/BS 2; *hier:* anzünden VI/BS 1

set out [ˌset ˈaʊt] *hier:* darlegen VI/3A4

set sail [ˌset ˈseɪl] in See stechen, auslaufen VI/2G9

set the table [ˌset ðə ˈteɪbl] den Tisch decken II/4B7

set up [ˌset ˈʌp] aufbauen VI/3A3

set up [ˌset ˈʌp] *hier:* aufstellen VI/4 Project 6

settle [ˈsetl] *hier:* (be)siedeln; sich niederlassen VI/2 Project 1

settlement [ˈsetlmənt] Siedlung VI/2 Project 1

settler [ˈsetlə] Siedler/in V/4A2

seven [ˈsevn] sieben I/2B4

several [ˈsevrəl] einige; verschiedene V/5B3

severe [sɪˈvɪə] schwer, schlimm; heftig VI/5A3

sew [səʊ] *hier:* stopfen VI/4 Project 1; nähen VI/5B2

sex [seks] Geschlecht VI/3A4

sexist [ˈseksɪst] sexistisch VI/3B8

°**shade** [ʃeɪd] Schatten VI/BS 2

shadow [ˈʃædəʊ] Schatten VI/1A3

°**shake** [ʃeɪk] schütteln VI/BS 5

nobody to shake a stick at *(informal)* [ˌnəʊbɒdi tə ˌʃeɪk ə ˈstɪk æt] niemand VI/4 Project 5

shall [ʃæl] sollen III/5A1

shame [ʃeɪm] Scham(gefühl); Schmach VI/4 Project 2

share [ʃeə] *hier:* weitergeben; austauschen V/2B1; teilen IV/3B2

°**sharp** [ʃɑːp] scharf VI/BS 1

°**shave** [ʃeɪv] sich rasieren VI/BS 3

shaving cream [ˈʃeɪvɪŋ kriːm] Rasiercreme VI/1A2

she [ʃi] sie I/1A3

sheep (*pl* **sheep**) [ʃiːp, ʃiːp] Schaf I/6B2

°**sheet metal** [ˈʃiːt ˌmetl] Blech VI/5O

sheet of paper [ˌʃiːt ɒv ˈpeɪpə] Blatt Papier VI/2I

shelf (*pl* **shelves**) [ʃelf, ʃelvz] Regal I/4A1

shelter [ˈʃeltə] schützen VI/6 Project 4

shield [ʃiːld] beschützen, abschirmen VI/4 Project 3

shift [ʃɪft] Verschiebung VI/4G3

shine [ʃaɪn] scheinen, glänzen VI/6 Project 5

ship [ʃɪp] Schiff II/2C1

ship [ʃɪp] verschiffen, transportieren VI/5B3

°**shit** [ʃɪt] Scheiße, Kacke VI/BS 3

°**shiver** [ˈʃɪvə] zittern, frösteln VI/BS 1

shocked [ʃɒkt] schockiert, entsetzt VI/1A8

shoe [ʃuː] Schuh I/2C7

shoot [ʃuːt] (er)schießen VI/3B4

shop [ʃɒp] Geschäft, Laden I/1B1

shop [ʃɒp] einkaufen VI/5B4

(shop) assistant [əˈsɪst(ə)nt] Verkäufer/in II/4C3

shopping [ˈʃɒpɪŋ] Einkaufen VI/5B2

°**shore** [ʃɔː] Küste, Ufer, Strand VI/BS 1

short [ʃɔːt] kurz; klein I/2A5

be short of money *(informal)* [bi ˌʃɔːt əv ˈmʌni] knapp bei Kasse sein III/6A2

shortage [ˈʃɔːtɪdʒ] Knappheit, Mangel VI/1B3

shorten [ˈʃɔːtn] (ver)kürzen VI/3P5

shot [ʃɒt] Aufnahme, Einstellung VI/1A3

should [ʃʊd] sollte/müsste I/3B1

shoulder [ˈʃəʊldə] Schulter III/7A2

°**shoulder blade** [ˈʃəʊldə ˌbleɪd] Schulterblatt VI/BS 9

shout [ʃaʊt] schreien; rufen I/6A6

°**shove** [ʃʌv] stecken VI/BS 3

show [ʃəʊ] zeigen I/3A1

°**show** [ʃəʊ] zu sehen sein; auftauchen VI/BS 1

shower [ˈʃaʊə] Dusche III/5B2

°**shunt around** [ˌʃʌnt əˈraʊnd] hin und her schieben VI/BS 6

shy [ʃaɪ] schüchtern IV/7A3

Siberia [saɪˈbɪəriə] Sibirien VI/2I

sick [sɪk] krank VI/1A5

°**be sick of** [bi ˈsɪk əv] die Nase voll haben von VI/BS 1

°**sickness** [ˈsɪknəs] Krankheit VI/BS 4

side [saɪd] Seite II/6B2

°**sidewalk** *(AE)* [ˈsaɪdˌwɔːk] Bürgersteig VI/BS 3

°**sigh** [saɪ] seufzen VI/BS 1

sight [saɪt] *hier:* Anblick IV/8B2

at first sight [æt ˌfɜːst ˈsaɪt] auf den ersten Blick VI/4 Project 3

sight(s) [saɪts] Sehenswürdigkeit(en) II/2B1

sightseeing *(no pl)* [ˈsaɪtˌsiːɪŋ] Besichtigungen, Sightseeing II/2C3

sign [saɪn] unterschreiben; *hier:* schreiben IV/7B5; Zeichen; (Straßen-/Verkehrs)schild II/5A7

°**stop sign** [ˈstɒpˌsaɪn] Stoppschild VI/BS 3

sign up [ˌsaɪn ˈʌp] sich einschreiben, sich anmelden V/5A2

°**signature** [ˈsɪgnətʃə] Signatur VI/BS 1

°**silence** [ˈsaɪləns] Stille VI/BS 1

silent [ˈsaɪlənt] *hier:* stumm VI/2 Project 4; still, ruhig VI/BS 1

silent letter [ˌsaɪlənt ˈletə] stummer Laut VI/1P6

°**silently** [ˈsaɪləntli] lautlos, schweigend VI/BS 2

silk [sɪlk] Seide VI/5A3

silky-smooth [ˌsɪlki ˈsmuːð] seidenweich VI/1A2

silly [ˈsɪli] albern, dumm II/3A1

silver [ˈsɪlvə] Silber VI/5A3

similar [ˈsɪmɪlə] ähnlich V/2B6

similarity [ˌsɪməˈlærəti] Ähnlichkeit, Parallele VI/1B1

simple [ˈsɪmpl] einfach VI/4 Project 2

simple past [ˌsɪmpl ˈpɑːst] einfache Vergangenheit II/1B4

since [sɪns] seit III/4B1

°**since** [sɪns] da, weil VI/BS 3; seitdem, seither VI/BS 3

sing [sɪŋ] singen I/1A4

sing along [ˌsɪŋ əˈlɒŋ] mitsingen IV/7A3

singer [ˈsɪŋə] Sänger/in II/5B9

single [ˈsɪŋgl] allein erziehend VI/4I

single [ˈsɪŋgl] einzige(r, s) VI/5A3

°**singsong** [ˈsɪŋsɒŋ] Singsang- VI/BS 3

singular [ˈsɪŋgjələ] Singular, Einzahl VI/3B6

sink [sɪŋk] untergehen, sinken VI/6 Project 5; *hier:* versenken VI/BS 1

°**Sir** [sɜː] Herr *(Anrede)* VI/BS 4

Dear Sir or Madam, (...) [ˌdɪə ˈsɜːr ɔː ˈmædəm] Sehr geehrte Damen und Herren! (...) V/2P4

sister [ˈsɪstə] Schwester I/1A4

sister-in-law [ˈsɪstər ɪn ˌlɔː] Schwägerin VI/3B4

sit [sɪt] sitzen I/5C4

Dictionary English – German

sit down [sɪt ˈdaʊn] sich (hin)setzen II/6B2
sit-down strike [ˌsɪtdaʊn ˈstraɪk] Sitzstreik VI/2 Project 4
site [saɪt] Stelle; *hier:* Website V/5A4
on site [ˌɒn ˈsaɪt] vor Ort VI/6 Project 4
situation [ˌsɪtʃuˈeɪʃn] Situation, Lage V/5A7
six [sɪks] sechs I/1A2
six-year-old [ˈsɪks jɪərˌəʊld] der/die/das sechsjährige III/3B1
size [saɪz] Größe I/3A1
°**sizeable** [ˈsaɪzəbl] ziemlich groß, beachtlich VI/BS 9
°**skeletal** [ˈskelɪtl] ausgemergelt, knochendürr VI/BS 2
sketch (*pl* sketches) [sketʃ, ˈsketʃɪz] Skizze VI/1B6
°**skewer** [ˈskjuːə] *hier:* hochstecken VI/BS 6
skill [skɪl] Fähigkeit, Fertigkeit IV/6B4
skim through [ˌskɪm ˈθruː] überfliegen III/7B1
skin [skɪn] Haut VI/1A2
skincare [ˈskɪnkeə] Hautpflege VI/1A2
skinny [ˈskɪni] dünn, mager VI/1A4
skirt [skɜːt] Rock I/4C7
sky [skaɪ] Himmel I/4C9
skyscraper [ˈskaɪˌskreɪpə] Wolkenkratzer IV/3A2
slave [sleɪv] Sklave/Sklavin VI/2I
slavery [ˈsleɪvəri] Sklaverei VI/5B6
sleep [sliːp] schlafen I/3B7
sleep over [sliːpˌˈəʊvə] über Nacht bleiben, übernachten II/6A1
sleepwear [ˈsliːpweə] Schlafkleidung VI/5A2
sleeve [sliːv] Ärmel VI/5B1
°**slice** [slaɪs] Scheibe VI/BS 3; schneiden VI/BS 3
°**slide** [slaɪd] rutschen, gleiten VI/BS 6
°**slightly** [ˈslaɪtli] ein wenig, etwas VI/BS 8
slim [slɪm] schlank, schmal, dünn VI/1A3
slippers (*only plural*) [ˈslɪpəz] Hausschuhe VI/4 Project 1
slow [sləʊ] langsam II/3C1
smack [smæk] Schmatz VI/4 Project 3
small [smɔːl] klein I/1B2
°**smear** [smɪə] beschmieren VI/BS 8
smell [smel] riechen; duften II/4B2

smile [smaɪl] lächeln IV/4A2
°**smoke** [sməʊk] rauchen VI/BS 5
°**smudge** [smʌdʒ] Fleck VI/BS 8
smuggle [ˈsmʌgl] schmuggeln VI/2 Project 4
snack bar [ˈsnæk ˌbɑː] Imbissstube II/4B2
snake [sneɪk] Schlange II/2B3
°**snatch** [snætʃ] Fetzen VI/BS 5
°**sneak** [sniːk] schleichen VI/BS 1
°**snot** [snɒt] Rotz VI/BS 3
snow [snəʊ] Schnee I/4B3
snow [snəʊ] schneien VI/4G11
so [səʊ] also III/1A3; daher, folglich I/3C4
so far [ˌsəʊ fɑː] bisher III/1A6
so that [ˌsəʊ ðæt] sodass, *hier:* damit VI/1A5
So what? (*informal*) [ˌsəʊ ˈwɒt] Na und?, Na wenn schon? II/6B6
so-called [ˌsəʊ kɔːld] so genannt VI/5A3
soap [səʊp] Seife VI/1A2
soap (opera) [ˈsəʊpˌɒprə] Seifenoper V/3I
soccer [ˈsɒkə] Fußball IV/2A1
social [ˈsəʊʃl] sozial, gesellschaftlich V/5A2
society [səˈsaɪəti] Gesellschaft VI/2 Project 3
sock [sɒk] Socke I/4C7
soft skill [ˈsɒft skɪl] *soziale und emotionale Kompetenz* V/2I
solar [ˈsəʊlər] Solar- VI/6G9
soldier [ˈsəʊldʒə] Soldat/in V/6I
°**sole** [səʊl] Sohle VI/BS 8
solution [səˈluːʃn] Lösung VI/3A5
solve [sɒlv] lösen V/2B6
some [sʌm] einige; etwas I/3B2
someday [ˈsʌmdeɪ] eines Tages, irgendwann einmal VI/4 Project 1
°**somehow** [ˈsʌmhaʊ] irgendwie VI/BS 6
someone (= **somebody**) [ˈsʌmwʌn] (irgend)jemand, irgendwer II/1C6
something [ˈsʌmθɪŋ] etwas I/4C5
something else [ˌsʌmθɪŋˌˈels] etwas anderes IV/3A2
sometimes [ˈsʌmtaɪmz] manchmal I/1B2
somewhere [ˈsʌmweə] irgendwo II/2A1
son [sʌn] Sohn I/5C7
song [sɒŋ] Lied I/5B2
soon [suːn] bald II/6A5
°**sophisticated** [səˈfɪstɪkeɪtɪd] kultiviert, hoch entwickelt VI/BS 2

feel sorry [ˌfiːl ˈsɒri] bedauern VI/3B8
be sorry (about/for) [ˌbiː ˈsɒri] bedauern V/2B7
Sorry. [ˈsɒri] Verzeihung., Entschuldigung. I/1A2
I'm sorry. [ˌaɪm ˈsɒri] Es tut mir leid. IV/4A4
sort [sɔːt] Sorte, Art IV/8A5; sortieren IV/6B1
°**sort of** [ˈsɔːtˌəv] irgendwie VI/BS 6
sort out [ˌsɔːtˌˈaʊt] *hier:* klären VI/1A2
sound [saʊnd] Geräusch, Klang VI/6I; klingen, sich anhören II/4A3
sound [saʊnd] *hier:* Ton VI/2 Project 4
sound check [ˈsaʊndˌtʃek] Tonprobe, Soundcheck IV/1P2
soup [suːp] Suppe III/1A2
°**sour** [ˈsaʊə] trüben; *hier:* verderben VI/BS 1
source [sɔːs] Quelle V/5A6
south [saʊθ] nach Süden VI/2I; Süden I/4C10
south [saʊθ] im Süden VI/4 Project 3
°**South American** [ˌsaʊθˌəˈmerɪkən] südamerikanisch VI/1O
South Asia [ˌsaʊθˌˈeɪʒə] Südasien VI/4 Project 2
South-East Asia [ˌsaʊθiːstˌˈeɪʒə] Südostasien VI/2 Project 5
south-west [ˌsaʊθˈwest] Südwest- VI/6 Project 4
southern [ˈsʌðən] südlich, Süd- VI/2 Project 1
Soviet Union [ˌsəʊviət ˈjuːniən] Sowjetunion (*historisch*) VI/2 Project 5
space [speɪs] Raum; *hier:* Weltraum III/5B1
Spain [speɪn] Spanien IV/7B4
Spanish [ˈspænɪʃ] Spanisch; spanisch V/5B2
spare [speə] verschonen VI/3B4; Ersatz- VI/BS 1
°**sparkler** [ˈspɑːklə] Wunderkerze VI/BS 1
speak out [ˌspiːkˈaʊt] seine Meinung deutlich vertreten VI/6 Project 3
speak (to/with) [spiːk] sprechen, reden (mit) III/7A7
°**speak up** [ˌspiːkˌˈʌp] lauter sprechen VI/BS 3
speakeasy (*informal*) [ˈspiːkˌiːzi] *Mondscheinkneipe* VI/2 Project 4

233

special [ˈspeʃl] besondere(r, s), spezielle(r, s) II/4A3; besonders IV/1A6
specific [spəˈsɪfɪk] genau; bestimmte(r, s), spezielle(r, s) V/5B3
specifically [spəˈsɪfɪkli] speziell; ausdrücklich VI/6 Project 4
speech [spiːtʃ] Sprache; Rede IV/7A2
inaugural speech [ɪˌnɔːɡjʊrəl ˈspiːtʃ] Antrittsrede VI/2 Project 3
speech bubble [ˈspiːtʃ ˌbʌbl] Sprechblase VI/2 Project 5
°**speed** [spiːd] Geschwindigkeit, Tempo VI/5O
cast a spell on sb [ˌkɑːst ə ˈspel ɒn ˌsʌmbədi] jdn verzaubern VI/4 Project 1
spelling [ˈspelɪŋ] Rechtschreibung V/2A4
spend [spend] verbringen *(Zeit)*; ausgeben *(Geld)* II/2C3
sphere [sfɪə] Kugel, Erdkugel VI/6 Project 5
spice [spaɪs] Gewürz VI/5A3
spicy [ˈspaɪsi] würzig; scharf IV/1A2
spider [ˈspaɪdə] Spinne II/2B3
spirit [ˈspɪrɪt] Geist VI/2 Project 4
spiritual advisor [ˌspɪrɪtʃuəl əd'vaɪzə] *hier:* geistl. Beistand VI/3B8
°**splash** [ˌsplæʃ ˈaʊt] planschen; spritzen; *hier:* springen VI/BS 1
split [splɪt] teilen VI/2 Project 5
sponge [spʌndʒ] Schwamm I/1C1
sponsor [ˈspɒnsə] sponsern VI/1B5; Sponsor/in VI/1A8
spoon [spuːn] Löffel I/2B3
sport [spɔːt] Sport(art) I/3A7
do sport [ˌduː ˈspɔːt] Sport treiben III/2A1
Be a sport! [ˌbiː ə ˈspɔːt] Sei kein/e Spielverderber/in! III/2I
spot [spɒt] Fleck; *hier:* Pickel VI/1A1
spray [spreɪ] (be)sprühen IV/7B2
°**spread** [spred] sich ausbreiten, sich verbreiten VI/BS 3
spread one's wings [ˌspred wʌnz ˈwɪŋz] sich auf neues Terrain vorwagen VI/6 Project 3
spring [sprɪŋ] Frühling I/4C8
spring [sprɪŋ] Quelle VI/6 Project 4; herrühren; *hier:* wachsen aus VI/BS 9
°**sb sprouts sth** [ˌsʌmbədi ˈspraʊts ˌsʌmθɪŋ] jdm wächst etw VI/BS 9
°**squeal** [skwiːl] kreischen, quietschen VI/BS 3

squeeze [skwiːz] drücken VI/4 Project 2
°**squeeze shut** [ˌskwiːz ˈʃʌt] zudrücken VI/BS 6
stable [ˈsteɪbl] stabil VI/6 Project 1
°**stacked** [stækt] gestapelt VI/BS 6
staff [stɑːf] Personal, Mitarbeiter IV/6B1
°**stage** [steɪdʒ] Etappe, Station VI/BS 6
at that stage [ət ˌðæt ˈsteɪdʒ] zu diesem Zeitpunkt, in dieser Phase VI/1A5
stagecoach [ˈsteɪdʒkəʊtʃ] Postkutsche VI/2 Project 2
stain [steɪn] Verfärbung, Fleck VI/1A2
stairs *(only plural)* [steəz] Treppe II/2C1
stall [stɔːl] (Verkaufs)stand III/3A4
stand [stænd] stehen I/2A4
stand for [ˈstænd fɔː] bedeuten, stehen für V/5A2
stand in line [ˌstænd ɪn ˈlaɪn] anstehen IV/8B2
stand up [ˌstænd ˈʌp] aufstehen I/5C1
°**standard** [ˈstændəd] Standard- VI/5O
standard of living [ˌstændəd əv ˈlɪvɪŋ] Lebensstandard VI/5B4
star [stɑː] Stern III/7A2
stare [steə] starren VI/6 Project 3; Starren, Blick VI/BS 3
°**stare at sb** [ˈsteər æt ˌsʌmbədi] jdn anstarren VI/BS 3
start [stɑːt] Anfang; Beginn V/2A8; anfangen (mit) I/5A2
start [stɑːt] Anfang, Beginn VI/4 Project 2
start a business [ˌstɑːt ə ˈbɪznəs] ein Unternehmen gründen VI/2 Project 5
start a family [ˌstɑːt ə ˈfæmli] eine Familie gründen VI/3A4
starter [ˈstɑːtə] Vorspeise III/1A2
starting point [ˈstɑːtɪŋ ˌpɔɪnt] Ausgangspunkt VI/6I
starvation [stɑːˈveɪʃn] Hunger(tod); Unterernährung VI/2 Project 1
starve [stɑːv] (ver)hungern V/5A4
state [steɪt] Bundesstaat V/4A3
statement [ˈsteɪtmənt] Äußerung II/5C3
statement [ˈsteɪtmənt] Stellungnahme VI/1B2
station [ˈsteɪʃn] Bahnhof VI/6G7

statistic(s) [stəˈtɪstɪks] Statistik V/1B1
Statue of Liberty [ˌstætʃuː əv ˈlɪbəti] Freiheitsstatue IV/3A2
stay [steɪ] Aufenthalt IV/2A1; bleiben I/3B4
stay cool [ˌsteɪ ˈkuːl] ruhig bleiben III/4B1
steal [stiːl] stehlen III/3A4
steep [stiːp] steil V/1A6
°**steering** [ˈstɪərɪŋ] Lenkung VI/5O
step [step] *hier:* Stufe IV/3A2
step [step] Schritt VI/2 Project 5; treten, steigen VI/BS 3
take a step [ˌteɪk ə ˈstep] einen Schritt machen VI/6 Project 2
°**stepladder** [ˈstepˌlædə] Stehleiter, Trittleiter VI/BS 5
°**stew** [ˈstjuː] Eintopf VI/1O
nobody to shake a stick at *(informal)* [ˌnəʊbɒdi tə ˌʃeɪk ə ˈstɪk æt] niemand VI/4 Project 5
still [stɪl] (immer) noch, noch immer II/3C1; trotzdem III/2A3
stock market [ˈstɒk ˌmɑːkɪt] Börse, Aktienmarkt VI/2 Project 4
stock price [ˈstɒk praɪs] Aktienkurs VI/2 Project 4
stocks *(AE, pl)* [stɒks] Aktien VI/2 Project 4
stomach [ˈstʌmək] Magen VI/1B4
stomach ache [ˈstʌmək eɪk] Magenschmerzen, Bauchschmerzen III/2B3
stop [stɒp] aufhören I/2A4; stehen bleiben; (an)halten II/1B4
°**stop** [stɒp] Halt VI/BS 2
°**stop sign** [ˈstɒpˌsaɪn] Stoppschild VI/BS 3
°**put a stop to sth** [ˌpʊt ə ˈstɒp tə ˌsʌmθɪŋ] etw ein Ende setzen VI/BS 3
Stop! [stɒp] Halt! I/6B2
stop-motion [ˌstɒp ˈməʊʃn] *Filmtechnik* VI/6 Project 5
store [stɔː] Laden, Geschäft V/2A5
storm [stɔːm] Sturm I/4C10
story [ˈstɔːri] Geschichte, Erzählung I/1A5
°**get sth straight** [ˌɡet sʌmθɪŋ ˈstreɪt] etw klarstellen VI/BS 3
straight (on) [streɪt] gerade(aus) II/2B4
°**straighten up** [ˌstreɪtn ˈʌp] sich aufrichten VI/BS 6
°**strain** [streɪn] *hier:* spannen VI/BS 2
strange [streɪndʒ] sonderbar, merkwürdig II/3C1

Dictionary English – German

°stranger ['streɪndʒə] Fremde/r VI/BS 6
straw [strɔ:] Stroh VI/6 Project 4
straw bale [strɔ: 'beɪl] Strohballen VI/6 Project 4
street [stri:t] Straße I/1B2
stress [stres] Betonung, Akzent VI/4G1
stressed [strest] gestresst VI/1A3
strict [strɪkt] streng III/7A2
strike [straɪk] hier: auffallen; beeindrucken VI/2 Project 3; schlagen VI/BS 3
string instrument [ˌstrɪŋ 'ɪnstrəmənt] Saiteninstrument VI/5A2
°strip off [ˌstrɪp 'ɒf] abziehen, abreißen VI/BS 1
°stroll [strəʊl] schlendern, bummeln VI/BS 3
strong [strɒŋ] stark I/4C10
structure ['strʌktʃə] Struktur, Aufbau VI/4 Project 6
°strut [strʌt] herumstolzieren VI/BS 3
student ['stju:dnt] Schüler/in; Student/in IV/2A1
study ['stʌdi] studieren; lernen V/2A2
stuff [stʌf] Zeug V/2A6
°stunned [stʌnd] fassungslos, sprachlos VI/BS 6
stupid ['stju:pɪd] dumm, blöd III/7A2
°stutter ['stʌtə] Stottern VI/BS 3
style [staɪl] Stil, Art IV/7B4
subject ['sʌbdʒɪkt] Thema; (Schul)fach I/5A1
be subjected to [ˌbi: səb'dʒektɪd tə] ausgesetzt sein VI/3A4
subtitle ['sʌbˌtaɪtl] Untertitel; hier: Bildunterschrift VI/1A3
°subtle ['sʌtl] subtil VI/BS 1
success [sək'ses] Erfolg VI/2 Project 4
successful [sək'sesfl] erfolgreich III/2A7
such [sʌtʃ] solche (r, s) V/4A3
such as ['sʌtʃ æz] wie V/2A8
°all of a sudden [ˌɔ:l əv ə 'sʌdn] ganz plötzlich VI/BS 3
suddenly ['sʌdnli] plötzlich, auf einmal I/6A3
suffer ['sʌfə] erleiden, ertragen VI/5A5
suffer from ['sʌfə ˌfrɒm] leiden an VI/1A5
sugar ['ʃʊgə] Zucker I/2B1

°sugar cane ['ʃʊgə ˌkeɪn] Zuckerrohr VI/BS 5
suggest [sə'dʒest] vorschlagen; hinweisen auf VI/2 Project 5
suitable ['su:təbl] geeignet, passend VI/6 Project 2
suitcase ['su:tˌkeɪs] Koffer II/6C5
sum [sʌm] Summe, Betrag VI/6 Project 1
sum up [ˌsʌm 'ʌp] zusammenfassen VI/1B3
summarize (= summarise) ['sʌməraɪz] zusammenfassen VI/3A4
summary ['sʌməri] Zusammenfassung IV/4B2
summer ['sʌmə] Sommer I/4C8
°summon ['sʌmən] rufen VI/BS 5
sun [sʌn] Sonne I/1A6
Sunday ['sʌndeɪ] Sonntag I/4C1
sunglasses *(only plural)* ['sʌnˌglɑ:sɪz] Sonnenbrille II/4B2
sunny ['sʌni] sonnig I/4C8
sunshine ['sʌnˌʃaɪn] Sonnenschein VI/6 Project 5
supermarket ['su:pəˌmɑ:kɪt] Supermarkt II/2A1
superpower ['su:pəˌpaʊə] Supermacht VI/2 Project 5
supper ['sʌpə] Abendessen V/5A4
supply [sə'plaɪ] Vorrat; Versorgung VI/6 Project 4
support [sə'pɔ:t] unterstützen V/1B5; Unterstützung VI/1B2
°suppose [sə'pəʊz] annehmen, denken VI/BS 6
be supposed to [ˌbi: sə'pəʊst tə] *hier:* sollen VI/3B7
sure [ʃɔ:] (aber) natürlich, (na) klar IV/1A2; sicher V/2A6
surf the Internet [ˌsɜ:f ði 'ɪntənet] im Internet surfen II/6A6
surname ['sɜ:neɪm] Familienname, Nachname V/2A3
surplus ['sɜ:pləs] überschüssig VI/1B2
surprise [sə'praɪz] überraschen VI/1B1
surprised [sə'praɪzd] überrascht, erstaunt IV/8B2
surprising [sə'praɪzɪŋ] überraschend V/4A2
surrender [sə'rendə] aufgeben, kapitulieren VI/2 Project 2
°surround [sə'raʊnd] umgeben VI/BS 3
surroundings *(only plural)* [sə'raʊndɪŋz] Umgebung VI/6 Project 1

survey ['sɜ:veɪ] Untersuchung, Umfrage IV/5A1
survival [sə'vaɪvl] Überleben VI/2 Project 1
survive [sə'vaɪv] überleben, am Leben bleiben VI/2 Project 1
°suspiciously [sə'spɪʃəsli] verdächtig VI/BS 6
sustainable [sə'steɪnəbl] nachhaltig VI/6 Project 4
swap [swɒp] tauschen V/1B1
°swear [sweə] fluchen VI/1O
sweater ['swetə] Pullover V/3I
sweatshop ['swetʃɒp] Ausbeuterbetrieb VI/5I
sweet [swi:t] süß I/2B1
swim [swɪm] schwimmen I/3A7
swimming ['swɪmɪŋ] Schwimmen I/6A1
swimming pool ['swɪmɪŋ pu:l] Schwimmbecken, Schwimmbad V/4B6
swing round [ˌswɪŋ 'raʊnd] herumschwingen VI/6 Project 3
°switch [swɪtʃ] Schalter VI/BS 5
switch off [ˌswɪtʃ 'ɒf] ausschalten IV/5B2
°swizzle stick ['swɪzl stɪk] Sektquirl VI/BS 6
°swollen ['swəʊlən] geschwollen VI/BS 3
syllable ['sɪləbəl] Silbe VI/4G1
°symbolism ['sɪmbəˌlɪzm] Symbolik VI/BS 8
symptom ['sɪmptəm] Symptom, Zeichen VI/3B7

T

table ['teɪbl] *hier:* Tabelle V/1A2; Tisch I/2B3
tablespoon ['teɪblˌspu:n] Esslöffel VI/4 Project 5
take [teɪk] bringen; nehmen I/3B5; *hier:* dauern V/4A2
take [teɪk] *hier:* erfordern VI/6 Project 3; *hier:* übernehmen VI/5A3
take a break [ˌteɪk ə 'breɪk] eine Pause machen VI/1A5
take a chance [ˌteɪk ə 'tʃɑ:ns] etw riskieren VI/6 Project 3
take a life [ˌteɪk ə 'laɪf] jdn umbringen VI/3B4
take a risk [ˌteɪk ə 'rɪsk] etw riskieren VI/6 Project 3
take a step [ˌteɪk ə 'step] einen Schritt machen VI/6 Project 2

take an exam [ˌteɪk ən ɪɡˈzæm] eine Prüfung ablegen IV/2B2
°**take away** [ˌteɪk əˈweɪ] wegnehmen VI/BS 2
take care of [teɪk ˈkeər əv] sich kümmern um, versorgen II/3A4
take control of sth [ˌteɪk kənˈtrəʊl əv ˌsʌmθɪŋ] *hier:* Kontrolle über etw gewinnen VI/1A5
°**take notice** [ˌteɪk ˈnəʊtɪs] Notiz nehmen VI/BS 6
°**take off** [ˌteɪk ˈɒf] ausziehen VI/BS 8
take over [ˌteɪk ˈəʊvə] übernehmen; die Macht ergreifen VI/2 Project 1
take part (in) [ˌteɪk ˈpɑːt] teilnehmen (an) IV/2A8
take photos [ˌteɪk ˈfəʊtəʊz] fotografieren III/3A2
take place [ˌteɪk ˈpleɪs] stattfinden III/6B2
take responsibility [ˌteɪk rɪˌspɒnsəˈbɪləti] Verantwortung übernehmen VI/3B8
take seriously [ˌteɪk ˈsɪəriəsli] ernst nehmen VI/3A7
take sth in [ˌteɪk ˌsʌmθɪŋ ˈɪn] etw erfassen, etw begreifen VI/6 Project 2
°**take sth too far** [ˌteɪk ˌsʌmθɪŋ tuː ˈfɑː] es zu weit treiben VI/BS 3
take the bus [ˌteɪk ðə ˈbʌs] mit dem Bus fahren II/5C2
take turns [ˌteɪk ˈtɜːnz] sich abwechseln IV/6B1
take/make notes (on) [teɪk meɪk ˈnəʊts] (sich) Notizen machen (über) II/3A4
talk [tɔːk] Gespräch, Unterhaltung; Vortrag VI/3B6
give a talk [ˌɡɪv ə ˈtɔːk] einen Vortrag halten VI/2 Project 2
talk (to) [tɔːk] sprechen/reden (mit) I/1A3
talkie *(informal)* [ˈtɔːki] Tonfilm VI/2 Project 4
tall [tɔːl] hoch; groß I/2A5
°**target** [ˈtɑːɡɪt] Ziel VI/BS 3
task [tɑːsk] Aufgabe III/1B6
taste [teɪst] schmecken III/1A10
tax [tæks] Steuer, Abgabe VI/5A3
tea [tiː] Tee II/5A5
teach [tiːtʃ] unterrichten; beibringen II/3C1
teacher [ˈtiːtʃə] Lehrer/in I/1A6
tear [tɪə] Träne VI/2 Project 2

teaspoon [ˈtiːˌspuːn] Teelöffel VI/4 Project 5
(car) technician [ˈkɑː tekˌnɪʃn] Mechatroniker/in V/2A8
technique [tekˈniːk] Technik, Verfahren VI/6 Project 4
technology [tekˈnɒlədʒi] Technologie, Technik I/5A2
teenage [ˈtiːneɪdʒ] jugendlich VI/3B6
brush one's teeth [ˌbrʌʃ wʌnz ˈtiːθ] sich die Zähne putzen III/4A3
telephone [ˈtelɪˌfəʊn] Telefon I/5C4
°**telescope** [ˈtelɪskəʊp] Teleskop VI/BS 3
tell [tel] sagen; erzählen I/6A4
have a temperature [ˌhæv ə ˈtemprɪtʃə] Fieber haben III/2B1
°**temple** [ˈtempl] Tempel VI/BS 8
°**temporary** [ˈtempərəri] *hier:* vorläufig VI/BS 3
ten [ten] zehn I/2B4
tense [tens] Zeitform, Tempus VI/4G3
term [tɜːm] Amtszeit VI/3B7; Ausdruck VI/4 Project 2
in terms of ... [ɪn ˈtɜːmz əv] was ... angeht VI/5A5
terrible [ˈterəbl] schrecklich, furchtbar I/5A1
°**terrified** [ˈterəfaɪd] erschrocken, verängstigt VI/BS 3
terrorist [ˈterərɪst] Terrorist/in VI/2 Project 5
terrorize [ˈterəraɪz] terrorisieren VI/2 Project 3
test [test] Prüfung, Test; Klassenarbeit II/5B9
°**test** [test] prüfen, testen VI/BS 2
text [tekst] (jdm) eine SMS senden VI/6G1
text block [ˈtekst ˌblɒk] Textbaustein VI/3B8
textbook [ˈtekstˌbʊk] Lehrbuch II/1C1
text message [ˈtekst ˌmesɪdʒ] SMS II/5C3
textile company [ˈtekstaɪl ˌkʌmpni] Textilunternehmen VI/5B3
textile factory [ˈtekstaɪl ˌfæktri] Textilfabrik VI/5B2
the Thames [ðə ˈtemz] Themse VI/6G7
than [ðæn] als *(bei Vergleich)* II/2C1
thank you [ˈθæŋk jə] danke (schön) II/1B5
Thank you very much. [ˌθæŋkjuː ˌveri ˈmʌtʃ] Vielen Dank. I/6B2

°**thankfully** [ˈθæŋkfli] dankbar VI/BS 6
thanks [θæŋks] danke I/4B5
°**thanks** [θæŋks] Dank VI/BS 5
Thanks a lot! [ˌθæŋks ə ˈlɒt] Vielen Dank! I/3C2
Thanksgiving [ˈθæŋksˌɡɪvɪŋ] Thanksgiving, amerik. Erntedankfest VI/2I
that [ðæt] das; der/die/das I/1A2; dass II/2A1
that's why [ˌðæts ˈwaɪ] deshalb IV/7A3
the [ðə] der/die/das I/W
the best [ðə ˈbest] der, die, das beste I/1A4
the British Isles *(only plural)* [ðə ˌbrɪtɪʃ ˈaɪlz] die Britischen Inseln II/LL1
the (River) Thames [ðə ˈtemz] die Themse II/2C1
the same [ðə ˈseɪm] gleich II/2C2
the tube [ðə ˈtjuːb] die (Londoner) U-Bahn II/2B1
the United States [ðə juːˌnaɪtɪd ˈsteɪts] die Vereinigten Staaten II/6C2
their [ðeə] ihr(e) I/1A5
theirs [ðeəz] ihre(r, s) IV/8A6
them [ðem] sie, ihnen I/1C1
theme [θiːm] Thema; *hier:* Lektion, Kapitel II/1I
themselves [ðəmˈselvz] sich; selbst IV/2A2
then [ðen] damals; *hier:* dann I/1C2
°**theology** [θiˈɒlədʒi] Glaubenslehre, Theologie VI/BS 8
therapist [ˈθerəpɪst] Therapeut/in VI/1B2
there [ðeə] dort(hin) I/1A2
there are [ðear ˈɑː] es gibt, da sind I/1B1
there is [ðear ˈɪz] es gibt, da ist I/1A5
°**thereby** [ˌðeəˈbaɪ] dadurch, damit VI/BS 3
°**therefore** [ˈðeəfɔː] deshalb, deswegen VI/BS 8
these *(pl of this)* [ðiːz] diese I/1A2
they [ðeɪ] sie I/1A3
°**thick** [θɪk] dick, dicht VI/BS 3
thin [θɪn] dünn I/4C9
thing [θɪŋ] Ding, Gegenstand I/1C1
How are things? *(informal)* [ˌhaʊ ə ˈθɪŋz] wie geht's? VI/1P5

Dictionary English – German

think [θɪŋk] denken, glauben, meinen I/1A4; *hier:* nachdenken, sich überlegen I/3C4
think about [ˈθɪŋk‿əˌbaʊt] denken an; nachdenken über II/3A6
think of [ˈθɪŋk‿əv] denken an, sich ausdenken VI/2I
think of [ˈθɪŋk‿əv] *hier:* halten von VI/3B10
third [θɜːd] dritte (r, s) III/4B1
this [ðɪs] diese(r, s); das I/1A2
this afternoon [ˌðɪs‿ɑːftəˈnuːn] heute Nachmittag II/2A3
this evening [ðɪsˈiːvnɪŋ] heute Abend II/5A2
this morning [ˌðɪsˈmɔːnɪŋ] heute Morgen I/5B2
those (*pl of* that) [ðəʊz] diese; jene I/2C7
though (*nachgestellt*) [ðəʊ] obwohl; jedoch VI/6 Project 3
thought [θɔːt] Nachdenken, Gedanke V/6I
freedom of thought [ˌfriːdəm‿əv ˈθɔːt] Gedankenfreiheit VI/3A4
thought bubble [ˈθɔːt ˌbʌbl] Gedankenblase VI/4 Project 3
thousand [ˈθaʊznd] Tausend III/3A2
threaten [ˈθretn] (be)drohen; gefährden V/5A6
three [θriː] drei I/1C3
thrilling [ˈθrɪlɪŋ] aufregend V/1A3
throat [θrəʊt] Hals III/2B1
through [θruː] durch V/1B3
throughout [θruːˈaʊt] *hier:* während VI/4 Project 6
throw [θrəʊ] werfen I/4B4
°throw a punch [ˌθrəʊ‿ə ˈpʌntʃ] jdm einen Faustschlag versetzen VI/BS 3
throw away [ˌθrəʊ‿əˈweɪ] wegwerfen VI/1B2
throw out [ˌθrəʊˈaʊt] hinauswerfen, wegwerfen VI/1B2
Thursday [ˈθɜːzdeɪ] Donnerstag I/4C5
ticket [ˈtɪkɪt] (Fahr)karte III/5A1; Karte II/2A2
tidy [ˈtaɪdi] aufräumen I/4B2
°tie back [ˌtaɪ ˈbæk] zurückbinden VI/BS 6
°tier [tɪə] Reihe VI/BS 5
tiger [ˈtaɪɡə] Tiger II/2A1
hold on tight [ˌhəʊldˌɒn ˈtaɪt] sich festhalten, sich festklammern V/1A6

°tile [taɪl] Fliese VI/BS 5
till (= until) [tɪl] bis VI/6 Project 3
timber [ˈtɪmbə] Bauholz, Nutzholz VI/6 Project 4
time [taɪm] (Uhr)zeit I/2B6
all the time [ˌɔːl ðə ˈtaɪm] die ganze Zeit VI/1A5
at the time [æt ðə ˈtaɪm] zu diesem Zeitpunkt VI/2 Project 4
by the time [ˌbaɪ ðə ˈtaɪm] bis VI/1A5; *hier:* als VI/2G8
on time [ɒn ˈtaɪm] pünktlich V/2A6
once upon a time [ˌwʌns‿əˌpɒn‿ə ˈtaɪm] es war einmal; vor langer Zeit VI/4 Project 1
time out [ˌtaɪm‿ˈaʊt] Auszeit III/2A4
timeline [ˈtaɪmˌlaɪn] *Zeitstrahl* V/4A3
... times [taɪmz] ... Mal II/1A4
timetable [ˈtaɪmteɪbl] Stundenplan I/5A1
°tinsel [ˈtɪnsl] Flitter, Lametta VI/BS 6
tiny [ˈtaɪni] winzig V/1B5
tip [tɪp] Rat(schlag), Tipp II/5C4
tire *(AE)* (= tyre *BE*) [ˈtaɪə] Reifen VI/4 Project 1
tired [ˈtaɪəd] müde II/2A1
title [ˈtaɪtl] Titel III/3A3
to [tuː] in, nach, zu I/1C5
tobacco [təˈbækəʊ] Tabak VI/2 Project 1
today [təˈdeɪ] heute I/2B3
together [təˈɡeðə] zusammen, gemeinsam I/3A1
go together [ˌɡəʊ təˈɡeðə] zusammenpassen VI/1B4
toilet [ˈtɔɪlət] Toilette IV/3A3
tomato (*pl* tomatoes) [təˈmɑːtəʊ, təˈmɑːtəʊz] Tomate I/2B1
tomorrow [təˈmɒrəʊ] morgen I/5C5
tone [təʊn] Farbton VI/6 Project 5
°mother tongue [ˌmʌðə ˈtʌŋ] Muttersprache VI/BS 4
tonight [təˈnaɪt] heute Abend I/4B5
too [tuː] (all)zu; auch I/1A3
°take sth too far [ˌteɪk ˌsʌmθɪŋ tuː ˈfɑː] es zu weit treiben VI/BS 3
(too) late [leɪt] (zu) spät II/1B5
tool [tuːl] Werkzeug V/2A6
tooth (*pl* teeth) [tuːθ, tiːθ] Zahn I/2A2
top [tɒp] überziehen mit, garnieren VI/4 Project 5; oberes Ende VI/BS 5
°on top [ɒn ˈtɒp] oben auf VI/BS 6

topic [ˈtɒpɪk] Thema IV/5A2
°torrent [ˈtɒrənt] Sturzbach VI/BS 5
torture *(no pl)* [ˈtɔːtʃə] Folter VI/3A4
total [ˈtəʊtl] Gesamtsumme; Anzahl VI/3B1
totally [ˈtəʊtli] völlig, total VI/3B4
touch [tʌtʃ] berühren II/5A7
get in touch [ˌɡet‿ɪn ˈtʌtʃ] in Kontakt treten IV/5A3
keep in touch [ˌkiːp‿ɪn ˈtʌtʃ] in Kontakt bleiben V/5A2
toward(s) [təˈwɔːdz] in Richtung II/6B2; gegen V/2A8
toward(s) [təˈwɔːdz] *hier:* gegenüber VI/2 Project 3
towel [ˈtaʊəl] Handtuch I/2A3
town [taʊn] Stadt I/1P4
toy [tɔɪ] Spielzeug II/6B1
trace [treɪs] Spur verfolgen VI/4 Project 3
tractor [ˈtræktə] Traktor VI/1B3
trade [treɪd] Handel VI/1B6
°trading post [ˈtreɪdɪŋ pəʊst] Laden VI/BS 3
tradition [trəˈdɪʃn] Tradition, Brauch VI/4 Project 2
traditional [trəˈdɪʃnəl] traditionell VI/4I
traffic [ˈtræfɪk] Verkehr IV/3A3
traffic jam [ˈtræfɪk dʒæm] Stau V/1B3
human trafficking [ˌhjuːmən ˈtræfɪkɪŋ] Menschenhandel VI/3A5
tragic [ˈtrædʒɪk] tragisch IV/4B1
trail [treɪl] Weg, Pfad VI/2 Project 2
train [treɪn] Zug III/5A1
trainer [ˈtreɪnə] Trainer/in VI/1A8; Turnschuh IV/6B1
training [ˈtreɪnɪŋ] Ausbildung IV/6B4; Training I/4C5
transcontinental [ˌtrænzˌkɒntɪˈnentl] transkontinental VI/2 Project 2
transient [ˈtrænziənt] vergänglich VI/6 Project 2
translate [trænsˈleɪt] übersetzen VI/4 Project 3
°translucent [trænsˈluːsnt] lichtdurchlässig VI/BS 3
transport [ˈtrænspɔːt] Transport; Verkehrsmittel VI/5A5
transport [trænsˈpɔːt] transportieren VI/2 Project 4
feel trapped [ˌfiːl ˈtræpt] sich gefangen fühlen VI/4 Project 5
travel [ˈtrævl] Reisen VI/5A5; reisen; fahren III/5B2

Dictionary English – German

traveller ['trævlə] Reisende/r III/8B1
travelling ['trævlɪŋ] Reisen III/8A2
treasure ['treʒə] schätzen VI/6 Project 5
treat [triːt] behandeln V/4A3
treatment ['triːtmənt] Behandlung, Umgang mit V/1B5
treaty ['triːti] Vertrag, Abkommen VI/2 Project 2
tree [triː] Baum I/3P5
°**tremulous** ['tremjʊləs] zitternd, bebend VI/BS 2
tribe [traɪb] Stamm VI/2 Project 1
°**trick** [trɪk] Trick; Kunststück; *hier:* Täuschung VI/BS 1
°**play a trick on sb** [ˌpleɪ ə 'trɪk ɒn ˌsʌmbədi] jdm einen Streich spielen VI/BS 1
tricky ['trɪki] schwierig, kompliziert VI/6 Project 4
trip [trɪp] Ausflug I/3A1; Reise, Fahrt III/8B1
troop [truːp] Truppe VI/2 Project 2
trouble ['trʌbl] Schwierigkeiten, Ärger; Problem V/2B9
be in trouble [ˌbiː ɪn 'trʌbl] in Schwierigkeiten stecken VI/4 Project 2
(pair of) trousers ['traʊzəz] Hose III/6A6
truck [trʌk] Lastwagen V/1B3
true [truː] wahr II/1B5
trust [trʌst] vertrauen VI/3B7
truth [truːθ] Wahrheit VI/1A2
try [traɪ] *hier:* (aus)probieren III/1A6; versuchen I/6A3
try [traɪ] Versuch VI/4 Project 3
try hard [ˌtraɪ 'hɑːd] sich sehr bemühen VI/6 Project 3
try on [ˌtraɪ 'ɒn] anprobieren II/5B5
try out [ˌtraɪ 'aʊt] ausprobieren V/1B9
try sb ['traɪ ˌsʌmbədi] jdn vor Gericht stellen VI/2 Project 4
Tuesday ['tjuːzdeɪ] Dienstag I/4C5
tummy *(informal)* ['tʌmi] Bauch I/2A4
turn [tɜːn] drehen VI/1A2
turn around [ˌtɜːn ə'raʊnd] sich umdrehen V/1B5
°**turn around** [ˌtɜːn ə'raʊnd] *hier:* umkehren VI/BS 3
turn back into [ˌtɜːn 'bæk ˌɪntʊ] *hier:* sich zurückverwandeln VI/4 Project 1
(turn) left [left] links (abbiegen) II/2B4

turn off [ˌtɜːn 'ɒf] abschalten IV/5B2
turn out [ˌtɜːn 'aʊt] sich herausstellen VI/2 Project 5
(turn) right [raɪt] rechts (abbiegen) II/2B4
turnaround ['tɜːnəˌraʊnd] Bearbeitungszeit, Lieferzeit VI/5B4
turnover ['tɜːnˌəʊvə] Umsatz VI/1B3
take turns [ˌteɪk 'tɜːnz] sich abwechseln IV/6B1
TV (= television) [ˌtiːˈviː, ˈtelɪˌvɪʒn] Fernseher; Fernsehen I/4A6
twelve [twelv] zwölf I/1A6
twice [twaɪs] zweimal II/1A4
twist [twɪst] drehen VI/1A2
two [tuː] zwei I/1A5
type [taɪp] Art VI/4I
typical ['tɪpɪkl] typisch; charakteristisch IV/1A2

U

ugly ['ʌgli] hässlich IV/7B1
°**Ugly** ['ʌgli] *hier:* eine hässliche Person VI/BS 1
UN (= United Nations) [juːˈen] UNO VI/3A7
un- [ʌn] nicht VI/4 Project 2
°**unable** [ʌn'eɪbl] unfähig, außerstande VI/BS 2
°**unbelievable** [ˌʌnbɪ'liːvəbl] unglaublich VI/BS 1
uncertain [ʌn'sɜːtn] unsicher, ungewiss VI/6 Project 2
unchristian [ʌn'krɪstʃən] unchristlich VI/2 Project 3
uncle ['ʌŋkl] Onkel I/W
uncover [ʌn'kʌvə] aufdecken VI/1A2
under ['ʌndə] unter I/2C3
underground [ˌʌndə'graʊnd] unterirdisch VI/5A3
underline [ˌʌndə'laɪn] unterstreichen IV/8B4
understand [ˌʌndə'stænd] verstehen II/3C1
understanding [ˌʌndə'stændɪŋ] Verständnis VI/6 Project 5
unemployment [ˌʌnɪm'plɔɪmənt] Arbeitslosigkeit VI/2 Project 4
unfairly [ʌn'feəli] unfair, ungerecht VI/1B3
unfamiliar [ˌʌnfə'mɪliə] unbekannt, nicht vertraut VI/1B1
unfit [ʌn'fɪt] nicht fit, in schlechter Form VI/1A11

unfortunately [ʌn'fɔːtʃnətli] unglücklicherweise IV/4B2
unfriend [ʌn'frend] *hier:* den Kontakt wieder löschen *(soz. Netzwerk)* V/5A4
unfriendly [ʌn'frenli] *hier:* feindlich VI/2 Project 1
unhappy [ʌn'hæpi] unglücklich VI/3B4
unhealthy [ʌn'helθi] ungesund V/1B5
unified ['juːnɪfaɪd] einheitlich, vereint VI/5A3
uniform ['juːnɪˌfɔːm] Uniform II/5B1
the Union [ðə 'juːniən] die Nordstaaten während des amerik. Bürgerkriegs VI/2 Project 2
unit ['juːnɪt] Einheit, Abteilung VI/3B10
unite [juː'naɪt] vereinigen VI/2 Project 3
United Kingdom of Great Britain and Northern Ireland (= UK) [ðə juːˌnaɪtɪd ˌkɪŋdəm əv greɪt ˌbrɪtn ənd ˌnɔːð(ə)n ˌaɪələnd] das Vereinigte Königreich *(Großbritannien und Nordirland)* II/LL1
the United Nations [ðə juːˌnaɪtɪd 'neɪʃnz] die Vereinten Nationen VI/1B5
the United States [ðə juːˌnaɪtɪd 'steɪts] die Vereinigten Staaten II/6C2
unity ['juːnəti] Einheit VI/6 Project 5
universal [ˌjuːnɪ'vɜːsl] allgemein, universell V/6I
university [ˌjuːnɪ'vɜːsəti] Universität VI/2 Project 5
°**unjust** [ˌʌn'dʒʌst] ungerecht VI/BS 2
unless [ən'les] *hier:* wenn nicht VI/3A7; außer wenn VI/BS 3
°**unlike** [ˌʌn'laɪk] anders als VI/BS 2
°**unlikely** [ˌʌn'laɪkli] unwahrscheinlich VI/BS 6
°**unlock** [ʌn'lɒk] aufschließen VI/BS 5
°**unmarried** [ʌn'mærɪd] unverheiratet, ledig VI/BS 8
°**unofficial** [ˌʌnə'fɪʃl] inoffiziell, nicht amtlich VI/BS 3
°**unpredictable** [ˌʌnprɪ'dɪktəbl] unvorhersehbar VI/BS 8
unrealistic [ˌʌnrɪə'lɪstɪk] unrealistisch, wirklichkeitsfremd VI/1P4
unresolved [ˌʌnrɪ'zɒlvd] ungelöst VI/6 Project 2

Dictionary English – German

unscramble [ʌnˈskræmbl] wieder ordnen VI/5A4
°unspoken [ˌʌnˈspəʊkən] unausgesprochen VI/BS 6
until [ənˈtɪl] bis I/6A3
right up until [ˌraɪt ʌp ənˈtɪl] noch bis (zu) VI/2G2
untouchable [ʌnˈtʌtʃəbl] Unberührbare/r VI/2 Project 4
unusual [ʌnˈjuːʒʊəl] ungewöhnlich IV/1A8
unwanted [ʌnˈwɒntɪd] unerwünscht; *hier:* nicht benötigt VI/1B2
°unwritten [ˌʌnˈrɪtn] ungeschrieben VI/BS 3
up [ʌp] nach oben, hinauf II/2C1
°up [ʌp] oben VI/BS 3
up and down [ˈʌp ənd ˌdaʊn] auf und ab II/3C1
up to date [ˌʌp tʊ ˈdeɪt] auf dem neuesten Stand VI/5B2
be up to sb [ˌbi ˈʌp tʊ ˌsʌmbədi] von jdm abhängen, jdm überlassen sein IV/7B4
up until [ˌʌp ənˈtɪl] bis VI/2 Project 2
right up until [ˌraɪt ʌp ənˈtɪl] noch bis (zu) VI/2G2
°upon [əˈpɒn] *hier:* bei VI/BS 8
once upon a time [ˌwʌns ə ˌpɒn ə ˈtaɪm] es war einmal; vor langer Zeit VI/4 Project 1
upper hand [ˌʌpə ˈhænd] die Oberhand haben über VI/6 Project 5
upper-class [ˌʌpə ˈklɑːs] der Oberschicht VI/4 Project 2
°upright [ˈʌpraɪt] aufrecht VI/BS 2
upsetting [ʌpˈsetɪŋ] schlimm, erschütternd V/5A6
upstairs [ʌpˈsteəz] (nach) oben II/5A5
°urban [ˈɜːbən] städtisch VI/BS 8
us [ʌs] uns I/3A1
US (= United States) [juːˈes] die USA VI/1A7; US- VI/2 Project 2
USA (= United States of America) [juːesˈeɪ, juːˌnaɪtɪd steɪts əv əˈmerɪkə] USA, Vereinigte Staaten von Amerika II/4A4
use [juːz] benutzen II/2B4
use [juːs] *hier:* Nutzen V/2A6; Verwendung, Gebrauch V/5A2
use [juːz] *hier:* anwenden VI/3B1
use [juːs] *hier:* Durchführung VI/3B1; *hier:* Einsatz VI/2 Project 5

be used to [ˌbi ˈjuːst tʊ] gewohnt sein VI/5A5
get used to [ˌget ˈjuːst tʊ] sich gewöhnen an VI/5A5
used to + *Verb* [ˈjuːst tʊ] früher IV/8A6
useful [ˈjuːsfl] nützlich, praktisch III/4B1
user [ˈjuːzə] Benutzer/in V/5A6
usual [ˈjuːʒʊəl] gewöhnlich, üblich V/4B6
usually [ˈjuːʒʊəli] gewöhnlich, normalerweise I/4B1
°utility [juːˈtɪləti] Nutzen VI/5O

V

vague [veɪg] vage VI/6 Project 2
°in vain [ɪn ˈveɪn] vergeblich, umsonst VI/BS 6
valley [ˈvæli] Tal IV/8B2
value [ˈvæljuː] Wert V/5B3
vandalism [ˈvændəˌlɪzm] Vandalismus, blinde Zerstörungswut IV/7B2
°vanish [ˈvænɪʃ] verschwinden, verloren gehen VI/BS 3
°vapid [ˈvæpɪd] banal; *hier:* geistlos VI/BS 1
variety [vəˈraɪəti] Vielfalt V/3I
various [ˈveəriəs] verschieden VI/6I
vary [ˈveəri] variieren VI/6 Project 4
vegetable [ˈvedʒtəbl] Gemüse I/5B1
vegetarian [ˌvedʒəˈteəriən] Vegetarier/in III/7A2; vegetarisch V/1B4
go vegetarian [ˌgəʊ vedʒəˈteəriən] Vegetarier/in werden V/1B4
veggie burger [ˈvedʒi ˌbɜːgə] Gemüseburger V/1B1
°vein [veɪn] Vene, Ader VI/BS 3
verb [vɜːb] Verb II/1A3
version [ˈvɜːʃn] Version, Fassung VI/6 Project 5
very [ˈveri] sehr I/1A6
life vest [ˈlaɪf ˌvest] Rettungsweste V/1A6
°vestigial [vesˈtɪdʒiəl] spärlich, nicht voll ausgebildet VI/BS 9
vet [vet] Tierarzt/Tierärztin IV/6A1
veteran [ˈvetərən] Veteran/in VI/2 Project 5
victim [ˈvɪktɪm] Opfer VI/3A4
victory [ˈvɪktəri] Sieg VI/2 Project 5
view [vjuː] Sicht; Ansicht, Meinung VI/4 Project 6
village [ˈvɪlɪdʒ] Dorf V/2A2

°villain [ˈvɪlən] Verbrecher/in, Schurke VI/BS 8
violate [ˈvaɪəleɪt] verletzen VI/3A3
violation [ˌvaɪəˈleɪʃn] Verletzung, Verstoß VI/3A3
violence [ˈvaɪələns] Gewalt VI/3A5
violent [ˈvaɪələnt] gewalttätig VI/3B4
visible [ˈvɪzəbl] sichtbar VI/1A2
vision [ˈvɪʒn] Vorstellung, Vision VI/2I
visit [ˈvɪzɪt] Besuch III/5A2; besuchen I/3A1
visitor [ˈvɪzɪtə] Besucher/in, Gast VI/2I
visualize [ˈvɪʒuəlaɪz] sich vorstellen, visualisieren VI/1B3
vocabulary [vəʊˈkæbjʊləri] Vokabular, Wortschatz V/2A8
°vodka [ˈvɒdkə] Wodka VI/BS 3
voice [vɔɪs] Stimme VI/2 Project 4
volume [ˈvɒljuːm] Volumen VI/1A2
voluntary [ˈvɒləntəri] freiwillig; ehrenamtlich V/2A2
volunteer [ˌvɒlənˈtɪə] ehrenamtliche/r Mitarbeiter/in V/2A2
volunteer [ˌvɒlənˈtɪə] ehrenamtlich VI/1B2
vomit [ˈvɒmɪt] (sich) erbrechen, sich übergeben VI/1A6
the vote *(no pl)* [ðə ˈvəʊt] Wahlrecht, Stimmrecht VI/2G7

W

wage [weɪdʒ] Lohn V/2A2
wait [weɪt] (ab)warten, (er)warten III/2B1
Wait a minute! [ˈweɪt ə ˌmɪnɪt] Moment mal! II/1B2
wait (for) [weɪt] warten (auf) I/4B2
waiter/waitress [ˈweɪtə/ˈweɪtrəs] Kellner/in III/1A3
waiting room [ˈweɪtɪŋ ˌruːm] Wartezimmer III/2B2
wake up [ˌweɪk ˈʌp] (auf)wecken V/2B9
Wales [weɪlz] Wales II/1A4
walk [wɔːk] (zu Fuß) gehen I/2A4; Gehen; Spaziergang I/4B4
walk past [ˌwɔːk ˈpɑːst] vorbeilaufen VI/4 Project 3
wall [wɔːl] Wand, Mauer IV/4B1
wanna *(informal)* (= want to) [ˈwɒnə] wollen VI/6 Project 5
want [wɒnt] wünschen; wollen I/2B3

Dictionary English – German

want sb to do sth [wɒnt ˌsʌmbədi tə ˈduː ˌsʌmθɪŋ] wollen, dass jd etw tut II/3C1
war [wɔː] Krieg V/6I
the Cold War [ðə ˌkəʊld ˈwɔː] der Kalte Krieg VI/2I
War of Independence [ˌwɔːr‿əv‿ˌɪndiˈpendəns] Unabhängigkeitskrieg VI/2 Project 1
declare war on sb [diˌkleə ˈwɔːr‿ɒn ˌsʌmbədi] jdm den Krieg erklären VI/2 Project 5
°**ward off** [ˌwɔːd‿ˈɒf] abwehren, abwenden VI/BS 8
°**warden** [ˈwɔːdn] Aufseher/in VI/BS 5
wardrobe [ˈwɔːdrəʊb] (Kleider)schrank I/4A1
warm [wɔːm] warm I/4C7
warn [wɔːn] warnen, ermahnen VI/5A3
°**warrior** [ˈwɒriə] Krieger/in VI/BS 3
wartime [ˈwɔːtaɪm] Kriegszeit(en) VI/3A5
wash [wɒʃ] (sich) waschen I/2A2
°**wash away** [ˌwɒʃ‿əˈweɪ] fortschwemmen, wegspülen VI/BS 1
washroom (AE) [ˈwɒʃruːm] Toilette IV/3A3
waste [weɪst] Exkremente; Abfall V/1B5
°**waste** [weɪst] Verschwendung VI/BS 7
watch [wɒtʃ] beobachten; zusehen, zuschauen I/3A3
watch [wɒtʃ] Wache VI/3A5
watch (pl **watches**) [wɒtʃ, ˈwɒtʃɪz] Armbanduhr III/3A4
watch TV [ˌwɒtʃ tiːˈviː] fernsehen I/4B4
°**watchful** [ˈwɒtʃfl] wachsam, aufmerksam VI/BS 2
water [ˈwɔːtə] Wasser I/2A2
°**wave** [weɪv] winken; fuchteln VI/BS 3
way [weɪ] Art und Weise V/4A3
°**way** (informal) [weɪ] weitaus; hier: viel VI/BS 1
we [wiː] wir I/1A3
°**weak** [wiːk] schwach VI/BS 3
weakness [ˈwiːknəs] Schwäche VI/1B4
wealth [welθ] Reichtum VI/5A3
°**the wealthy** [ðə ˈwelθi] die Reichen VI/BS 2
weapon [ˈwepən] Waffe VI/2I

wear [weə] tragen I/5A1; tragen; anziehen II/5A2
weary [ˈwɪəri] müde, erschöpft VI/2I
weather [ˈweðə] Wetter I/4C8
weave [wiːv] weben, flechten VI/6 Project 5
web [web] Netz V/5A6
web page [ˈwebˌpeɪdʒ] Webseite, Internetseite VI/4 Project 1
wedding [ˈwedɪŋ] Hochzeit VI/4 Project 1
Wednesday [ˈwenzdeɪ] Mittwoch I/3A1
week [wiːk] Woche I/4C5
a week [ə ˈwiːk] in der Woche VI/3A3
weekday [ˈwiːkdeɪ] Wochentag VI/1B2
weekend [ˌwiːkˈend] Wochenende I/2B2
weigh [weɪ] wiegen VI/1A5
weight [weɪt] Gewicht VI/1A5
gain weight [ˌgeɪn ˈweɪt] zunehmen VI/1A6
lose weight [ˌluːz ˈweɪt] abnehmen VI/1A5
put on weight [ˌpʊt‿ɒn ˈweɪt] zunehmen VI/1A8
weird [wɪəd] merkwürdig, komisch V/5A4
welcome [ˈwelkəm] willkommen V/4A4
You're welcome. [jɔː ˈwelkəm] Nichts zu danken!, Gern geschehen! III/2B1
°**welding** [ˈweldɪŋ] Schweißen VI/5O
well [wel] gut II/3B1; nun (ja), tja I/3A4
Well done! [ˌwel ˈdʌn] Gut gemacht! II/1B2
°**well-fed** [ˌwel ˈfed] wohlgenährt VI/1O
well-known [ˌwelˈnəʊn] (allgemein) bekannt; berühmt VI/2 Project 3
well-paid [welˈpeɪd] gut bezahlt VI/6 Project 1
°**well-pressed** [ˌwel ˈprest] gut gebügelt VI/BS 2
well-suited [ˌwelˈsuːt ɪd] gut zusammenpassend VI/4G2
Welsh [welʃ] walisisch VI/4 Project 4
west [west] Westen III/4A9
west [west] westlich VI/2 Project 2; westwärts, nach Westen VI/2 Project 2
the West Indies [ðə ˌwest‿ˈɪndiz] die Westindischen Inseln VI/2 Project 2

what [wɒt] was I/W; hier: welche(r, s) I/1C1
What about ...? (informal) [ˌwɒt‿əˈbaʊt] Was ist mit ...? II/1B2
What are you having? [ˌwɒtˈɑː juː ˌhævɪŋ] Was nimmst du/nehmen Sie? III/1A3
What time is it? [wɒtˈtaɪm ˌɪz ˌɪt] Wie spät ist es? II/3C3
What was it like? [ˌwɒt wəz‿ɪt ˈlaɪk] Wie war es? III/1A10
What's on offer? [ˌwɒts‿ɒn ˈɒfə] Was ist im Angebot? III/6A7
What's on? [ˌwɒtsˈɒn] Was läuft? Was geht ab? III/7B1
What's the matter? [wɒts ðə ˈmætə] Was ist los? II/2A1
whatever [wɒtˈevə] was (auch immer) VI/3A4
wheelchair [ˈwiːlˌtʃeə] Rollstuhl III/6B2
when [wen] als I/5C5; wann; wenn I/1C1
whenever [wenˈevə] jedes Mal, wenn V/5B2
where [weə] wo(hin) I/W
whether [ˈweðə] ob IV/2A8
which [wɪtʃ] welche(r, s) I/3A1
while [waɪl] während III/3B1
while [waɪl] Weile VI/4 Project 2
for a while [fər‿ə ˈwaɪl] eine Weile VI/1A8
whilst [waɪlst] während VI/4 Project 5
°**whisper** [ˈwɪspə] Flüstern, Geflüster VI/BS 3
white [waɪt] weiß I/2A5
white [waɪt] Weiße/r VI/2 Project 2
who [huː] wem, wen II/3A8; wer; der/die/das I/1A1
°**whoever** [huˈevə] wer auch immer VI/BS 7
whole [həʊl] ganz, gesamt III/5B1
°**whom** [huːm] wem, wen VI/BS 1
whose [huːz] wessen I/5C7
why [waɪ] warum I/2A4
wide [waɪd] breit III/5B2
widely [ˈwaɪdli] weithin VI/6 Project 4
widower [ˈwɪdəʊə] Witwer VI/4 Project 6
°**width** [wɪdθ] Breite VI/5O
wife (pl **wives**) [waɪf, waɪvz] Ehefrau I/5C7
wild [waɪld] wild I/3B2
Wild West [ˌwaɪld ˈwest] Wilder Westen; Wildwest- VI/2 Project 2

Dictionary English – German

willing ['wɪlɪŋ] bereit, gewillt V/2A2
willow ['wɪləʊ] Weide VI/6 Project 4
win [wɪn] gewinnen II/1B2
°**win** [wɪn] Sieg VI/BS 3
wind [wɪnd] Wind I/6A2
°**wind down** [ˌwaɪnd ˈdaʊn] herunterkurbeln VI/5O
window ['wɪndəʊ] Fenster I/1B2
°**windscreen wiper** ['wɪndskriːn ˌwaɪpə] Scheibenwischer VI/5O
wine [waɪn] Wein VI/4 Project 1
wing [wɪŋ] Flügel V/1B3
°**wing span** ['wɪŋ ˌspæn] Flügelspannweite VI/BS 9
spread one's wings [ˌspred wʌnz 'wɪŋz] sich auf neues Terrain vorwagen VI/6 Project 3
winner ['wɪnə] Gewinner/in; Sieger/in I/3A5
winter ['wɪntə] Winter I/4B4
°**wipe off** [ˌwaɪp ˈɒf] wegwischen VI/BS 1
wish [wɪʃ] wünschen II/4B7
make a wish [ˌmeɪk ə ˈwɪʃ] sich etwas wünschen VI/6 Project 3
witch (pl **witches**) [wɪtʃ, 'wɪtʃɪz] Hexe VI/4 Project 1
with [wɪð] mit I/W
within [wɪˈðɪn] innerhalb VI/3B6
without [wɪˈðaʊt] ohne II/4C3
°**witness** ['wɪtnəs] beobachten VI/BS 2; Zeuge/Zeugin VI/BS 5
°**wobble** ['wɒbl] wackeln; zittern VI/BS 2
wolf (pl **wolves**) [wʊlf, wʊlvz] Wolf VI/1B4
woman (pl **women**) ['wʊmən, 'wɪmɪn] Frau I/2A7
wonder ['wʌndə] sich fragen IV/2A1
wonderful ['wʌndəfl] wunderbar, wundervoll II/5B9
wood [wʊd] Holz II/4C4
woodland ['wʊdlənd] Wald(land) VI/6 Project 4
°**woods** (only plural) [wʊdz] Wald VI/BS 3
word [wɜːd] Wort I/1A4
word web ['wɜːd ˌweb] Wortnetz II/4B9
wordbank ['wɜːdbæŋk] Wortfeld II/1A3
work [wɜːk] Arbeit I/5A1; arbeiten I/1A6; hier: funktionieren, laufen III/6A7

be out of work [biːˌ aʊt əv ˈwɜːk] arbeitslos sein III/4B2
work experience [ˌwɜːk ɪkˈspɪərɪəns] Berufserfahrung; hier: Praktikum IV/6B1
work out [ˌwɜːk ˈaʊt] ausarbeiten VI/1A8
workbook ['wɜːkˌbʊk] Arbeitsbuch II/1A2
worker ['wɜːkə] Arbeiter/in IV/6A1
railroad worker ['reɪlrəʊd ˌwɜːkə] Bahnarbeiter/in VI/2 Project 2
working conditions ['wɜːkɪŋ kənˌdɪʃnz] Arbeitsbedingungen VI/5B4
working day ['wɜːkɪŋ deɪ] Arbeitstag IV/6B4
workshop ['wɜːkˌʃɒp] hier: Workshop, Seminar VI/3A6
world [wɜːld] Welt III/5I
all over the world [ɔːlˌ əʊvə ðə ˈwɜːld] auf der ganzen Welt IV/2A8
around the world [əˌraʊnd ðə ˈwɜːld] in der ganzen Welt VI/2 Project 5
world-famous [ˌwɜːldˈfeɪməs] weltberühmt VI/2 Project 2
developing world (no pl) [dɪˈveləpɪŋ ˌwɜːld] Entwicklungsländer VI/5B4
world record [ˌwɜːld ˈrekɔːd] Weltrekord III/6B2
world war [ˌwɜːld ˈwɔː] Weltkrieg V/4A3
World War II [ˌwɜːld ˌwɔː ˈtuː] 2. Weltkrieg VI/2 Project 5
°**worldly** ['wɜːldli] weltgewandt VI/BS 8
worldwide [ˌwɜːldˈwaɪd] weltweit IV/7B5
worried ['wʌrɪd] beunruhigt, besorgt III/4B2
worry ['wʌri] sich Sorgen machen II/3B2
be worth [biː ˈwɜːθ] wert sein IV/5B1
°**worthless** ['wɜːθləs] wertlos VI/BS 3
would [wʊd] würde(n/st/t) II/4B8
wrap up [ˌræp ˈʌp] einwickeln, einpacken IV/1A2
wrench open [ˌrentʃ ˈəʊpən] aufreißen VI/4 Project 3
°**wristwatch** ['rɪstwɒtʃ] Armbanduhr VI/BS 3

write [raɪt] schreiben I/1A4
write down [raɪt ˈdaʊn] aufschreiben I/1C4
writer ['raɪtə] Autor/in VI/1B1
in writing [ɪn ˈraɪtɪŋ] schriftlich VI/6 Project 3
wrong [rɒŋ] falsch I/3P6
wrong [rɒŋ] Unrecht VI/3I
go wrong [ˌgəʊ ˈrɒŋ] schiefgehen VI/1A1
wrong sb ['rɒŋ ˌsʌmbədi] jdm Unrecht tun VI/2 Project 2
be wrong with sb [biː ˈrɒŋ wɪð ˌsʌmbədi] nicht stimmen, los sein III/2B1

Y

ya (= you) (informal) [jə] du VI/6 Project 5
yard [jɑːd] Hof VI/3B4
year [jɪə] Jahr I/W; hier: Schuljahr, Klasse I/3A1
all year [ˌɔːl ˈjɪə] das ganze Jahr (über) VI/1P2
half a year [ˌhɑːf ə ˈjɪə] ein halbes Jahr VI/2 Project 1
yearly ['jɪəli] jährlich VI/1B3
°**yell** [jel] schreien VI/BS 3
yellow ['jeləʊ] gelb I/3B8
Yemen ['jemən] Jemen VI/3B1
yes [jes] ja I/1B4
yesterday ['jestədeɪ] gestern II/1B4
yet [jet] und doch, und trotzdem VI/1B2
°**not yet** [nɒt ˈjet] noch nicht VI/BS 5
°**yet again** [jetˌ əˈgen] schon wieder VI/BS 4
you [juː] du, dich, dir, Sie, Ihnen; ihr, euch I/W; man III/1B1
young [jʌŋ] jung I/3A1
your [jɔː] dein(e); euer/eure; Ihr(e) I/W
yours [jɔːz] deine(r, s); eure(r, s); Ihre(r, s) IV/8A6
yours faithfully [ˌjɔːz ˈfeɪθfli] mit freundlichen Grüßen V/2A5
yourself (pl **yourselves**) [jəˈself, jəˈselvz] dich; dir; selbst I/6C6

Z

zebra ['zebrə] Zebra II/2B3
zilch (informal) [zɪltʃ] null VI/1A8
zoo [zuː] Zoo II/2A1

Dictionary German – English

A

(links/rechts) abbiegen turn (left/right)
abdecken cover
Abend evening; night
am Abend in the evening
Abendessen dinner, supper
abends *(nur hinter Uhrzeit zwischen 12 Uhr mittags und Mitternacht)* pm (= post meridiem)
Abenteuer adventure
abenteuerlustig, risikofreudig adventurous
aber but
Abfall; Exkremente waste
abgepackt packaged
von jdm abhängen, jdm überlassen sein be up to sb
abhängen von depend on
abnehmen lose weight
Abreise, Abfahrt departure
Absatz, Abschnitt paragraph
abschaffen abolish
abschalten turn off
abschreiben copy
abspülen do the washing up
(ab)warten, (er)warten wait
sich abwechseln take turns
acht eight
achten auf make sure
Adjektiv adjective
adoptiert adopted
Adresse, Anschrift address
Affe monkey
ähnlich similar
Ähnlichkeit, Parallele similarity
(Akten)mappe portfolio
Aktivität, Unternehmung activity
Akzent accent
albern silly
allein alone
allein erziehend single
alle möglichen all kinds of
alles everything
alles in allem all in all
Alles Gute! All the best!
Alles Gute zum Geburtstag! Happy birthday (to you)!
alles Liebe love *(in Briefen)*
alle(s) all (the)
(all)zu too
allgemein, universell universal
als when, as; than *(bei Vergleich)*
als ob as if
also so
alt old
Alter age
im Alter von aged, at the age of
Amerika America
Amerikaner/in; amerikanisch American
amerikanische/r Ureinwohner/in Native (American)
sich amüsieren enjoy oneself, have a good time
analysieren, untersuchen analyse (= analyze)
anbieten offer
Anblick sight
andere(r, s) other
ein(e) andere(r, s) another
anders, andere(r, s) different
anerkennen respect
Anfang beginning; start
am Anfang at the beginning
anfangen (mit) start, begin
sich anfreunden make friends
Was ist im Angebot? What's on offer?
Angehörige/r member
Angestellte/r employee
angreifen attack
Angst haben (vor) be afraid (of), be scared of
hier: anhängen attach
(an)heben raise
sich anhören sound
ankämpfen gegen fight off
ankommen arrive
Ankunft arrival
Anmeldeformular registration form
sich anmelden sign up
annehmen, akzeptieren accept
anprobieren try on
anrufen phone; call; telephone
anschließend afterwards
Anschluss connection
sich ansehen have a look (at)
anstatt rather than
anstehen stand in line
hier: anstrengend hard
Antwort answer, reply
antworten answer, reply
Anweisung instruction
Anzeige, Inserat advert (= advertisement)
anziehen put on, wear
sich anziehen dress
Apfel apple
Apfelsine orange
April April
Arbeit work; job
arbeiten work
Arbeiter/in worker
Arbeitgeber/in employer
Arbeitsbedingungen working conditions
Arbeitsbuch workbook
arbeitslos sein be out of work
Arbeitstag working day
Ärger trouble
sich ärgern über be angry about
Argument argument
Arm arm
arm poor
Armbanduhr watch *(pl watches)*
Armut poverty
Art, Sorte kind, type
Art und Weise way
Artikel article
Artikel; Gegenstand item
Arzt/Ärztin doctor
Aspekt, Gesichtspunkt aspect
Atem(zug), Luft breath
atmen breathe
attraktiv, verlockend attractive
auch nicht neither, not … either
auch too; also; as well
auf onto
aufbauen set up
auf Deutsch in German
auf Englisch in English
auf und ab up and down
Auf Wiedersehen. Goodbye.
auf, an, in on; at
aufbewahren keep
Aufenthalt stay
hier: aufführen present
Aufgabe task, job
aufgeben give up
aufgeregt excited
aufhängen hang (up)
hier: aufheben save
aufhören (mit) stop; quit; finish
auflisten list
aufmachen open
Aufmachung, Layout Layout
Aufnahme recording
aufräumen tidy
aufregend exciting, thrilling
aufschreiben write down
aufstehen get up, stand up
(auf)teilen in divide into
aufwachsen grow up
(auf)wecken wake up
aufzeichnen; aufnehmen record
aufziehen raise
Aufzug, Fahrstuhl elevator *(AE)*
Auge eye
im Augenblick at the moment
August August
aus out of
Ausbildung training; apprenticeship; education
(sich) ausdenken make up
Ausdruck expression; phrase
ausdrucken print out
ausdrücken express
Auseinandersetzung argument
Ausflug trip
ausfüllen fill in; fill out *(Formular)*

Dictionary German – English

Ausgangspunkt starting point
ausgeben *(Geld)* spend
(gut) ausgebildet educated
ausgehen go out
(aus)helfen, unterstützen help out
(im/ins) Ausland abroad
ausländisch, fremd foreign
(aus)probieren try; try out
ausschalten switch off
aussehen look
Aussehen look
außerdem also
sich äußern comment
Ausstellung exhibition; display
Austausch exchange
hier: **austauschen, weitergeben** share
Australien Australia
(in / nach) Australien down under *(informal)*
Australier/in; australisch Australian
austral. Ureinwohner/in Aborigine, Aboriginal
auswandern emigrate
Auswanderung emigration
auswendig by heart
Auswirkung, Effekt effect
Auszeit time out
(Text)auszug excerpt
Auto car
automatisierte Viehhaltung factory farming
Autor/in writer
außen, außerhalb outside
äußerst extremely
Äußerung statement

B

babysitten babysit
Bad(ewanne) bath
Bad(ezimmer) bathroom
Bahnhof (railway) station
bald soon
Ball ball
Banane banana
Bargeld cash
Großes Barriereriff Great Barrier Reef
basieren auf, beruhen auf be based on
Bauch tummy *(informal)*
Bauchschmerzen stomach ache
bauen build
Bauer/Bäuerin farmer
Bauernhof farm
Baum tree
(be)antworten answer
bedauern be sorry (about/for)
bedecken cover
bedeuten, stehen für mean; stand for
bedeutend, wichtig; *hier:* **Haupt-** major
Bedeutung meaning
Bedingungen, Verhältnisse conditions *(only plural)*
(be)drohen threaten
sich beeilen hurry up
(be)enden finish, end
sich befassen mit deal with
Befehlsform imperative
befestigen; beilegen attach
begeistert excited
Beginn beginning, start
zu Beginn at the beginning
beginnen begin; get started
behalten keep
behandeln treat
Behandlung, Umgang mit treatment
behaupten claim
bei at
bei Gillian (zu Hause) at Gillian's
bei jdm zu Hause at sb's house
beide both
beilegen, beifügen enclose
beim Arzt/bei der Ärztin at the doctor's
Bein leg
beinhalten, mit sich bringen, betreffen involve
Beispiel example
beisteuern, spenden contribute
Beitrag contribution
beitreten join
(be)kämpfen fight
bekommen get, receive; develop
bekommern, erlangen gain
beleidigend insulting
beliebt, populär popular
bemerken notice
Bemerkung comment
(be)nennen name
benutzen use
Benutzer/in user
beobachten watch
bereit sein be prepared
bereit, gewillt willing
Berg mountain
Bericht report
berichten report (to)
Beruf career
Berufserfahrung work experience
berühmt famous
berühren touch
beschäftigen, einstellen employ
beschäftigt; arbeitsreich busy
jdn beschimpfen call sb names
beschreiben describe
Beschreibung description
Besichtigungen sightseeing *(no pl)*
besiegen beat
besitzen own
Besitzer/in owner
besondere(r, s) special
besonders especially
besprechen discuss
(be)sprühen spray
besser better
der/die/das beste the best
beste(r, s) best
bestellen order
Möchten Sie schon bestellen? Are you ready to order?
bestimmt certainly
bestimmte (r, s) specific
Bestrafung, Strafe punishment
Besuch visit
besuchen visit; attend
Besucher/in, Gast visitor
beten pray
betrachten look at
Betrag amount
hier: **betreiben** run
betreffen; gelten apply
Bett bed
beunruhigt, besorgt worried
Beutel; Sack sack
Bevölkerung population
bevor before
bevorzugen prefer
Bewegung exercise
(sich) bewegen move
sich bewerben (um) apply (for)
Bewerbungsschreiben letter of application
bewusst aware
sich bewusst sein über realise (= realize)
(be)zahlen pay
Beziehung relationship
Bibliothek, Bücherei library
bieten offer
Bild picture
Bild, Gemälde painting
Bildung education
billig, preiswert cheap
Bindewort conjunction
bis until, till
bis bald see you (later)
Bis bald! See you soon!
bisher so far
ein bisschen a little, a bit
bitte please
Bitte schön! Here you are!
Blatt leaf *(pl leaves)*
Blatt Papier sheet of paper
blau blue
bleiben stay
Bleistift pencil
Blick look
blöd stupid, silly
Blume flower
Bluse blouse
Boden earth
Bombe bomb
Boot; Schiff boat
an Bord on board
braten cook
brauchen need
braun brown
(sich) brechen break
breit wide
Brett board

243

D

Dictionary German – English

Brief letter
Brille (pair of) glasses *(only plural)*
bringen take
(mit)bringen bring
jdn dazu bringen, etw zu tun make sb do sth
britisch British
die Britischen Inseln the British Isles *(only plural)*
Broschüre brochure
Brot bread
Brücke bridge
Bruder brother
Buch book
Buchladen bookshop
Buchstabe letter
Bundesstaat state
bunt colourful
Burg, Schloss castle
Büro office
Büroangestellte/r office worker
Bus bus
mit dem Bus fahren take the bus
Bushaltestelle bus stop
Butter butter

C

Chance chance
Charakter character
charakteristisch typical
Checkliste checklist
Chef/in boss
Chips crisps *(only plural)*
n. Chr., nach Christus AD (= Anno Domini)
v. Chr., vor Christus BC (= before Christ)
Cousin/e cousin

D

da as
Dach roof *(pl roofs or rooves)*
daher, folglich so
damals; dann then
danach after that, afterwards, after
danke thanks
danke (schön) thank you
daran denken remember
das; der/die/das; dass that
Datum date
dauern take
Debatte, Diskussion debate
den Tisch decken set the table
Definition, Erklärung definition
dein(e) your
deine(r, s) yours
denken think
denken, vermuten guess
denken an think about
denken an, sich ausdenken think of
der/die/das the; who
derjenige/diejenige/dasjenige the one
deshalb that's why
Detail, Einzelheit detail
Deutsche/r; deutsch German
Deutschland Germany
Dezember December
Dialog dialogue
dich; dir; selbst yourself *(pl yourselves)*
dick fat
Dienstag Tuesday
diese these *(pl of this)*
diese; jene those *(pl of that)*
diese(r, s); das this
Ding thing
Dinosaurier dinosaur
diskutieren discuss
Diskussion, Erörterung discussion
und doch, und trotzdem yet
Donnerstag Thursday
Dorf village
dort drüben over there
dort(hin) there
Dossier, Akte dossier
draußen outside
dreckig dirty
drehen turn
drei three
dritte (r, s) third
Droge drug
(be)drohen threaten
Druck pressure
du, dich, dir you
duften smell
dumm stupid, silly
dunkel dark
Dunkelheit, Finsternis darkness
dünn thin; slim
etw tun dürfen be allowed to do sth
durch through
durchsehen look through
Dusche shower

E

echt, richtig; *hier:* **gut** proper
(an der) Ecke (at the) corner
Ehe marriage
Ehefrau wife *(pl wives)*
Ehemann husband
ehrenamtlich voluntary
ehrenamtliche/r Mitarbeiter/in volunteer
ehrlich honest
Ei egg
Eifersucht jealousy
eigene(r, s) own
Eigenschaft feature; quality
eigentlich, wirklich; tatsächlich actually
einander each other
eindeutig, definitiv definitely
ein(e) a / an
einerseits ... andererseits ... on the one hand ..., on the other hand ...
einfache Vergangenheit simple past
jdm einfallen come to sb's mind
sich einfügen fit in
einige a couple of, a few
einige; etwas some
einige; verschiedene several
sich einigen auf agree on
einkaufen (gehen) do the shopping, go shopping
(große) Einkaufspassage mall
Einkommen, Lohn income
einladen invite
einmal once
einmal im/pro Jahr once a year
eins; ein(e) one
einsam lonely
einschlafen fall asleep
sich einschreiben sign up
einsteigen get on
Einstellung, Haltung attitude
Eintrag entry
eintragen fill in
nicht einverstanden sein disagree
Einwanderer/in immigrant
Einwanderung, Immigration immigration
einwickeln, einpacken wrap up
Einwohner/in inhabitant
Einzelheit detail
einzeln, individuell individual
einzige(r, s) only
Eiskrem, Eis ice cream
Eislaufen ice-skating
Elefant elephant
Elektrizität electricity
elf eleven
Eltern parents *(only plural)*
Emigration emigration
emigrieren emigrate
Empfehlungsschreiben reference
Ende end; ending
Energie, Kraft energy
endlich at last
eng; knapp narrow
sich engagieren, kämpfen campaign
England England
englisch; Englisch English
englischsprachig English-speaking
entdecken discover
enthalten contain
sich entscheiden choose
(sich) entscheiden; beschließen decide
Entscheidung decision
sich entschuldigen apologize (= apologise)
Entschuldigen Sie bitte!, Entschuldigung! Excuse me!
Entschuldigung. Sorry.
entweder ... oder ... either ... or ...
entwickeln, erarbeiten develop
Entwicklungsland developing country
er he

Dictionary German – English

(Erd)boden, Erde ground
Erde earth
Erdgeschoss ground floor
Erdkunde, Geografie geography
Ereignis event
erfahren learn
Erfahrung; Erlebnis experience
Erfahrungen sammeln gain experience
erfinden invent; make up
Erfinder/in inventor
Erfindung invention
erfolgreich successful
(er)forschen, untersuchen research
Ergebnis result
erhalten get, receive
jdn erinnern remind sb
sich erinnern (an) remember
Erinnerung memory
(starke) Erkältung (bad) cold
erkennen recognize
erklären explain
Erklärung explanation; declaration
erlauben, gestatten allow
Erlebnis adventure
erleiden, ertragen suffer
ernähren feed
Ernährungslehre food technology
Das ist doch nicht dein Ernst! You're kidding! (informal)
Das meinst du doch nicht im Ernst! You must be joking!
(er)raten guess
erreichen achieve
erschaffen, erzeugen create
(er)scheinen; auftauchen appear
(er)schießen shoot
erschöpft exhausted
erstaunlich, toll amazing
erste(r, s) first
erwachsen werden grow up
Erwachsene/r adult
erwähnen mention
erwidern reply

erzählen tell
Erzählung story
es it
es gibt, da ist there is
es gibt, da sind there are
essen eat; have
Ich werde ... nehmen/ essen. I'll have ...
Essen food, meal
essen gehen eat out
Essstörung eating disorder
(Etagen)wohnung flat
euch you
euer/eure your
eure(r, s) yours
etwas something
etwas anderes something else
Europa Europe
Europäer/in; europäisch European
existieren, bestehen exist
Experte/Expertin expert
Extremsport(art) extreme sport(s)

F

Fabrik, Werk factory
(Schul)fach subject
hier: Fach course
Fachkompetenz hard skill
Fähigkeit, Fertigkeit skill
Fahne, Flagge flag
Fähre ferry
fahren drive; travel; go
fahren (mit) ride
mit dem Bus fahren take the bus
(Fahr)karte ticket
Fahrrad bicycle, bike
Fahrt ride, trip, journey
Fall case
fallen fall
falsch wrong
Familie family
Familienname surname
Familienstammbaum family tree
fangen catch
fantastisch, super fantastic
Farbe colour
farbenfroh colourful
fast, beinahe almost, nearly
Februar February
Federmäppchen pencil case
Fehler mistake

Feier celebration
feiern celebrate
fern; weit entfernt far away
Fenster window
fernsehen watch TV
Fernseher; Fernsehen TV (= television)
fertig, bereit ready
Fest, Festival festival
sich festhalten hold on tight
festmachen fix
Fett fat
Feuer; Brand fire
Feuerwerkskörper firework
Fieber haben have a temperature
hier: Figur character
Film movie
Filzstift felt-tip
finanziell financial
finden find; discover
Finger finger
Firma, Unternehmen company
Fisch fish (*pl* fish *or* fishes)
Flasche bottle
Fleisch meat
fliegen fly
Flügel wing
Flug, Fliegen flight
Flughafen airport
Flugsteig, Gate gate
Flugzeug (aero)plane
Fluss river
folgen follow
folgende(r, s) following
Form, Art form
Forschung, Nachforschung research
Foto photo
Fotoapparat camera
fotografieren take photos
Frage question
Frage, Angelegenheit issue
Fragen stellen ask questions
fragen; bitten ask
sich fragen wonder
Frankreich France
Franzose/Französin; französisch; Französisch French
Frau woman (*pl* women)
Frau *(Anrede)* Mrs

frei free
Freiheit freedom
Freiheitsstatue Statue of Liberty
Freitag Friday
freiwillig voluntary
Freizeit free time
Fremdenführer/in guide
Freude, Vergnügen pleasure
Freund *(Partner)* boyfriend
Freund/in friend
Freundin; Partnerin girlfriend
freundlich friendly
mit freundlichen Grüßen yours faithfully
Freundschaft friendship
Freundschaften schließen make friends
Frieden peace
friedlich peaceful
frisch fresh
fröhlich happy
Frucht fruit
früh early
früher used to + *Verb*
frühere(r, s) past
Frühling spring
Frühstück breakfast
frühstücken have breakfast
Frühstückspension B&B (= bed and breakfast)
(sich) fühlen feel
sich schlecht fühlen feel bad
sich sicher fühlen feel safe
führen lead
Führer/in leader
Führerschein driving licence
füllen fill
fünf five
für ..., ... lang for ... (+ *Zeitraum*)
für; *hier:* zu(m) for
füttern feed
funktionieren, laufen work
furchtbar awful, terrible
Fuß foot (*pl* feet)
zu Fuß on foot
(zu Fuß) gehen walk
Fußball football, soccer
(Fuß)boden floor

245

G

Gabel fork
ganz, gesamt whole
der/die/das ganze all (the)
auf der ganzen Welt all over the world
den ganzen Tag all day
Ganztags- full-time
Garten garden
Gast guest
Gebäude, Bau building
geben give
Gebiet, Region area
geboren werden be born
Gebrauch, Verwendung use
gebrochen broken
Geburtsdatum date of birth
Geburtsort place of birth
Geburtstag birthday
Gedächtnis memory
Gedanke thought
Gedicht poem
Geduld patience
Sehr geehrte Damen und Herren! (...) Dear Sir or Madam, (...)
gefährden threaten
gefährlich dangerous
Gefangene/r prisoner
Gefängnis prison
Gefühl feeling
gegen against; towards (in Richtung)
Gegend part
Gegenstand thing
gegenüber opposite
Gehalt salary
gehen go
(zu Fuß) gehen walk
mit jdm gehen go out with sb (informal)
Gehen; Spaziergang walk
gehören (zu) belong (to)
gelangweilt bored
gelb yellow
Geld money
Geld verdienen make money
Gelegenheit chance; opportunity
gelten; betreffen apply
Gemeinde, Gemeinschaft community
gemeinsam together

Gemüse vegetable
Gemüseburger veggie burger
genannt called
genau; bestimmte(r, s) specific
(genau)so ... wie ... as ... as
Genesungskarte get well card
genießen enjoy
genug enough
hier: **gerade (eben)** just
gerade(aus) straight (on)
Geräusch noise
Geräusch, Klang sound
Gericht *(Speise)* dish *(pl dishes)*
Gern geschehen! You're welcome.
Gesamtsumme; Anzahl total
Geschäft, Laden shop; store; business
geschehen happen
Geschenk gift, present
Geschichte history; story *(Erzählung)*
Geschlecht sex
geschlossen, zu; gesperrt closed
Geschwister brothers and sisters
Gesetz law
Gesicht face
Gesichtspunkt, Standpunkt point of view; aspect
Gespräch dialogue, conversation; talk
Gestalt, Figur figure
gestern yesterday
gesund healthy
Gesundheit health
Getränk drink
Gewicht weight
gewinnen win
Gewinner/in winner
sich gewöhnen an get used to
gewöhnlich usually
gewohnt sein be used to
Gewürz spice
Giraffe giraffe
Gitarre guitar
Gitter grid
Glas glass
glauben believe; think

Ich glaube nicht. I don't think so.
gleich equal
gleich; der/die/das Gleiche the same
gleichzeitig, zur gleichen Zeit at the same time
Glück, Zufriedenheit happiness
Glück haben be lucky
glücklich happy
Gold gold
Graffiti piece (of graffiti)
Grammatik grammar
Gras grass
gratis (for) free
grau grey
grausam, gemein cruel
groß big, large
groß, riesig; großartig great
Großbritannien (Great) Britain
Größe size
Großeltern grandparents (only plural)
Großes Barriereriff Great Barrier Reef
Großmutter grandmother
(Groß)stadt city
Großvater grandfather
grün green
Grund reason
Grund, Absicht, Ziel purpose
gründen found
grundlegend basic
mit freundlichen Grüßen yours faithfully
viele Grüße love (in Briefen)
Gruppe group
in Gruppen, gruppenweise in groups
Gummi; Radiergummi rubber
gut good, well
Es geht mir gut. I'm fine.
(gut) ausgebildet educated
etw gut können be good at sth
Alles Gute zum Geburtstag! Happy birthday (to you)!
Alles Gute! All the best!

Gut gemacht! Well done!
Guten Abend. Good evening.
Guten Tag! How do you do?
Gutes/Frohes neues Jahr! Happy New Year!

H

Haar(e) hair *(no pl)*
haben have (got)
Hafen harbour
halb elf half past ten
eine halbe Stunde half an hour
Hälfte half (*pl* halves)
Hallo. Hello.
Hals throat
Hals; Nacken neck
halten hold; keep
Haltung, Einstellung attitude
Hamster hamster
Hand hand
handeln; sich benehmen act
handeln von be about
Händler/in trader
Handlung, Tat action
Handschuh glove
Handtuch towel
Handy mobile (phone), cellphone *(AE)*
hart; schwer hard
hassen, nicht ausstehen können hate
hässlich ugly
Ich hätte/würde gern ... I'd like (to) ...
hier: **häufig, oft** much
Haupt- main
Hauptgericht main course
hauptsächlich mainly
Hauptstadt capital
Hauptwort noun
Haus house
nach Hause home
zu Hause at home
Hausaufgaben homework *(no pl)*
Haustier pet
Haut skin
Heft exercise book
Heiligabend Christmas Eve
Heimat home
Heirat; Ehe marriage

Dictionary German – English

heiraten marry
heiß hot
heißen be called
helfen help
(aus)helfen, unterstützen help out
hell; strahlend, glänzend bright
herausfinden find out; discover
(heraus)fordernd challenging
Herbst autumn
hereinkommen come in
Herkunft origin; background
Herr *(Anrede)* Mr
herstellen produce
herumkommen get around
herunterladen download
Herz heart
heute today
heute Abend this evening, tonight
heute Morgen/Nachmittag this morning/afternoon
Hier, bitte! Here you are!
hier(her) here
hiesig local
Highschool *(weiterführende Schule)* high school *(AE)*
(Zu) Hilfe! Help!
hilfreich, hilfsbereit helpful
Himmel sky
hinab down
(hinauf)steigen climb (up)
hineinsetzen/-legen/-stellen put in
hinkommen get there
sich hinlegen lie down
hinrichten execute
Hinrichtung, Exekution execution
hinten at the back (of)
hinter behind
Hinterland (Australiens) outback
hinunter down
hinzufügen add
Hitze heat
hoch high
hoch; groß tall
höchst extremely
hochziehen raise

hoffen hope
Ich hoffe, von Ihnen zu hören. I look forward to hearing from you.
Hoffnung hope
höflich polite
holen, kaufen get
Holz wood
hören hear
Hose (pair of) trousers
hübsch pretty
Hügel hill
Huhn chicken
Hund dog
Hunger hunger
hungrig hungry
Hut; Mütze hat
Hütte hut

I

ich I
Idee idea
Igel hedgehog
ihm, ihn him
Ihnen; ihr you
ihr(e) their
ihre(r, s) hers
ihre(r, s) theirs
Ihr(e) your
Ihre(r, s) yours
illustrieren illustrate
Imbissstube snack bar
immer always
(immer) noch still
Imperativ imperative
importieren import
in in; into; at
indem by
innerhalb within
in Ordnung, gut fine
in Richtung toward(s)
in, nach, zu to
Inder/in; indisch Indian
Indien India
indirekte Frage reported question
Industrie industry
Informationstechnologie; Informatik information technology
sich informieren über find out about
innen, drinnen inside
Insel island
interessant interesting
Interesse interest
sich interessieren für be interested in

Internat boarding school
Internet, Netz Internet, Net
im Internet on the Internet
im Internet suchen search the Internet
im Internet surfen surf the Internet
interviewen, befragen interview
(irgend)ein(e); jede(r, s) any
(irgend)etwas anything
(irgend)etwas anderes anything else
(irgend)jemand, irgendwer someone (= somebody)
irgendwo somewhere
irgendwo anders anywhere else
irisch Irish
(Republik) Irland (republic of) Ireland
Italien Italy
Italiener/in; italienisch Italian

J

ja yes
Jacke jacket
Jahr year
Jahreszeit season
Jahrgangsstufe form; year
Jahrhundert century
Januar January
jede(r, s) each, every
jede(r); alle everybody, everyone
jede(r); jemand anybody
jedes Mal, wenn whenever
jedoch however
jemals, schon einmal ever
jetzt now
hier: **Jetzt hör aber auf!** Come on!
Journalist/in journalist
Jugendliche(r) kid
Juli July
jung young
Junge boy
jüngste(r, s) *(aktuell)* late(st)
Juni June

K

Käfig cage
Kaffee coffee
Kalender calendar
kalt cold
Kamera camera
Kampagne, Aktion campaign
(be)kämpfen fight
Kandidat/in candidate
Kapitän/in; Mannschaftsführer/in captain
Kapitel theme; chapter
Kappe cap
kaputt broken
Karneval, Volksfest carnival
Karriere career
Karte ticket
Kartoffel potato *(pl* potatoes)
Karton; Karte card
Käse cheese
Kasse cash desk
Kasten box
Katze cat
kauen chew
kaufen buy
kaufen, holen get
Kaufhaus department store
Kaugummi (chewing) gum
kein/keine not any
kein(e) no
keine(r, s) not ... any
Kellner/in waiter/waitress
Es freut mich, Sie/dich kennen zu lernen. Nice to meet you.
jdn kennen lernen get to know sb
Kenntnisse knowledge
(Kfz-)Werkstatt garage
Kilo kilo
Kilometer kilometre
Kind child *(pl* children); kid
Kinderarbeit child labour
Kindheit childhood
Kino cinema
Kirche church
Kiste; Schachtel box
klar; rein clear
(na) klar sure
Klasse form; year
Klassenarbeit test
Klassenkamerad/in classmate
Klassenzimmer classroom
Klebstoff glue *(no pl)*

247

Dictionary German – English

Kleid dress
Kleider, Kleidung clothes *(only plural)*
(Kleider)schrank wardrobe
Kleidung clothing
klein little, small
klettern (auf) climb (up)
klingen, sich anhören sound
Klub club
klug, schlau clever
km/h kph (= kilometres per hour)
knapp bei Kasse sein be short of money *(informal)*
Knie knee
Knopf; *hier:* **Taste** button
Koch/Köchin cook
kochen do the cooking, cook
Koffer suitcase
Kollege/Kollegin colleague
Kolonie colony
komisch weird
kommen come
Ich bin/komme (aus …) I'm (from …)
Kommentar comment
einen Kommentar abgeben comment
Kommode chest of drawers
Komm(t) schon!; Mach(t) jetzt! Come on!
Kommunikation communication
Kommunikationsfähigkeit communication skills
kommunizieren communicate
Konflikt conflict
Kongress, Tagung congress
König king
Königin queen
Konjunktion conjunction
können can
etw tun können be able to do sth
können, mögen may
könnte(st/n/t) could, might
in Kontakt bleiben keep in touch

in Kontakt treten get in touch
hier: **den Kontakt wieder löschen** unfriend
Kontra, Wider con
kontrollieren, steuern control
sich konzentrieren (auf) concentrate (on)
Konzert concert
Kopf head
(Kopf)kissen, Polster pillow
Korb basket
Körper body
körperlich physical
korrigieren correct
kosten cost
Es kostet … Pfund. It's … £ (pounds).
köstlich delicious
Kostüm costume
Kraft, Stärke power
krank ill, sick
(Kranken)schwester, (Kranken)pfleger nurse
Krankheit disease, illness
kreativ, schöpferisch creative
Kreditkarte credit card
Krieg war
Krise crisis *(pl* crises)
Kritik, Rezension review
Kritiker/in critic
kritisch, missbilligend critical
kritisieren criticize
Küche kitchen
Kuchen cake
Kuh cow
Kühlschrank fridge
sich kümmern um look after
sich kümmern um, versorgen take care of
Kultur culture; civilization
kulturell cultural
Kunde/Kundin customer, client
Künstler/in artist
(bildende) Kunst art
(Kunst)maler/in painter
Kunstwerk piece of art
Kurs course
kurz; klein short
kürzlich, in letzter Zeit lately

kürzlich, vor kurzem recently
küssen kiss
Küste coast

L

lächeln smile
lachen laugh
Laden store
Lage location
Land country, countryside, land, nation
(Land)karte map
lang long
eine Stunde lang for an hour
langsam slow
langweilig boring
Lärm noise
lassen let
lass(t) uns … let's (= let us) …
etw machen lassen get sth done, have sth done
Lastwagen lorry, truck
laufen, rennen run
Läufer/in runner
laut loud, noisy
Leben life *(pl* lives)
leben, am Leben sein be alive
leben live
Lebenslauf CV (= curriculum vitae)
Lebensmittel groceries *(only plural)*
Lebensstandard standard of living
Lebensstil lifestyle
seinen Lebensunterhalt verdienen make a living
lecker delicious
leer empty
legen put
Lehrbuch textbook
Lehre apprenticeship
Lehrer/in teacher
leicht, einfach easy
Es tut mir leid. I'm sorry.
leiden an suffer from
leihen lend
leise, ruhig quiet
sich leisten afford
hier: **Leistung** performance
Lektion theme
lernen learn; study
lesen read
letzten Endes in the end

letzte(r, s) last; late(st) *(aktuell)*
in letzter Zeit lately
Leute people
Licht light
Liebe love
Liebe(r, s) … Dear … *(in Briefen)*
alles Liebe love *(in Briefen)*
lieben; sehr gern mögen love
am liebsten mögen like best
Liebling; Favorit/in favourite
Lieblings- favourite
Lied song
(Lied)text lyrics *(only plural)*
liefern, ausliefern deliver
liegen; sich hinlegen lie
Lineal ruler
Linie; Zeile line
linke(r, s) left
links (abbiegen) (turn) left
links, auf der linken Seite on the left
Liste list
Literatur literature
Loch hole
Löffel spoon
Lohn, Gehalt pay
hier: **den Kontakt wieder löschen** unfriend
lösen solve
Löwe lion
Lohn wage
Luft air
lustig good fun
lustig, witzig, komisch funny

M

machen make
etw machen lassen get sth done, have sth done
Macht, Einfluss power
Mädchen girl
Magazin, Zeitschrift magazine
Magenschmerzen stomach ache
Mahlzeit meal
Mai May
… Mal … times
jedes Mal, wenn whenever

malen, streichen paint
Mama, Mutti mum *(informal)*
man you
manchmal sometimes
Manieren manners
Mann man *(pl men)*
männlich male
Mantel coat
(Akten)mappe portfolio
Mappe, Ordner folder
markieren, kennzeichnen mark
Markt market
März March
Maschine, Motor engine
Material, Stoff material
Mathe maths
Mauer wall
Maus mouse *(pl mice)*
Mechatroniker/in (car) technician
die Medien the media *(only plural)*
Medikament, Droge drug
Medizin, Medikamente medicine
Meer, (die) See sea
mehr more
Meile *(= 1,609 km)* mile
mein(e) my
meine(r, s) mine
meinen mean; think
Meinung, Ansicht opinion
meiner Meinung nach in my opinion
am meisten most
die meisten most
meistens mostly
Menge amount
Mensch man *(pl men)*; person
Menschen people
Menschenrechte human rights *(only plural)*
merkwürdig strange
Merkmal feature
Messer knife *(pl knives)*
Meter metre
Metzgerei butcher's
Mietwohnung flat
Milch milk
mindestens, zumindest at least
Minute minute
mir, mich; ich me

mir, mich; selbst myself
mit by *(+ Verkehrsmittel)*, with
Mitarbeiter staff
Mitarbeiter/in employee
(mit)bringen bring
Mitglied member
Mitglied werden; mitmachen bei join
mitlesen read along
Mitschüler/in classmate
mitsingen sing along
Mittagessen lunch, dinner
in der Mitte; mitten in/auf in the middle
Mittwoch Wednesday
Mobbing bullying
Mobiltelefon mobile (phone)
Mode fashion
Modell model
mögen like
am liebsten mögen like best
möglich possible
alle möglichen all kinds of
möglicherweise maybe
Möglichkeit chance
Möhre, Karotte, Mohrrübe carrot
Moment mal! Wait a minute!
momentan at the moment
Monat month
Mond moon
Montag Monday
Mord murder
Mörder/in murderer
morgen tomorrow
Morgen morning
am Morgen in the morning
morgens *(nur hinter Uhrzeit zwischen Mitternacht und 12 Uhr mittags)* am *(= ante meridiem)*
Motor engine
müde tired
Müll, Abfall rubbish, garbage *(AE)*
Mülleimer, Mülltonne bin
Müllmann dustbin man *(pl dustbin men)*
Mund mouth
Münze, Geldstück coin
Museum museum

Musik music
Musiker/in musician
(Musik)gruppe group
Muskel muscle
müssen must, need to
etw tun müssen have to do sth
Mustertext model (text)
Mut, Tapferkeit courage
Mutter mother
Mütze cap

N
Na und?, Na wenn schon! So what? *(informal)*
nach after
nach oben, hinauf up; upstairs
Nachbar/in neighbour
nachdem after
Nachdenken thought
nachdenken, sich überlegen think
nachdenken über think about
nachher after
Nachmittag afternoon
am Nachmittag in the afternoon
nachmittags *(nur hinter Uhrzeit zwischen 12 Uhr mittags und Mitternacht)* pm *(= post meridiem)*
Nachname surname
Nachricht, Botschaft message
Nachrichten news *(no pl)*
Nachrichten schicken message
nachschlagen look up
nachspielen act out
nächste(r, s) next
Nacht night
Nachtisch dessert
nachts at night
nahe (bei) near
Name name
Nase nose
Nation, Land nation
Nationalität nationality
Natur nature
natürlich of course; natural
(aber) natürlich sure
(Natur)wissenschaft science
neben next to

Neffe nephew
negativ negative
nehmen take
nein no
nennen call; name
nennen, angeben *(Grund)* give
nervös nervous
nett, liebenswürdig lovely
Netz web
Netzwerk network
neu new
neueste(r, s) *(aktuell)* late(st)
Neuigkeit news *(no pl)*
Neujahr New Year
neun nine
nicht not
nicht dürfen must not
nicht einverstanden sein disagree
nicht mehr not anymore
nicht nur ..., sondern auch ... not only ... but also ...
nicht stimmen, los sein be wrong with sb
nichts not anything, nothing
Nichts zu danken! You're welcome.
nie(mals) never
niemand not anyone, nobody
niemand anderes no one else
nirgendwo(hin) not ... anywhere
Niveau; Ebene level
noch eine(r, s) another
noch einmal once more
noch immer still
noch mehr; weitere(r, s) more
noch nicht einmal not even
Nord-, nördlich northern
Norden; in nördliche Richtung north
Nordirland Northern Ireland
normalerweise normally; usually
Note, Zensur mark
nötig, notwendig necessary
Notiz note

Dictionary German – English

(sich) Notizen machen (über) take/make notes (on)
November November
Nummer number
nun (ja), tja well
nur only
nur, bloß, einfach just
Nutzen use
nützlich useful; handy

O

ob whether; if
als ob as if
(nach) oben upstairs
oberhalb; *hier:* oben above
Objekt object
Obst fruit
obwohl even though, though, although
obwohl, jedoch though *(nachgestellt)*
oder or
offen, geöffnet open
offensichtlich obviously
öffentlich public
offiziell official
öffnen open
sich öffnen, aufgehen open
ökologisch green
Opfer victim
örtlich local
oft, häufig often
ohne without
ohne etw auskommen do without sth
Ohr ear
Ohrring earring
Oktober October
Olympische Spiele Olympic Games
Oma, Omi grandma *(informal)*
Onkel uncle
Opa, Opi grandpa *(informal)*
optimistisch optimistic
orange orange
Orange orange
Ordnung order
Organisation organization
organisieren; koordinieren; ordnen organize
Ort; Platz place
(Stand)ort location
örtlich, hiesig local

Osten east
östlich, Ost- eastern
Ozean, Meer ocean

P

Paar pair
ein paar a couple of
Papa, Vati dad *(informal)*
Papier paper
Pappe card
Parade, Umzug parade
Parterre ground floor
Partner/in partner
eine Party machen have a party
passen zu go with, match
passend matching
passieren happen; go on
Passiv passive
Passwort password
Patient/in patient
Patrone cartridge
Pause break
Pech bad luck
Penny p (= penny; *pl* pennies *or* pence)
Person, Mensch person
Personal staff
persönlich personal
Pferd horse
Pflanze plant
Pfund *(engl. Währung)* pound
Pinguin penguin
planen; vorbereiten plan
Plastik, Kunststoff plastic
Platz, Raum; Zimmer room
plaudern mit, chatten mit chat with/to
plötzlich, auf einmal suddenly
plus, zuzüglich plus
die Polizei the police
Polizeibeamter/-beamtin police officer
Pommes frites chips *(only plural)*
positiv positive
Post mail
Präsentation, Vortrag presentation
präsentieren present
Präsident/in president
Praktikant/in intern
Praktikum work experience

praktisch useful
praktisch, nützlich handy
Preis price
preiswert cheap
Premierminister/in prime minister
privat private
Pro, Für pro
(zweimal) pro (Woche) (twice) a (week)
Problem problem; trouble
Produkt, Erzeugnis product
produzieren produce
Profil, Porträt profile
Programm, Plan programme *(BE)*, program *(AE)*
Projekt project
protestieren protest
Prozent per cent
Prüfung exam, test
eine Prüfung ablegen take an exam
Pullover sweater
Punkt; Komma *(bei Zahlen)* point
pünktlich on time, punctual

Q

Qualifikation; Voraussetzung qualification
Qualität quality
Quelle source

R

Rad fahren cycle
Radiergummi eraser, rubber
Rasse race
jdm raten(, etw zu tun) advise sb (to do sth)
Rate mal! Guess what!
Rat(schlag) (piece of) advice, tip
Raum room
Raum; Weltraum space
realistisch realistic
Realität, Wirklichkeit reality
Rechnung bill
Die Rechnung, bitte! Could we have the bill, please?
Recht right
Recht haben be right
rechte(r, s) right

rechts (abbiegen) (turn) right
rechts, auf der rechten Seite on the right
Rechtschreibung spelling
(Rede)wendung phrase
Regal shelf *(pl* shelves*)*
Regel rule
Regen rain
Regenbogen rainbow
Regierung government
regnen rain
regnerisch rainy
reich rich
Reihenfolge order
Reim rhyme *(no pl)*
Reis rice
Reise trip, journey
reisen travel
Reisen travelling, travel
Reisende/r traveller
reiten ride
Religionslehre religious education
Reparatur repair
reparieren repair, fix
Reporter/in reporter
repräsentieren; darstellen represent
Republik republic
Respekt, Achtung respect
respektieren respect
Restaurant, Gaststätte restaurant
Rettungsweste life vest
Rezept recipe
richtig, in Ordnung right
richtig, korrekt correct
riechen smell
riesig, riesengroß huge
Rinder, Vieh cattle
Rock skirt
Rolle part; role
Rollstuhl wheelchair
Rose rose
rot red
Rücken; Rückseite back
Rückmeldung, Feedback feedback
(an)rufen call
rufen shout
Ruhe peace
ruhig bleiben stay cool

S

Sack; Beutel sack
Saft juice
sagen say; tell

Dictionary German – English

hier: **Saison** season
Salat salad
Salz salt
sammeln collect; gain
Sammlung collection
Samstag Saturday
Sand sand
Sänger/in singer
satt machen feed
Satz sentence; phrase
Satzgegenstand object
sauber clean
sauber machen clean
Säulendiagramm bar chart
Schaf sheep (*pl* sheep)
es schaffen manage
Schal scarf (*pl* scarves)
Schale, Schüssel dish (*pl* dishes)
scharf hot
schätzen, zu schätzen wissen appreciate
Schaubild diagram
Schauspieler/in actor/actress
scheinen seem
schicken; bekannt geben post
schießen (*Tor*) score
Schiff ship
Schlange, Reihe queue
schlank, schmal, dünn slim
(Straßen-/Verkehrs)schild sign
Schinken ham
schlafen be asleep, sleep
Schlafzimmer bedroom
schlagen (*besiegen*) beat
schlagen; treffen hit
Schlagzeile headline
Schlange snake
schlecht; schlimm bad
sich schlecht fühlen feel bad
schließen, zumachen close
schließlich after all; in the end; at last; lastly
schließlich, endlich finally
schlimm, erschütternd upsetting
Schlittschuhlaufen ice-skating
Schluss ending
Schlüsselwort keyword
schmecken taste

Schmerz pain
schmutzig dirty
Schnee snow
schneiden cut
schnell fast, quick
Schnellgerichte, ungesundes Essen junk food
Schokolade chocolate
schön beautiful
schon, bereits already
schön, hübsch; herrlich lovely
schön; nett nice
Schottland Scotland
Schrank cupboard
schrecklich terrible, awful, horrible
schreiben write
Schreibtisch desk
schreien shout, scream
schüchtern shy
Schuh shoe
Schul-AG club
Schule school
Schüler/in pupil, student
(Schul)fach subject
Schuljahr year
(Schul)klasse class
Schultasche schoolbag
Schulter shoulder
schützen protect
Schwamm sponge
schwarz black
Schwein pig
schwer; stark heavy
schwer, schlimm; heftig severe
Schwester sister
hier: **schwierig** hard
schwierig, schwer difficult
Schwierigkeiten trouble
Schwimmbecken, Schwimmbad swimming pool
Schwimmen swimming
schwimmen swim
schwimmen gehen go swimming
sechs six
der/die/das sechsjährige six-year-old
See lake
seekrank seasick
segeln sail
sehen see
sehen, schauen look (at)

Sehenswürdigkeit(en) sight(s)
sehr very
Sehr geehrte(r) ..., Liebe(r, s) ... Dear ...
Sehr geehrte Damen und Herren! (...) Dear Sir or Madam, (...)
Seife soap
Seifenoper soap (opera)
sein be
sein(e), ihr(e) its
sein(e, r) his
seit since
Seite page, side
Sekunde second
selbst; sogar even
selbstsicher, selbstbewusst confident
selbst wenn even though
selten, nicht oft rarely
September September
setzen, stellen, legen put
sich; selbst herself, himself, themselves
sicher safe; sure
sich sicher fühlen feel safe
sicherlich certainly
sie she, they
sie, ihnen them
sie; ihr(e, n) her
Sie you
sieben seven
Siedler/in settler
Sieger/in winner
Sightseeing sightseeing (*no pl*)
singen sing
Situation, Lage situation
sitzen sit
Sklave/Sklavin slave
Sklaverei slavery
SMS text (message)
so; auf diese Weise like this/that
Socke sock
sodass; damit so that
sofort right away; at once
sogenannt so-called
Sohn son
solang(e) as long as
solche(r/s) such
Soldat soldier
sollen shall
sollte/müsste should
Sommer summer
sonderbar, merkwürdig strange

Sonne sun
Sonnenbrille sunglasses (*only plural*)
sonnig sunny
Sonntag Sunday
sonntags (on) Sundays
Was sonst ...? What else ...?
sich Sorgen machen worry
Sorte, Art sort
sortieren sort
Soße, Sauce sauce
sowieso, überhaupt; jedenfalls anyway
sowohl ... als auch ... both ... and ...
sozial, gesellschaftlich social
soziale und emotionale Kompetenz soft skill
Spanien Spain
Spanisch, spanisch Spanish
spannend exciting
sparen save
(zu) spät (too) late
später later; afterwards
(spätestens) bis by (+ *Zeitpunkt*)
Spaß fun
Spaß haben have fun
Spaziergang walk
Speisekarte menu
spezielle(r, s) special; specific
Spiel game; match
spielen play
Spieler/in player
Sei kein/e Spielverderber/in! Be a sport!
Spielzeug toy
Spinne spider
Sport treiben do sport
Sport(art) sport
Sport(unterricht) PE (= physical education)
Sprache language
Sprache; Rede speech
sprechen, reden (mit) speak (to/with), talk (to)
springen jump
Stadt town
Stadtteil borough
stark strong
statt instead of
stattfinden take place
Stau traffic jam
stehen stand

D

Dictionary German – English

stehen bleiben; (an)halten stop
stehen für stand for
stehlen steal
steil steep
Stein; Fels rock
Stelle (Arbeit) job, placement
Stelle; hier: Website site
stellen put
sterben die
Stern star
Steuer, Abgabe tax
steuern control
Stiefel boot
Stift pen
Stil, Art style
Stock, Stockwerk floor
Stoff, Material material
stolz proud
stoßen (gegen) hit
Strafe punishment
Strand beach
Straße road, street
auf der Straße in the street
Strecke, Route route
(sich) streiten fight
streng strict
Strom electricity
Student/in student
studieren study
Stück, Werk piece
Stufe step
Stuhl chair
Stunde hour, lesson
Stundenplan timetable
Sturm storm
Substantiv noun
suchen nach look for, search for
Suchmaschine search engine
Süden, nach Süden south
super fantastic
Supermarkt supermarket
Suppe soup
süß sweet

T

Tabelle table, grid
Tafel blackboard, board
Tag day
den ganzen Tag all day
jeden Tag, täglich daily
Tagebuch diary
Tal valley

Tante aunt
Tanz dance
tanzen dance
Tasche bag; pocket (an Kleidungsstücken)
Taschendieb/in pickpocket
Taschengeld pocket money
Tasse cup
hier: Taste button
Tatsache fact
tatsächlich actually
tauschen swap
Tausend thousand
Technologie, Technik technology
Tee tea
Tee trinken have tea
Teil part
(auf)teilen in divide into
teilen share
teilnehmen (an) take part (in), participate (in)
Teilnehmer/in participant
Teilzeit part-time
Telefon telephone
(am) Telefon (on the) phone
(Telefon)anruf call
telefonieren make a call
Teller plate
Test test
teuer expensive
(Text)auszug excerpt
Textilfabrik textile factory
Theater(kurs); Schauspielerei drama
(Theater)stück play
Thema topic; theme; subject; issue
die Themse the (River) Thames
tief deep
tiefgekühlt frozen
Tier animal
Tierarzt/Tierärztin vet
Tiger tiger
Tipp tip
Tisch table
Titel title
Tochter daughter
Tod death
Todesstrafe death penalty
Todestrakt death row
Toilette toilet, washroom (AE)
toll, klasse brilliant

Tomate tomato (pl tomatoes)
Tonprobe, Soundcheck sound check
Tor gate; goal (Sport)
Torte cake
Tortendiagramm pie chart
tot dead
töten kill
traditionell traditional
tragen carry; wear (anziehen)
tragisch tragic
Trainer/in coach; trainer
Training training
Traum dream
träumen dream
traurig sad
Treffen meeting
(sich) treffen meet; see
sich trennen, Schluss machen break up
Treppe stairs (only plural)
treten, schießen kick
trinken drink; have
etw trinken have a drink
trotz despite
trotzdem still
und trotzdem, und doch yet
Tschüss. Bye. (informal)
tun, machen do
Tür door
Turnen gym (= gymnastics)
Turnschuh trainer
typisch typical

U

die (Londoner) U-Bahn the tube
üben practise
über about, above, across, over
über Nacht bleiben, übernachten sleep over
überall anywhere, everywhere
überfliegen (Text) skim through
überfliegen, absuchen (Text) scan
Übernachtung mit Frühstück B&B (= bed and breakfast)
überprüfen, kontrollieren check

überraschen surprise
überraschend surprising
überrascht, erstaunt surprised
überreden; überzeugen persuade
Überschrift headline, heading
üblich, gewöhnlich usual, common
übrig, restlich remaining
Übung exercise
etwa: Übung macht den Meister. Practice matters.
Uhr clock
(acht) Uhr (eight) o'clock
(Uhr)zeit time
hier: um at
um (… herum) around
um Hilfe bitten ask for help
(um) wie viel Uhr (at) what time
sich umdrehen turn around
umgehen mit deal with
umsonst (for) free
umsteigen change
Umwelt environment
um zu in order to
umweltfreundlich green; environmentally friendly
unabhängig, selbständig independent
Unabhängigkeit independence
und and
und auch nicht, noch nor
Unfall accident
ungefähr about; around
Ungerechtigkeit injustice
ungesetzlich, illegal illegal
ungesund unhealthy
ungewöhnlich unusual
unglücklich unhappy
unglücklicherweise unfortunately
Uniform uniform
universell, allgemein universal
uns us
uns; selbst ourselves
unschuldig innocent
unser(e) our
unsere(r, s) ours
unten, darunter below
unter below, under
unterbrechen interrupt

Dictionary German – English

Unterhaltung conversation; talk
Unterkunft accomodation
unterrichten; beibringen teach
Unterricht(sstunde) class
Unterschied difference
unterschiedlich different
unterschreiben; *hier:* **schreiben** sign
unterstreichen underline
unterstützen support
Unterstützung support
Untersuchung, Umfrage survey
Untertitel; *hier:* **Bildunterschrift** subtitle
austral. **Ureinwohner/in** Aborigine
Urlaub, Ferien holiday
Urlaub/Ferien haben be on holiday
in Urlaub gehen/fahren go on holiday
ursprünglich originally
USA (= Vereinigte Staaten von Amerika) USA (= United States of America)

V

Vandalismus, blinde Zerstörungswut vandalism
Vater father
Vegetarier/in vegetarian
Vegetarier/in werden go vegetarian
vegetarisch vegetarian
(ver)ändern; austauschen change
(Ver)änderung change
veranschaulichen illustrate
Veranstaltung event
verärgert; zornig angry
verantwortlich responsible
Verb verb
Verband bandage
verbessern improve
verbieten; ausschließen ban
Verbindung connection
sich in Verbindung setzen mit contact
Verbraucher/in consumer
Verbrechen crime

(ver)brennen burn
verbringen *(Zeit)* spend
verbunden werden get connected
verdienen earn
Verein club
das Vereinigte Königreich *(Großbritannien und Nordirland)* United Kingdom of Great Britain and Northern Ireland (= UK)
die Vereinigten Staaten the United States
verfügbar, zur Verfügung stehend available
vergangen past
Vergangenheit past
einfache Vergangenheit simple past
vergessen forget
Vergleich comparison
vergleichen compare
verheiraten marry
verheiratet married
verhindern prevent
(ver)hungern starve
sich verirren lose one's way
verkaufen sell
zu verkaufen for sale
Verkäufer/in (shop) assistant, seller
(Verkaufs)stand stall
Verkehr traffic
sich verkleiden dress up
verkünden, bekannt geben announce
verlassen leave
verlässlich reliable
verletzen violate *(Rechte)*
verletzt, verwundet hurt
Verletzung, Verstoß violation
sich verlieben (in) fall in love (with)
verliebt sein (in) be in love (with)
verlieren lose
vermeiden avoid
vermissen; verpassen miss
veröffentlichen publish
verrückt crazy
verschieden different
verschiedene several
verschmutzen pollute
versprechen promise

Versprechen promise
sich verständigen communicate
Verständigung communication
verstecken hide
verstehen understand
Ich verstehe. I see.
versuchen try
Vertrauen; Glaube faith
verursachen, hervorrufen cause
verurteilen sentence
verteidigen defend
vervollständigen complete
Verwaltungsbezirk borough
Verwandte(r) relative
Verwendung, Gebrauch use
Verzeihung. Sorry.
auf etw verzichten do without sth
Vieh cattle
automatisierte Viehhaltung factory farming
viel Glück good luck
viel, jede Menge lots *(informal)*, lots of
viel; sehr much
viel(e) a lot (of)
viele many
Vielen Dank! Thanks a lot!, Thank you very much!
Vielfalt variety
vielleicht perhaps, maybe
vier four
Viertel (vor/nach) quarter (to/past)
Viertel, Gegend area
Viertel; Umgebung neighbourhood (*BE* = neighborhood *AE*)
Viertelstunde quarter of an hour
Vogel bird
Vokabular, Wortschatz vocabulary
Volk people
voll full
völlig, total totally
vollkommen, perfekt perfect
Vollzeit- full-time
hier: **von** by
von of

von, aus from
vor before, in front of
vor (langer Zeit) (long) ago
vorbei an; hinter, nach past
(sich) vorbereiten (auf) prepare (for)
Vorführung, Aufführung performance
vorgeben pretend
(laut) vorlesen read out
Vormittag morning
vormittags *(nur hinter Uhrzeit zwischen Mitternacht und 12 Uhr mittags)* am (= ante meridiem)
vorne at the front (of)
vorsichtig careful
Vorspeise starter
Vorsprechen, Vorsingen, Vortanzen audition
jdn vorstellen introduce sb
sich vorstellen imagine
Vorstellung idea
Vorstellung; Einführung introduction
Vorstellungsgespräch interview
Vortrag talk
vorziehen prefer

W

wachsam, vorsichtig aware
wachsen, größer werden grow
Wahl election
wählen; sich entscheiden choose
wahnsinnig crazy
wahr true
Wahrheit truth
wahrscheinlich probably
während during, while
Wald forest
Wales Wales
Wand wall
wann; wenn when
warm warm
warnen, ermahnen warn
(ab)warten, (er)warten wait
warten hold on
warten auf wait (for)

253

Dictionary German – English

Wartezimmer waiting room
warum why
was what
Was ist im Angebot? What's on offer?
Was ist los? What's the matter?
Was ist mit …? What about …? *(informal)*
Was kostet/kosten …? How much is/are …?
Was läuft? Was geht ab? What's on?
was man tun und was man nicht tun sollte dos and don'ts
Was nimmst du/nehmen Sie? What are you having?
Was sonst …? What else …?
(sich) waschen wash
Wasser water
Website website, site
Wechselgeld change
(auf)wecken wake up
weder … noch … neither … nor …
(jdm) den Weg beschreiben give (sb) directions
nach dem Weg fragen ask for directions
(weg)gehen; abfahren leave
weggehen, fortgehen go away; go out
wegwerfen throw away
wehtun, schmerzen hurt
weiblich female
Weihnachten Christmas
erster Weihnachtsfeiertag Christmas Day
weil, da because
weinen; schreien cry
weit far
weiter, (noch) mehr further
hier: **weitergeben, austauschen** share
etw weiter(hin) tun keep on doing sth
weitermachen mit continue
weiß white
welche(r, s) which; what

Welt world
auf der ganzen Welt all over the world
Weltkrieg world war
Weltraum space
Weltrekord world record
weltweit worldwide
wem, wen who
wenig little
ein wenig a little
wenige a few
weniger less
am wenigsten least
wenn, falls if
wer who
werden become, get
werfen throw
(Kfz-)Werkstatt garage
Werkzeug tool
Wert value
wert sein be worth
wessen whose
Westen west
Wettbewerb competition
Wetter weather
wichtig important
wie how, like, as, such as
Wie alt bist du/seid ihr? How old are you?
Wie geht es dir/Ihnen/euch? How are you?
wie man how to
Wie spät ist es? What time is it?
(um) wie viel Uhr (at) what time
wie viele how many
Wie war es? What was it like?
wieder; noch (ein)mal again
wiederholen repeat
Auf Wiedersehen. Goodbye.
wild wild
willkommen welcome
Wind wind
Winter winter
winzig tiny
wir we
wirklich really
wirklich, echt real
Wirklichkeit reality
Wirkung effect
Wirtschaft economy
Wissen knowledge
wissen; kennen know

Das soll wohl ein Witz sein! You must be joking!
Woche week
Wochenende weekend
am Wochenende at the weekend
Wochentag weekday
wo(hin) where
Wohltätigkeitsorganisation charity
wohnen live
Wohnung flat; apartment *(AE)*
Wohnzimmer living room
Wolkenkratzer skyscraper
wollen want
wollen, dass jd etw tut want sb to do sth
Wort word
Wörterbuch dictionary
Wortfeld wordbank
Wortnetz word web
Wortschatz vocabulary
wunderbar, wundervoll wonderful
wünschen wish; want
würde(st/n/t) would
Wurst, Würstchen sausage
würzig; scharf spicy
wütend angry

Z

Zahl; Ziffer number; figure
zählen count
Wir möchten bitte zahlen! Could we have the bill, please?
Zahn tooth *(pl* teeth*)*
sich die Zähne putzen brush one's teeth
Zebra zebra
zehn ten
Zeichen sign
zeichnen draw
Zeichnung, Skizze drawing
zeigen show
Zeile line
in letzter Zeit lately
Zeitschrift magazine
Zeitstrahl timeline
Zeitung newspaper
Zensur mark
Zentrum centre *(BE)*; center *(AE)*

Zeug stuff
Zeugnis; Empfehlungsschreiben reference
Ziel goal
zielen; anstreben aim
ziemlich quite; pretty *(informal)*
Zimmer room
Zitat quote
Zitrone lemon
Zivilisation, Kultur civilization
Zoo zoo
zu Fuß on foot
(Zu) Hilfe! Help!
Zucker sugar
zuerst, als Erstes (at) first
zufrieden happy
mit jdm zufrieden sein be pleased with sb
Zug train
Zuhause; Heimat home
zuhause home
(zu)hören listen (to)
Zukunft future
zum Beispiel for example (= e.g.)
zunehmen put on weight
zuordnen match (with/to)
zurück back
zurückblicken look back
zurückkehren return
zurückkommen come back
zurücklassen leave behind
zusammen together
Zusammenfassung summary
zusammenkommen get together
zusammenpassen match
zusätzlich additional
(zu)schicken send
zusehen, zuschauen watch
zustimmen agree
zuverlässig reliable
zuvor, vorher before
Zweck purpose
zwei two
zweimal twice
zweite(r, s) second
Zwiebel onion
zwischen between
zwölf twelve

Names

Girls/Women
Alice ['ælɪs]
Alison ['ælɪsən]
Amy ['eɪmi]
Avril ['ævrəl]
Barbara ['bɑːbrə]
Bhumika ['bʊmɪkə]
Bridget ['brɪdʒɪt]
Buffy ['bʌfi]
Caitlin [,keɪtlɪn]
Carol ['kærəl]
Carrie ['kæri]
Chantelle [,ʃɑːn'tel]
Devina [di'viːnə]
Eleanor ['elənə]
Ella ['elə]
Faith [feɪθ]
Farah ['færə]
Helen ['helən]
Indira ['ɪndɪrə]
Jennifer ['dʒenɪfə]
Joanna [dʒəʊ'ænə]
Joyce [dʒɔɪs]
Juno ['dʒuːnəʊ]
Kate [keɪt]
Kathy ['kæθi]
Katrina [kə'triːnə]
Kirsty ['kɜːsti]
Leah [liːə]
Lisa ['liːsə]
Loretta [lə'retə]
Lou Ann [luː'æn]
Louise [luˈiːz]
Mantheesh [mən'tiːʃ]
Marie [məˈriː]
Melinda [məˈlɪndə]
Nazneen [,næz'niːn]
Neena ['niːnə]
Pandora [pænˈdɔːrə]
Peggy ['pegi]
Penelope [pəˈneləpi]
Peris ['perɪs]
Pocahontas [,pɒkəˈhɒntəs]
Ramona [rəˈməʊnə]
Ronni ['rɒni]
Rosa ['rəʊzə]
Sally ['sæli]
Sandra ['sændrə]
Shay [ʃeɪ]
Shirley ['ʃɜːli]
Skinny ['skɪni]
Sonya ['sɒnjə]
Stacy ['steɪsi]
Star [stɑː]
Sue [suː]
Suniti [sʊ'niːti]
Tally ['tæli]
Taylor ['teɪlə]
Tortolita [,tɔːtəʊ'liːtə]
Victoria [vɪkˈtɔːriə]
Virgie ['vɜːdʒi]

Boys/Men
Abdul ['æbdʊl]
Abraham ['eɪbrəhæm]
Adrian ['eɪdriən]
Al [æl]
Alexander [,ælɪgˈzɑːndə]
Allan ['ælən]
André ['ɒndreɪ]
Andrew ['ændruː]
Arnold ['ɑːnld]
Bali ['bɑːli]
Barack ['bæræk]
Bobby ['bɒbi]
Buzz [bʌz]
Charles [tʃɑːlz]
Charlie ['tʃɑːli]
Chris [krɪs]
Colin ['kɒlɪn]
Cyril ['sɪrəl]
D. (= Delano) [diː, 'delənəʊ]
Dan [dæn]
David ['deɪvɪd]
Desmond ['dezmənd]
Dinyar ['diːndʒɑː]
Dylan ['dɪlən]
Eddie ['edi]
Estevan ['estəvæn]
F. (= Fitzgerald) [ef, fɪtsˈdʒerəld]
Felix ['fiːlɪks]
Franklin ['fræŋklɪn]
Frederick ['fredrɪk]
Gavin ['gævɪn]
Geoffrey ['dʒefri]
George [dʒɔːdʒ]
Geronimo [dʒəˈrɒnɪməʊ]
Godfrey ['gɒdfri]
Gordon ['gɔːdən]
Graham ['greɪəm]
Gregory ['gregəri]
Henry ['henri]
Jack [dʒæk]
Jamie ['dʒeɪmi]
Jeffrey ['dʒefri]
Jesus ['dʒiːzəs]
John [dʒɒn]
Junior ['dʒuːniə]
Kalaya'an ['kɑːləjɑːn]
Langston ['læŋkstən]
Leroy ['liːrɔɪ]
Leslie ['lezli]
Luther ['luːθə]
Mahatma [məˈhɑːtmə]
Manjit ['mʌndʒɪt]
Manny ['mæni]
Marcus ['mɑːkəs]
Martin ['mɑːtɪn]
Matthew ['mæθjuː]
Micah ['maɪkə]
Nat [næt]
Nathan ['neɪθn]
Neil [niːl]
Nick [nɪk]
Paris ['pærɪs]
Pat [pæt]
Paul [pɔːl]
Paulie ['pɔːli]
Peter ['piːtə]
Phil [fɪl]
Powhatan ['paʊətæn]
Printz [prɪnts]
Ralph [rælf]
Ratan [rəˈtæn]
Robert ['rɒbət]
Roger ['rɒdʒə]
Rowdy ['raʊdi]
Saddam [səˈdæm]
Saju ['sɑːwuː]
Sam [sæm]
Scott [skɒt]
Shel [ʃel]
Squanto ['skwɒntəʊ]
Sunil ['sʊnɪl]
Tariq ['tærɪk]
Tom [tɒm]
Tommy ['tɒmi]
Vasco ['væskəʊ]
Will [wɪl]
William ['wɪljəm]

Families
Adams ['ædəmz]
Aldrin ['ɔːldrɪn]
Armstrong ['ɑːmstrɒŋ]
Barber ['bɑːbə]
Been [biːn]
Benenate ['benəneɪt]
Bhandari [,bæn'dæri]
Black [blæk]
Board [bɔːd]
Bourque [bɜːk]
Bricusse ['braɪkʌs]
Brookshire ['brʊkʃə]
Brown [braʊn]
Burns [bɜːnz]
Bush [bʊʃ]
Capone [kəˈpəʊn]
Celeste [səˈlest]
Chahal [ʃæˈhɑːl]
Chaplin ['tʃæplɪn]
Charles [tʃɑːlz]
Chaturvedia [,tʃɑːtʊr'vediə]
Chettira ['tʃetɪrə]
Chisholm ['tʃɪzəm]
Churchill ['tʃɜːtʃɪl]
Cisneros [,sɪsˈneərəʊs]
Cody ['kəʊdi]
Columbus [kəˈlʌmbəs]
Cooper ['kuːpə]
Custer ['kʌstə]
D'Aluisio [dəluˈiːʒəʊ]
da Gama [dəˈgɑːmə]
Darbyshire ['dɑːbɪʃə]
Delacroix [,deləˈkrwɑː]
Ferguson ['fɜːgəsən]
Ford [fɔːd]
Forshaw ['fɔːʃɔː]
Gandhi ['gændi]
Gerrard ['dʒerɑːd]
Godrej ['gɒdreɪ]
Gomez ['gəʊmez]
Grant [grɑːnt]
Greer [grɪə]
Harlow ['hɑːləʊ]
Hewlett ['hjuːlɪt]
Hilfiger ['hɪlfɪgə]
Hitler ['hɪtlə]
Hughes [hjuːz]
Hussein [hʊˈseɪn]
Jackson ['dʒæksən]
Kahn [kɑːn]

255

Names

Kennedy [ˈkenədi]
Khan [kɑːn]
King [kɪŋ]
Kingsolver [ˈkɪŋsɒlvə]
Kowalik [kɒˈvɑːlɪk]
Lauren [ˈlɔːrən]
Lavigne [ləˈviːn]
Le Blanc [ləˈblɑ̃ː]
Lincoln [ˈlɪŋkən]
Lindbergh [ˈlɪndbɜːg]
Maggio [ˈmægiəʊ]
Mendoza [menˈdəʊzə]
Menzel [ˈmensl]
Mole [məʊl]
Namjoshi [næmˈjɒʃi]
Nehru [ˈneəruː]
Obama [əʊˈbɑːmə]
Ornadel [ɔːnəˈdel]
Packard [ˈpækɑːd]
Parks [pɑːks]
Parsons [pɑːsnz]
Percy [ˈpɜːsi]
Pineda [pɪˈniːdə]
Poncelet [ˈpɒnslət]
Prejean [ˈpreɪʒɑːn]
Rabelais [ˈræbəleɪ]
Rai [reɪ]
Ramsay [ˈræmzi]
Reddie [ˈredi]
Reuben [ˈruːbən]
Rolfe [rəʊf]
Roosevelt [ˈrəʊzəvelt]
Ruff [rʌf]
Ryan [ˈraɪən]
Sacco [ˈsækəʊ]
Sainte-Marie [ˌseɪnt məˈriː]
Shakespeare [ˈʃeɪkspɪə]
Silverstein [ˈsɪlvəstaɪn]
Smith [smɪθ]
Sonnier [ˈsɒniə]
Spirit [ˈspɪrɪt]
Stalin [ˈstɑːlɪn]
Stetson [ˈstetsən]
Tata [tæˈtɑː]
Taylor [ˈteɪlə]
Thomas [ˈtɒməs]
Townsend [ˈtaʊnzənd]
Trollope [ˈtrɒləp]
Tutu [ˈtuːtuː]
Vanzetti [vænˈzeti]
Washington [ˈwɒʃɪŋtən]

Westerfeld [ˈwestəfeld]
Weymouth [ˈweɪməθ]
White [waɪt]
Wood [wʊd]
Woodhouse [ˈwʊdhaʊs]

Other Names

agri-food [ˈægrɪ ˌfuːd]
Air Jordan [ˌeə ˈdʒɔːdn]
the Alamo [ðiˈæləməʊ]
Alexander the Great [ˌælɪɡˌzɑːndə ðə ˈɡreɪt]
Allah [ˈælə]
Amnesty [ˈæmnəsti]
Amnesty International [ˌæmnəstiˌɪntəˈnæʃnl]
Apache [əˈpætʃi]
Apollo [əˈpɒləʊ]
Apollo 11 [əˌpɒləʊ ɪˈlevn]
Arapaho [əˈræpəhəʊ]
Banbury Road [ˈbænbəri ˌrəʊd]
Barbie [ˈbɑːbi]
BBC [ˌbiː biː ˈsiː]
Bigfoot [ˈbɪɡfʊt]
bindi [ˈbɪndi]
Bollywhat [ˈbɒliwɒt]
Bollywood [ˈbɒliwʊd]
Brahman [ˈbrɑːmən]
Buckingham Palace [ˌbʌkɪŋəm ˈpæləs]
Buffalo Bill [ˌbʌfələʊ ˈbɪl]
cent [sent]
chakra [ˈtʃʌkrə]
Cheyenne [ˌʃaɪˈæn]
Chief [tʃiːf]
Clearasil [ˈklɪərəsɪl]
Coco Pop [ˈkəʊkəʊ ˌpɒp]
Comanche [kəˈmæntʃi]
Council of Europe [ˌkaʊnsl əv ˈjʊərəp]
Dead Man Walking [ˌded mæn ˈwɔːkɪŋ]
Diwali [dɪˈwɑːli]
dollar [ˈdɒlə]
East India Company [ˌiːst ˈɪndiə ˌkʌmpni]
the Eiffel Tower [ðiˌaɪfəl ˈtaʊə]
Ellis [ˈelis]

EU (= European Union) [ˌiː ˈjuː, ˌjʊərəˌpiːən ˈjuːnjən]
Euro [ˈjʊərəʊ]
Facebook [ˈfeɪsbʊk]
Flopnik [ˈflɒpnɪk]
Glad [ɡlæd]
the Great Wall of China [ðə ˌɡreɪt ˌwɔːl əv ˈtʃaɪnə]
Hallelujah [ˌhælɪˈluːjə]
Harlem Renaissance [ˌhɑːləm rɪˈneɪsəns]
Heathrow Airport [ˌhiːθrəʊ ˈeəpɔːt]
Hindi [ˈhɪndi]
hip hop [ˈhɪp hɒp]
Human Rights Watch [ˌhjuːmən ˈraɪts ˌwɒtʃ]
Inuit [ˈɪnuɪt]
Isaiah [aɪˈzaɪə]
Islam [ˈɪslɑːm]
IT (= Information Technology) [ˌaɪ ˈtiː]
jambalaya [ˌdʒæmbəˈlaɪə]
jazz [dʒæz]
Kiowa [ˈkiːəwɑː]
Kiwi [ˈkiːwiː]
KKK (= Ku Klux Klan) [ˌkeɪ keɪ ˈkeɪ, ˌkuː klʌks ˈklæn]
Kmart [ˈkeɪmɑːt]
La Esperanza [lɑːˌespəˈrænzə]
Lacrosse [ləˈkrɒs]
Lakota [ləˈkəʊtə]
Latino [læˈtiːnəʊ]
Lord [lɔːd]
Mafia [ðə ˈmæfiə]
Malcolm X [ˌmælkəm ˈeks]
Marshall Plan [ˈmɑːʃl plæn]
Mayflower [ˈmeɪˌflaʊə]
Model T [ˌmɒdl ˈtiː]
monster [ˈmɒnstə]
Motorola [ˌməʊtəˈrəʊlə]
Namaste [nʌmʌsˈteɪ]
Nano [ˈnɑːnəʊ]
NASA [ˈnæsə]
Navaho [ˈnævəhəʊ]
Nazi [ˈnɑːtsi]
Nemi [ˈnemi]
New Deal [ˌnjuː ˈdiːl]
Newspaper Rock [ˈnjuːzˌpeɪpə rɒk]

Nivea [ˈnɪviə]
OzHarvest [ˌɒz ˈhɑːvɪst]
Paddington [ˈpædɪŋtən]
Pangaea [pænˈdʒiːə]
the Boston Tea Party [ðə ˌbɒstən ˈtiː ˌpɑːti]
Pontiac [ˈpɒntiæk]
pop [pɒp]
Poseidon [pəˈsaɪdn]
Prohibition [ˌprəʊɪˈbɪʃn]
Walking Purchase [ˈwɔːkɪŋ ˌpɜːtʃəs]
Random [ˈrændəm]
the Red Fort [ðə red ˈfɔːt]
Harlem Renaissance [ˌhɑːləm rɪˈneɪsəns]
rez [rez]
rugby [ˈrʌɡbi]
Safeway [ˈseɪfweɪ]
sari [ˈsɑːri]
Scouting for girls [ˌskaʊtɪŋ fə ˈɡɜːlz]
Sears [sɪəz]
Silicon Valley [ˌsɪlɪkən ˈvæli]
Sioux [suː]
sitar [sɪˈtɑː]
Sitting Bull [ˌsɪtɪŋ ˈbʊl]
Spirit of St Louis [ˌspɪrɪt əv sənt ˈluːɪs]
Spokane [spəʊˈkæn]
Sputnik [ˈspʊtnɪk]
Squaw Boy [ˈskwɔː ˌbɔɪ]
St Louis [sənt ˈluːɪs]
Steppenwolf [ˈstepnwʊlf]
Sting [stɪŋ]
Taj Mahal [ˌtɑːdʒ məˈhɑːl]
Tata [tæˈtɑː]
Tata Motor Limited [tæˌtɑː ˈməʊtə ˌlɪmɪtɪd]
The Bean Trees [ðə ˈbiːn ˌtriːz]
Timex [ˈtaɪmeks]
Tonto [ˈtɒntəʊ]
Twitter [ˈtwɪtə]
UFO [ˌjuː ef ˈəʊ]
Uglies [ˈʌɡliz]
UN (= United Nations) [ˌjuː ˈen]
Underground Railroad [ˌʌndəɡraʊnd ˈreɪlrəʊd]

Names

the United Nations [ðə juːˌnaɪtɪd ˈneɪʃnz]
Venus [ˈviːnəs]
Walking Purchase [ˈwɔːkɪŋ ˌpɜːtʃəs]
Wampanoag [ˌwɒmpəˈnəʊæɡ]
War of Independence [ˌwɔːr əv ˌɪndɪˈpendəns]
World Congress [ˌwɜːld ˈkɒŋɡres]
Young Minds [jʌŋ ˈmaɪndz]

Geographical Names
Afghanistan [æfˈɡænɪstɑːn]
Africa [ˈæfrɪkə]
Alabama [ˌæləˈbæmə]
Alaska [əˈlæskə]
Asia [ˈeɪʒə]
Australia [ɒˈstreɪliə]
Bahamas [bəˈhɑːməz]
Bangladesh [ˌbæŋɡləˈdeʃ]
Beijing [ˌbeɪˈdʒɪŋ]
Belarus [ˌbeləˈruːs]
Berlin [bɜːˈlɪn]
Bombay [ˌbɒmˈbeɪ]
Boston [ˈbɒstən]
Bristol [ˈbrɪstəl]
Burma [ˈbɜːmə]
Calcutta [kælˈkʌtə]
Cambodia [kæmˈbəʊdiə]
Canada [ˈkænədə]
Canary Islands [kəˌneəri ˈaɪləndz]
Canyonlands National Park [ˌkænjənˌlændz ˌnæʃnəl ˈpɑːk]
Cardiff [ˈkɑːdɪf]
Carnegie Hall [ˌkɑːnəɡi ˈhɔːl]
Chicago [ʃɪˈkɑːɡəʊ]
China [ˈtʃaɪnə]
Croydon [ˈkrɔɪdən]
Cuba [ˈkjuːbə]
the Czech Republic [ðə ˌtʃek rɪˈpʌblɪk]
Delaware [ˈdeləweə]
Delhi [ˈdeli]
Denmark [ˈdenmɑːk]
Ecuador [ˈekwədɔː]
Ellis Island [ˌelɪs ˈaɪlənd]
Florida [ˈflɒrɪdə]
Frankfurt [ˈfræŋkfɜːt]
Ganges [ˈɡændʒiːz]
Geneva [dʒəˈniːvə]
Georgia [ˈdʒɔːdʒə]
Gettysburg [ˈɡetɪzbɜːɡ]
Greece [ɡriːs]
Gulf of Mexico [ˌɡʌlf əv ˈmeksɪkəʊ]
Gurgaon [ˈɡɜːrɡaʊn]
Hawaii [həˈwaɪi]
Hiroshima [hɪˈrɒʃɪmə]
Hollywood [ˈhɒliwʊd]
Illinois [ˌɪləˈnɔɪ]
India [ˈɪndiə]
Indore [ɪnˈdɔː]
Indus [ˈɪndəs]
Iran [ɪˈrɑːn]
Iraq [ɪˈrɑːk]
Jamestown [ˈdʒeɪmztaʊn]
Japan [dʒəˈpæn]
Johannesburg [dʒəʊˈhænɪsbɜːɡ]
Kansas [ˈkænzəs]
Kashmir [ˌkæʃˈmɪə]
Korea [kəˈrɪə]
Lammas [ˈlæməs]
Lebanon [ˈlebənən]
Little Bighorn [ˌlɪtl ˌbɪɡˈhɔːn]
London [ˈlʌndən]
Macedonia [ˌmæsɪˈdəʊniə]
Malaga [ˈmæləɡə]
Mali [ˈmɑːli]
Massachusetts [ˌmæsəˈtʃuːsɪts]
Memphis [ˈmemfɪs]
Mexico [ˈmeksɪkəʊ]
Middle East [ˌmɪdl ˈiːst]
Mississippi [ˌmɪsɪˈsɪpi]
Missouri [mɪˈzʊəri]
Moscow [ˈmɒskəʊ]
Mount Everest [ˌmaʊnt ˈevərɪst]
Mount Snowdon [ˌmaʊnt ˈsnəʊdn]
Mumbai [ˌmʊmˈbaɪ]
Myanmar [ˈmiːənmɑː]
Nagasaki [ˌnæɡəˈsɑːki]
the Netherlands [ðə ˈneðələndz]
New Amsterdam [ˌnjuː ˈæmstədæm]
New Delhi [njuː ˈdeli]
New Hampshire [njuː ˈhæmpʃə]
New York [njuː ˈjɔːk]
New Zealand [njuː ˈziːlənd]
the Nile [ðə ˈnaɪl]
North America [ˌnɔːθ əˈmerɪkə]
North Carolina [ˌnɔːθ kærəˈlaɪnə]
North Korea [ˌnɔːθ kəˈrɪə]
the North Sea [ðə ˌnɔːθ ˈsiː]
Northern California [ˌnɔːðn kæləˈfɔːniə]
Notting Hill Gate [ˌnɒtɪŋ hɪl ˈɡeɪt]
Ohio [əʊˈhaɪəʊ]
Oklahoma [ˌəʊkləˈhəʊmə]
Ottawa [ˈɒtəwə]
Oxford [ˈɒksfəd]
Pakistan [ˌpɑːkɪˈstɑːn]
Paris [ˈpærɪs]
Pawtucket [pɔːˈtʌkɪt]
Pearl Harbo(u)r [ˌpɜːl ˈhɑːbə]
Pembrokeshire [ˈpembrʊkʃə]
Plymouth [ˈplɪməθ]
Plymouth Rock [ˌplɪməθ ˈrɒk]
Poland [ˈpəʊlənd]
Portugal [ˈpɔːtʃʊɡl]
Reardan [ˈrɪədn]
Salford [ˈsɔːlfəd]
Sand Creek [ˌsænd ˈkriːk]
Saudi Arabia [ˌsaʊdi əˈreɪbiə]
Siberia [saɪˈbɪəriə]
Somalia [səˈmɑːliə]
Somerset [ˈsʌməset]
South Asia [ˌsaʊθ ˈeɪʒə]
South Carolina [ˌsaʊθ kærəˈlaɪnə]
South-East Asia [ˌsaʊθiːst ˈeɪʒə]
Soviet Union [ˌsəʊviət ˈjuːniən]
Spain [speɪn]
Sri Lanka [srɪ ˈlæŋkə]
Stanford [ˈstænfəd]
Summertown [ˈsʌməˌtaʊn]
Sydney [ˈsɪdni]
Taunton [ˈtɔːntən]
Texas [ˈteksəs]
Tibet [tɪˈbet]
Tokyo [ˈtəʊkiəʊ]
the United States [ðə juːˌnaɪtɪd ˈsteɪts]
Utah [ˈjuːtɑː]
Vietnam [ˌviːetˈnæm]
Virginia [vəˈdʒɪniə]
Wellpinit [ˈwelpɪnɪt]
the West Indies [ðə ˌwest ˈɪndiz]
Wounded Knee [ˌwuːndɪd ˈniː]
Yalta [ˈjæltə]
Yemen [ˈjemən]

Numbers/Months

Numbers

0	oh, zero, nil [əʊ, ˈzɪərəʊ, nɪl]	101	one hundred and one [wʌn ˌhʌndrəd ən ˈwʌn]	11th	eleventh [ɪˈlevnθ]
1	one [wʌn]	102	one hundred and two [wʌn ˌhʌndrəd ən ˈtuː]	12th	twelfth [twelfθ]
2	two [tuː]			13th	thirteenth [ˌθɜːˈtiːnθ]
3	three [θriː]	110	one hundred and ten [wʌn ˌhʌndrəd ən ˈten]	14th	fourteenth [ˌfɔːˈtiːnθ]
4	four [fɔː]			15th	fifteenth [ˌfɪfˈtiːnθ]
5	five [faɪv]	200	two hundred [tuː ˈhʌndrəd]	16th	sixteenth [ˌsɪksˈtiːnθ]
6	six [sɪks]			17th	seventeenth [ˌsevnˈtiːnθ]
7	seven [sevn]				
8	eight [eɪt]	1,000	a/one thousand [ə/wʌn ˈθauznd]	18th	eighteenth [ˌeɪˈtiːnθ]
9	nine [naɪn]			19th	nineteenth [ˌnaɪnˈtiːnθ]
10	ten [ten]	1,001	one thousand and one [wʌn ˌθauznd ən ˈwʌn]	20th	twentieth [ˈtwentiəθ]
11	eleven [ɪˈlevn]			21st	twenty-first [ˌtwentiˈfɜːst]
12	twelve [twelv]	1,111	one thousand one hundred and eleven [wʌn ˈθauznd wʌn ˌhʌndrəd ən ɪˈlevn]	22nd	twenty-second [ˌtwentiˈsekənd]
13	thirteen [ˌθɜːˈtiːn]				
14	fourteen [ˌfɔːˈtiːn]			23rd	twenty-third [ˌtwentiˈθɜːd]
15	fifteen [ˌfɪfˈtiːn]	2,000	two thousand [tuː ˈθauznd]		
16	sixteen [ˌsɪksˈtiːn]	10,000	ten thousand [ten ˈθauznd]		
17	seventeen [ˌsevnˈtiːn]	100,000	a/one hundred thousand [ə/wʌn ˌhʌndrəd ˈθauznd]	30th	thirtieth [ˈθɜːtiəθ]
18	eighteen [ˌeɪˈtiːn]			40th	fortieth [ˈfɔːtiəθ]
19	nineteen [ˌnaɪnˈtiːn]	1,000,000	a/one million [ə/wʌn ˈmɪljən]	50th	fiftieth [ˈfɪftiəθ]
20	twenty [ˈtwenti]			60th	sixtieth [ˈsɪkstiəθ]
21	twenty-one [ˌtwentiˈwʌn]	1,000,000,000	a/one billion [ə/wʌn ˈbɪljən]	70th	seventieth [ˈsevntiəθ]
22	twenty-two [ˌtwentiˈtuː]			80th	eightieth [ˈeɪtiəθ]
				90th	ninetieth [ˈnaɪntiəθ]
30	thirty [ˈθɜːti]	1st	first [fɜːst]	100th	hundredth [ˈhʌndrədθ]
40	forty [ˈfɔːti]	2nd	second [ˈsekənd]		
50	fifty [ˈfɪfti]	3rd	third [θɜːd]	½	a/one half [ə/wʌn ˈhɑːf]
60	sixty [ˈsɪksti]	4th	fourth [fɔːθ]	⅓	a/one third [ə/wʌn ˈθɜːd]
70	seventy [ˈsevnti]	5th	fifth [fɪfθ]	¼	a/one quarter [ə/wʌn ˈkwɔːtə]
80	eighty [ˈeɪti]	6th	sixth [sɪksθ]	⅛	a/one eighth [ə/wʌn ˈeɪtθ]
90	ninety [ˈnaɪnti]	7th	seventh [sevnθ]	¾	three quarters [θriː ˈkwɔːtəz]
100	a/one hundred [ə/wʌn ˈhʌndrəd]	8th	eighth [eɪtθ]		
		9th	ninth [naɪnθ]		
		10th	tenth [tenθ]		

Months

January [ˈdʒænjuəri]
February [ˈfebruəri]
March [mɑːtʃ]
April [ˈeɪprəl]

May [meɪ]
June [dʒuːn]
July [dʒʊˈlaɪ]
August [ˈɔːgəst]

September [sepˈtembə]
October [ɒkˈtəʊbə]
November [nəʊˈvembə]
December [dɪˈsembə]

Irregular verbs

infinitive	simple past	past participle	
babysit ['beɪbɪˌsɪt]	babysat ['beɪbɪˌsæt]	babysat ['beɪbɪˌsæt]	babysitten
be [biː]	was/were [wɒz/wɜː]	been [biːn]	sein
beat [biːt]	beat [biːt]	beaten [biːtn]	schlagen; besiegen
become [bɪˈkʌm]	became [bɪˈkeɪm]	become [bɪˈkʌm]	werden
begin [bɪˈgɪn]	began [bɪˈgæn]	begun [bɪˈgʌn]	anfangen, beginnen
bend [bend]	bent [bent]	bent [bent]	biegen
bet [bet]	bet/betted [bet/ˈbetɪd]	bet/betted [bet/ˈbetɪd]	wetten
bleed [bliːd]	bled [bled]	bled [bled]	bluten
break [breɪk]	broke [brəʊk]	broken [ˈbrəʊkən]	(sich) brechen
bring [brɪŋ]	brought [brɔːt]	brought [brɔːt]	(mit)bringen
build [bɪld]	built [bɪlt]	built [bɪlt]	bauen
burn [bɜːn]	burnt/burned [bɜːnt/bɜːnd]	burnt/burned [bɜːnt/bɜːnd]	(ver)brennen
buy [baɪ]	bought [bɔːt]	bought [bɔːt]	kaufen
cast [kɑːst]	cast [kɑːst]	cast [kɑːst]	werfen über, verteilen
catch [kætʃ]	caught [kɔːt]	caught [kɔːt]	fangen
choose [tʃuːz]	chose [tʃəʊz]	chosen [tʃəʊzn]	wählen; sich entscheiden
come [kʌm]	came [keɪm]	come [kʌm]	kommen
cost [kɒst]	cost [kɒst]	cost [kɒst]	kosten
cut [kʌt]	cut [kʌt]	cut [kʌt]	schneiden
do [duː]	did [dɪd]	done [dʌn]	tun, machen
draw [drɔː]	drew [druː]	drawn [drɔːn]	zeichnen; hineinziehen, verwickeln
dream [driːm]	dreamt/dreamed [dremt/driːmd]	dreamt/dreamed [dremt/driːmd]	träumen
drink [drɪŋk]	drank [dræŋk]	drunk [drʌŋk]	trinken
drive [draɪv]	drove [drəʊv]	driven [drɪvn]	fahren; vertreiben
eat [iːt]	ate [eɪt]	eaten [iːtn]	essen
fall [fɔːl]	fell [fel]	fallen [ˈfɔːlən]	fallen
feed [fiːd]	fed [fed]	fed [fed]	satt machen, ernähren, zu essen geben, füttern
feel [fiːl]	felt [felt]	felt [felt]	(sich) fühlen
fight [faɪt]	fought [fɔːt]	fought [fɔːt]	(sich) streiten; (be)kämpfen
find [faɪnd]	found [faʊnd]	found [faʊnd]	finden
fly [flaɪ]	flew [fluː]	flown [fləʊn]	fliegen
forbid [fəˈbɪd]	forbade [fəˈbæd]	forbidden [fəˈbɪdn]	verbieten
forget [fəˈget]	forgot [fəˈgɒt]	forgotten [fəˈgɒtn]	vergessen
forgive [fəˈgɪv]	forgave [fəˈgeɪv]	forgiven [fəˈgɪvn]	vergeben, verzeihen
get [get]	got [gɒt]	got [gɒt]	erhalten, bekommen; werden; holen, kaufen
give [gɪv]	gave [geɪv]	given [gɪvn]	geben; nennen, angeben
go [gəʊ]	went [went]	gone [gɒn]	gehen; fahren
grow [grəʊ]	grew [gruː]	grown [grəʊn]	wachsen, größer werden; anbauen; werden
hang [hæŋ]	hung [hʌŋ]	hung [hʌŋ]	(auf)hängen; fallen
have [hæv]	had [hæd]	had [hæd]	haben; essen, trinken
hear [hɪə]	heard [hɜːd]	heard [hɜːd]	hören
hide [haɪd]	hid [hɪd]	hidden [hɪdn]	verstecken
hit [hɪt]	hit [hɪt]	hit [hɪt]	schlagen; treffen; stoßen
hold [həʊld]	held [held]	held [held]	halten
hurt [hɜːt]	hurt [hɜːt]	hurt [hɜːt]	wehtun, schmerzen
keep [kiːp]	kept [kept]	kept [kept]	aufbewahren; (be)halten; halten; unterbringen
know [nəʊ]	knew [njuː]	known [nəʊn]	wissen; kennen
lead [liːd]	led [led]	led [led]	(an)führen
learn [lɜːn]	learnt/learned [lɜːnt/lɜːnd]	learnt/learned [lɜːnt/lɜːnd]	lernen

Irregular verbs

leave [liːv]	left [left]	left [left]	(weg)gehen; abfahren; verlassen
lend [lend]	lent [lent]	lent [lent]	leihen
let [let]	let [let]	let [let]	lassen
lie [laɪ]	lay [leɪ]	lain [leɪn]	liegen; sich hinlegen
lose [luːz]	lost [lɒst]	lost [lɒst]	verlieren
make [meɪk]	made [meɪd]	made [meɪd]	machen; lassen
mean [miːn]	meant [ment]	meant [ment]	bedeuten; meinen
meet [miːt]	met [met]	met [met]	(sich) treffen
pay [peɪ]	paid [peɪd]	paid [peɪd]	(be)zahlen
put [pʊt]	put [pʊt]	put [pʊt]	setzen, legen, stellen
read [riːd]	read [red]	read [red]	lesen
ride [raɪd]	rode [rəʊd]	ridden [rɪdn]	fahren (mit); reiten
ring [rɪŋ]	rang [ræŋ]	rung [rʌŋ]	anrufen
rise [raɪz]	rose [rəʊz]	risen [rɪzn]	steigen
run [rʌn]	ran [ræn]	run [rʌn]	laufen, rennen; fließen
say [seɪ]	said [sed]	said [sed]	sagen
see [siː]	saw [sɔː]	seen [siːn]	sehen; treffen
sell [sel]	sold [səʊld]	sold [səʊld]	verkaufen
send [send]	sent [sent]	sent [sent]	(zu)schicken
set [set]	set [set]	set [set]	setzen
sew [səʊ]	sewed [səʊd]	sewed/sewn [səʊd/səʊn]	nähen; stopfen
shine [ʃaɪn]	shone/shined [ʃɒn/ʃaɪnd]	shone/shined [ʃɒn/ʃaɪnd]	scheinen, glänzen
shoot [ʃuːt]	shot [ʃɒt]	shot [ʃɒt]	(er)schießen
show [ʃəʊ]	showed [ʃəʊd]	shown [ʃəʊn]	zeigen
sing [sɪŋ]	sang [sæŋ]	sung [sʌŋ]	singen
sink [sɪŋk]	sank/sunk [sæŋk/sʌŋk]	sunk [sʌŋk]	untergehen, sinken
sit [sɪt]	sat [sæt]	sat [sæt]	sitzen
slay [sleɪ]	slew [sluː]	slain [sleɪn]	ermorden
sleep [sliːp]	slept [slept]	slept [slept]	schlafen
smell [smel]	smelt/smelled [smelt/smeld]	smelt/smelled [smelt/smeld]	riechen; duften
speak [spiːk]	spoke [spəʊk]	spoken [ˈspəʊkən]	sprechen, reden
spend [spend]	spent [spend]	spent [spent]	verbringen *(Zeit)*; ausgeben *(Geld)*
spit [spɪt]	spat/spit [spæt/spɪt]	spat/spit [spæt/spɪt]	spucken
split [splɪt]	split [splɪt]	split [splɪt]	teilen
spread [spred]	spred [spred]	spred [spred]	sich aus-/verbreiten
spring [sprɪŋ]	sprang [spræŋ]	sprung [sprʌŋ]	herrühren; wachsen aus
stand [stænd]	stood [stʊd]	stood [stʊd]	stehen
steal [stiːl]	stole [stəʊl]	stolen [ˈstəʊlən]	stehlen
strike [straɪk]	struck [strʌk]	struck [strʌk]	schlagen
swim [swɪm]	swam [swæm]	swum [swʌm]	schwimmen
take [teɪk]	took [tʊk]	taken [ˈteɪkən]	bringen; nehmen; dauern; erfordern; übernehmen
teach [tiːtʃ]	taught [tɔːt]	taught [tɔːt]	unterrichten; beibringen
tell [tel]	told [təʊld]	told [təʊld]	sagen; erzählen
think [θɪŋk]	thought [θɔːt]	thought [θɔːt]	denken, glauben, meinen; nachdenken, sich überlegen
throw [θrəʊ]	threw [θruː]	thrown [θrəʊn]	werfen
understand [ˌʌndəˈstænd]	understood [ˌʌndəˈstʊd]	understood [ˌʌndəˈstʊd]	verstehen
wake [weɪk]	woke [wəʊk]	woken [ˈwəʊkən]	(auf)wecken; aufwachen
wear [weə]	wore [wɔː]	worn [wɔːn]	tragen; anziehen
weave [wiːv]	wove [wəʊv]	woven [wəʊvn]	weben, flechten
win [wɪn]	won [wʌn]	won [wʌn]	gewinnen
write [raɪt]	wrote [rəʊt]	written [rɪtn]	schreiben

Bild- und Textquellen

Bildquellen

|akg-images GmbH, Berlin: 36 (Lincoln), 38 (Lindbergh), 43; ap 40 (Napalmangriff). |alamy images, Abingdon/Oxfordshire: 15 (Teenager), 22, 69 (Mann), 78; Frazier Photolibrary 113 (Obdachloser); GODONG/DELOCHE/BSIP 145; Robert Harding 32 (Gedenkstein); © AJSHowden Photography 97 (Mann), 99; © Archive Images 36; © dbimages 99 (Muslimin); © Michael Dwyer / Alamy 28 (Museum); © stockex 99 (Frau). |alimdi.net, Deisenhofen: Michael Peuckert 108. |Art Resource, New York: 30 (Pocahontas). |Associated Press, Frankfurt/M.: AP Photo/H. Rumph J 28. |Blickwinkel, Witten: M. Lohmann 93 (Mädchen). |Bos, Doris, Hanau: 80 (Fahrzeug), 82 (Zeichnung), 86, 150 (Inder). |bpk–Bildagentur, Berlin: Dietmar Katz 31 (Hafen). |Bridgeman Images, Berlin: 27 (Flugblatt), 36. |Bulls Pressedienst GmbH, Frankfurt am Main: Lise Myhre/Strandcomics 63 (Comic), 70. |dreamstime.com, Brentwood: 33. |Druwe & Polastri, Cremlingen/Weddel: 73. |Eckardt-Scheurig, Wiesbaden: 86 (Europäer und Inder), 88 (Schileder). |Focus Photo- u. Presseagentur GmbH, Hamburg: 145 (Ernährung Afrika); Peter Menzel 145 (Ernährung Amerika); © Peter Menzel /Hungry Planet, China, Buch: So isst der Mensch 17, 19. |Fotodesign Matthias Stolt, Hamburg: 65 (Senioren und Asiatin). |fotolia.com, New York: 63 (Blumen), 63 (Piktogramm), 64 (Ingenieur), 72, 73, 74, 80 (Kuh), 80 (Markt), 97, 98 (Fahrbahnmarkierung), 105, 108 (Schwangere); Bilderjet 89 (Verkäuferin); Monkey Business 23; RioPatuca Images 144; Sunnydays 126 (Elefant); © absolut 65 (Seniorin und Frau); © jo 108 (Wolken). |Getty Images, München: 32, 44 (Sitting Bull), 97, 101, 152 (Hand); AFP 37 (Martin Luther King); Alex Wong 42 (Obama); WireImage 144 (Laufsteg); © Bettmann/CORBIS 36 (Rosa Parks). |Hardy, Helen: 62, 62, 62. |Henrich, Nina, Hamburg: 124, 125. |Huber, André, Ingolstadt: 3. |Human Rights Convention: 49 (Shirts). |IBM Almaden Research Center, San Jose/Californien: Courtesy of International Business Machines Corporation, © 2013 International Business Machines Corporation. 41 (Silicon Valley). |Interfoto, München: 63 (Dan - Mitten im Leben), 74, 75, 140, 140, 140, 140; Mary Evans / United Artists / Ronald Grand Archive 27, 38. |iStockphoto.com, Calgary: 27 (Mayflower), 30, 63 (Comic), 64, 64, 64 (Hände), 65 (Kinder), 65 (Senior und Jugendlicher), 66, 71, 97, 149 (Gruppenbild); junkal22 115; Ridofranz 99; Steve Corrigan 81 (Flagge); © Carmen Martínez Banús 65 (Familie); © Christopher Steer 103, 152 (Fußabdruck); © Claudia Dewald 108 (Kleinkind); © Rich Legg 108 (Braut). |Jackson, Amanda: 97 (Hütte), 102, 102. |K. und U. Schuster, Oberursel: Liaison 28 (Freiheitsstatue). |Keystone Pressedienst, Hamburg: 27 (Mondlandung), 41, 64 (PC). |KNA - Katholische Nachrichten-Agentur, Bonn: 79 (Mumbai). |Leinonen, Seppo / seppo.net: Seppo Leinonen 93 (Cartoon). |Maciej Dakowicz Photography: 46 (Schule). |mauritius images GmbH, Mittenwald: Jose Fuster 107. |MEV Verlag GmbH, Augsburg: 80 (Taj Mahal). |Michael Biermann, Bröthen: 73. |Michael, M., Ilsenburg: 20. |Microsoft Deutschland GmbH, München: 23, 23, 23, 23, 23, 23, 23, 23, 23, 56, 102. |Neuss, Evelyn, Hannover: 141. |Otfried Börner, Hamburg: 54. |Pätzold, Kathrin, Berlin: 141, 141 (Puppen). |Pedder, Penelope Rose: 62. |Picture-Alliance GmbH, Frankfurt/M.: 27 (Freiheitsstatue), 140; Abaca 57, 148 (Supreme Court); Bildagentur Huber/Gräfenhain 29; dpa 37 (Obama), 63 (Indische Hochzeit), 69; dpa/ Rieger 41 (Ground Zero); dpa/K.-J. Hildenbrand 148; Everett Collection 37 (Malcolm X); KPA/TopFoto 80 (Gandhi); Mary Evans / National Archives 33 (Plakat); The Advertising Archives 11, 11; united archives 39 (Wall Street Crash). |pixelio media GmbH, München: Marcel Klinger 29. |Rogge, Bernd, Gründau-Breitenborn: 84. |Shutterstock.com, New York: 31 (Washington), 80, 97, 106. |Stöber, Georg Dr., Braunschweig: 82 (Mohenjo Daro). |Süddeutsche Zeitung - Photo, München: Scherl 39. |The Advertising Archives, London: 11. |Tia Ralhan: 62. |Tonn, Dieter, Bovenden-Lenglern: 40. |TV-yesterday, München: W. M. Weber 28. |ullstein bild, Berlin: 9, 34 (Petroglyphen), 36 (Ku Klux Klan), 46, 46 (Inderin), 51 (Eleanor Roosevelt), 58, 58 (DEAD MAN WALKING), 80 (cricket), 80 (sari), 82 (Medaillon), 83 (Gandhi), 86 (Call Center), 96, 121 (Penn und Sarandon), 147 (Flüchtlingslager), 150 (Nano); ddp 40 (Atombombenexplosion); Granger Collection 27, 29, 30, 32, 146 (THE TRAIL OF TEARS); Imagno 38; SIPA 126 (Lisa Ray); united archives 82 ((East India Company). |Unilever Deutschland GmbH, Hamburg: 12. |Visum Foto GmbH, Hannover: Panos Pictures 89, 151 (Textilfabrik). |wikimedia.commons: 32 (Dollar). |Xinhua, Berlin: 108 (Paralympics). |Zwick, Joachim, Gießen: 264.

Bild- und Textquellen

Textquellen

20	„Hunger in a land of plenty", extracted from IPS-Inter Press Service report (http://ipsnews.net/news.asp?idnews=52061);
21	„Not fair", vereinfachte Version, Oxfam Canada, Toronto, Canada;
26	"How they eat in heaven". In: Barbara Kingsolver. *The Bean Trees*. Harper and Row, New York, 2007;
37	„I, too, sing America". Langston Hughes;
54	Leroy White's (†) letters to Britta Stehle and class, Heinrich-Böll-Schule, 2009;
56	„Kids Against the death penalty". Gavin Been et al. (http://www.kadp.org);
66	Auszug aus *The Secret Diary of Adrian Mole Aged 13 ¾* © Susan Townsend. *The Secret Diary of Adrian Mole Aged 13 ¾*. Verlag Moritz Diesterweg, Frankfurt, 1990, S. 133;
68	Auszug aus *(Un)Arranged Marriage* © Bali Rai. *(Un)Arranged Marriage*. Corgi Books, 2009;
70	„The letter" © Alison Chisholm;
72	„Cat my Cat", Dylan Thomas, 1950;
73	„A house of my own" © Sandra Cisneros;
93	"Child labour in India" © Oxfam UK, 2007 (http://www.oxfam.org.uk/coolplanet/kidsweb/world/india/indioxf3.htm);
100	„Dreams", Langston Hughes, „Look to the future", Leah Harlow, „The future", David Darbyshire, „Features of the Future", Robert Reuben;
102	Vereinfachter Internetauftritt (http://www.lammas.org.uk/);
110/111	Auszug aus *Uglies* © Scott Westerfeld. *Uglies*. New York, Simon Pulse, 2005, S. 77-81;
112/113	„Hunger in a world of plenty", Dinyar Godrej © New Internationalist 1995;
114/117	"How to fight monsters". In: Sherman Alexie. *The Absolute True Diary of a Part-Time Indian*. Little, Brown and Company, New York/Boston, 2007, S. 54–66;
120/121	Auszug aus *Dead Man Walking* © Helen Prejean. *Dead Man Walking*. London, Harper Collins, 1993, S. 115–118;
122/123	Auszug aus „*Star Rubbish*" © Joanna Trollope. In: Brown, Sarah & Gil McNeil (Hgg.). *Summer Magic*. Bloomsbury, 2003;
126/127	*BollyWhat? The Bollywood FAQs* (http://www.bollywhat.com/faq.html);
127	„Bird woman" © Suniti Namjoshi. In: Suniti Namjoshi. *Feminist fables*. Sheba Feminist Press, London, 1981, S. 16.

Bild- und Textquellen

Liedquellen

22	„Hunger song", Text und Musik: Joyce Brookshire ℗ & © Emworld Records;
28	Auszug aus „Monster", Text und Musik: John Kay und Jerry Edmonton ℗ & © Rainman, Inc;
29	Auszug aus „Englishman in New York", Text und Musik: Sting ℗ & © A&M/Universal music;
33	„Now that the buffalo's gone", Text und Musik: Buffy Sainte-Marie ℗ & © Vanguard;
66	„Put another log on the fire", Text und Musik: Shel Silverstein;
72	„This ain't a love song", Text und Musik: Scouting for girls ℗ & © 2010 Sony Music Entertainment UK Limited;
101	„Breakaway", Text und Musik: Bridget Louise Benenate, Matthew R.T. Gerrard und Avril Ramona Lavigne.
104/5	„One Tribe", Text und Musik: Stacy Ferguson, William Adams, Jamie Gomez, Allan Pineda und Printz Board ℗ & © Interscope Records;
105	„If I ruled the world", Text und Musik: Cyril Ornadel und Leslie Bricusse.

Nicht alle Copyrightinhaber konnten ermittelt werden. Deren Rechte werden hiermit vorsorglich anerkannt.

263

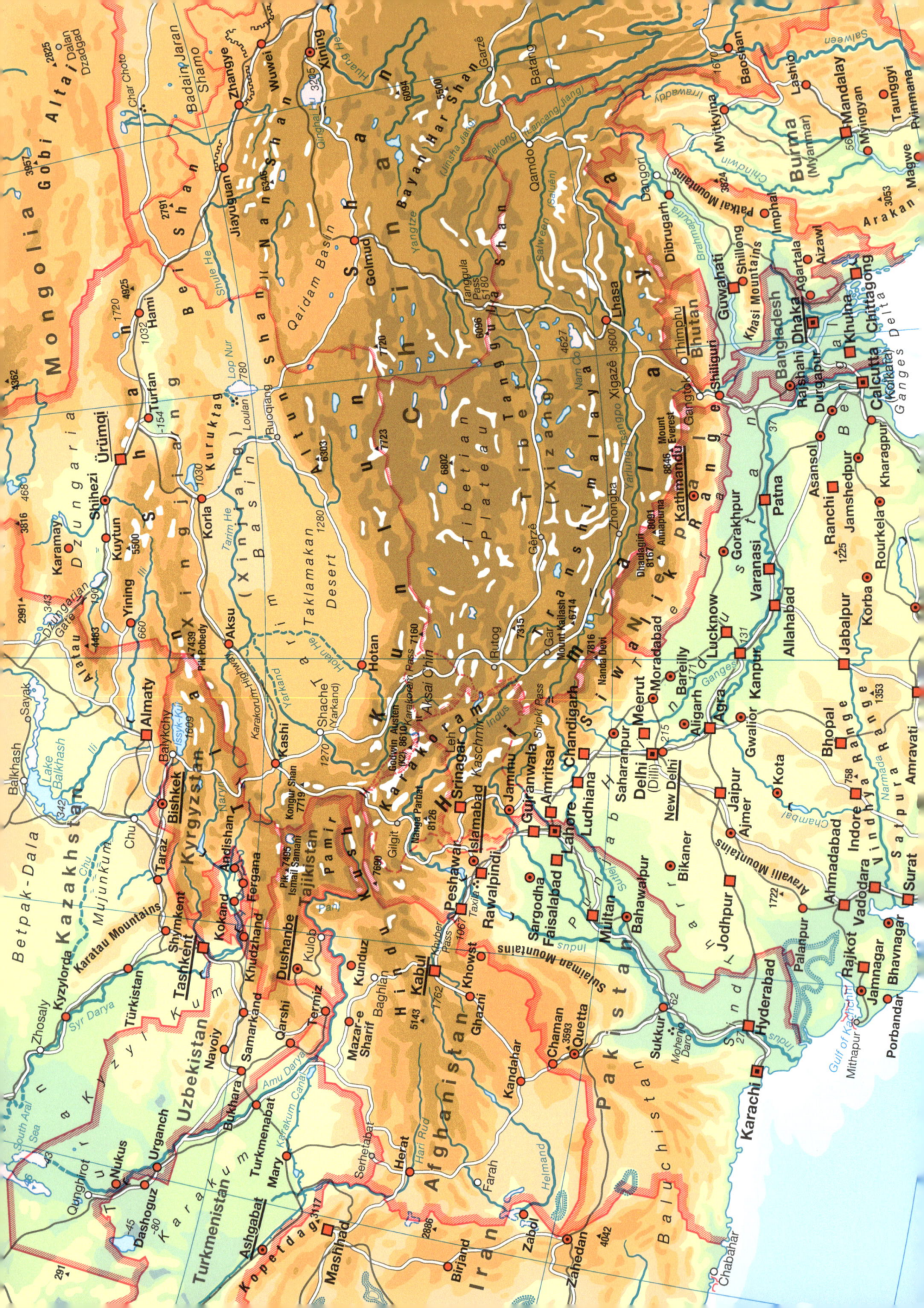